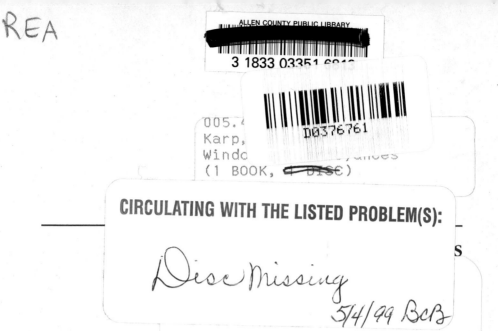

Windows 98 Annoyances

David A. Karp

O'REILLY™

Beijing · Cambridge · Köln · Paris · Sebastopol · Taipei · Tokyo

Windows 98 Annoyances
by David A. Karp

Printed in the United States of America.

Published by O'Reilly & Associates, Inc., 101 Morris Street, Sebastopol, CA 95472.

Editor: Ron Petrusha

Production Editor: Madeleine Newell

Printing History:

October 1998: First Edition.

This book is printed on acid-free paper with 85% recycled content, 15% post-consumer waste. O'Reilly & Associates is committed to using paper with the highest recycled content available consistent with high quality.

ISBN: 1-56592-417-7

Table of Contents

Preface

What Is an Annoyance?

More than anything else, an annoyance is a way of looking at a problem or an unfamiliar task. It's an attitude that puts you in a position to solve the problem, rather than being powerless, frustrated, or feeling like a dummy.

Your computer should *not* be a "black box," something for which you must adjust the way you work and think. It's a hands-on, flexible tool with many capabilities and limitations. Computers and the software that runs on them are designed by humans, and by their very nature are imperfect and often troublesome.

I've written this book with the philosophy that the more you know about a tool you use—specifically, Microsoft Windows 98—the better your day-to-day experience with it will be. If this contradicts what you've seen in other books or in the Windows manual, it's completely intentional.

The Interface

In this book, one of the most frequently examined aspects of Windows 98 is the user interface, and this is no accident. The user interface in Windows 98 includes everything from the visual components that are used to make up every window to the way that individual dialog boxes are laid out. The interface is how you communicate with your computer and how your computer communicates with you; it directly influences how quickly you learn the various tasks in Windows and how efficiently you carry them out once you've learned them. An interface must be designed carefully and meticulously; it should be intuitive enough for beginners, yet not too dumbed down to annoy experienced users.

One of the strengths of Windows 98, and one of the reasons that the Windows PC is the dominant home-computer platform, is that its interface is extremely flexible and configurable. This is not to say, however, that the default interface is the most effective one possible.

Now, I believe that it's better to light a single candle than to curse the darkness, which is why this book is full of solutions rather than gripes. It should be evident from even a brief look at the vast amount of information here that this is *not* a book of "Microsoft-bashing" or complaining of any kind. The focus is on solving problems, and that sometimes means taking a critical view of the Windows interface or the design of a particular Windows component.

The default configuration of Windows 98—the settings that are in use when Windows is first installed—has been designed to showcase the various features of the product, rather than to make the operating system easy to use. One problem with this approach is that most users don't take time to customize the interface and otherwise streamline the operating system. Whether this is due to the quite valid fear of screwing something up, or simply to a lack of time and patience, *Windows 98 Annoyances* can help.

Take the solutions in this book seriously, but don't follow them blindly. Anything that indeed improves the interface can streamline your work and make the overall Windows experience less painful and more enjoyable. However, one person's annoyance is another's feature; what's important is to construct an interface that works best for you.

Throughout this book, I mention third-party software and utilities that you can use to customize your version of Windows 98. Some of these programs are included on the accompanying CD-ROM. Links to others can be found on my website, *www.annoyances.org*. For details, see Appendix F.

A Brief History of Time

My first impression of Windows 95 was how much of an improvement it was over Windows 3.x.

Back in early 1995, I was using a pre-release (beta version) of Windows 95 on my machine, and within only a few hours of installing it, I became aware of the extent to which the previous version of Windows had been stunting my machine. A well-designed operating system unleashes the power of the hardware on which it runs, while a poorly designed operating system can make you want to throw all that expensive hardware in the thresher. Windows is a little bit of both.

Now, not being the patient type, I immediately started compiling a list of questions and complaints about the operating system, some of which had solutions, and some of which did not. This was the start of the *Windows 95 Annoyances* web site, which was one of the first web sites devoted to Windows 95. Later in the summer of 1995, other pre-release users began writing in with their own questions and complaints, and even with occasional solutions to the problems I couldn't solve.

As readers' requests for information and additional solutions became more diverse, so did the web site. The site quickly evolved from a simple list of annoyances to an extensive collection of tips and tricks, and then to a more general support center for Windows 95. In the beginning of 1997, I wrote the book *Windows Annoyances*, which quickly became a bestseller.

Windows 98 Annoyances, the sequel to that popular volume, is more than just an update that covers the changes in the newest version of Windows. This book contains many more solutions, more undocumented secrets, and more information than the previous book, yet it's presented in the same clear, straightforward format. I hope you enjoy it!

Organization of This Book

Chapter 1, *Making the Most of Windows 98*, discusses some of the more common annoyances in the Windows 98 operating system. This chapter also covers many of the improvements made since Windows 95, and notes some of the problems that *weren't* fixed.

Chapter 2, *Customizing the Interface*, starts by examining the Windows user interface and how to overcome its limitations. What follows is a discussion of the way you work with Windows and how to take advantage of some of its lesser-known tricks and customization features. This includes advanced Explorer tips, file manipulation tricks, and undocumented interface tweaks.

Chapter 3, *The Registry*, covers the structure of the Registry and the use of the Registry Editor. This is important, because most of the solutions hereafter make use of this knowledge. In addition to registry basics, there are some advanced topics, such as effective searching techniques, finding the right registry keys, and restoring a corrupted Registry.

Chapter 4, *Tinkering Techniques*, continues with customization and problem-solving topics that take advantage of the registry techniques discussed earlier. There are solutions for reducing clutter, protecting your file types, and customizing Windows 98 beyond Microsoft's intentions: editing the Start Menu has a whole new meaning in this chapter.

Chapter 5, *Maximizing Performance*, is often a neglected topic. The goal is to get the best possible performance from your system without spending a lot of money or time. If and when you decide to upgrade, you'll also find tips here to help make informed decisions.

Chapter 6, *Troubleshooting*, starts with preventative maintenance; in addition to backing up your system effectively, there's extensive coverage of disaster recovery and emergency restoration. Detailed attention is given to error messages and to hardware and software conflicts. There's also a section on troubleshooting specific hardware components.

Chapter 7, *Networking*, allows you to expand your desktop and your repertoire by setting up a local area network and connecting to the Internet. Going beyond the basics, the chapter explores protocols, troubleshooting, and new technologies such as virtual private networking and connecting a LAN to the Internet.

Chapter 8, *Taking Control of Web Integration*, is an in-depth examination of the controversial so-called *integration* of Microsoft's web browser, Internet Explorer, with the fundamental Windows interface. This chapter explores the components that constitute web integration and how to configure them, including customizing the "Web View" and choosing a default web browser.

Chapter 9, *Scripting and Automation*, rounds out the book with a discussion of simple programming using the Windows Scripting Host included with Windows 98, as well as DOS batch files, which have been around since the beginning of time, yet are still undocumented in Windows 98. In addition to a rapid introduction to both scripting platforms, you'll find advanced solutions, such as functions for registry access and file system access, and ready-to-run scripts and batch files to solve a wide range of problems. The chapter concludes with a look at the seemingly simple Scheduled Tasks feature, and how it can be used in conjunction with scripts for a truly automated environment.

Six appendixes are included as references:

Appendix A, *Setting Locator*, is a comprehensive list of nearly every setting scattered throughout Windows 98, from folder options to removing tray icons.

Appendix B, *DOS Lives*, covers DOS commands, which can be surprisingly useful in the Windows world.

Appendix C, *Contents of the MSDOS.SYS File*, documents the *Msdos.sys* file, which controls many aspects of the Windows 98 boot procedure.

Appendix D, *Class IDs of System Objects*, is a listing of common Class IDs (special registry codes for identifying system objects) used throughout the book.

Appendix E, *Interface Terminology and the Basics*, examines the user interface of Windows 98, which will be of interest to beginners and experienced users alike; it covers everything from the nomenclature of common interface elements to annoyances related to the changes in the Taskbar and Start Menu.

Appendix F, *Software to Solve Annoyances*, is a launching point for obtaining additional information, as well as the software mentioned in this book, primarily, but not exclusively, over the Internet.

About the Accompanying CD-ROM

The accompanying CD-ROM has been included with *Windows 98 Annoyances* at no additional charge. It contains the sample scripts presented in Chapter 9, and features an evaluation copy of *O'Reilly Utilities—Quick Solutions for Windows 98 Annoyances*, a commercial software product that automates some of the fixes discussed in this book and supports numerous other customizations and enhancements.

This trial version of the software has a 30-day evaluation period. For details about the software, see Appendix F.

Getting the Most Out of This Book

This book is arranged so that it can be used as a learning tool as well as a reference. More than just a bag of tricks, it covers a wide range of topics, some informational and some instructional. While you certainly don't need to read the chapters in order, it is structured so that you can progress easily from one topic to the next, expanding your knowledge and experience as you go. You should be able to jump to any topic as needed; if you find that you don't have the proficiency required by a particular solution, such as knowledge of the Registry, you should be able to learn about it elsewhere in the book (Chapter 3, in the case of the Registry). For additional software and corrections, check out the Windows 98 Annoyances web site at *www.annoyances.org*, or see Appendix F.

Most topics are presented as problems or annoyances with corresponding solutions. Topics usually begin with a few introductory paragraphs explaining why you'd want to complete the particular solution, and including some useful background information. In some cases, you may want to skip ahead to the actual solution procedure, easily identifiable by the bullets or numbered steps. Don't forget to look at the "Notes and other issues" at the end of most solutions for exceptions, pitfalls, and related information. You'll also find an "Undo" section where applicable, which will explain how to undo the solution if you so desire.

Conventions in This Book

We used some style conventions to assist you in reading this book:

- Captions, menus, buttons, checkboxes, tabs, and other interface elements are all **bold** to make the text easier to follow, for example:

  Select **Options** from Explorer's **View** menu, and choose the **File Types** tab.

- When any typing is involved, the text is in a `monospaced` typeface; the same goes for registry paths (`HKEY_CURRENT_USER\Software`) and DOS commands (`ATTRIB`).
- Items that can be replaced in typed text are in a *`monospaced italic`* font, as are variable and object names.
- Filenames, folder names, Internet addresses, and function names appear in *italic*. Among other things, this frees up quotation marks so that they're only included when necessary; if you see quotation marks around something to type, for example, it means that you should type the quotation marks as well (unless otherwise specified).

This symbol indicates a tip.

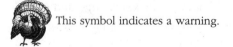

This symbol indicates a warning.

How to Contact Us

We have tested and verified all the information in this book to the best of our ability, but you may find that features have changed (or even that we have made mistakes!). Please let us know about any errors you find, as well as your suggestions for future editions, by writing to:

O'Reilly & Associates
101 Morris Street
Sebastopol, CA 95472
800-998-9938 (in the U.S. or Canada)
707-829-0515 (international/local)
707-829-0104 (FAX)

You can also send messages electronically. To be put on our mailing list or to request a catalog, send email to:

nuts@oreilly.com

To ask technical questions or comment on the book, send email to:

bookquestions@oreilly.com

Acknowledgments

While you may have noticed that the Internet seems to get a lot of attention in this book, you may not know it's not that way for marketing reasons, but rather because this book has its roots on the Web. Part of my thanks goes to the five million or so visitors to the web site (*www.annoyances.org*), most of whom were just looking for solutions to one or two of life's little problems.

I'd like to start by thanking the folks at O'Reilly & Associates. It's a supreme pleasure to work with people who are dedicated to quality and passionate about their work. In particular: my exceptional editor, Ron Petrusha; the project manager, Troy Mott; and the editorial assistant, Katie Gardner. Thanks to Tim O'Reilly for his enthusiasm; Gina Blaber, John Blaber, John Dockery, and Susan Peck, for helping to get the book out on time and for questioning the status quo; Mark Bracewell for his opinions and advice; J.D. Butler for additional comments; and Andrew Schulman for getting the ball rolling.

I'd like to thank my family, friends, and well-wishers (in that they didn't wish me any particular harm), all of whom put up with my deadlines and late-night writing binges. Special thanks to Ruth Kampmann. Finally, my everlasting gratitude to Torey Bookstein, whose love and support never failed to put a smile on my face.

And thank you, the reader, for your time with this book; I hope it's helpful in alleviating some of the annoyances in your life.

In this chapter:
- *What's Wrong with Windows*
- *Flavors of Windows—Past and Present*
- *Transition to Windows 98*

1

Making the Most of Windows 98

Windows 98 is the latest version of Microsoft's dominant operating system, just in case you didn't know. Odds are you either have Windows 98 on your computer, are in the process of upgrading to it, or are at least thinking of using it. It probably hasn't taken long for the luster to wear off and for certain aspects of the software to grate on your nerves.

For those of you who've upgraded to Windows 98 from Win95, probably the biggest irritant is the fact that Microsoft programmers seem to have put more effort into integrating the Internet Explorer web browser with the operating system than into fixing the basic problems that have plagued Windows 95 since day one. For example, if you've become accustomed to Windows crashing at least once a day, don't expect it to get much better.

Admittedly, Windows 98 isn't much different than Windows 95, at least on the surface. In fact, if you install Internet Explorer 4.x and all of the available program updates and bug fixes on top of Windows 95 OSR2 (the second release of Win95, only available preinstalled on new computers), it's superficially indistinguishable from Win98. The fact that Win98 comes with all the patches and updates preinstalled makes for a very convenient upgrade. In addition to some minor interface changes (not including the silly web view), Windows 98 also includes fairly good support for newer hardware, some performance improvements and additional utilities, and several nit-picky updates that more experienced Windows users will appreciate (see "Transition to Windows 98" later in this chapter).

If Windows 98 is your first foray into Windows, you're lucky to have escaped the early days of changing jumpers, editing *Config.sys,* and suffering with the Program Manager found in Windows 3.x. However, dealing with the early problems of Windows was a good way to build coping skills. Getting under the hood of Windows is not only a great way to take charge of the operating system and make it conform to the way you work and think, but also a very effective method for learning more about Windows. When you delve into the Registry to turn off the annoying little bouncing arrow that tells you "Click here to begin," you'll learn how to make other changes, solve problems, and work around the inherent problems in Windows.

While nobody's particular requirements and preferences will be the same, everyone can benefit from some light being shed on the inner workings of the operating system. And while a little knowledge can be dangerous, a lot of knowledge can keep your system running smoothly and make your Windows experience relatively pain free.

What's Wrong with Windows

There are many reasons that software in general, and Windows 98 in particular, annoys us. One of the most common excuses is that software is designed to be used by a large number of people as well as to be compatible with a vast array of hardware components, and that no single program can be expected to satisfy everyone. While that's true to some extent, this excuse is too often used as a scapegoat for other problems. Part of the problem is that software designers often don't understand good user interface design, or simply don't understand users, and therefore create products that annoy us. And part of the problem is that users don't understand software designers, and therefore don't understand the products they create.

Another truth that most computer companies will never admit is that computer technology, in general, is still quite infantile on the evolutionary scale. Personal computers really haven't been around that long, and we humans are still getting used to them. Regardless of the excuses, you should *not* be required to adjust the way you think in order to complete a task on a computer, but rather you should learn how to adjust the computer to work in a way that makes sense to you. That is what this book is about.

Windows 98 Annoyances presents solutions that enable you to both customize and troubleshoot Windows. This is an important distinction, as many times solving a problem requires that you know whether something irritating is a bug or a feature of the software, and the dividing line isn't always clear. It's important to realize that if software doesn't respond in a way that *you* think it should, it should be regarded as poor design, which is not necessarily the same as a bug. A bug is an action carried out by a piece of software that wasn't intended by the *designer* of the product.

We can speculate as to the intentions of the various developers of Windows, and sometimes even uncover the motivations behind a particular aspect of the software we don't like, but what it really comes down to is *attitude*. By labeling something a bug, we are placing the burden of resolving the problem on Microsoft, and waiting for Microsoft developers to fix a bug that they consider to be a feature can definitely be considered a lost cause.

However, if we lump together the crash-a-day tendency of Windows, the irritating little animations, the clutter on the desktop, the lack of decent documentation, and the fact that performance rarely meets expectations, and call them all *annoyances*, we empower ourselves. This is a valuable attitude to adopt; it motivates us to learn more about the operating system so that we can work more efficiently. And more importantly, it gives us the power to resolve the problems we encounter, so that we can get through the day with some degree of sanity.

What, in particular, is annoying about Windows? Let me give you a very simple, yet not readily apparent, example. Common file dialogs—the little windows that allow you to choose a file to open, or specify a filename to save—look basically the same in nearly all applications, since they're a function provided by Windows itself. An annoyance that plagued these boxes in Windows 95 was that they were not resizable, and therefore were awkward to use with large displays. This problem, fortunately, was fixed in Windows 98, making most file dialogs easier to live with.

A more serious problem (in my opinion) was *not* remedied—that of the "Look in" (or "Save in") list. When you go to open or save a file, the only clue to where the current folder is located in the grand hierarchy is the name—not the entire path—of the folder. So, for example, if the current folder shown in a file dialog is called *images*, there's no way to immediately determine if the folder you're looking at is *c:\projects\images*, or *d:\webpages\personal\images*.

What's worse is that Microsoft knows about the problem and has done nothing about it. The smoking gun, if you will, is the online help; if you click on the ? button and then click on the "Look in" list, you'll see, "To see how the current folder fits in the hierarchy on your computer, click the down arrow."

The simple truth is that this would be very easy for Microsoft to remedy. Windows Explorer has an option that allows you to fix a similar problem with folder windows by turning on the **Display the full path in title bar** option in the Folder Windows dialog. Yet this option has no effect on the file dialogs, which could easily be programmed to display the full path of the current folder just below the "Look in" list. Why has Microsoft neglected to fix this very basic design flaw?

My guess is that it's part of Microsoft's strategy to hide as much information as possible from the user, in an effort to make the computer easier to use. This is the same type of thinking that resulted in folder titles that don't show the full path, hidden filename extensions, and the Windows 98 installation program, which overwrites file associations without asking.* Microsoft fails to realize that making users ignorant is not a good way to make the product easier to use.

Of course, it could also be a question of priority—it was obviously more of a priority to integrate a web browser with the desktop interface than to fix the little irritants in Windows by making changes that Microsoft couldn't list on the outside of the box as marketable "improvements" to Windows. Or perhaps the designers of Windows didn't want to admit that they had done anything wrong in the first place.

So how does Microsoft get away with it? Microsoft is in a unique position: the company is powerful and wealthy enough to devote substantial marketing resources to ensuring the commercial success of their products regardless of the quality or intelligence of design. For example, we put up with Windows because the competing products were outmarketed years ago—there simply are no other practical choices available at the moment. The closest competitor to Windows 98 is Windows NT 5.0, also produced by Microsoft; in any other industry, this would be considered a monopoly.

In extreme cases, marketing can influence design, rather than just compensate for it. A stellar example of this is the *Web View* feature found in Windows 98. The concept of viewing one's desktop as though it were a web page was certainly not the brainchild of any self-respecting interface designer. The irresistible marketing appeal of the Internet, combined with Microsoft's undying need to squelch Netscape in the web browser market, has led Microsoft to tie in Internet Explorer to their almost ubiquitous operating system, leaving users to suffer with this ridiculous interface.

The good news is that this creates jobs for countless thousands—those employed to release patchwork software, provide technical support and training, or otherwise pick up the pieces left by Microsoft Windows.

---

* See "Protect Your File Types" in Chapter 4, *Tinkering Techniques*, for more information on file associations and how to keep applications from overwriting yours.

Ultimately, the commercial success of any particular product depends on you and me, the consumers. In other words, every purchase is a vote. The problem is that extensive marketing in the computer industry creates standards to which we must adhere. Purchase decisions are often based upon these standards rather than on quality or usability, which helps to explain the success of inferior products like Microsoft Word. It is the goal of this book to help readers live with their purchase decisions.

Flavors of Windows—Past and Present

Windows 98 will most likely be the last version of a graphical operating system from Microsoft built on top of DOS, with the exception of minor maintenance releases and bug fixes to Windows 98. Windows' successor will be a later version of Windows NT, to be released around 2001. Combining both versions of Windows is something Microsoft has been talking about for years, but they've yet to win the industry support for Windows NT required to take such a plunge.

Whether Windows 98 is your first foray into computing, or just another step in a long line of upgrades, you should be aware of its position among the other operating systems available for the PC platform. A few years ago, this discussion might have included IBM's OS/2 or even NeXTstep, but today's choice of OS software is unfortunately limited to Microsoft's offerings.

Windows 95 was Microsoft's major upgrade to Windows 3.1, and is designed to run the largest variety of software on the majority of home PCs. Some users who received Windows 95 with new computers after about the middle of 1996 got a slightly improved version, known as Windows 95 OEM Service Release 2 (OSR2). OSR2 included some welcome improvements to Dial-Up Networking, support for new hardware such as universal serial bus devices and Intel's then new MMX processors, better support for PCMCIA devices, and a more efficient file system known as FAT32 (discussed at length in Chapter 5, *Maximizing Performance*). Strangely enough, and to the frustration of many Windows 95 users, OSR2 wasn't available shrink-wrapped on store shelves or on Microsoft's web site, so these improvements weren't widely available until the release of Windows 98.

Relative to previous releases, Windows 98 is considered a minor upgrade to its predecessor. The basic interface and feature set is essentially unchanged from Windows 95, with a few notable exceptions. Among the more obvious changes are added animation here and there, built-in support for new hardware, and the controversial integration with the web browser. While some of the refinements in this release, such as fixes to dial-up networking and improved Plug-and-Play, solve a few of the annoyances of Windows 95, Windows 98 introduces plenty of new ways to annoy its users.

Meanwhile, Microsoft continues to develop Windows NT, an operating system that has remained outside the reach of most home computer users. Until the release of Version 4.0, about six months after that of Windows 95, the role of NT wasn't very clearly defined. The media didn't know what it was for, and Microsoft's marketing efforts for NT were fragmented at best. Windows NT was born as Version 3.1, which was nothing more than a lumbering big brother of Windows 3.1 (the current version of Windows at the time) that ran 32-bit applications (nonexistent at the time), and had more extensive network support and much higher hardware requirements. Microsoft quickly developed this product into Windows NT 3.5, which had better security but poorly implemented support for long filenames. NT 3.5 was marketed in two variants: the "Workstation" version positioned as a high-end desktop OS, and the "Server" version positioned as a network server platform to compete with Unix. While NT Workstation suffered due to total lack of consumer interest and poor industry support, the Server version began to make inroads as an Internet web server, which helped it win limited support from some software and hardware vendors, although Unix dominates the server market to this day. Not until the release of Windows 95, however, did substantial support surface for 32-bit Windows applications, and consequently, for Windows NT.

Windows NT 4.0 inherited Windows 95's interface and some of its popularity, but not Plug-and-Play, advanced power management, or the supposedly rigorous testing that put Windows 95 through its paces. Version 5.0, slated to be released some time after Windows 98, includes the same subtle interface updates and web integration found in Windows 98, as well as some features that allow it to catch up to Windows 95, such as Plug-and-Play and better hardware support. Perhaps the most significant change, albeit long overdue, is NT's support for the Win32 driver model, which essentially means that Windows NT 5.0 and Windows 98 can both use the same hardware drivers, and NT 5 users supposedly will not encounter the compatibility headaches associated with previous releases. This should provide some of the footing necessary for a future version of NT to become a more universal desktop platform, allowing Microsoft to finally axe the DOS-based Windows platform and concentrate solely on NT.

For most users, Windows 98 will yield better performance and compatibility with less of an investment than Windows NT, due mostly to NT's higher hardware requirements. Some users, however, may require the added benefits that Windows NT provides, such as better multitasking (including support for multiple processors) and stability for 3-D, CAD, and video applications, and better security and network support for Internet and LAN server applications. The interfaces of the two operating systems, thankfully, are virtually the same, which makes migration and support much easier. In fact, many of the solutions in this book apply to NT 5.0 as well as to Windows 98, mostly because the program that provides the user interface, called the shell, is essentially the same for both platforms. This is possible because of the modular design of all flavors of Windows, wherein the shell and the core operating system, called the Kernel, are separate entities. While the operating system takes care of things like communicating with your printer, storing files on your hard disk, and displaying graphics (things that the two platforms do somewhat differently), the shell includes interface basics like your Start Menu, the desktop, and the Control Panel.

The default Windows shell is the Windows Explorer (hereon called simply "Explorer"), which in its most recent incarnation has been combined with Internet Explorer (IE), Microsoft's web browser, to form a sort of Frankenstein's monster of operating system interfaces. Since most of the interface changes in the latest versions of Windows are due to this integration, it's possible for users of Windows 95 and Windows NT 4.0 to configure their systems to look and feel like Win98 and NT 5.0, respectively, should they be so inclined, without going through the pain and expense of installing a new operating system. IE Version 4.0 and later, complete with Microsoft's insidious shell integration, has been available for free download from Microsoft's web site since it was released, and is available on CD for about $5.00, which may be more cost-effective than a three-hour download. That said, you can jump right into Chapter 8, *Taking Control of Web Integration*, for help with taming web integration.

For the record, the solutions in this edition assume that you have the original shipping version of Windows 98. Microsoft may release a service version (much like OSR2 for Windows 95) or make certain patches publicly available, which may either solve existing annoyances or create new ones. Rest assured that such changes will be documented on the web site accompanying this book, *www.annoyances.org*, along with other news, updates, and relevant information.

Transition to Windows 98

If you're new to computers, you probably weren't paying much attention to the introduction of Windows 95 to the computing populace back in August 1995. With a $200 million advertising budget, Microsoft released the most substantial upgrade to the operating system since its introduction. Windows 98, however, is not as revolutionary an upgrade as its predecessor.

In my opinion, much of the value of the Windows 98 upgrade lies in the numerous minor improvements that Microsoft decided to include. Of course, I don't think they went far enough, but that's what the rest of the book is about. Readers of this book are likely to share my active interest in the many small details that make up Windows. Following is a list of some of the changes in Windows 98, both large and small, as well as good and bad:

Better file copy boxes

When copying or moving a bunch of files in Explorer, the progress indicator now reflects the status of the *entire* job, not each individual file, which means that the estimated time to completion now actually means something. Unfortunately, this can result in a "Preparing to copy" delay before copying a group of files from floppies or CDs, as Windows must add up all the file sizes before continuing. The other improvement is that the copy/move boxes are no longer *owned* by the target window; that is, when you drag-drop a group of files to the desktop, you can now access other items on the desktop while you're copying (the same goes with folder and Explorer windows). If only they let us turn off the silly flying paper animations. . . .

Resizable file dialogs

As described in "What's Wrong with Windows" earlier in this chapter, most of the file dialogs in Windows 98 can now be resized. While Windows does actually remember the dialog sizes for each application, it doesn't save the settings to disk, and forgets them when you shut down. There is no apparent way to set the default size of the file dialogs, and some common dialogs, as well as the custom dialogs found in Microsoft Office 97, still don't allow resizing, so this is an incomplete solution at best.

Direct manipulation of Start Menu items

Among the many problems with the Start Menu in Windows 95 was that you had to open a window somewhere else to customize the contents of the *Programs* subfolder; the menu items could not be *directly* manipulated. This problem has been fixed, at least somewhat, in Windows 98. You can now drag-drop shortcuts directly onto the Start Menu, drag items *from* the Start Menu, and even reorder Start Menu items in place. You can also right-click on Start Menu items just as though you were right-clicking on the respective shortcuts in Explorer, providing easy access to their Properties sheets, although, strangely, you cannot rename shortcuts in this way. Naturally, this functionality does not extend to intrinsic items like **Find** or **Shut Down**. See Appendix E, *Interface Terminology and the Basics*, for more information on using the Start Menu, and "Customize Start Menu Components" in Chapter 4 for more information on the intrinsic components.

More aware Explorer tree

You probably know that if you drag an object towards the top or bottom of the tree pane in Explorer and hold it for about a half-second, the tree will start to scroll either until you move away, or until the top or bottom of the tree is reached. This has been taken a step further in Windows 98. If you drag an object and hold it over a collapsed folder (one with subfolders that aren't visible), Windows will automatically expand the branch, allowing you to drop the items anywhere in the file system. This is great for those of us who don't want to take the time before the drag-drop to make sure that the target is visible. While I think this is a step in the right direction, I must point out that it can also be disconcerting when the tree starts moving while you're trying to drop something in just the right place.

Of course, with every minor improvement comes a minor disappointment. For example, it's nearly impossible to see the free space on your drive in Explorer's status bar without maximizing Explorer. The little panes aren't user-resizable, and don't adjust with the contents of the information they display. For this inconvenience, there's no fix—it's just another annoyance.

Menu animation and tooltips

Microsoft designers asked themselves, "How do we make a brand-new Pentium II class computer feel like a 15-year-old 286?" Their answer was, of course, the silly animated menus, trees, and list boxes that have replaced the quick controls we were used to. And to add insult to injury, those little yellow tooltips now appear on top of nearly every interface component, just in case you forget what the [X] button at the top of every window does. What's worse is that there's no way to turn any of it off without installing the TweakUI utility; see Appendix A, *Setting Locator*, for more information.

Internet Explorer integration

The hot topic in Windows 98 is the so-called *integration* with Internet Explorer, Microsoft's web browser. Neglecting Microsoft's intentions for a moment, this means you have a web browser that cannot be removed, a Web View of your desktop and the folders on your hard disk, and an Active Desktop, essentially allowing you to display a web page that can't cover up another window. All of Chapter 8 is devoted to this new interface and how to cope with it.

Taskbar button bars

In an effort to augment the less than ideal Start Menu, Microsoft has added tiny toolbars that can be docked to the taskbar. These toolbars have buttons that can be used to launch programs, open folders, and, of course, open Internet Explorer. There's also a toolbar that mimics the Internet Explorer address bar (see Appendix C, *Contents of the MSDOS.SYS File*). While Windows doesn't come with any useful predefined toolbars, new ones are easy to create, albeit not very flexible. See Appendix E for more information.

Year 2000 (Y2K) compliance

Partially rectifying an industry-wide blunder, wherein apparently nobody saw the year 2000 coming, Microsoft has claimed that Windows 98 is fully year 2000 compliant. When your computer's clock rolls over from December 31, 1999, to January 1, 2000, you supposedly won't experience the Armageddon the media soothsayers have been forecasting.

The global panic surrounding this problem is caused by the fact that most computer software stores dates with double-digit years, meaning that 1998 is stored as "98" and 2017 is stored as "17." Everything from sorting files by date to calculating compounded interest could be affected by the year 2000 bug if the software is not prepared for it.

You can test any software or hardware on your own for year 2000 compliance by setting your computer's clock ahead. Try setting it to 2001, 2061, 2081, 2093. Of course, I recommend doing a full system backup beforehand, just to be on the safe side.

Better backup, finally

Microsoft has included a backup program with each release of Windows since Version 3.1, and each time the program has been remarkably feeble. The limited backup program included with Windows 95, for example, was licensed from Hewlett-Packard, and while that meant it worked with most HP drives, many users of other products were required to purchase a third-party backup program.

Luckily, Microsoft licensed the backup utility for Windows 98 from Seagate Software. The new backup program is essentially a scaled-down version of Seagate Backup Exec 2.0 (32-bit), which is an updated version of Arcada Backup for Windows 95 (which Seagate purchased in 1997). This is an excellent program, which I have been using for years. It should support nearly any backup device you throw at it, actually has a functional restore, and is very fast and flexible. Plus, I expect Seagate to do a much better job of supporting and updating it than Hewlett-Packard did with their release. Microsoft gets a hearty thumbs up for this one.

FAT32

The *File Allocation Table* (FAT) is the method by which files and directories were stored on a hard disk in every version of DOS (and therefore Windows) before the release of Windows 98. While Windows NT has always supported a more reliable and secure file system called NTFS, it is to this day not supported by Windows 95/98.

FAT32 is a more efficient version of FAT, supporting much larger partitions and smaller cluster sizes, which in turn allow larger disks with less wasted space. While Windows 95 OSR2 was the first OS to include FAT32, Windows 98 is the first commercially available release to support it. What's more, Windows NT 5.0 also supports FAT32, meaning that you can use it even if you have a dual-boot system with NT 5.0.

Note, however, that your drives will not be automatically converted to FAT32 when you upgrade, and some system vendors who don't understand FAT32 may not enable it for you. Using the FAT32 converter, or a third-party program (like Partition Magic 3.0), you'll be able to easily convert your drives. See Chapter 5 for more information on converting to FAT32, including the advantages and pitfalls.

Better hardware support and Win32 drivers

Windows 95 came with an impressive collection of drivers, supporting thousands of video cards, controllers, multimedia devices, network cards, and just about anything else that was on the market in 1995. Of course, this being the computer industry, that wasn't good enough a year later. To catch up with new technologies, Windows 98 includes support for MMX processors, universal serial bus (USB) controllers and devices, firewire (IEEE 1394), AGP 3D-accelerated video cards, DVD players and encoders, and TV tuner cards. Note that Windows 95 OSR2 supported MMX and OSR2.5 supported USB, but Windows 98 is the first version in which these features will be commercially available.

Additionally, many specific devices are now supported by Windows 98 out of the box, meaning that fewer third-party drivers will need to be installed, at least for now.

Windows 98 also supports the Win32 hardware driver model, a driver specification that will work with both Windows 98 and Windows NT 5.0—something Microsoft should have done long ago. Until now, manufacturers had to supply separate drivers for Windows 95 and Windows NT 4.0, and given the low consumer popularity of NT, Windows 95 had significantly better industry support. Microsoft hopes that the Win32 driver model will level the availability of hardware support for the two platforms, which should make a global migration to NT possible, and allow Microsoft to abandon the DOS-based Windows 9x platform.

Whether or not this will actually happen remains to be seen.

Performance

Supposedly, any computer that was competent enough to run Windows 95 should be able to handle Windows 98 with the same ease. Considering Windows' propensity for making fast Pentium II systems perform as though they were old 286s, that's not saying much.

However, there are many factors that can influence system performance, and Windows 98 does improve a few of them. For example, Win98 purportedly contains an algorithm that allows applications to start three times faster; if you've used the Norton SpeedStart utility that comes with Symantec's Norton Utilities 3.0, you'll find that the Win98 algorithm is pretty much the same thing. While it probably won't blow you away, it's a step in the right direction.

On the down side, Windows 98 requires quite a bit more disk space (you'll need to store the graphics for all those *Channels*, after all) although it does save some space with FAT32, discussed earlier in this chapter.

Regardless of how much Windows 98 has changed your life, you'll benefit from Chapter 5, which covers some upgrading issues as well as some neat little tricks for turning your copy of Windows 98 into a lean, responsive operating system—you probably won't even recognize it.

In this chapter:
- *Coping with Explorer*
- *Get Control of the Desktop*
- *Fundamental Interface Tweaks*

2

Customizing the Interface

Windows can be annoying. So much of your time on a computer is spent in Windows: starting programs, finding files, copying folders, configuring the interface. The first steps in dealing with annoyances include learning how to accomplish common tasks more easily and how to adjust various aspects of the Windows interface, making it easier to use, more pleasant to look at, and less irritating to work with. The ideal user interface should adapt to you, rather than the other way around, but this isn't a perfect world, and the Windows interface is far from ideal.

Perhaps the least ideal interface component is the new Web View, and one of the most common questions about Windows 98 is "How do I turn off the Web View?" Discussion of the Web View and the rest of the fallout from the integration of the Internet Explorer web browser with the core interface is found in Chapter 8, *Taking Control of Web Integration.*

There are some fundamental features of the interface that simply can't be changed, such as using icons and folders, and drag-and-drop. Even if it were possible, for example, to change the way Windows responds to drag-and-drop, the user would be ill-advised to mess with it, as such a change would go against the consistency (what little there is) of the interface.

There are times, however, when the design of certain basic Windows functionality is so confusing that it makes you want to tear your hair out: for example, when Explorer allows you to go through the paces of saving folder settings (**View → Folder Options → View → Make all folders like current folder**), and then pretty much ignores those settings.

The goal of all solutions in this book is to arrive at the best possible compromise between the actual usefulness of a solution and general interface consistency, while, of course, maintaining the lowest "annoyance coefficient."

Therefore, a good place to start is with Explorer, the desktop, the Start Menu, and their interaction. We'll cover some basic tips and tricks for mastering the finer points of what's technically referred to as the default shell in Windows 98, and discuss how to get around many of its hurdles. Once that's out of the way, the section on interface tweaks will start us on our path to enlightenment by covering some basic aspects of Windows we *can* change. Now, I don't mean to presume that you'll become a better human being if you replace those seemingly serene clouds in the Windows 98 startup screen with something else, but I do think most of us will benefit from reducing the annoyances in our lives.

Many of the topics discussed throughout this book require knowledge of the Windows Registry, with the exception of this chapter—I figured you'd want to jump right in. When you're ready, read through Chapter 3, *The Registry*; this should prepare you for the rest of the material in the book. The present chapter assumes a basic working knowledge of files and folders, double-clicking on icons, and right-clicking.

Coping with Explorer

Explorer is the all-encompassing program that provides the basic working interface allowing you to manage the files and folders on your hard drive. The Windows desktop, the My Computer window, the single-folder windows, the Exploring tree view window, and the Start Menu are all part of the Explorer application. However, in most Windows lore, and most of the solutions in this book, the term "Explorer" refers specifically to the window labeled "Exploring" with the folder tree visible, which is opened by selecting **Windows Explorer** from the Start Menu or by launching *Explorer.exe* from the Start Menu's **Run** command. All other windows used to browse folders—those windows accessible from the My Computer window—are referred to as folder windows, or the single-folder view.

Explorer Techniques

Files, folders, and most other system objects are copied, moved, opened, closed, and deleted in virtually the same way in all of these places. If you learn how to combine mouse movements with keystrokes effectively, for example, you'll see how much easier it is to use Explorer to accomplish everyday management tasks. See Appendix E, *Interface Terminology and*

the Basics, for accomplishing basic Explorer tasks, such as customizing the Start Menu and using context menus.

One of the primary annoyances with Windows is the need for special combinations of keystrokes and mouse clicks to perform simple operations, such as having to use the **Ctrl** key to copy a file, or having to make sure the source and destination folders are both visible before trying to copy or move a file. Many aspects of the way Windows works can be controlled by changing certain settings that are scattered throughout several different dialog boxes. The key here is to configure Windows as best you can to behave how you expect it to behave, which depends on your level of experience and how you work. The Folder Options window is a good place to start:

- Select **Folder Options** from the **View** menu in a single-folder window or in Explorer, choose the **Custom, based on settings you choose** option, and then click **Settings**.

  Figure 2-1 shows the settings that will make Windows 98 behave most like Windows 95, which may be desirable for those who are upgrading. It's ironic that the **Classic View** setting doesn't strictly mimic the standard interface in Windows 95, but only approximates it.

Most of the settings in the dialog shown in Figure 2-1 should be self-explanatory. For more information on the **Active Desktop** and **View Web Content** options, see Chapter 8. The best way to figure out any of these options is to try them.

Browse folders as follows

If you have become accustomed to using the **Ctrl** key in Windows 95 to control on the fly whether or not new windows were opened when you double-clicked on folder icons, you'll probably be discouraged by the fact that Windows 98 doesn't respond to it at all. There's no way to choose on the fly whether new folder windows are opened or the same folder window is reused when you double-click on folder icons. It may sound like nitpicking, but when Microsoft periodically changes the fundamental behavior of the interface, it can be very frustrating for users.

- My advice: choose the **Open each folder in its own window** option, and when the screen becomes cluttered with too many folder windows, hold the **Shift** key while closing the top window to get rid of all of the folder windows from that branch.

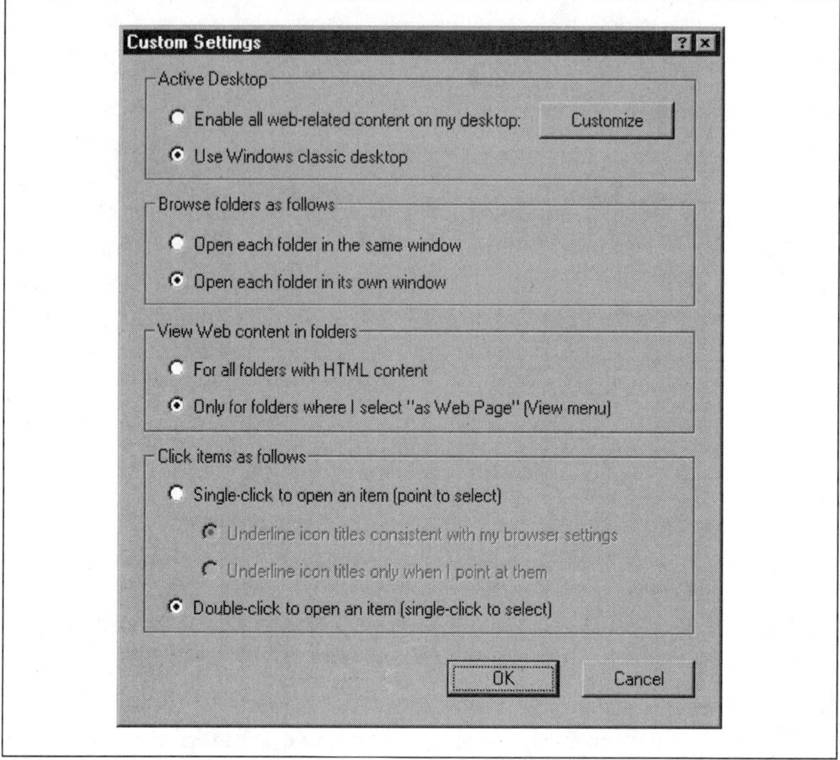

Figure 2-1: The Custom Settings dialog box is a good place to start messing around with some basic Explorer settings

Click items as follows

- In order to conform to Microsoft's Web View paradigm, you now have the option of single-clicking to open icons. This has the advantage of allowing you to navigate most of Windows without having to double-click (something you could've done before with the right mouse button). One note: if you select the single-click interface, you can't click twice slowly on an item anymore to rename it—you must either right-click on it and select **Rename**, or move the mouse pointer so that it is hovering over the icon and press the **F2** key.
- Double-clicking certainly can be a pain in the neck for beginners and experienced users alike, but there are significant advantages of using double-clicks to open icons. For example, it virtually eliminates the possibility of accidentally opening a program or folder when you try to drag-drop or rename an item. Most important, double-clicking is consistent with every other graphical operating system currently in

existence. While this may not seem like a great argument, good user interface design starts with what users are accustomed to.

What it comes down to is that you should use what works best for you. Don't blindly accept the defaults just because that's the way it came out of the box.

Helpful navigation keystrokes (assuming standard double-clicking)

- Hold the **Alt** key while double-clicking on a file or folder to view the **Properties** window for that object.
- Hold the **Shift** key while double-clicking on a folder to open **Explorer** at that location (careful when using this, as **Shift** is also used to select multiple files).
- Press **Backspace** in an open folder to go to the parent (containing) folder. (Whether or not a new window appears depends on the **Browse Folders** setting described above.)
- Hold the **Shift** key while clicking on the close button **[X]** to close *all* open folders that were used to get to that folder. (This makes sense only if there is more than one window open, which depends on the **Browse Folders** setting described above.)
- Right-click on any folder icon to present all of the exploring options, such as **Open** (folder view) and **Explore** (tree view).

Keystrokes for use with navigating and selecting files

- A quick way to choose a new program to be used with a certain file type is to hold the **Shift** key while *right-clicking* on a file, and selecting **Open With...** from the list. You could use this technique, for example, if Internet Explorer is your default browser and you want to view an HTML file with Netscape Navigator. If a file is unregistered (not associated with any program), this box will appear simply by double-clicking the file.

  If you have the *Open With* utility, part of *O'Reilly Utilities—Quick Solutions for Windows 98 Annoyances* (see Appendix F, *Software to Solve Annoyances*), you can right-click on any file, registered or not, and select **Open With** to choose a new default program, as well as to add non-default context menu items.
- Hold the **Ctrl** key to select or deselect multiple items, one by one. Or select one icon, and then hold the **Shift** key while clicking on another to select a range of items. You can also drag a *rubber band* around multiple files to select them; start in a blank portion of a folder win-

dow, and drag the mouse to the opposite corner to select everything in the rectangle. If you use a rubber band or the **Shift** key to select a bunch of files, you can still use the **Ctrl** key to deselect items one by one.

- Press **Ctrl-A** to quickly select all the contents of a folder, both files and folders.

Notes and other issues

For more information, see the next section, "Move or Copy Files at Will," and "Force Windows to Remember Folder Settings," later in this chapter.

While all settings in the Folder Options dialog box theoretically apply to all folders on your system (rather than just the currently open folder), you may find yourself returning often to this box when Windows forgets your settings.

Move or Copy Files at Will

Intuitively, when one drags a file from one place on the screen to another, it would seem reasonable that the file would be moved instead of copied. That is, when you see an object disappear from a location, it shouldn't still be there the next time you look. One of the worst inconsistencies in Windows is what actually happens to files when they're dragged.

Dragging from one place to another on the same disk ends up moving the files, while dragging from one disk to another copies them. If you're just dragging *.exe* files, however, only a shortcut to the file is created, and the file is neither copied nor moved. If you're dragging system objects, such as items in the My Computer window or the Control Panel, shortcuts to the items are always created, since they can't be copied or moved. However, if you drag a Dial-Up Networking connection out of the Dial-Up Networking window, a new "Dial-Up Networking Exported file" will be created that is neither a copy of nor a shortcut to the original item (see Chapter 7, *Networking*, for details).

The best way to cope with this confusion is to use a combination of keystrokes and the right mouse button to ensure the desired results every time:

- To *copy* a file under any situation, hold the **Ctrl** key while dragging. If you press **Ctrl** before you click, Windows assumes you're still selecting files. This won't work for system objects like Control Panel items—a shortcut will be created regardless.

- To *move* a file under any situation, hold the **Shift** key while dragging. Accordingly, if you press **Shift** before you click, Windows assumes you're still selecting files. This won't work for system objects like Control Panel items—a shortcut will be created regardless.
- To choose what happens to dragged files each time without pressing keys, drag your files with the right mouse button, and a special menu like the one shown in Figure 2-2 will appear when the files are dropped. This context menu is also helpful, as it will display only appropriate options, depending on the type of objects you're dragging and where you've dropped them.

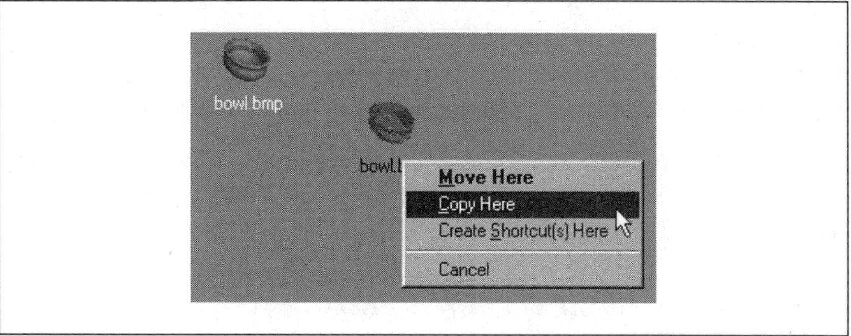

Figure 2-2: Drag files with the right mouse button for more control

- To open the context menu without using the right mouse button, hold the **Ctrl** and **Shift** keys simultaneously while dragging. You'll see a shortcut arrow appear next to the mouse cursor, but the context menu will appear anyway.
- There's no way to force the creation of a shortcut by using keystrokes alone—you'll have to use the context menu (either with the right mouse button or with the **Ctrl** and **Shift** keys as described above).
- To aid in learning the keystrokes, you'll notice that the mouse cursor changes depending on the action being taken. A small plus sign [+] appears when copying, and a curved arrow appears when creating a shortcut.
- Using the **Ctrl** key as described above will also work when dragging a file from one part of a folder to another part of the same folder. See "Make a Duplicate of a File or Folder" later in this chapter for more information.

Notes and other issues

There is no way to set the default action when dragging files in Windows 98, and therefore no way to avoid using keystrokes or the right mouse button to achieve the desired results.

Explorer's **Undo** command, available in the **Edit** menu as well as by right-clicking in an empty area of Explorer, allows you to undo the last file operation. If you've copied or moved any files, the command will read **Undo Copy** or **Undo Move**, respectively. Additionally, if your Recycle Bin is configured to store files, **Undo Delete** will also appear. However, if you're doing a lot of copying, moving, and deleting of files, it's hard to know to which operation, in particular, it refers. The easiest way to tell is to click and hold the mouse button on the **Undo** command, and look in the status bar (select **Status Bar** from the **View** menu if it's not visible), which will tell you exactly which files the operation dealt with.

If you use *.zip* files, you may like the WinZip utility (*http://www.winzip.com*), which effectively utilizes the right-drag menu described above to zip and unzip files.

Copy or Move to a Specified Path

To copy or move a file in Windows by drag-and-drop, both the source folder and the destination folder must be open and visible. There is no provision for specifying a destination folder, such as typing it with the keyboard when copying or moving a file, making this task nearly impossible without a mouse. To add this functionality, which makes file management far less awkward, use the following solutions.

Solution 1: Be patient when dragging

1. Open Explorer with the tree view and navigate to the source folder.
2. Drag one or more items over the tree pane on the left, and hold the mouse over the visible root of the destination folder. After two or three seconds, Explorer should automatically expand the branch and make the subfolders visible.

   If the destination folder you're looking for is buried several layers deep, you'll have to wait for Explorer to expand each level. This requires a steady hand and a lot of patience. It's an improvement over Windows 95, but it's usually quicker and easier to either open the folders before you start to drag, or follow one of the other solutions.

   This works in Network Neighborhood, even when the host computer (the machine on which the folders are located) is running Windows 95 or NT and doesn't support it natively.

Solution 2: Use Copy and Paste

1. Select the file you want to copy, right-click on it, and select **Copy** to copy the file, or **Cut** to move the file. If the file is cut, its icon will appear semitransparent, as though it were a hidden file. If the file is copied, its icon will have no visual distinction.
2. Open the destination folder, right-click on an empty area, and select **Paste**. Whether the file is copied or moved or a whether a shortcut is made depends on the same criteria that apply when dragging and dropping an item.

Solution 3: Use a third-party add-on

- *O'Reilly Utilities—Quick Solutions for Windows 98 Annoyances* (see Appendix F) comes with an add-on that enables easier copying and moving in Explorer. Just right-click on any file or folder, select **Move To** or **Copy To**, and then type or point to the destination folder. The utility allows you to create new folders on the fly, and saves the last ten folders you copied or moved to.
- One of Microsoft's Power Toys, OtherFolder (see Appendix F), adds copy and move functionality to the Send To menu. Right-click on one or more files, select **Send To**, and then **Other Folder**. You can then type a destination, or click **Browse** to select one.

Notes and other issues

The **Copy** and **Paste** solution isn't exactly intuitive, but it can be convenient if you don't have a mouse, or if your screen size limits the number of open windows.

What's even less intuitive is that if you cut a file and never get around to pasting it, or even cut another file, the first file that was cut is magically restored. It's inconsistent with the way that *information* is cut and pasted from application to application, which is what most of us are used to. If you cut text from one application, and don't bother pasting it, the text is lost. Cut, copy, and paste in the context of files work with file *references* rather than the files themselves, so unless you cut and paste a file into the Recycle Bin, there isn't much danger of losing anything. Note that you can abort any cut operation by pressing the **Esc** key, which will do little more than return the file icon to its normal state. The cut/copy/paste behavior in Explorer is similar to that of Microsoft Excel.

While you can drag-drop files from Explorer or the desktop into a running application to open the file in that application, the same isn't necessarily true for **Copy** and **Paste**. If you try to copy a file and then paste it into an application like Word or WordPerfect, the file is inserted as an icon object directly into the document, which isn't of any use to anyone. Additionally, files cannot be pasted into most other applications at all.

Rename Files Without a Hassle

If you have Windows configured to display your registered file extensions, and have ever tried to rename a file and change the extension, you'll see that Windows doesn't let you do it without a stern warning, shown in Figure 2-3. If you can't see your extensions (usually three letters following a period at the end of your files—*.xls* for Excel files, for example), you can show them by selecting **Folder Options** from Explorer's **View** menu, choosing the **View** tab, and turning off the **Hide file extensions for known file types** option.

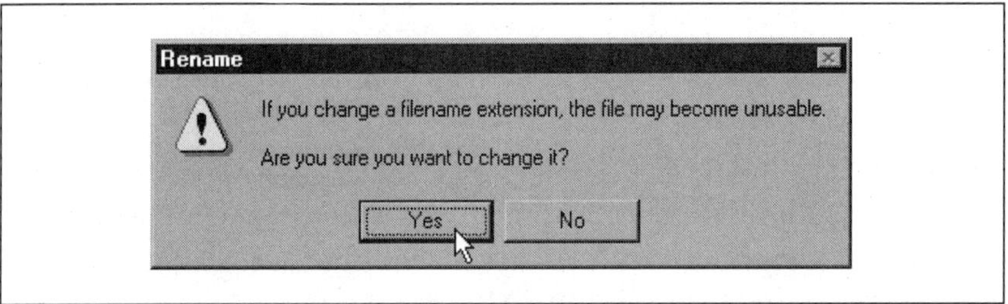

Figure 2-3: Why does Windows hassle you when you try to do something as simple as renaming a file?

There are many reasons why one might want to change the extension of a file. For example, when you try to save a document in Microsoft Word 97 so that it's readable in an earlier version of Word, the file is actually saved as a Rich Text Format (*.rtf*) file, yet it's named with the *.doc* extension. Since this can cause a whole slew of problems, you might want to rename the file so that it has the proper *.rtf* extension.

Since Windows doesn't have the technical ability to sense your intentions or determine if you know what you're doing, it assumes you're an idiot, and displays this useless message every time. Although there is no explicit way to disable this message, there are other ways to rename files that won't trigger this message.

Solution 1: Use the Command Prompt

1. Open the **Command Prompt**, change to the directory containing the file you want to rename, and use the `REN` command. For example, to rename *myfile.doc* to *myfile.txt*, type the following command:

   ```
   REN MYFILE.DOC MYFILE.TXT
   ```

2. The `REN` command also has the definite advantage of allowing you to rename multiple files simultaneously. For example, to rename all the files with the extension *.doc* to *.txt*, type the following command:

   ```
   REN *.DOC *.TXT
   ```

   See Appendix B, *DOS Lives*, for more information on `REN` and the command prompt.

Solution 2: Use the File Manager

- If you can bear it, fire up the old Windows 3.x-style File Manager (*Winfile.exe*). Not only will it *not* display the warning message, but it will allow you to rename multiple files as described for the `REN` command above. You might also be pleased to learn that File Manager won't display the flying paper animation when you move or copy files—an added bonus.

Solution 3: Use the Send To menu

If you find yourself renaming files to the same extension all the time, you can set up an entry in your **Send To** menu to do it for you, without any typing, and without the useless warning message:

1. Open a text editor, such as Notepad, and type the following line:

   ```
   REN %1 *.TXT
   ```

   Here, *`%1`* represents the file being selected with the mouse. Of course, you'll probably want to change *`*.TXT`* to whatever extension you need; just remember the asterisk.
2. Save the file in a folder on your hard disk, and call it something like `Rename to TXT.bat`. Make sure you use the *.bat* extension at the end, so that Windows knows this is a DOS batch file. Then make a shortcut to the batch file in your *Send To* folder (it's in your Windows folder), and call it something like `Rename to TXT`.
3. From now on, you can right-click on a file in Explorer or a folder window, select **Send To** and then **Rename to TXT** (or whatever you've called it), and the file will be renamed automatically.
4. You can configure the DOS window to close automatically by right-clicking on the shortcut you created, selecting **Properties**, choosing the **Program** tab, and turning on the **Close on exit** option. Click **OK** when you're finished.

Solution 4: Power Rename

Power Rename, which comes with *O'Reilly Utilities—Quick Solutions for Windows 98 Annoyances*, provides powerful renaming functions, allowing you to rename any number of files with a minimum of typing and a maximum of flexibility.

- Just select one or more files, right-click on them, and select **Power Rename**. Or start Power Rename and drag any files you want to rename onto the window.

Power Rename is also a good way to quickly get rid of the "Shortcut to" prefix on new shortcuts (see "Get Rid of Shortcut Residue" later in this chapter) and the "Copy of" prefix on file duplicates (see "Make a Duplicate of a File or Folder" later in this chapter).

Notes and other issues

Windows warns you when you try to change a filename extension because extensions show Windows what type of file a certain file is. If, for example, you have a file with the extension *.doc*, Windows knows it's a Word file. When you double-click it, Word is started and the file is opened. Also, when opening files from within the application, Word only lets you see Word files (**.doc*) by default. This link between file extensions and the programs that edit them is stored in the Registry (see Chapter 3 for more information). If you change the extension, this link can be broken. If you don't know what you're doing, you can temporarily lose the ability to open the file.

No file can be altered by simply changing its name or extension; even if you change *Myfile.txt* to *Food.dog*, the file can *still* be opened in Notepad (or whatever your default text editor is), but not by double-clicking on it in Explorer. You'll have to open the application manually, select **Open** from the application's **File** menu, and choose **All Files (*.*)** from the **Files of type** list to see files other than the default type.*

Some *applications* (as opposed to Windows itself) also determine a file's type by its extension, rather than its contents. For example, if you change *Myfile.gif* to *Myfile.dog*, and then try to open the file, an application might report something like, "This is not a valid dog file." In that case, the file really will become unusable if you change the extension. This occurs most often with *.gif* and *.jpg* files, the graphic file formats used in web pages. Many people mistakenly switch their extensions, most likely in a failed attempt to convert between formats. While web browsers don't seem to

* An exception to this rule is Microsoft Office 97. Any documents created with one of the applications in Office (e.g., Word, Excel, etc.) are aware of their file type. If you change the extension of a Word file, for example, to *.hula*, it will still be opened in Word. However, this doesn't work if you change the extension to that of an already registered file type, such as *.txt*.

mind this, most graphics programs, which rely on file extensions, will tell you the file is corrupt.

See Appendix B and Chapter 9, *Scripting and Automation*, for more information on DOS commands and DOS batch files, respectively.

Make a Duplicate of a File or Folder

Windows lets you copy and move files from one folder to another by dragging them with different combinations of keystrokes (see "Move or Copy Files at Will" earlier in this chapter). You can also rename a file by clicking on its name or pressing the **F2** key. However, if you want to make a duplicate of a file in the same directory and assign it a different name, the process might not be as obvious. Here are a few ways to do it:

- Hold the **Ctrl** key while dragging a file from one part of the window to another part of the same window. This works in folder windows, on the desktop, and (unlike Windows 95) in Explorer.
- Use the right mouse button to drag the file from one part of the window to another part of the same window, and then select **Copy Here** (see Figure 2-2).
- For keyboard enthusiasts, press **Ctrl-C** and then **Ctrl-V** to create a duplicate of a file using the clipboard.
- Use the Power Rename utility (see "Rename Files Without a Hassle" earlier in this chapter) to quickly duplicate large numbers of files.

  First, right-click on the file you want to duplicate, select **Send To**, and then **Power Rename**. Or, open Power Rename and drag-drop the file into the window. Select **With Operation**, and check the **Increment** option. Choose the **name** option here. Leave the **position** field blank, and specify the correct **number of digits**: type **1** if you want to make fewer than 10 duplicates, **2** if you want to make fewer than 100 duplicates, and so on. Turn off all other operations.

  Turn on the **Leave original (copy)** option, and turn on the **Show what files will look like** option to see what the new file will look like. Click **Accept** to duplicate the file once, or click **Accept** repeatedly to make lots of duplicates. Use Power Rename to quickly make numbered duplicates of a file, and to avoid the "Copy of" prefix.

Notes and other issues

For all of the solutions above except for the use of Power Rename, the duplicate of a file called, say, *Myfile.txt* would automatically be named *Copy of Myfile.txt*. An additional copy of *Myfile.txt* will be called *Copy (2) of Myfile.txt*, while a copy of *Copy of Myfile.txt* will be called *Copy of Copy of Myfile.txt*. Since the filename keeps changing (albeit inconveniently), you can duplicate multiple files simultaneously to quickly fill a directory with dozens of identical files.

If you duplicate a folder, all the contents of the folder will be duplicated, but only the name of the duplicated folder will be changed.

Turn Off Delete Confirmation

A common complaint about Windows, especially among advanced users, is the inability to configure the Recycle Bin to immediately delete a file without one or more nag windows.

At worst, you may get up to four confirmation messages when you try to delete a series of files. You'll get a nag window when you first drop files into the Recycle Bin, a second when you empty the Recycle Bin, a third if the file that's being deleted is an *.exe* file (but this does not happen for *.dll* files, which are just as necessary as *.exe* files), and a fourth if the file has a read-only or system attribute set.

The number and type of confirmation messages you get will depend on the settings of your Recycle Bin. For example, if your Recycle Bin is configured to simply hold files (the default) rather than delete them, you might not see any message at all when you throw files away. However, if you find that multiple warnings are driving you crazy, there are several ways to reduce nag windows to a bare minimum, and in some circumstances, to circumvent them altogether.

To delete files immediately after they are dropped

1. Right-click on the Recycle Bin, and select **Properties**.
2. Under the **Global** tab, select **Use one setting for all drives**.
3. Turn on the option labeled **Do not move files to the recycle bin**. (For some reason, decreasing the **Maximum size of Recycle Bin** option to 0% doesn't do the trick.) Note that when this option is chosen, the **Display delete confirmation dialog** option immediately becomes inaccessible. This is a clue that the designers of Windows did not intend to permit the deletion of files without at least one prompt. Now, this safety feature is probably worthwhile for the majority of users, but the inflexibility here is a bit too strict for some.

   If you don't use this setting, and instead have Recycle Bin store deleted files, they won't be deleted until you right-click on the Recycle Bin and select **Empty Recycle Bin**. However, since the Recycle

Bin can be configured to empty files automatically when there are too many being kept around, it is possible for files to disappear without any confirmations at all.

To delete a file permanently without disabling the Recycle Bin's ability to store other files

1. Turn off the **Do not move files to the recycle bin** option (as described above) if it's on.
2. Hold the **Shift** key while dropping files into the Recycle Bin. You'll still get a prompt, but any files currently in the Recycle Bin will remain there, and future dropped files will also be stored.

To delete files without confirmation, and without storing them in the Recycle Bin

1. Create a shortcut to the **Recycle Bin** in your *Send To* folder.
2. To delete a file, right-click on it and select **Recycle Bin** from the **Send To** menu.

To automatically skip the prompts

- Obtain and install RtvReco (see Appendix F), which can be configured to bypass many useless, repetitive screens.

For faster, nag-free deletes

Using the command prompt can be a big time saver, as well as a big sanity saver.

- Use the `DEL` command (see Appendix B) to delete one or more files without any prompt at all. Added benefits of using this method include the ability to quickly delete all files sharing a common trait, such as a filename extension. Just type `DEL *.TMP` to delete all files with the *.tmp* extension. For a large number of files, you'll also notice that the DOS commands are completed much more quickly than their Windows counterparts.
- Use the `DELTREE` command (see Appendix B) to delete an entire folder and all its subfolders. Similar to `DEL`, above, `DELTREE` is substantially faster at deleting a large number of files; an entire branch can be deleted in seconds, while deleting them in Windows can take several minutes. `DELTREE` also works without nag windows, and without any flying paper animations at all.

Notes and other issues

Undo. If the Recycle Bin is configured to store deleted files, you can get back accidental deletions by opening the Recycle Bin and pulling files out of it. If you've configured the Recycle Bin to delete files immediately, you'll need an undelete program (such as the one that comes with Norton Utilities) to get them back. If you delete files with the `DEL` or `DELTREE` commands, the files will *not* be stored in the Recycle Bin, regardless of its configuration.

Coping with Loss: Using the New Windows Help System

The central Windows help system has undergone many transformations, but unfortunately, each successive version loses some of the functionality or usability of its predecessor.

First introduced in Windows 3.0, WinHelp provided a common interface and functionality for online documentation. Multiple pages of "rich" text (containing formatting and graphics) could be linked together and condensed into a single WinHelp (*.hlp*) file, which in turn was accessible directly from the application that it accompanied. In Windows 95, Microsoft added a global text-search feature, as well as an irritating little "Contents" window. While the new system didn't necessarily remove any of the functionality of the old system, those help files that utilized the new design were less flexible and harder to use than those without the new features.

WinHelp's latest incarnation, supported in Windows 98, adds some flexibility and a somewhat new architecture. Driven by the proliferation of the Web, Microsoft created the Compiled HTML Manual (**.chm*) format, also known as HTML Help. HTML Help files essentially serve the same purpose as the older HLP counterparts, but have more of a web look and feel, and present both advantages and disadvantages over the previous version.

The following tips should help you overcome some of the limitations in either type of help system, as both are used in Windows 98 applications.

Classic WinHelp files

WinHelp files use four types of windows to either display help content or control the display of help content: the small, yellow popup windows that appear when you press the **F1** key in a dialog box; the tabbed help dialog with the **Contents**, **Index**, and **Find** features; the main help window; and the occasional secondary popup help window. The problem with this system is the inconvenience of moving from one type of window to another. The following are solutions to the two major obstacles WinHelp places in the way of effortless navigation.

First, the main help window has buttons that allow you to jump to the **Contents**, **Index**, and **Find** features, if they're available. However, this window is not the first one to appear when you select **Help Topics** from an application's **Help** menu. If the author of the help file has followed Microsoft's standards, the first thing you'll see is the **Contents** window, a preprogrammed outline of the help file that forces users to hunt for information by double-clicking on tiny icons of books and paper.

Instead of seeing a friendly and familiar introductory page and being presented with an *option* to view the outline, you are forced to mess with this ridiculous hierarchy in order to get to any actual documentation. Furthermore, rather than allowing you to quickly navigate the actual structure of the help file, this window merely contains a simple hierarchy set up by the author of the help file that links to only some of the help pages.

This counterintuitive and counterproductive design is only available on applications which specifically support it; thankfully, not all applications use the new window. Fortunately, it's easy to disable this window, but that requires some knowledge of how the help system works. Along with an application's main help file (*.hlp*), there can be up to three other files, each with the following extensions:

.gid

This file is created the first time the help file is opened, and helps Windows find the help file next time. It can be deleted without consequence as long as the help file isn't currently open. The next time you access the help file, the file will be recreated.

.fts

This file is created when the file is indexed, and can become quite large—up to 75% of the size of the *.hlp* file. It can take quite a bit of time to create and read, especially on slower systems. The first time you choose the **Find** tab in the **Help Topics** window of a particular help file, the *.fts* file is created. It can be deleted to save disk space (at least temporarily) as along as the help file isn't open; the only consequence is that you'll have to wait for Windows to recreate this index file the next time you use the **Find** feature for that particular help file.

.cnt

This file may be included with an application's help file, but is not created on the fly. You can delete this file (as long as the help file isn't currently open), and the Contents screen will never appear again. If you delete the file, and select **Help Topics** from the application's **Help** menu, the **Index** tab will be selected instead of the **Contents** tab. Also, if you double-click on the *.hlp* file, the help file's main introductory page, which may be blank, will be displayed.

Note that you will also have to delete the *.gid* file (if it exists) for the change to take effect. The consequence of deleting the *.cnt* file is that you won't be able to get it back without reinstalling the application with which it came; you might want to rename the file instead. In some rare circumstances, deleting the *.cnt* file will make the help file totally unusable, so it's best to simply rename it and test the help system before you do away with it for good.

Second, the small yellow popup windows, which are actually located in the same *.hlp* file, can't easily be accessed from the main help file. Conversely, you can't access the main help file to view other topics when you're viewing one of the small, yellow popup windows—you must close the popup window, close the dialog box, return to the main application screen, and access the help contents window from there.

Occasionally, the information in the small, yellow popup windows has been included in the preprogrammed **Index** feature. If it's not there, you can almost always use the **Find** feature to find the information you seek (assuming you want to sacrifice the time and disk space to create an index), as long as you can guess one of the words on that page.

HTML help

There are two advantages to the contents screen in HTML Help (which otherwise hasn't been improved) over its classic WinHelp counterpart: it's resizable, and you aren't forced to use it. Whether or not it's open, you can begin using the actual help material in the right pane right away. Although you can close the **Contents** pane by clicking the **Hide** button on the HTML Help toolbar, this also makes the **Index** and **Search** features inaccessible, so it's not exactly a good solution.

Now, it may seem frustrating that if you hide the tabbed pane, and then close the help window and reopen it, the tabbed pane is again visible. The good news is that it doesn't always default back to the **Contents** tab—whatever tab you've last selected becomes the default, so if you find yourself using the **Search** tab most often, you won't have to keep switching to it.

And unlike classic WinHelp files, the *Contents* file is integrated into the *.chm* file, so it's impossible to disable it permanently. However, you can still reclaim some disk space by deleting the following unnecessary file:

.chw

This file is created automatically the first time the help file is opened, and is the HTML Help counterpart to the *.gid* and *.fts* files used in the Classic WinHelp system. It can be deleted as long as the help file isn't currently open. The next time you access the help file, the file will be recreated; the only consequence is that it can take 10–20 seconds, depending on its size, for this to happen. The only advantage to deleting this file is the amount of disk space you'll recover temporarily; deleting it won't change any help functionality. To give you an idea of how much space you'll get back, *Windows.chm*, the main online help file for Windows, is about 570KB. The accompanying *.chw* file (*Windows.chw*), which can be deleted, is a whopping 660KB.

The most significant difference between the new help system supported by Windows 98 and the classic WinHelp system is the way the help file is constructed, something many users will never have reason to notice. Classic WinHelp files are almost exclusively authored by using Microsoft Word to create *.rtf* files, and then combining those files with graphics, a WinHelp project file, and several other files using the Help Compiler. This system is convoluted, arduous, and relies heavily on Word (although authoring with other applications is possible; the Help Compiler is available from Microsoft for free). The new system uses HTML, the file format used for web pages, which can be authored with any plain text editor, such as Notepad. The only thing that is required is the tool that compiles the HTML files and graphics into a single distribution file—the HTML Help Workshop—which is available for free from Microsoft (see Appendix F).

Note that HTML Help is a new technology, and will undoubtedly undergo many revisions, especially as Microsoft has apparently abandoned development of WinHelp.

Notes and other issues

For Classic WinHelp files, there may not be a *.cnt* file for every help file on your hard disk. Deleting a single *.cnt* file (if it exists) will only disable the contents window for that particular help file.

Go ahead and use Windows' **Find** feature to find all of the *.cnt*, *.fts*, *.gid*, and *.chw* files on your system. You'll be pleasantly surprised at the hard drive space you'll retrieve as a result of deleting these files. If you're really low on disk space, you can also delete any or all of your *.hlp* and *.chm* files, although, of course, it will consequently make those help files inaccessible. The Disk Cleanup wizard that comes with Microsoft Plus! 98 actually recommends this practice, and has a nice interface for doing so.

If you find yourself using a particular *.hlp* file often, yet are disappointed with the searching capabilities provided (for example, if you are not able to locate a specific word on a page), you can convert the *.hlp* file to one or more *.html* files. Use the HTML Help Workshop to perform the conversion, and then use your favorite web browser to view the files.

See "What to Throw Away" in Chapter 5, *Maximizing Performance*, for more files that can be deleted to reclaim disk space and improve overall system performance.

Get Control of the Desktop

The desktop is the root of all evils . . . well, at least the root of all folders. The desktop paradigm to which Windows supposedly adheres commands that the desktop be the base upon which all other system objects are placed. This includes all drives, the Control Panel, the Network Neighborhood, and even all running applications.

However, internally, the desktop is simply part of the Explorer application, and its contents are a combination of namespace objects (see Appendix D, *Class IDs of System Objects*) and the files in a special folder on your hard disk. As for controlling the desktop, one might think that a good place to start is the **Desktop Properties** (accessible by right-clicking); however, this gets you to the **Display Properties**—perhaps convenient, but not very intuitive. Most of the settings for the desktop are shared with Explorer and the single folder windows, and therefore are discussed throughout this book.

The following sections cover some fundamental tasks involved in dealing with the desktop: what refreshing the desktop means and when it can be done instead of restarting, and how to make sure your desktop configuration remains intact. For details on the Active Desktop and other web integration topics, see Chapter 8.

Force Windows to Remember Folder Settings

For most users, Windows' most irritating behavior is its inability to save the settings for folder windows, and its corresponding tendency to set defaults for new, unopened folder windows. Settings like position, size, sort order, auto-arrange, and icon size are often reset to Windows' default values when folders are opened. The Explorer window (tree view) is a little better behaved, although it's far from perfect. For example, one would expect that once a sort order has been set in a particular folder, the items in that folder would remain sorted in the same way the next time the folder is opened.

Other than a vague memory of the two dozen most recently opened windows, Windows won't automatically save many of your settings, either for use when reopening the same windows, or for viewing new ones. The problem is that these settings are stored in the Registry, instead of saved in the file system as properties of the folders themselves. This inherent design flaw will never allow Windows to remember settings for more than a finite number of windows. Windows NT has a partial fix for a similar problem, at least in the context of security. If you specify which users have rights to read or modify the files in a certain folder on your hard disk, those settings are saved as properties of the folders, meaning that there's no limit—no central database of saved settings that will eventually get full.

At any rate, Windows 98 introduces some new functionality that theoretically helps deal with the problem, although it doesn't work as well as many of us would like.

Using Explorer

- Use the Explorer window with the folder tree labeled Exploring visible, instead of the single-folder view accessible from the My Computer window when browsing your files.
- When you make a change, such as the sort order or icon size, the change will be saved with Explorer, and not with any individual folders. That means that when you click on any other folder in the tree, it will be displayed in the same way—the settings won't revert to the folder's "memory."
- Additionally, when you close the Explorer window, or open others, the changes (for the most part) will remain intact. This applies to icon size, sort order, window size and placement, any toolbar settings, the sizes of the columns in the **Details** view, and the position of the vertical divider. Any changes made to the Explorer window will not affect the single-folder view.

Using single-folder windows

The settings for single-folder windows are saved differently than for Explorer. Instead of using the most recent setting to view all folder windows, the individual settings for the last two dozen or so folders are stored in the Registry. Here are some tips for using single-folder windows:

- When you open an existing folder, set the sort order or icon size to your liking, and then close the window, your settings should be remembered the next time you open it. Those settings, however, are stored only for that folder, and are used only when it's viewed in the single-folder view. Furthermore, after a while, and after you open a sufficient number of other folders, the settings for the first folder will be discarded.* Note also that if you make a copy of a folder for which you've changed the settings (see "Make a Duplicate of a File or Folder" earlier in this chapter), the new folder won't inherit any of the original folder's settings.

- To change this, select **Folder Options** from the folder's **View** menu, and choose the **View** tab. Then, click **Like Current Folder**, and answer **Yes** to the confirmation box. As the warning states, all folders on the system, including those you've configured previously as well as those ones that don't yet exist, will be reset to use the settings of the latest window.
- Lastly, make sure the **Remember each folder's view settings** option is checked. Click **OK** when you're finished.

Notes and other issues

Using the **Like Current Folder** feature in a single-folder window will make some of those settings carry over to the Explorer window, although the converse isn't necessarily true.

Another major annoyance is that if you change any of the "Custom Settings" in the **Folder Options** box in single-folder windows or in Explorer, any settings you thought you saved with the **Like Current Folder** feature described above are discarded.

In Windows 95, if you configured a single-folder window to use the same window for successive folders—that is, when you double-click on a folder icon, a separate window isn't created—your settings for the first window would remain intact, much like the first solution for Explorer. This isn't the case in Windows 98. While it's less consistent for users who've upgraded, it's probably a better design.

Toolbar settings don't follow the same rules as the rest of the settings here. When you turn on one of the three standard toolbars in Explorer, they stay on until you turn them off, even if you close and reopen Explorer. Likewise, if you turn on or off any toolbars in a single-folder window, that setting remains in effect in *all* single-folder windows until it's changed again. This behavior is inconsistent from the way that other settings are saved in folders, which makes the whole process that much more confusing.

* Shouldn't Windows show more respect for your preferences than to simply discard them?

See "Explorer Techniques" later in this chapter for more information on controlling this behavior on the fly.

If you've taken steps to "Get Rid of the Unwanted Explorer Windows at Startup," discussed later in this chapter, the setting may be preventing Windows from saving your Explorer settings.

Refresh the Desktop Without Restarting Windows

When Windows starts, it loads the Explorer application, which provides the desktop and the Start Menu. While it's loading, Explorer reads its settings from the Registry (see Chapter 3). If you make a change to the Registry, such as when following some of the procedures in this book, it might not take effect until you reload Explorer, which usually means restarting Windows. However, restarting Windows can take several minutes, and, for example, if you're using Dial-Up Networking, you'll be forced to disconnect. To refresh the desktop *without* restarting Windows, follow these directions. Whether or not any of these solutions will cause any changes you've made to take effect depends on the type of setting you've changed.

Solution 1

- Click on any empty area of your desktop or any icon on your desktop with the left mouse button, and press the **F5** key to refresh the desktop.

Solution 2

In such cases where Solution 1 is not sufficient to implement your changes, you can force Explorer to reload without restarting:

1. Press **Ctrl-Alt-Del**, and select **Explorer** from the list (don't select **Exploring...**). Don't worry; this shouldn't affect your other running applications, although they may be paused temporarily while the Close Program window is being shown.
2. Click **End Task**. In a few seconds, you'll see a message window asking if you wish to shut down Windows. Click **No**.
3. Wait about ten seconds until another window appears confirming that you wish to close Explorer, and click **End Task** here.

The Taskbar and all desktop icons will disappear temporarily, but then will reappear in a few seconds when Explorer is reloaded.

Solution 3

In such cases where Solution 2 is not sufficient to implement your changes, the following will not only reload Explorer, but reinitialize all your user settings:

- If you have any network components installed (the option will be unavailable otherwise), you can select **Log Off *username*** from the Start Menu, where *username* is the currently logged on user. This will cause all your programs to close, but it doesn't take nearly as long as restarting.

Notes and other issues

If you have the Resource Meter utility running, make sure to close it before using Solution 2.

See the next section for more information.

Restart Windows Without Restarting Your Computer

Choosing **Shut Down** from the Start Menu gives you several choices, including restarting your computer. However, in most cases, you'll be able to simply reload Windows *without* restarting your computer, saving time and aggravation. This concept should sound familiar to any of you who once used Windows 3.x.

Solution 1: Using keystrokes

- Select **Shut Down** from the Start Menu, select **Restart**, and hold down the **Shift** key while pressing **OK**.

Solution 2: Make a Restart icon on your desktop

1. Using a text editor, such as Notepad, type the following by itself:

   ```
   @EXIT
   ```

2. Save the one-line file somewhere on your hard disk, and call it whatever you like, as long as it has the *.bat* extension.
3. Place a shortcut to this new batch file on your desktop or Start Menu, and name it **Restart Windows**.
4. Right-click on the shortcut, select **Properties**, choose the **Program** tab, and make sure the **Close on Exit** option is turned on.

5. Then, click the **Advanced** button, and make sure the **MS-DOS mode** option is selected and the **Warn before entering MS-DOS mode** option is turned off.
6. Click **OK** twice, and then double-click on the icon to use it.

Notes and other issues

See "Refresh the Desktop Without Restarting Windows" earlier in this chapter for a few alternatives to restarting Windows.

Save Your Desktop Layout

After meticulously arranging all the icons on your desktop, you may have found that Windows either rearranges them for no particular reason, or simply forgets their positions the next time you start Windows. Sometimes a system crash is the cause; at other times, Windows can do this right when you're staring at it. Here are some workarounds.

Solution 1

If you're also experiencing other settings being lost, such as Taskbar settings or display colors, it may be that you're not logged in. Windows saves some of these settings only for configured users of the system, and if there is no current user, it can't save your settings.

- Double-click on the **Passwords** icon in **Control Panel**, and click **Change Windows Password**. Choosing a new password should convince Windows that you're an actual user with feelings and preferences.

  You may have to log off and log back on for this setting to take effect (see Solution 2).

Solution 2

If you find that Windows has spontaneously forgotten your desktop layout, you can "save" it by logging off and then logging back on again.

- Select **Log Off *username*** from the **Start Menu**, where *username* is the currently logged on user. When the logon box appears, enter your username (you can leave the password field blank) and click **OK**.
- If the **Log Off *username*** menu item does not appear in your Start Menu, there are two things you can try. First, double-click on the **Network** icon in **Control Panel**. If there aren't any network drivers loaded whatsoever, click **Add**, double-click **Client**, select **Microsoft** in the left column and **Client for Microsoft Networks** in the right column, click

OK, and then **OK** again. If there *are* network drivers loaded, close the **Network Properties** box, double-click on the **Users** icon in **Control Panel**, and follow the onscreen instructions to create a new user.

Solution 3

- If neither of the first two solutions seem to work, try the EzDesk utility—see Appendix F for more information.

Notes and other issues

If you're unable to move the icons on your desktop, right-click on an empty portion of the desktop, select **Arrange Icons**, and turn off the **Auto-Arrange** option.

Windows seems to refresh the desktop under certain situations, such as when files are copied to or deleted from the desktop, or when settings are changed in Explorer. There's no way to completely predict or control this behavior.

Get Rid of the Unwanted Explorer Windows at Startup

You may have noticed that any Explorer and single-folder windows that were left open whenever you shut down Windows are reopened the next time you start. Under some circumstances, these Windows are opened automatically at startup regardless of whether they were left open or not. There are a few things that can cause this:

- Make sure you close *all* Explorer and single-folder windows before shutting down.
- You might not be shutting down completely; make sure you see the screen that says, "It is now safe to turn off your computer."
- You may have *Explorer.exe* specified in your *StartUp* folder in the Start Menu, or in the `RUN=` or `LOAD=` lines of *Win.ini* (see Chapter 3).

You can also configure Windows to not save the states of open Explorer and single-folder windows, although this setting will negate any other saved settings, as described in "Force Windows to Remember Folder Settings" earlier in this chapter. To stop Windows from saving window states and positions when you shut down, complete either of the following solutions.

Solution 1

1. Double-click on the **TweakUI** icon (see Appendix A, *Setting Locator*) in Control Panel and choose the **Explorer** tab.
2. Turn off the **Save Explorer window settings** option and then click **OK**.

This setting should take effect the next time you shut down.

Solution 2

1. Open the System Policy Editor (see Appendix A) and select **Open Registry** from the **File** menu.
2. Double-click on the **Local User** icon, and expand the branches to `Local User\Windows 98 System\Shell\Restrictions`.
3. Turn on the **Don't save settings at exit** option.
4. Click **OK**, select **Save** from the **File** menu, and close the System Policy Editor.

This setting should take effect the next time you shut down.

Notes and other issues

If you turn off this setting, Windows will not remember any of your window positions or settings such as icon sizes or sort order. See "Force Windows to Remember Folder Settings" earlier in this chapter.

Fundamental Interface Tweaks

You should already know how to change your desktop wallpaper, specify screen colors, and rearrange the items in your Start Menu. The material in this section covers more specific changes to the Taskbar, the Tray, and desktop icons to make them a bit more usable. Some of the concepts covered in this section include:

- Using command-line parameters with Windows programs
- Referencing virtual folders
- Making shortcuts to system objects
- Using TweakUI
- Tricking Windows by adding and removing key files

Probably the most important customizations in this section are illustrated in "Force Explorer to Start with the Folder You Want" and "Customize Drive Icons." Both of these solutions utilize built-in features of the operating system in ways for which they weren't intended. The rest of this section should help you tame the Tray, the Control Panel, and the Start Menu—stuff you won't find in the manual. You may want to skip down to "Replace the Startup and Shutdown Screens" right away, if you can't stand to look at the clouds another minute.

Get Rid of Shortcut Residue

Shortcuts have three ways of telling you that they're shortcuts. When a shortcut is first created, its caption begins with the text *Shortcut To*. The shortcut's icon also has a small curved arrow in the lower-left corner (see the *before* icon in Figure 2-4). If you're viewing the folder containing the shortcut in **Details** mode, the **Type** column will read either **Shortcut**, **Shortcut to MS-DOS Program**, or **Internet Shortcut** for *.lnk*, *.pif*, and *.url* shortcut files, respectively. Note that even if you've configured Windows to display your filename extensions, the extensions for shortcuts will always be hidden.

Figure 2-4: Cleaning up shortcuts: before (left) and after (right)

Although one can simply rename the icon so that the *Shortcut To* prefix isn't there, there is no quick way to remove the little arrow for just one shortcut. To turn off these artifacts for good on all shortcuts, follow these instructions.

Solution 1

- According to Microsoft, if you remove the *Shortcut To* prefix by hand (by renaming the file) immediately after creating the shortcut at least *eight times*, it will stop coming back. Unfortunately, this doesn't seem to always work. Proceed immediately to Solution 2. Do not pass Go; do not collect $200.

Solution 2

1. To turn off the prefix immediately, and without a hassle, double-click on the **TweakUI** icon (see Appendix A) in Control Panel.
2. Choose the **Explorer** tab and turn off the **Prefix "Shortcut to" on new shortcuts** option in the **Settings** section.

3. To disable or change the curved arrow icon, choose the desired option in the **Shortcut overlay** section. If you choose **Custom**, you can choose any icon, although it should be partially transparent, so as not to obscure the original icon.
4. Click **OK** when you're done. After you've made these changes, your shortcuts should resemble the *after* icon in Figure 2-4.

Notes and other issues

The curved arrow icon can also be changed with the Microangelo Engineer utility.

If you disable both the *Shortcut To* prefix and the curved arrow icon, the only ways to distinguish a shortcut from the actual program or file to which it's linked are either through the shortcut's **Properties** sheet, or by its description in the **Type** column in Explorer.

Undo. Any of these items can be restored to their defaults using TweakUI. You can use the **Restore Factory Settings** button, but it will undo all of the settings on the page. It may be easier just to change the individual settings you changed originally.

Customize the Tray

The Tray is the little box (usually in the lower right-hand corner of your screen, at the end of your Taskbar) that, by default, contains the clock and the little yellow speaker. Figure 2-5 shows a more or less typical Tray.

Figure 2-5: The Tray contains several icons as well as the clock

You'll notice some other icons appearing in the Tray, used either to start a program or to show the options for a program that is already running. What's irritating is that there doesn't seem to be any sort of consistent standard for items in the Tray; some icons get double-clicked, some require a single right- or left-click, and some don't get clicked at all. However, it's possible to remove most of the icons that appear in the Tray, or to add your own icons.

Add your own programs to the Tray

1. Obtain and install the Tray utility.
2. Run *Tray.exe*, right-click on the new icon in the Tray, and select **Help** for instructions.

Hide the Tray entirely (without manually removing all of its contents)

- Obtain *O'Reilly Utilities—Quick Solutions for Windows 98 Annoyances* (see Appendix F). It allows you to hide the Tray as well as restore it, and even works the next time you start Windows.

Remove unwanted icons from the Tray

- To remove the yellow speaker icon used for volume control, double-click on the **Multimedia** icon in the Control Panel. Choose the **Audio** tab, and turn off the **Show volume control on the Taskbar** option.
- To remove the little modem icon with the blinking lights used with Dial-Up Networking, open the Dial-Up Networking folder. Right-click on a connection icon and select **Properties**. If you have more than one connection, you'll need to repeat these steps for each one. In the **Connect using** section, click **Configure**; this will display a box similar, but not identical to, the modem settings in the Control Panel. Click on the **Options** tab, and turn off **Display modem status** in the **Status control** section.
- To remove the little modem icon with the blinking lights used with HyperTerminal, first open a connection in HyperTerminal. If you have more than one connection, you'll need to repeat these steps for each one. Select **Properties** from the **File** menu, and in the **Connect using** section, click **Configure**; this will display a box similar, but not identical to, the modem settings in the Control Panel. Click on the **Options** tab, and turn off **Display modem status** in the **Status control** section.
- To remove additional Tray icons, see Appendix A.

Notes and other issues

If you remove the yellow speaker, you can still adjust the volume with the Volume Control utility included with Windows. Removing the flashing modem icon will not have any effect on modem performance or functionality.

Undo. You can restore any of the removed Tray icons by simply reversing the process you used to hide them.

Force Explorer to Start with the Folder You Want

As you've undoubtedly discovered, Windows Explorer always opens at the root folder of the drive on which Windows is installed. Since there are several ways to start Explorer, there are several ways to specify where it opens.

Launching Explorer from a shortcut

1. Open Explorer, and go to your *\Windows\Start Menu* folder (you can right-click on the **Start** button and select **Explore** to get there quickly—see the next method).
2. Find the shortcut for Explorer (or create one if it doesn't exist), right-click on it, and select **Properties**.
3. Click on the **Shortcut** tab, and change the text in the **Target** field so it reads:

   ```
   Explorer.exe /n, /e, d:\myfolder
   ```

   where *`d:\myfolder`* is the drive and folder where you want Explorer to start.
4. If you want Explorer to start at the top level, My Computer, so no drive branches are initially expanded, type the following:

   ```
   Explorer.exe /n, /e, /select, c:\
   ```

Explore the Start Menu

- Right-click on the **Start** button and select **Explore**.

  This will always open Explorer pointed at your *\Windows\Start Menu* folder. This behavior follows the object paradigm; right-clicking on that object and selecting (in this case) **Explore** will carry out that action on *that* object. There's no way to change this particular instance of the **Explore** command so that Explorer displays another folder. Use the first technique discussed to achieve the closest approximation.

Explore a folder

- You can right-click on any folder icon and select **Explore**; this will open Explorer expanded to that folder. This works in the same way as the previous example. Although there's no equivalent command for the desktop, the desktop folder is located at the top of the Explorer tree, so it's always easy to get to.

Notes and other issues

The command-line parameters Explorer accepts (as discussed previously in "Launching Explorer from a shortcut") are as follows:

```
explorer [/n] [/e][,/root,object][[,/select],subobject]
```

The `/n` switch tells Explorer to always open a new window (even if the specified folder is already open), and the `/e` switch tells Explorer to use the tree view rather than the default single-folder view. The ***`/root,object`*** parameter allows you to choose what appears as the root of all folders in the new window. The default is the desktop, but you can specify any other namespace object (see Appendix D). The ***`subobject`*** parameter specifies the folder that you want to select. Use the ***`/select`*** switch to ensure that ***`subobject`*** is selected, which is useful if ***`subobject`*** is a file.

Customize Drive Icons

At this point, you've probably figured out that you can create shortcuts to all your drive icons in My Computer, place them in a folder or on the desktop, and then change the icons of the shortcuts to something other than the default generic hard disk and floppy drive icons. That solution, while relatively easy, is quite limited, especially since the icons aren't reflected in Explorer or My Computer, and you can't customize your own icons for floppy and removable drives.

Using the functionality built into the CD-ROM *Autorun* feature (see Chapter 4, *Tinkering Techniques*), which allows you to start a CD just by inserting the disc, there's a simple way to customize your drive icons (for hard, floppy, and removable drives):

1. Using a text editor such as Notepad, type the following:

   ```
   [autorun]
   icon=filename, number
   ```

   where ***`filename`*** is the name of the file (an *.exe*, *.dll*, *.ico*, or *.bmp* file) containing the icon, and ***`number`*** is the index of the icon to use. Leave ***`number`*** blank or specify 0 (zero) to use the first icon in the file, 1 for the second, and so on.*

2. Save the file as *Autorun.inf* in the root folder of the hard disk, floppy, or removable drive you wish to customize.

* There are different kinds of icon files. Most icon editors read and write *.ico* files, which usually only contain a single icon. However, *.ico* files, *.dll* files, and *.exe* files all can contain many icons, each in several resolutions. If you wish to use, say, the *third* icon in a file, you would specify an icon index of 2. The Microangelo Studio utility can be used to create and edit all types of icon files.

3. Double-click on the **My Computer** icon or open Explorer, and press the **F5** key to refresh the display and read the new icons.

Figure 2-6 shows a My Computer window that's been customized in this way.

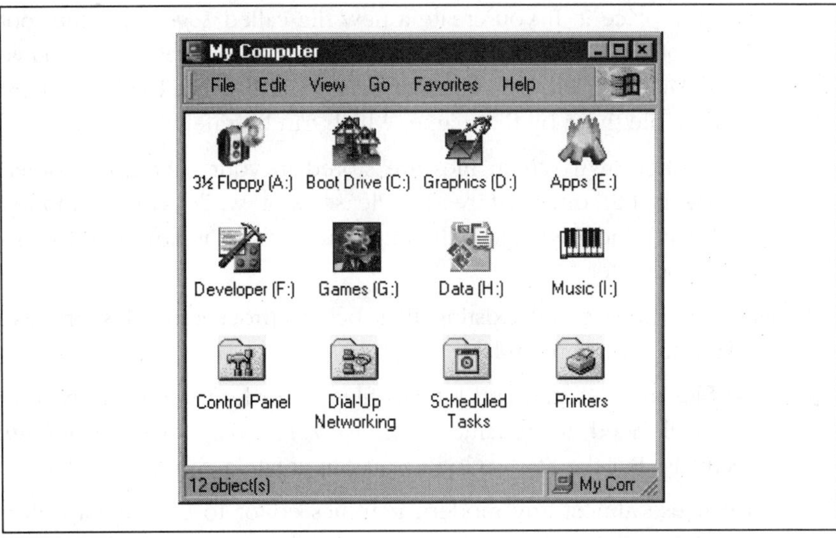

Figure 2-6: The My Computer window may be a little more inviting with customized icons

Notes and other issues

This will work even if you've turned off CD-ROM Autorun.

This will also work for removable drives (floppies, Syquest and Zip drives, CD recorders, optical disks), but since Windows isn't able to determine when you insert and remove removable media (like it can for CD-ROMs), you need to manually refresh the My Computer or Explorer window every time by pressing the **F5** key.

To turn the display of certain drive icons on or off in the My Computer window, use the **My Computer** tab in TweakUI (see Appendix A for more information).

Replace the Startup and Shutdown Screens

You spend at least a few seconds every time you turn on your computer staring at the huge Windows logo floating in the clouds while you wait for it to load. The screens that tell you to "Please wait while Windows is shutting down" and that "It is now safe to turn off your computer" are even uglier. The three screens are simply bitmaps on your hard disk, and can be replaced with your own designs:

1. The startup logo—the blue clouds with the pulsating lights at the bottom—is embedded in the Windows *io.sys* file, located in the root folder of drive *C:*. However, don't look for it there, because that's not how you replace it. If you create a new file called *Logo.sys* in the root directory of drive *C:*, it will be used instead of the default. If you've installed Microsoft Plus! or a newer version of Internet Explorer, there might be a file there by that name, which can be safely replaced.

   The two shutdown screen files are stored in your *\Windows* folder. *Logow.sys* is the one that reads "Please wait while your computer shuts down," and *Logos.sys* is the one that reads "It is now safe to turn off your computer."

2. Make duplicates of all existing files before proceeding, just in case you want to restore them later.

3. These files are just standard bitmap files. In order to edit the existing files, you'll need to rename them to *Logow.bmp* and *Logos.bmp*, respectively. For the Startup logo, you can create a new bitmap file.

4. You can use almost any modern graphics editor to edit bitmap files, such as MS Paint, Paint Shop Pro (*http://www.jasc.com*), or my favorite, Adobe Photoshop (*http://www.adobe.com*).

   The specifications of the logo files are as follows: **256-color** (8-bit) Windows bitmaps (RGB Windows-encoded, but *not* "RGB mode," for you Photoshop users), and 320×400 pixels in size. Since the aspect ratio (width/height) of these files is not the standard 4:3 of most computer screens, the bitmaps will appear vertically elongated in your graphics program, but will be squeezed to display properly when in use.

   To make a new design conform to this strange aspect ratio, begin with a bitmap size of 534×400 while you're working on it, or resize one of the existing images to those dimensions, which will elongate it horizontally and achieve the correct 4:3 aspect ratio.

5. When you're done making your screens, resize them to **320×400** pixels, and save. If the dimensions are incorrect, or you're not using the correct number of colors, the screens won't work.

6. Once you're done, rename the extensions of your new files from *.bmp* back to *.sys* and move them to your Windows folder if they're not already there.

Notes and other issues

For the best results, you might want to convert the images to 24-bit mode (RGB mode in Photoshop) after you open them. That way, when they're resized, the edges will be smoothed. Just before you save, convert the images back to 256-color mode (indexed, 8-bit mode in Photoshop).

If your machine reboots instead of shutting down when these logos are replaced, make sure the bitmaps are not corrupted and use no more than 256 colors.

If you're using a disk compression program like Stacker or DriveSpace, and have compressed drive *C:*, your boot drive may not be drive *C:*. If this applies to you, consult your settings for the particular program you're using to find which letter is your host drive for *C:*, and place the *Logo.sys* file in the root directory of that drive instead.

See Appendix F for information on some sample Windows screens you can download.

You can turn off the display of the startup logo altogether by editing the file *Msdos.sys* (usually located in *C:*) and adding the line `LOGO=0` to the end of the `[Options]` section. However, this may only work if you have a *Logo.sys* file in the root directory of drive *C:*. See Appendix C, *Contents of the MSDOS.SYS File*, for more information on the *Msdos.sys* file. This setting can also be changed with TweakUI (see Appendix A).

If you delete *logow.sys* and *logos.sys* altogether, and follow the instructions in "How to exit to DOS" in Chapter 5, Windows will exit to DOS automatically instead of shutting down.

It's a good idea to back up your logos, as some programs (such as Microsoft Plus! and updates to Internet Explorer) tend to overwrite them without asking. If you install Plus! 98, for example, the installation program will rename your custom *logo.sys* to *logo.w98*, and put its own ugly *logo.sys* in place of your custom file. It's safe to delete this *logo.sys* file, and rename *logo.w98* back to *logo.sys*. The same goes for *logow.sys* in your Windows folder.

Undo. Assuming you've made backups of the shutdown screen files before replacing them, you can just copy them over the ones you've customized to restore them to the defaults. For the startup logo, just delete *c:\logo.sys* to revert to the default Windows 98 startup screen.

Make Control Panel Applets More Accessible

When you open the Control Panel, you are presented with a few dozen icons allowing you to control many aspects of the Windows environment. There's a way that not only makes these Control Panel applets more easily accessible, but allows you to exclude the ones you don't want and to add your own custom icons. The first solution takes advantage of the fact that Windows shortcuts can be used with system objects (such as Control Panel applets) as well as files, folders, drives, and programs.

The second solution shows you how to exploit one of the properties of *virtual folders*, the folders in windows that aren't actually on your hard disk, like the Control Panel and Dial-Up Networking.

Solution 1

1. Open both the Control Panel and Explorer, and place them side by side on your screen.
2. In Explorer, navigate to the *\Windows\Start Menu* folder, and make a new folder inside it called *Control Panel.*
3. Select some or all of the icons in Control Panel, and drag them into this new folder. Windows will display a message stating that, "You cannot move or copy this item to this location." Select **Yes** to confirm that you "want to create a shortcut to the item instead."

   Windows will make a shortcut to each icon you drop into the folder, forming new menu items accessible right off the **Start Menu**. The resulting menu is shown in Figure 2-7.
4. Not only can you rename or remove any of the entries you wish, but you can add non-Control Panel items to the list, such as the Volume Control, the System Policy Editor, and Dial-up Networking (which logically should reside in the Control Panel anyway). Note that any items that are installed into the Control Panel hereafter will have to be added to your custom Control Panel menu manually.

Solution 2

1. In Explorer, navigate to your *\Windows\Start Menu* folder, and make a new folder inside it called *Control Panel.{21EC2020-3AEA-1069-A2DD-08002B30309D}.* Make sure to include the period between the Control Panel and the code in the curly brackets. When you press **Enter**, the numeric code will disappear, and the icon will change to the standard Control Panel icon.

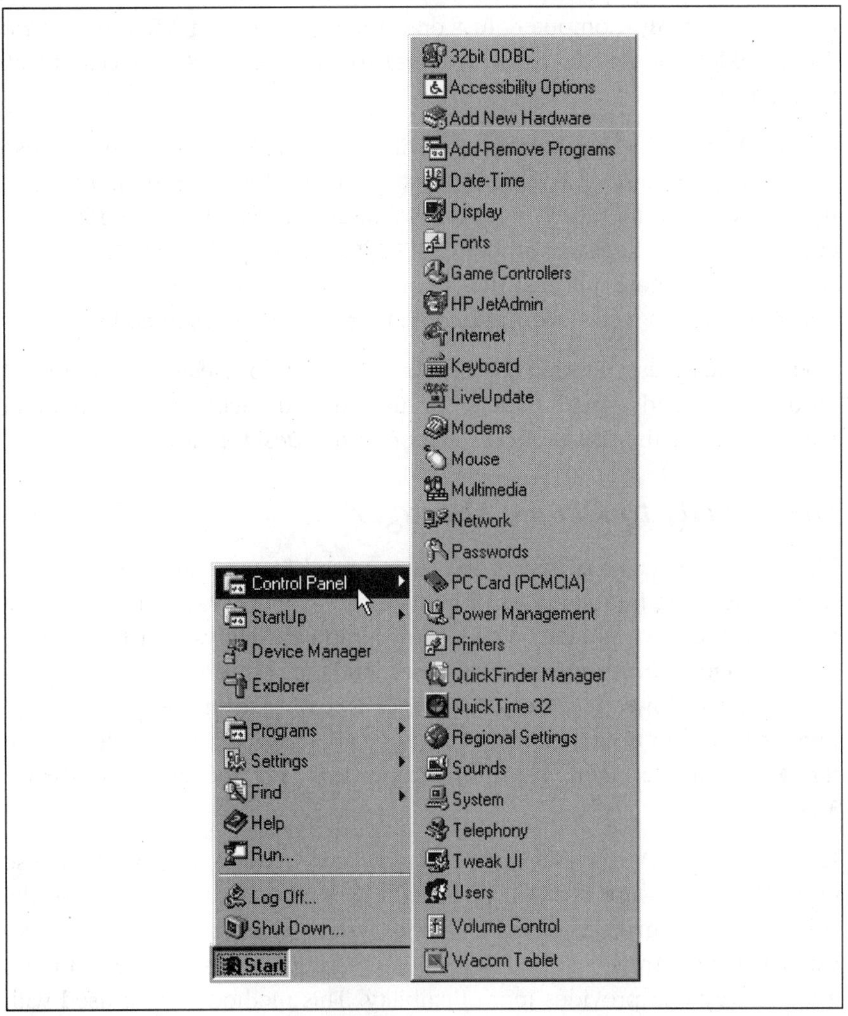

Figure 2-7: Putting the contents of the Control Panel in the Start Menu can make it much easier to get to the items you actually use

2. This will create a menu right off the Start Menu (similar to Solution 1), although you can't change its contents. A benefit is that this process is automatic, and newly added Control Panel items will automatically show up in this menu.

Notes and other issues

To configure any of the shortcuts in Solution 1 to automatically open the Control Panel applet to the second or third tab, see the next section, "Go Directly to Device Manager."

Solution 1 can also be applied to other parts of Windows, such as the drive icons in My Computer. Just drag them all into the *\Windows\Start Menu* folder (or one of its subfolders) to provide quicker access to all your drives.

Control Panel is what's known as a virtual folder. Virtual folders are also discussed in "Change the Icons of System Objects" in Chapter 4. The long numeric code in the curly braces in Solution 2 is called a Class ID (referenced in the Registry under `HKEY_CLASSES_ROOT\CLSID\`; see Chapter 3 for more information). You can apply this solution to other system folders as well—see Appendix D for commonly used codes.

You can also use TweakUI (see Appendix A) to create duplicates of virtual icons and virtual folders for use in your Start Menu and other places. Just use the **Create As File** button in the **Desktop** tab.

Go Directly to Device Manager

The Device Manager is one of the most useful features in Windows, and one of the most frequently used items in the Control Panel. It provides a list of all the devices attached to your computer, allows you to examine and change the resources they use, and refreshes that list without restarting Windows. The **Device Manager** is just a tab in the System Properties window in Control Panel. You can also access it by right-clicking on the **My Computer** icon, selecting **Properties**, and choosing the **Device Manager** tab.

Getting to the Device Manager this way can require up to six mouse clicks, but if you use it often, you might as well make it more accessible. While you can make a shortcut to the System icon (described in "Make Control Panel Applets More Accessible" earlier in this chapter), there's another way that provides more flexibility. This method can be used with nearly all other Control Panel icons, as well:

1. Open Explorer, and navigate to the folder in which you want to place the shortcut to the Device Manager, such as the *\Windows\Start Menu* folder, or the desktop.
2. Select **New** from the **File** menu and then select **Shortcut**.
3. In the field labeled **Command Line**, type:

   ```
   C:\Windows\Control.exe Sysdm.cpl, System, 1
   ```

   replacing *`C:\Windows\`* with your Windows folder, if different.
4. Click **Next**, type `Device Manager` for the name of this shortcut, and press **Finish** when you're done.

This will create a standard Windows shortcut that will take you directly to Device Manager. You can, of course, place this shortcut anywhere else, change its icon, or call it something different.

Notes and other issues

If you examine the command line above, you'll see what makes it work. *Control.exe* is the program filename for Control Panel, *Sysdm.cpl* is the filename for the System Properties applet, and "System" is the caption underneath the icon in the Control Panel (also required, as there are sometimes multiple applets stored in a single *.cpl* file). The last parameter (note that they're all separated by commas) specifies the tab to open, where `0` (zero) is the first tab, and `1` (one) is the second tab. In this case, Device Manager is the second tab in this dialog.

While it's easier to drag-drop the System icon from Control Panel into the Start Menu, the resulting shortcut doesn't have the flexibility to allow you to specify the tab to open automatically.

As with any shortcut, if you right-click on our new shortcut and select **Properties**, you can change the icon, any of the command-line options, and even specify a hotkey.

For a more in-depth examination of the Control Panel and its various command lines, see *Windows 95 in a Nutshell*, by Tim O'Reilly and Troy Mott (O'Reilly & Associates).

What to Do if You Hate the Start Menu

Nobody liked Program Manager, the shell that came with Windows 3.x. Fortunately, Windows 95 and 98 both come with something better, if only because they have several different interfaces built in. Explorer, the default shell in Windows 98, contains the desktop, the Start Menu, the My Computer window, the Explorer tree-view window, as well as several other components (the Tray and Dial-Up Networking, for example).

As a user interface, the Start Menu is somewhat of a disaster. You're forced to navigate through several levels of menus, any of which can disappear if your mouse strays even a few millimeters, just to get to the icon that opens the word processor you use every day. If it weren't for the **Programs** section, and the fact that the entire menu is labeled "Start," the idea of having a central location for **Help**, **Run**, **Find**, **Shut Down**, and **Settings** is a good one—in fact, every Macintosh has had a menu like this for the past 15 years.

There are better ways to get to your applications and your files (the actual reason you use a computer). The following are good replacements for the Start Menu.

The desktop

While the desktop is certainly not a great place to store a link to every program on your computer, it's a prime location for the most frequently used programs. If you only use your computer for a handful of applications, you can move all your Start Menu shortcuts directly onto the desktop and forget about the Start Menu entirely:

- Start by right-clicking on the **Start Menu** button and selecting **Explore**. You can then navigate through your *Start Menu* folders and move (or copy, by holding the **Ctrl** key) any shortcuts onto the desktop.
- For those programs that don't have shortcuts in your Start Menu, or to make shortcuts for a document or folder on your desktop, you'll have to first find the actual location of the item(s) you want to link. Then, use the right mouse button to drag-drop it to your desktop (see "Move or Copy Files at Will" earlier in this chapter for more information).

Taskbar toolbars

As a partial fix for the inaccessibility of items in the Start Menu, Windows 98 has new configurable, dockable toolbars. Like the Start Menu, the contents of these toolbars just mirror the contents of folders on your hard disk, but you don't have to fish through your Start Menu to find them. By placing icons for your most frequently used applications, folders, and documents directly on the Taskbar, you can make it easier and quicker to open the tasks you need:

- To display one of the preconfigured toolbars, right-click on an empty area of the Taskbar, select **Toolbar**, and choose the one you want. In addition to the Address and Links toolbars from Internet Explorer (see Chapter 8), there's a Desktop toolbar that mirrors the contents of your desktop, and the customizable Quick Launch bar. Select **New Toolbar** to make a new, blank toolbar.
- Icons on the customizable toolbars are, like the Start Menu, just shortcuts on your hard disk, located in subfolders of the *\Windows\Application Data\Microsoft\Internet Explorer* folder. The exceptions are the Address Bar (discussed in Chapter 8 and Appendix B) and the desktop, which is linked directly to your desktop folder.
- You can drag items into these folders as well as directly onto the toolbars to add them. Note that right-clicking on toolbar icons allows you

to open them, change their properties, and even delete them, as though you were right-clicking on the actual shortcuts.

Replace Explorer with another program

1. The Start Menu and the desktop are just part of the *Explorer.exe* program. To configure Windows to use another program as the system shell, select Run from the **Start Menu**, type `system.ini`, and click **OK**. Notepad or another plain text editor should then appear with *system.ini* loaded. This file is a *.ini* configuration file, a type discussed in Chapter 3.
2. In the `[Boot]` section, which should be first, look for a line that begins with `shell=`. If it doesn't exist, add it to the end of the `[Boot]` section.
3. Change the line so it reads `shell=some_progman.exe`, where *`some_progman.exe`* is the filename for the program you wish to use as your system shell. If the *.exe* file is not in the Windows folder, you'll have to specify the full path. If you *only* use your computer for word processing, you can put your word processor here, although you'll probably want a program that serves the necessary shell functions, such as launching programs and viewing folders.

Notes and other issues

If you replace Explorer as the system shell (using the second solution above), you'll also lose all your desktop icons, the Start Menu, and the Taskbar. Any minimized programs will be reduced to small rectangles instead of Taskbar items. Make sure the new program you choose is able to launch programs, or you may get stuck. Additionally, the program should be able to shut down your system if you exit directly from the software, which isn't always the case.

Undo. If you change your system shell to another program, and find that you're unable to start Windows, you'll have to edit *system.ini* from DOS and remove the `shell=` line. See Chapter 6, *Troubleshooting*, for information on booting directly into DOS. Once you're there, type `edit c:\windows\ system.ini` (assuming your Windows directory is *c:\windows*) to open a DOS-based text editor.

Route 1 Pro, an interface enhancement for Windows 95/98 and Windows NT 4.0/5.0, implements a simple row of buttons providing quick access to your programs and files. Its operation is much slicker and more flexible than either the Start Menu or the Taskbar toolbars mentioned above. If you're looking for a better primary interface for Windows, it may suit your needs. An evaluation version is available for free at *http://www.creativelement.com/software/route1.html.*

Stop Menus from Following the Mouse

One of the fundamental changes to the traditional Windows 3.x interface included in Windows 95/98 is the way that menus seem to be magnetically attracted to the mouse pointer. The problem with this design is that it can be very difficult to navigate menus unless you're able to hold your mouse very steady. Even the smallest unintentional move in the wrong direction can cause the menu you're using to disappear. This can be even more annoying to those with more sensitive pointing devices, such as touchpads, pens, and other digitizers. Here's how to disable this behavior.

Solution 1

- Obtain and install the Old Mouse Mode utility (see Appendix F), which forces the menus in Windows to behave pretty much like Windows 3.x menus.

Solution 2

1. Double-click on the **TweakUI** icon in Control Panel (see Appendix A).
2. Choose the **Mouse** tab, and move the Menu Speed slider all the way to the right (towards **Slow**).

This will increase the delay when opening menus to its maximum setting, virtually disabling it. While it will prevent *submenus* from opening automatically, the top-level menus will still follow the mouse like starving alley cats.

Taming Mindless Animation

One of the most obvious differences between Windows 95 and Windows 98 is the addition of animation throughout most of the interface. Sure, it's cute; but it can make the fastest Pentium II class systems seem to perform like antiquated 386s. Rather than watch your Start Menu slowly crawl to its open position, you can easily configure your menus and listboxes to simply snap to position. You'll be surprised at how much faster and more responsive Windows will feel.

Solution 1: All for one and one for all

1. Double-click on the **Display** icon in Control Panel, and choose the **Effects** tab.
2. Turn off the **Animate windows, menus and lists** option, and click **OK**.

Solution 2: Individual animation

1. Double-click on the **TweakUI** icon in Control Panel (see Appendix A), and choose the **General** tab. In the **Effects** list, you'll find settings for **Window animation** (used when maximizing and minimizing windows), **Smooth scrolling** (used in Explorer and Internet Explorer), **Menu animation** (used in standard menus and in the Start Menu), **Combo box animation** (also known as drop-down listboxes), and **List box animation** (similar to Smooth scrolling).
2. The **Mouse hot tracking effects** option turns off the tooltips everywhere (although not necessarily animation, they're annoying just the same), rather than turning off the way that menus and toolbar buttons follow the mouse around, as you'd expect.
3. Click **OK** when you're finished.

Notes and other issues

If you have both the **AutoHide** setting turned on in Taskbar Properties and the **Show window contents while dragging** option enabled in Display Properties, turning off the **Window animation** option will also disable the animation for the disappearing Taskbar.

To turn off the animated **Click here to begin** arrow at system startup, see "Turn Off the Bouncing 'Click Here to Begin' Arrow" in Chapter 4.

3

In this chapter:
- *Getting to Know the Registry*
- *Tips and Tricks*
- *Registry Tools*

The Registry

Whenever you change your system colors, install an application, or change a setting in Control Panel, the relevant information is stored in your Registry. The Registry is a database of all the settings for Windows, as well as for the applications installed on your system. Knowing how to use the Registry is important for the advanced operation of Windows and for the troubleshooting and extended customizing techniques discussed in this book.

All of your file types (see "Customize Context Menus" in Chapter 4, *Tinkering Techniques*) are stored in the Registry, as well as all of the network, hardware, and software settings for Windows, and all of the particular configuration options for most of the software you've installed. While the particular settings for each of your applications and Windows components can differ substantially, there are some techniques you can use to figure out undocumented settings and uncover hidden functionality. What's especially helpful is that most of the settings stored in the Registry are named in plain English rather than obscure codes and acronyms. While you shouldn't take this fact for granted, it does help quite a bit in finding settings and troubleshooting problems.

For more information and programming techniques regarding the Windows Registry, see *Inside the Windows 95 Registry*, by Ron Petrusha (O'Reilly & Associates).

You can irreversibly disable certain components of Windows by changing settings in the Registry, so do so with caution. However, if you take the simple precaution of backing up the Registry, you'll virtually eliminate the possibility of disaster. Furthermore, backing up your *entire system*, a more involved process than just backing up the Registry, will ensure that none of your valuable data or programs are compromised, and undoubtedly save you hours of hard work and a painful headache.

Getting to Know the Registry

While the Registry is stored in multiple files on your hard disk, it is represented in a single logical hierarchical structure, like the directories on your hard disk. The Registry Editor (*Regedit.exe,* located in your Windows folder) is included with Windows to enable you to view and edit the contents of the Registry. Most of the access to the Registry is performed behind the scenes by the applications that you run, as well as by Windows—settings and other information are constantly read from and written to the Registry.

When you open the Registry Editor, you'll see a window divided into two panes (see Figure 3-1). The left side shows a tree with folders, and the right side shows the contents (named *values*) of the currently selected folder. Now, the items in the left pane aren't really folders; this is just a convenient and familiar method of organizing and displaying the information stored in your registry files.

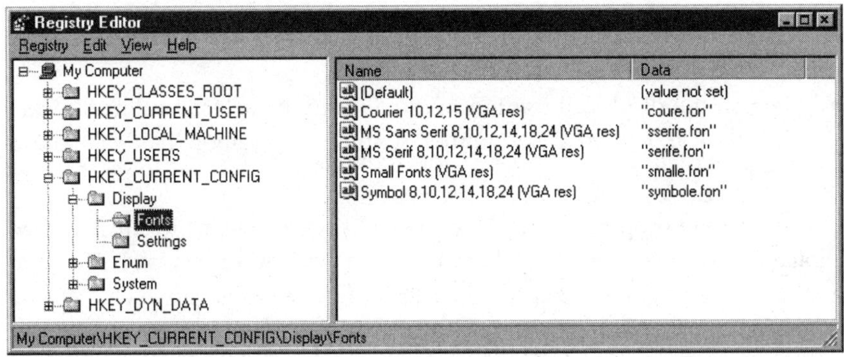

Figure 3-1: The Registry Editor enables you to view and change the contents of the Registry

Each branch (denoted by a folder icon in the Registry Editor) is called a *key*. Each key can contain other keys, as well as *values*. Each value contains the actual information stored in the Registry. Keys are shown only in the left pane and values are shown only in the right pane.

The Registry Editor shows three types of values: String, Binary, and DWORD. Their use is determined by the program that created them. To display the contents of a key (folder), just click the desired key name on the left, and look at the values listed on the right side. To expand a certain branch to show its subkeys, click on the plus sign [+] to the left of any folder, or just double-click on the folder.

An important thing to notice at this point is the value at the top of the right pane labeled `(Default)`. The default value cannot be removed, although its contents can be erased, leading to the (`value not set`) caption. In the more simplistic Registry found in Windows 3.1 and Windows NT 3.x, there was only one value in each key. In Windows 95/98 and Windows NT 4/5, where a key can contain any number of values, the default value takes the place of the lone value from previous versions. In most cases, the default value doesn't have any special meaning, other than what might have been assigned by the application that owns the key.

The Registry Editor allows you to perform the following operations:

- Add a new key or value by first choosing the location for the new object, and then selecting **New** from the **Edit** menu.
- Rename any existing value and *almost* any key with the same method used to rename files: right-click on an object and click **Rename**, click on it twice (slowly), or just select it and press the **F2** key.
- Delete a key or value by clicking on it and pressing the **Del** key, or by right-clicking on it and selecting **Delete**.
- Search for text in the names of keys or values by selecting **Find** from the **Edit** menu.
- Refresh the displayed portion of the Registry by selecting **Refresh** from the **View** menu, in case another running application has changed a setting.

You can't drag-drop any keys or values as you can with files in Explorer. Similar to Explorer, though, is the notion of a *path*. A registry path is a location in the Registry described by the series of nested keys in which a setting is located. For example, if a particular value is in the `Microsoft` key under `SOFTWARE`, which is under `HKEY_LOCAL_MACHINE`, the registry path would be `HKEY_LOCAL_MACHINE\SOFTWARE\Microsoft`. Elsewhere in this book, when a setting is changed in the Registry, this type of registry path is always given.

There are six primary, or "root" branches, each containing a specific portion of the information stored in the Registry. These root keys can't be deleted, renamed, or moved, as they are the basis for the organization of the Registry. They are:

HKEY_CLASSES_ROOT

This branch contains all of your file types, filename extensions, and OLE information for all your OLE-aware applications. See "Understanding File Types" later in this chapter for details on the structure of this branch. One special key here, called `CLSID` (short for *Class ID*), contains all registered components of the applications and ActiveX controls (application building blocks) installed on the system. While the contents of `HKEY_CLASSES_ROOT` are easy to edit, it's best not to mess with anything in the `CLSID` branch, as almost none of it is in plain English.

This entire branch is a "mirror" of `HKEY_LOCAL_MACHINE\SOFTWARE\Classes`, but is displayed separately in this branch for clarity and easy access.

HKEY_USERS

This branch contains a sub-branch named for the currently logged in user, usually called `.default`.

In each user's branch are the settings for that user, such as Control Panel settings and Explorer preferences. Some applications store user-specific information here as well. The `HKEY_CURRENT_USER` branch is simply a "mirror" of any one of the branches here, depending on which user is currently logged on. Its contents are explained below.

If the system is configured for a single user, there is only a single `.default` branch; if the system is configured for multiple users, only the `.default` branch and the branch for the current user are visible.

HKEY_CURRENT_USER

This branch simply points to a portion of `HKEY_USERS`, signifying the current user. This way, any application can read the settings for the current user without having to know which user is currently logged on.

The settings for the current user are divided into several categories; `AppEvents`, `Control Panel`, `InstallLocationsMRU`, `keyboard layout`, `Network`, `RemoteAccess`, and `Software`. The most useful of these branches, `Software`, contains a branch for almost every application installed on your computer, arranged by manufacturer. You'll find Windows settings under the Microsoft branch.

HKEY_LOCAL_MACHINE

This branch contains information about all of the hardware and software installed on your computer that isn't specific to which user is currently logged in.

Be very careful when changing any information pertaining to installed hardware, as it can make certain devices unavailable. Most of the settings in the `Hardware` key can be configured in the Device Manager (see Chapter 6, *Troubleshooting*).

The sub-branch of interest here is the `SOFTWARE` branch, which contains all of the information specific to the applications installed on your computer. Both this branch and `HKEY_CURRENT_USER\Software` are used to store application-specific information. Those settings which are specific to each user (even if your computer has only one user), such as toolbar configurations, are stored in the `HKEY_CURRENT_USER` branch, and those settings which are user-independent, such as installation directories, are stored in the `HKEY_LOCAL_MACHINE` branch.

You'll also notice the `Config` branch—it contains one or more numbered `Hardware Profiles`. The current hardware profile is mirrored in `HKEY_CURRENT_CONFIG`.

HKEY_CURRENT_CONFIG

This branch points to a branch of `HKEY_LOCAL_MACHINE\Config`, corresponding to the currently selected hardware configuration. In most cases, there's only one; this branch is usually a mirror of `HKEY_LOCAL_MACHINE\Config\0001`.

HKEY_DYN_DATA

This is the only *dynamic* branch of the Registry. That is, while all other branches are *static* and stored on the hard disk, this branch is created every time you start Windows and is held in memory. Its contents represent the various VxDs (device drivers) and Plug-and-Play devices installed on your system, as reported by the Configuration Manager. This branch is not much use in completing the material discussed in this book.

`HKEY_USERS` and `HKEY_LOCAL_MACHINE` are the only two *original* root keys stored on the hard disk. Other than `HKEY_DYN_DATA`, the root keys simply mirror different portions of the first two, which are stored on the hard disk as *User.dat* and *System.dat*, respectively. Knowing which files comprise the Registry is important only for backup and emergency recovery procedures (see "Backing Up the Registry," later in this chapter). The contents of the Registry are viewed and changed with the Registry Editor, which works independently of the actual files used to make up the Registry.

Tips and Tricks

Once you're somewhat familiar with the Registry and the Registry Editor application, you can begin to make use of them to diagnose problems, implement new features, and customize the operating system and its software. The first topic discussed here, "Backing Up the Registry," is the most important, and can eliminate nearly all problems that occur when changing settings in the Registry. The information covered in the rest of this section should provide you with enough knowledge to complete any procedure involving the Registry in this book.

Backing Up the Registry

Since the Registry is stored in certain files on your hard disk, you can create a backup by simply copying the files to another location. While the Registry is rarely small enough to fit on a single floppy, most backup software made for Windows 95/98, such as the Backup utility that comes with Windows, includes a feature to back up the Registry. It's always a good idea to exploit this functionality.

When you start Windows, the information in the Registry is loaded into memory. While Windows is running, some changes may not be physically written to the registry files until you shut down your computer, while others (such as those made by the Registry Editor) are written immediately. For this reason, if you've made any substantial changes to the contents of the Registry, you'll probably want to restart Windows before backing it up to ensure that the files on the disk reflect the most recent changes.

If your system is not configured for multiple users, the Registry is stored in two hidden files in your Windows directory, *User.dat* and *System.dat.* If there are multiple users, however, each user's *User.dat* file will be located in the *\Windows\Profiles\username* folder (where *username* is the name of the user).

These files are all hidden, meaning that with Explorer's default settings, you won't be able to see or find them. To view hidden files, select **Folder Options** from Explorer's **View** menu, choose the **View** tab, click the **Show all files** option, and click **OK**.

Using the Windows Registry Checker

A new feature in Windows 98 is the Registry Checker (ScanReg), a simple utility that handles several registry maintenance tasks. Windows automatically runs ScanReg at startup, at which time it makes a backup of the registry files, checks them for errors, and, if needed, optimizes them.

Although ScanReg runs automatically and transparently, you can also manually check and back up the Registry at any time. While this interactive mode isn't strictly necessary, it does let you perform a registry backup or check it for errors without having to restart Windows and test new configuration options (see "Performing a manual backup," later in this chapter).

You won't find the Registry Checker on the Start Menu; to run ScanReg manually, select **Run** from the Start Menu, and type `scanregw.exe`. There's also a DOS version (*Scanreg.exe*), but if you try to run it from within Windows, it'll switch to its Windows sibling automatically.

ScanReg maintains, by default, five separate backups of your registry files, as well as some other important system files, including *win.ini* and *system.ini*. It compresses the backups into five separate *.cab* files,* named *rb000.cab*, *rb001.cab*, and so on. Any registry backups in which ScanReg has detected corruption will, however, be stored in *Rbbad.cab*.

You'll have to check the file dates for the most recent backup (view the files in Explorer's **Details** view, or type `DIR` if you're in DOS), as their numbers aren't a reliable indicator of their age. The *.cab* backup files are located in the hidden *\Windows\sysbckup* folder; you'll see this folder if you've configured Windows to display hidden files.

You can configure how many simultaneous backups are kept by editing the *Scanreg.ini* file, located in the *\Windows* folder, and setting the `MaxBackupCopies=5` line to any value you want. A higher setting will increase the likelihood of finding a good copy in the event of a serious problem, but will also consume more disk space. The size of your registry backup files depends upon the combined sizes of your registry files, as well as how effectively they can be compressed. Assuming that your two registry files add up to about two megabytes (this varies significantly,

---

* Cabinet files (**.cab*) are the files in which Microsoft compresses and distributes their applications. They're similar to *.zip* files in their use, but you'll find far less support for them in the computer industry. To view the contents of a *.cab* file, just double-click on it in Explorer. You can extract files embedded in *.cab* files by drag-dropping them out of the *.cab* window into a folder or the desktop. This is especially handy for retrieving individual files from the Windows distribution CD. To create *.cab* files, you'll need the Cab Maker utility, available for download on the Internet (see Appendix F, *Software to Solve Annoyances*).

depending on how many applications you've installed, as well as other factors), and that Windows will be able to compress them about 50%, the default setting of 5 backups would therefore consume about 5MB of disk space (5×2MB×50%). The default setting is a good compromise, and should suit most configurations. You can reduce the number if you need the extra space or increase it if you do a lot of tinkering and feel you'll be more likely to need them. If you rely on and trust another backup procedure, and you need the space, you can disable the automatic backup altogether by changing the line `Backup=1` to `Backup=0` in the *Scanreg.ini* file.

See "Restoring a Corrupted Registry" later in this chapter for more information on getting at the Registry Checker's Backups. ScanReg also optimizes your Registry when needed; see "Compacting the Registry," later in this chapter, for more information.

Extra Registry Checker duties

You can configure ScanReg to back up additional files along with the Registry, although it should by no means be considered a substitute for a full system backup. This is helpful for saving prior versions of important system files, allowing their easy retrieval if something happens. Of course, if your hard disk crashes, or your computer is stolen, these automated backups are lost along with everything else. It is therefore a good policy to make solid backups of your Registry and other important configuration files to tape or diskette. Since the compressed registry backups are smaller than the actual registry files, they're more likely to fit on a standard floppy diskette (your mileage may vary), and make for an easy and convenient backup.

In addition to your two registry files, *System.ini* and *Win.ini*, ScanReg will include in its backup any additional files you specify in the *Scanreg.ini* file, as follows:

```
Files = c:\msdos.sys, c:\logo.sys
Files = c:\autoexec.bat, c:\config.sys
Files = c:\windows\bob.pwl
```

Multiple filenames can be combined on a single line, or separated so each has its own line, as shown. You can ignore the `dir code` setting that's explained in the *.ini* file—its only purpose is to allow you to specify files in key directories without having to spell out the directory names, which is useful only if you're writing one file for use on several computers.

Of the files included in the above example, the only one you should definitely include in your own backups is *Msdos.sys*. The others can be included or left out at your discretion. For example, *Logo.sys* is simply the startup screen (see Chapter 2, *Customizing the Interface*), although you may want to back it up if you've spent a long time on it and fear that installing a future Microsoft upgrade will cause it to be overwritten. Feel free to include any other *.ini* or other configuration files you deem important, keeping in mind that the more files you back up, the longer it will take (which could slow system boots marginally).

Performing a manual backup

While the ScanReg utility is helpful for keeping several copies of your Registry in case one of them becomes corrupted, it certainly can't prepare your computer for an actual disaster. If your hard disk crashes or gets infected with a virus, or if your computer is stolen or dropped out of a seven-story building, those registry backups on your hard disk won't do you much good.

Backing up your Registry is simply a matter of making a copy of your two registry files and keeping that copy somewhere other than inside your computer. If you back up your entire system regularly, such as to a tape drive or other backup device, the backup software you use should specifically support safeguarding the Registry.

The quickest way to do this is to first locate the two files, by either navigating to your Windows folder or by using the **Find** feature and searching for `*.dat`. Remember, the files are hidden, so you won't be able to see them by default. To view them in Windows, see the beginning of this section; to see them in DOS, use the `ATTRIB` command (refer to Appendix B, *DOS Lives*, for more information).

Select both files, right-click on one of them, and select **Properties**. This dialog box will tell you how much space the two files consume collectively. If the total is less than about 1.4 megabytes, you can just drag both of the files onto a floppy diskette. If they're larger and won't fit on a single floppy, you'll have to use a program like WinZip (*http://www.winzip.com*) to compress them. If you have a tape drive or a removable cartridge drive (Syquest, Zip, Jaz), that's even better, although an advantage to a floppy drive registry backup is that you don't need any special drivers to access it.

Note that the automated backup *.cab* files (described in the previous section) are already compressed, and therefore will be smaller and more convenient to copy to a floppy or other device. The downside is that the files inside of the *.cab* backups can be a few days old, and if you're a stickler, that just won't do.

If you don't already back up your entire system regularly, you should make a habit of backing up your Registry at least once a week, as it can save you hours of work if your system should fail.

Automate off-disk backups

The Registry Checker provides automated backups of your Registry every time you start your computer, right out of the box. However, if you're diligent enough to make manual backups, you'll benefit from a more automated procedure for that, as well. If you use a backup program to back up your entire system (highly recommended), then you probably also have the option of using the built-in scheduler that comes with most backup software.

The following example uses a DOS batch file (see Chapter 9, *Scripting and Automation* and Appendix B) in conjunction with the *PKZIP* utility (see Appendix F) to compress the latest versions of your registry files into a single archive, and then copy that archive to a floppy disk. Open a plain text editor, such as Notepad, and type the code shown in Example 3-1.

Example 3-1: A Simple Batch File Used to Automate Manual Backups of the Registry

```
@echo off
format a: /u/q
pkzip -& -whs a:\regback.zip c:\windows\system.dat
c:\windows\user.dat
```

Replace *`c:\windows`* if your copy of Windows 98 is installed in a different location. If you'd rather back up to a different location, replace `a:` with the drive of your choice.

The first line turns off the display of the commands that follow. The second line takes care of two things: it prompts for a floppy, and then erases it. The final line also does two things: it compresses the two registry files and copies them to the floppy. The `&` parameter tells PKZip to use more than one floppy diskette, if necessary, and the *`whs`* parameter (which is required and case-sensitive—don't use uppercase) tells PKZip to include hidden and system files.

To include additional files in the backup, just list them at the end of the `pkzip` line; see "Using the Windows Registry Checker," earlier in this chapter, for suggestions of other important system files.

Restoring a Corrupted Registry

There are several ways to restore a corrupted Registry. The appropriate method depends on how serious the problem is, and how diligent you've been about keeping backups.

If you encounter a problem with the Registry, the first thing you should do is run Scandisk (either *scandisk.exe* from DOS, or *scandskw.exe* from Windows) to check for disk and file problems, since they're much more likely to occur than registry corruption. If you can't get into Windows, and need to run the DOS version of Scandisk, you'll first have to get to the command prompt. Press the **F8** key just after you turn on your computer, and when Windows first begins to load, press **Shift-F5** to drop into the plain command prompt. Then just type `Scandisk` at the prompt to start the program. Make sure you check all drives on your system, if you have more than just drive *C:*.

Only if the problem persists after running Scandisk should you resort to restoring your Registry. Unfortunately, there's not much you can do to repair a damaged registry file other than to replace it with a backup. Registry corruption comes in the following two forms, both of which can be alleviated by restoring from a backup:

- One of the files that make up the Registry is actually physically corrupted, meaning that Windows has trouble reading the file from the hard disk, or the file has been truncated in some way. This can be caused by a system crash, a power outage while the file was being written, a physical error on the hard disk, or even a virus. If Scandisk can't correct the problem, you'll have to replace the file with a recent backup. The more often you've backed up, the more recent your backup will be.
- The registry files are intact, but there are one or more registry settings that are causing a problem with Windows or a piece of hardware connected to the computer. This can be caused by an errant program that has written to a Registry, a faulty device driver, or most commonly, user error. This can often be very hard to diagnose, but is most easily solved by replacing the registry files with a recent backup, so it's important to make backups of the Registry before messing with any settings inside. Note also that having multiple, successive backups makes it easier to fix a problem like this; if the most recent backup *also* contains the errant entry that's causing the problem, you can try earlier backups.

Regardless of the cause of the problem, the process of restoring the Registry is the same, with the following exception: if the problem is of the first type, and one of the registry files has become corrupted, it's possible that other files on your hard disk have also become corrupted, including the backups made by the Registry Checker. This is why it's important to have off-disk backups, either on tape or diskette.

Restoring a Registry Checker backup

If, when scanning your Registry for errors at system startup, the Registry Checker encounters an error, it's supposed to automatically restore the most recent backup after asking. However, there are times—either when this process doesn't restore the correct backup, or ScanReg simply doesn't recognize that there's a problem—when you'll need to restore the backup yourself. Here's how you do it:

- If you're in Windows, just double-click on the most recent *.cab* file. The *.cab* backup files are located in the hidden *\Windows\sysbckup* folder. If you don't see this folder, you'll need to configure Windows to display your hidden files by selecting **Folder Options** from Explorer's **View** menu, choosing the **View** tab, and clicking the **Show all files** option. You'll have to check the file dates for the most recent backup (view the files with Explorer's **Details** view), as their numbers aren't a reliable indicator of their age.

  To extract a file from the *.cab* file, just drag it out of the Cabinet window that appears when you double-click on the *.cab* file, and drop it in your Windows folder. Do this for each of the registry files (*System.dat* and *User.dat*); if you're asked, click **Yes** to confirm that you wish to replace the file that's there.

- If you're in DOS (since registry corruption can often prevent Windows from starting), type `scanreg /restore` to start the DOS version of the Registry Checker. The screen should present a list with the five most recent backups; there may be more or fewer backups, depending on your configuration. Highlight the most recent backup, and press **Restore**. If that backup doesn't solve the problem, repeat the above steps, and choose the *next*-most recent backup.

  When you use the DOS Registry Checker's restore feature, all of the files in a particular backup set will be restored; there's no way to choose which files are restored, and which aren't. If you know which file is corrupted, there's no sense in overwriting all of the files with older versions. To extract only a single file from a backup set (leaving the others intact), type the following:

```
extract  c:\windows\sysbckup\rb003.cab c:\windows\system.dat
```

This example extracts the file *System.dat* from the *rb003* backup and places it in the Windows directory. Make sure to replace *c:\windows* with your Windows directory, if different. Type `Extract /?` for more options for the extract command, and see Appendix B for more information on DOS commands.

Restoring a manual backup

If you've made manual backups as described in the previous section, all you need to do is copy them over the damaged files and restart your computer:

1. Assuming you can't start Windows, the first thing you need to do is get into DOS. Press the **F8** key just after you turn on your computer, and when Windows first begins to load, press **Shift-F5** to drop into the plain command prompt.
2. Next, you'll need to turn off the *system* and *hidden* attributes of the registry files so that they can be overwritten. At the DOS prompt, type:

   ```
   attrib -r -s -h c:\windows\system.dat
   attrib -r -s -h c:\windows\user.dat
   ```

3. Then, copy your backups over the original files. If, when backing up, you've just copied the files to another location, such as your floppy drive, just type the following:

   ```
   copy a:\system.dat c:\windows
   copy a:\user.dat c:\windows
   ```

   Or, if you've done your manual backup with the batch file described in "Automate off-disk backups" earlier in this chapter, type the following:

   ```
   pkunzip a:\regback.zip c:\windows
   ```

4. Now, for all of these, you'll have to substitute `c:\windows` with the correct path if you've installed Windows into a different location. Also, replace `a:\` with the correct letter of your floppy drive, if necessary.
5. When you're done, restart your computer to test the restored registry files.

Notes and other issues

While backing up the Registry is easy, it doesn't provide the level of protection achieved by a full system backup (see Chapter 6).

When you install Windows 98, a file named *System.1st* is placed in the root directory of your boot drive. This file is a copy of your *System.dat* file from when Windows was first installed. If you ever reinstall Windows over an existing installation, this file will become the last version of *System.dat* before you reinstalled. If you lose your backups and there's a problem with your Registry, a last resort would be to rename this file to *System.dat* and copy it over your corrupted registry file. While it won't have your most recent settings, it may allow you to start Windows without reinstalling.

To back up certain portions of the Registry, or to share certain settings in the Registry, see the next section.

Using Registry Patches

Although you can edit the Registry with the Registry Editor (see "Getting to Know the Registry," earlier in this chapter), you can also make changes by using registry patches. A registry patch is simply a text file with the *.reg* extension that contains one or more registry keys or values. If you double-click on a *.reg* file, the patch is applied to the Registry, meaning that the contents of the patch are merged with the contents of the Registry. This is a good way to share or back up small portions of the Registry for use on your own computer or someone else's, because it's much simpler and quicker than manually editing the Registry.

Create a registry patch

1. Open the Registry Editor and select a branch you wish to use. The branch can be anywhere from one of the top level branches to a branch a dozen layers deep. Registry patches include not only the branch you select, but all of the values and subkeys in the branch. Don't select anything more than what you absolutely need.
2. Select **Export Registry File** from the **Registry** menu, type a filename, and press **OK**. All of the values and subkeys in the selected branch will then be duplicated in the patch. Make sure the filename of the new registry patch has the extension *.reg*.

Edit a registry patch

Since registry patches are plain text files, you can edit them with any plain text editor, such as Notepad. The contents of the registry patch will look like the text shown in Example 3-2.

Example 3-2: The Contents of a Registry Patch of HKEY_CLASSES_ROOT\.txt

```
REGEDIT4

[HKEY_CLASSES_ROOT\.txt]
@="txtfile"
"Content Type"="text/plain"

[HKEY_CLASSES_ROOT\.txt\ShellNew]
"FileName"="template.txt"
```

The first line, `REGEDIT4`, tells Windows that this file is a valid registry patch; don't remove this line. The rest of the registry patch is a series of key names and values. The key names appear in brackets and are the full path of the key. The values contained within each key follow. The name of the value is given first, followed by an equals sign, and then the data stored in each value. The value names and value data are all enclosed in quotation marks. A value name of `@` tells the Registry Editor to place the value data in the `(Default)` value.

If you are familiar with the particular information contained within the registry patch you've just created, you can edit anything you wish, and save the changes when you're done. Note that making changes to a registry patch doesn't mean that anything is written to the Registry. Your changes won't take effect in the Registry until the registry patch is applied.

Apply a registry patch

1. When you apply a registry patch, you are merging the keys and values stored in a patch file with the Registry. Double-click on a registry patch file (with the *.reg* extension) in Explorer to apply it. Answer **Yes** to the warning message that asks, "Are you sure you want to add the information in *C:\Windows\Desktop\MyPatch.reg* to the Registry?"
2. Once you've applied the registry patch, you'll see a message that looks something like "Information in *MyPatch.reg* has been successfully entered into the Registry."
3. If the Registry Editor utility is currently open, you can also select **Import Registry File** from the **Registry** menu, select the patch, and click **OK** to merge the file. It's best not to apply registry patches by double-clicking patch files if the Registry Editor is open.
4. Any keys or values in the patch that don't already exist will be added to the Registry. If a key in the patch already exists, its contents will be updated with the contents in the patch file. If a specific value already exists, the value will be changed to whatever is in the patch, but any values already in an existing key that *aren't* in the registry patch will be left alone.

Notes and other issues

Backing up the Registry is a good safeguard against any mistakes made when applying registry patches.

If you're creating a registry patch on your computer for use on another, make sure any folder names or drive letters are corrected for the new computer. If, for example, your registry patch created on one computer references *c:\my_folder\my_program.exe*, you'll need to make sure to change it to *d:\her_folder\my_program.exe* to reflect any differences in the computer to which you'll be applying the patch.

Although the Registry Editor has a search feature, it doesn't allow you to search and replace. If you wish to change a branch of settings—for example, if you've moved an application from one drive to another—you can use a registry patch. Just create a patch of the branch in question, and use your favorite text editor's search-and-replace feature to change the values in the patch (for example, replace all occurrences of *c:\big_program* to *e:\big_program*). When you apply the patch, all the settings will be changed for you. Note that you should use this with caution, as you can screw up many settings unwittingly. See "Search the Registry Effectively" later in this chapter for more information.

To apply a registry patch without displaying the two annoying confirmation messages (which can be useful when applying patches from DOS batch files or VBScript files), you'll need to launch them with *regedit.exe* and the `/s` parameter, as follows:

```
regedit /s c:\path\regfile.reg
```

See Chapter 9 for a discussion on the Windows Scripting Host, which documents a method for automating changes to the Registry.

Finding the Right Registry Key

The most prevalent obstacle you'll encounter when trying to make a change to the Registry is finding not only where a setting is located in the Registry, but also how it is changed. Sometimes it's obvious how to change a setting: by changing a zero to a one, or by substituting one directory name with another. At other times, you'll see only a long, seemingly meaningless series of numbers or characters.

For this example, we'll find the registry setting associated with turning off the silly "click here to begin" arrow that's shown when you first boot Windows 98, and create the appropriate registry patch.

The idea is to take *snapshots* (make registry patches) of your entire Registry *before* and *after* a change is made in Explorer (or another program). By comparing the two snapshots, we can easily see which registry keys and values were affected:

1. Start by opening the Registry Editor, and select the `HKEY_CURRENT_USER` branch. Select **Export Registry File** from the **Registry** menu, and export the entire branch to a file called, for example, *User1.reg*, stored somewhere convenient, such as on your desktop. Then, select the `HKEY_LOCAL_MACHINE` branch and repeat the steps, exporting it instead to *System1.reg*.

2. Next, we will make our desired change. In this case, double-click on the **TweakUI** icon (see Appendix A, *Setting Locator*) in Control Panel, and choose the **Explorer** tab. The option we're interested in is the **Animated "Click here to begin" (if room)** option. Turn it off, or if it's already off, find another option to change, just for the sake of argument. Click **OK** when you're done.

3. Immediately switch back to the Registry Editor, and re-export the `HKEY_CURRENT_USER` and `HKEY_LOCAL_MACHINE` branches into new files, such as *User2.reg* and *System2.reg*, respectively.

   What we now have is a snapshot of the entire Registry taken before and after the change (or changes) were made. It's important that the snapshots be taken immediately before and after the change, so that other trivial settings, such as changes in Explorer window positions, aren't included with the changes we care about.

4. All that remains to be done is to distill the changed information into a useful format. Windows comes with the DOS File Compare utility (*fc.exe*, located in *\windows\command*), which can be used to find the differences between the "before" and "after" files. There are several superior, Windows-based third-party alternatives, such as UltraEdit-32 (available at *http://www.ultraedit.com*) and the Compare utility, part of the *O'Reilly Utilities—Quick Solutions for Windows 98 Annoyances* (see Appendix F). At the command prompt, first use the CD command to change to the directory containing the registry patches, and then type the following:

   ```
   fc user1.reg user2.reg > user.txt
   fc system1.reg system2.reg > system.txt
   ```

   This will write *only* the differences between the files into new text files: *user.txt* for the changes in `HKEY_CURRENT_USER`, and *System.txt* for the changes in `HKEY_LOCAL_MACHINE`. The *User.txt* file should look something like this:

```
Comparing files user1.txt and user2.txt
****** user1.txt
"NoFileMenu"=dword:00000000
"NoStartBanner"=hex:00,00,00,00
"NoRecentDocsHistory"=hex:01,00,00,00
****** user2.txt
"NoFileMenu"=dword:00000000
"NoStartBanner"=hex:01,00,00,00
"NoRecentDocsHistory"=hex:01,00,00,00
******
```

From the listing above, it's evident that the only change was the `NoStartBanner` value (hardly an intuitive name), located in the *user* branch. No changes were recorded in the *system* branch, so *System.txt* ends up empty. Note also that the lines surrounding the differing lines are also included, but only as an aide in finding the differing lines, and can be removed.

5. Next, you'll need to convert the output from File Compare into a valid registry patch. This is done by first removing all but the *second* version of the changed line (representing the "after" file).

   You may notice that some changes—namely the removal of a key or value—cannot be put in registry patch form. For example, the use of TweakUI to remove an icon from the desktop or an item from Explorer's New menu results in a key being deleted, and keys cannot be deleted with registry patches. See "Automate the Deletion of Registry Items" later in this chapter for more information.

6. You'll need to search one of the original registry patch files (either the *before* or *after* snapshots will do) for the registry key path in which the changed line is located. This is simply the line enclosed in square brackets immediately *above* the changed line. The `NoStartBanner` line in our example is located in the `[HKEY_CURRENT_USER\Software\Microsoft\Windows\CurrentVersion\Policies\Explorer]` section.

7. Copy the entire line in brackets and paste it into *User.txt* directly above the line as shown below. Lastly, add the text `REGEDIT4` followed by a blank line at the beginning of the file. The final result should look something like this:

```
REGEDIT4

[HKEY_CURRENT_
USER\Software\Microsoft\Windows\CurrentVersion\Policies\Explorer]
"NoStartBanner"=hex:01,00,00,00
```

8. Save this file into a new file called *User-final.reg* (or something like that). If the settings you've changed have resulted in changes in the HKEY_LOCAL_MACHINE branch, simply repeat the above steps for the *system.txt* file as well.
9. You can then apply the registry patch(es) to any computer.

Notes and other issues

This solution should help you find the appropriate keys and values associated with a particular Windows or application setting, although it's not much use in finding keys that have no corresponding "interface." This comes in very handy, for example, when you want to create a registry patch for a group of settings, which can then be applied to any number of computers. This makes the task of configuring a room full of computers substantially less daunting.

There are some caveats to this approach, mostly that the File Compare utility will often pull out more differences than are really appropriate to the change you wish to make. It's important to look closely at each key in the resulting registry patch to see if it's really necessary. In the example above, if you wait until after you export the first registry patch to open Control Panel, you may find some cryptic Explorer registry information representing the Control Panel's window position. This can, of course, be omitted.

See Chapter 9 for a discussion on the Windows Scripting Host, which documents a method for automating changes to the Registry.

Undo. It's always smart to create a corresponding "undo" registry patch while you're following the above instructions. For example, since our registry patch contains the differences in the "after" file, *user2.reg,* the corresponding *undo* patch would contain the corresponding lines in the "before" file, *user1.reg.* Applying the *undo* patch effectively returns the keys and values stored within to their state before the setting was changed. Obviously, an important caveat is that an undo patch for one computer won't necessarily be an effective undo for another computer.

Automate the Deletion of Registry Items

An important drawback to using registry patches is that they can be used only to replace or augment information in the Registry. For some reason, no provision for removing keys or values is included in registry patches, yet some changes can only be made by removing keys. For example, to remove the **Bitmap Image** entry from Explorer's **New** menu, you need to delete the key **HKEY_CLASSES_ROOT\.bmp\ShellNew** entirely, and no registry patch can do that.

Luckily, Windows 98 now comes with the Windows Scripting Host, which includes a command for deleting registry information. See "Scripting Goodies" in Chapter 9 for more information on this use of the Windows Scripting Host:

1. Open a plain text editor, such as Notepad, and type the following:

   ```
   Call RegistryDelete("HKEY_CURRENT_USER\.bmp\ShellNew", "")

   Sub RegistryDelete(KeyName, ValueName)
     Set WshShell = WScript.CreateObject("WScript.Shell")
     WshShell.RegWrite KeyName & "\" & ValueName, ""
     WshShell.RegDelete KeyName & "\" & ValueName
   End Sub
   ```

   The first line invokes the **RegistryDelete** subroutine, listed immediately after. Simply put the full path of the registry key you wish to delete between the quotation marks, making sure not to include a trailing slash.

   To delete a single value (such as a value named **Editflags**, if it were present) rather than an entire key, replace the first line above with the following:

   ```
   Call RegistryDelete("HKEY_CURRENT_USER\.bmp", "EditFlags")
   ```

   To remove the `(Default)` value of a key, you'll need to use a standard registry patch, and simply set the default value to an empty string (`@=""`).

2. Save the file and call it something like *Delete.vbs*. Double-click on the script file to execute it.

3. Another useful example is the following script:

   ```
   Call RegistryDelete("HKEY_LOCAL_
   MACHINE\Software\Microsoft\Windows\CurrentVersion\explorer\
   Desktop\NameSpace\{FBF23B42-E3F0-101B-8488-00AA003E56F8}\", "")

   Sub RegistryDelete(KeyName, ValueName)
     Set WshShell = WScript.CreateObject("WScript.Shell")
     WshShell.RegWrite KeyName & "\" & ValueName, ""
     WshShell.RegDelete KeyName & "\" & ValueName
   End Sub
   ```

   which will remove the Internet icon from the desktop. Note that most of this script is identical to the previous script, except that a different registry path is being deleted.

   See Appendix D, *Class IDs of System Objects*, for a list of other class IDs (the stuff between the curly braces). See "Clear the Desktop of

Unwanted Icons" in Chapter 4 for more information on getting icons off the desktop.

Notes and other issues

If you wish to use VBScript files on any NT 4.0 or Windows 95 systems, you'll need to download and install the Windows Scripting Host (WSH); see "Further Study" in Chapter 9 for more information. The WSH comes with NT 5.0 and Windows 98, so no external application is required.

Currently, there is no provision for *renaming* a registry branch using either registry patches or WSH scripts. However, there are a few more involved ways to do it. For example, you can export the branch to a registry patch, and using a program with a search-and-replace feature (such as WordPad), rename the keys as desired. Then, you can apply the revised patch normally, and use a script as described above to remove the old branch. From a programmatic standpoint, you can recursively read an entire branch and write it to its new location, deleting the original when you're done.

See "Clear Unwanted Entries from Explorer's New Menu" in Chapter 4 for more information on the **New** menu.

See Chapter 9 for a full discussion on the Windows Scripting Host, which documents a method for automating changes to the Registry.

Search the Registry Effectively

The Registry Editor has a simple search feature, allowing you to search through all the keys and values for text. (Note that you can't search for the contents of binary or `DWORD` values.) Just select **Find** from the Registry Editor's **Edit** menu, type the desired text, and click **Find Next**. Since the Registry can become quite large and have a wide variety of settings and information, it is important to learn to search effectively, so you don't miss anything or waste a lot of time. Additionally, since the Registry Editor doesn't have a search-and-replace feature, doing something as simple as changing every occurrence of `c:\program files` to `d:\program files` can be a monumental chore. Here are some tips that may help:

- Make sure that all three options in the **Find** window's **Look at** section are checked, unless you know specifically that what you're looking for is solely a **Key**, **Value** (value name), or **Data** (value contents). You'll also usually want the **Match whole string only** option turned off.

- Many folder names in the Registry are stored in both long and short versions. For example, say you want to move your *Program Files* folder from one drive to another (see "Clean Up and Customize System Folders" in Chapter 4 for more information). When you install Windows, any settings pertaining to this folder may be stored in the Registry as *c:\Program Files* or *c:\Progra~1.* Make sure you search for both.
- If you're searching the Registry for both `Program Files` and `Progra~1`, you may want to just search for `progra`, which will trigger both variations. Since this will trip upon other uses of the word `program`, try placing a backslash (\) in front of it (i.e., `\progra`) to limit the search to directory names beginning with those letters. A minute of mental preparation can save you an hour of searching.
- You may want to search the Registry for an interface element, such as a new item added to a context menu, or the text in a dialog box. If the text contains an underlined character, which indicates an accelerator key, you'll need to add an ampersand (&) to the search string. For example, say you've installed a program that creates *.zip* files (such as WinZip; see Appendix F), and the program has added the command **Add to Zip** (with the Z underlined) to the context menu of all files that you wish to remove. You'll need to search for `add to &zip` to match the text properly; a search for `add to zip` will probably turn up nothing. Note also that text searches are *not* case-sensitive.
- Searching begins at the currently selected key. If you want to be sure to search the entire Registry, make sure the `My Computer` entry at the top of the registry tree is highlighted before you begin. However, if you know the setting you want to change is in, for example, `HKEY_LOCAL_MACHINE`, you should highlight that key beforehand to reduce the search time.
- Although the Registry Editor has a search feature, it doesn't allow you to search and replace. If you have a branch of settings you wish to change, for example, if you've moved an application from one drive to another, or want to replace every occurrence of *notepad.exe* with another text editor, you can use a registry patch—see "Using Registry Patches" earlier in this chapter. Just create a patch of the branch in question, and use your favorite text editor's search-and-replace feature to change the values in the patch. When you apply the patch, all the settings will be changed for you. Note that you should use this with caution, as you can screw up many settings unwittingly by searching and replacing common pieces of text.

- If you find yourself wanting to use search-and-replace more often, and the registry patch tip above isn't sufficient, you may want to try the registry Search and Replace utility. It's a bit safer and more flexible, too. See the section "Registry Tools" at the end of this chapter for more information.

Compacting the Registry

As you may have noticed, your Registry can become quite large. This is due, in part, to the empty space inside your registry files. If you're familiar with the way that data is stored in the Registry, you know that the Registry is a database. As with all databases, when information is removed or added, the entire database file is *not* rewritten entirely, in order to improve performance. Instead, new information is simply appended to the end of the file, and gaps are left in the file where information has been removed. After a lot of use, this can cause the files that make up the Registry to become enormous. See Figure 3-2 for a diagram of this process.

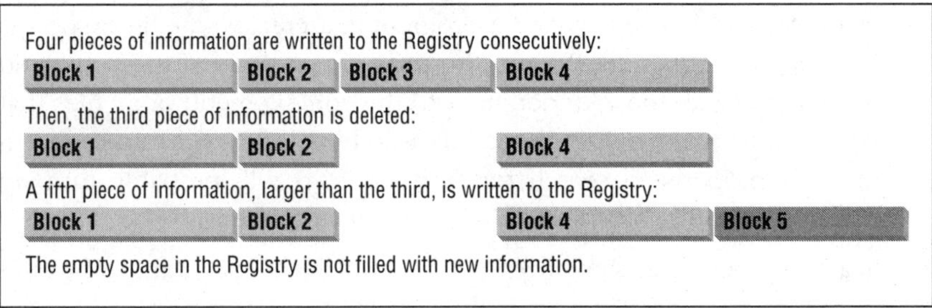

Figure 3-2: The process by which the Registry accumulates empty space

Compacting any database file like the Registry involves reading all of the settings and then writing them, in order, into a new file. This way, the empty space is eliminated and the entries are stored consecutively, resulting in less wasted space and better performance.

If you wanted to compact your Registry in Windows 95, you had to go through a long, convoluted process that involved making a registry patch of the entire Registry, then rebuilding it from within DOS. Windows 98 not only includes a utility that can compact the Registry, it does this for you automatically whenever the amount of wasted space goes above 500KB.

To optimize the Registry manually, you must first exit Windows. Select **Shut Down** from the Start Menu, and choose **Restart the computer in MS-DOS mode**. Type `SCANREG /OPT` at the DOS prompt. If you try to do this from within Windows, it won't work.

If you find that the automatic registry optimization noticeably slows your boot process, you can disable it by changing the line `Optimize=1` to `Optimize=0` in the *Scanreg.ini* file. For more information on the *Scanreg.ini* file and the Registry Checker utility, see "Backing Up the Registry" earlier in this chapter.

Understanding File Types

The term "File Types" describes the collection of associations between documents and the applications that created them. The most apparent use of this feature is that, for example, Windows knows to run Notepad when you double-click on a file with the *.txt* extension. The traditional method for configuring these associations to suit your needs is discussed in "Customize Context Menus" in Chapter 4, but it goes quite a bit deeper than that.

File configuration starts with file extensions, the letters (usually three) that follow the period in most filenames. For example, the extension of the file *Readme.txt* is *.txt*, signifying a plain text file; the extension of *Resume.wpd* is *.wpd*, signifying a document created in WordPerfect. By default, Windows hides the extensions of registered file types in Explorer and on the desktop, but it's best to have them displayed. File extensions not only allow you to determine easily what kind of file a certain file is (icons are almost never descriptive enough), but also allow you to change Windows' perception of the type of a file by simply renaming the extension.

Note that changing a file's extension doesn't actually change the contents or the format of the file, only how Windows interacts with it. For more information on changing file extensions, see "Rename Files Without a Hassle" in Chapter 2. To display your file extensions, select **Folder Options** in Explorer's **View** menu, choose the **View** tab, and turn off the **Hide MS-DOS file extensions for known file types** option.

By hiding file extensions, Microsoft hoped to make Windows easier to use—a plan that backfired for several reasons. Since only the extensions of registered files are hidden, the extensions of files which aren't yet in the File Types database are still shown. When one of those file types finally becomes registered either by an application or by Windows itself, it can appear to the inexperienced user as though all of the old files of that type have been renamed, since their extensions will mysteriously vanish. (Windows never hides extensions for file types that have not yet been registered.) This creates a knowledge gap between those who understand file types and those who don't; try telling someone whose computer still has hidden extensions to find *Readme.txt* in a directory full of files. Other problems have arisen, such as trying to differentiate *Excel.exe* and *Excel.xls* in Explorer when the extensions are hidden; one file is an application and the other is a document, but they may have the same icon.

The `HKEY_CLASSES_ROOT` branch of the Registry stores information on all your file types. File extensions, preceded by periods, are listed first, followed by the actual file types. The keys named for file extensions contain information that points to the keys describing the file types. For example, if you locate the key `HKEY_CLASSES_ROOT\.txt` (note that the period *is* included), you'll notice that there's not a lot there. The important piece of information is the `(Default)` value, which is set to the name of another key down the tree. In the case of *.txt*, the `(Default)` value contains the text `txtfile`. This, in effect, points to `HKEY_CLASSES_ROOT\txtfile`, which is the actual file type (see Figure 3-3).

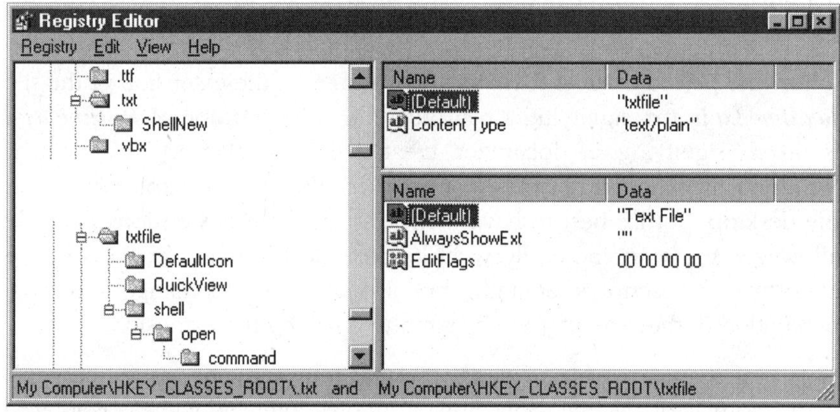

Figure 3-3: These two portions of the Registry make up a basic file type

All of the details of the file type are stored in the `txtfile` branch, such as the formal name (in this case, "Text File"), the icon used in Explorer, and the application used to edit the file. Since many different extension keys can point to this branch, a file type like `txtfile` can have many extensions pointing to (associated with) it. This is important, as there's no way to assign more than one extension to any given file type in the File Types editor in Explorer.

Creating file types

There are several ways to create file types:

- The structure shown in Figure 3-3 is what you'll usually get when an application claims a file type. In this case, the **Text File** file type was created when Windows was first installed. If you use the File Types editor in Explorer (see "Customize Context Menus" in Chapter 4) to create a new file type, you'll get something similar.

- If you've ever double-clicked on a file with an unregistered file type, you've seen the **Open With** window (also accessible by right-clicking on any file while holding the **Shift** key and selecting **Open With**) asking you which program you want to use with that type of file. File types created in this way are recognized by the `_auto_file` suffix; for example, choosing a program this way for a file with the *.dat* extension will create a file type key called `dat_auto_file`.
- The final way to create a file type is manually, either by editing the Registry directly or by applying a registry patch.

Regardless of the method by which a file type has been created, the structure in the Registry is virtually the same. All the major components of a file type are shown in Figure 3-3. First, a key is created for each extension associated with the file type. The `(Default)` value of the extension key contains the name of the key containing the file type, but not the formal name of the file type itself. For example, put `txtfile` here and not `Text File`. The `Content Type` value shown may appear for some file types, but is not necessary for normal operation.

A key called `ShellNew` may also appear underneath the file extension key. This key tells Windows to include the extension in the **New** menu (found in Explorer's **File** menu), allowing one to create a new, empty file of that type right in Explorer, without starting the file's application. The reason that the `ShellNew` key is located underneath the extension key and not the file type key (discussed below) is that a file type may have more than one extension, and Windows needs to know which extension to use when creating a new file. The `ShellNew` key is usually empty, although there may be a value called `FileName` which points to a *template*—a file on your hard disk that Windows will use to create a new, blank document (see Example 3-2). In most cases, the `FileName` value is omitted, and Windows will create a zero-byte (empty) file with the appropriate extension.

Most of a file type's definition is located in the main file type key, the name of which is specified in each of the extension keys listed above. In Figure 3-3, the `txtfile` key is the main key containing all of the settings for the "Text File" file type. First of all, the `(Default)` value here is the descriptive name of the file type—the text that appears in the File Types editor in Explorer and in the **Type** column in Explorer's **Details** view.

If the value named `AlwaysShowExt` is present (it is always empty), the extension for this file type will be displayed in Explorer, even if the user has elected to hide extensions for file types that are registered. You may also see a binary value entitled `EditFlags`. If this value is omitted or set to `00 00 00 00`, you will be allowed to edit this file type in Explorer. If `EditFlags` is set to `01 00 00 00`, the file type won't be visible in Explorer's File Types editor.

Underneath the file type key are three or four independent subkeys. `DefaultIcon` contains only the `(Default)` value, set to the filename of the icon used for the file type. Icons are specified by filename and icon index, such as:

```
d:\path\filename, ###
```

where *`d:\path\filename`* is the full path and filename of an *.exe*, *.dll*, *.ico*, or *.bmp* file containing one or more icons, and *###* represents the number of the icon (you won't actually see pound signs). To use the first icon in the file, specify `0` (zero); the second icon is `1` (one), and so on. The easiest way to choose an icon is through Explorer, as the File Types editor will allow you to browse and choose icons without typing.

If a key entitled `QuickView` is present, the context menu for the file type will include QuickView. See "Use QuickView with Any File" in Chapter 4 for more information. This key normally has the `(Default)` value set to an asterisk (*).

Most of the meat is stored in the `shell` key. Its subkeys define what happens when a file of this type is double-clicked and which commands appear in the file type's context menu. Underneath `shell` is a separate key for each command in the file's context menu; that is, when you right-click on a file of this type, these are the commands that will appear at the top of the list. Most file types have an **open** command (with a key by the same name). You may also see **Edit**, **Print**, **PrintTo**, and **View** here. You can add, remove, or change any of these commands. Underneath each one of these keys is a key called `command`. The `command` key's `(Default)` value is set to the program filename used to carry out the command.

For example, if Notepad is associated with the **Open** command for text files, the contents of `HKEY_CLASSES_ROOT\txtfile\shell\open\command` will be `Notepad.exe "%1"`. Now, the *`"%1"`* (including the quotation marks) is very important—*`%1`* is what Windows substitutes in the application's command line, and the quotation marks are necessary in case there are any spaces in the filename of the clicked file. So, if one were to right-click on any file with the *.txt* extension (say, *c:\documents\my file.txt*), and select **Open** from the context menu that appears,

Windows will carry out the following command, which will launch *Notepad* and instruct it to open the document:

```
Notepad "c:\documents\my file.txt"
```

If there is more than one command for a given file type, *one* of the commands will appear in bold (see the **View** command in Figure 3-4). This command is called the *default* and is the one that Windows uses when you double-click on a file instead of right-clicking. Usually, **Open** is the default, but any command can be the default. To set the default to a different command, specify the name of the command in the `(Default)` value in the `shell` key. For example, if a file type contains **Open**, **Edit**, and **Print**, and you type `edit` in the `(Default)` value, the **Edit** command will appear bold in the file type's context menu, and **Edit** will be the command carried out when you double-click. Note that while the word `open` is often spelled with all lowercase letters, it still appears as **Open** in the context menu. Windows will preserve the case of all other commands as you've typed them, but will automatically capitalize **Open**.

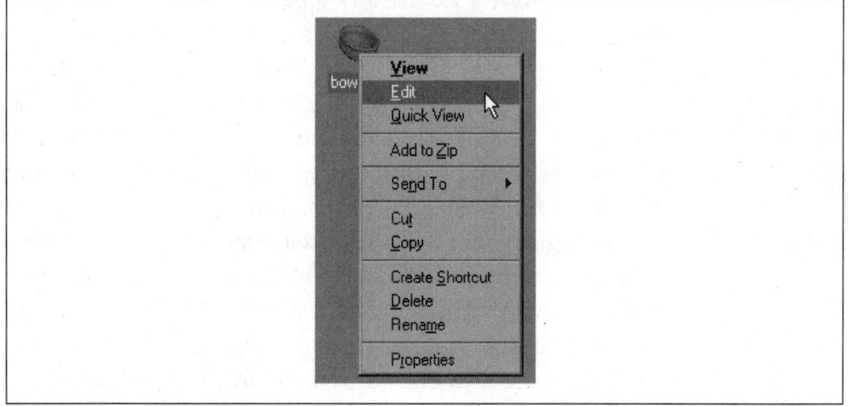

Figure 3-4: A context menu for the bitmap file type shows the default View option, as well as the extra Edit and Add to Zip options

Lastly, the `shellex` key contains references to shell extensions, and unless you're a programmer, these items will be of little use to you. Note that you can remove some unwanted context menu commands and extra tabs in the property sheets of certain file types by removing the corresponding keys to shell extensions here; just use caution. You might also see `CLSID` and `ddeexec` keys scattered around the Registry. These also have special uses, but are of little interest to most users.

Since there are so many parts to a standard file type, the best way to duplicate or safeguard a file type is to create a registry patch (see "Using

Registry Patches" earlier in this chapter). If you're creating an entirely new file type, it might be easiest to start by exporting an existing file type and then changing the particular components.

Notes and other issues

Having a good grasp of file types can be very useful for resolving annoyances. For example, you can create individual registry patches for any file types that get commonly overwritten, such as *.jpg*, *.gif*, *.bmp*, *.txt*, *.doc*, and *.html*. If an unwanted application claims a file type you have backed up, simply apply the registry patch to restore your preferences. See "Protect Your File Types" in Chapter 4 for more information.

For more information on the File Types editor in Explorer, see "Customize Context Menus" in Chapter 4. See "Change the Icons of System Objects" in Chapter 4 for another use of the `DefaultIcon` key.

Using .ini Files

If you've been using a Windows PC for any length of time, you've probably come across initialization (*.ini*) files. Initialization files (or *Configuration Files* in Windows 95/98) were used to store settings for many applications as well as previous versions of Windows before the Registry was implemented. *.ini* files are simply text files (editable with any plain text editor, such as Notepad) that are specially formatted to store such settings. Since *.ini* files are limited in their maximum file size and are not as efficient as the Registry, application developers have been encouraged to abandon *.ini* files and instead store settings in the Registry. Since some older applications, written before the release of Windows 95, and even some newer ones still use *.ini* files to store certain settings, it may become necessary to look for and change settings in *.ini* files as well. A stellar example is the Registry Checker and its *Scanreg.ini* file, discussed earlier in this chapter. The settings are stored in an *.ini* file instead of the Registry, which, among other things, makes it easy to configure in DOS.

Here are some tips on working with *.ini* files.

Edit an .ini file

- Double-click on any *.ini* file to open it in Notepad. To configure another text editor to be used with *.ini* files, see "Creating file types" earlier in this chapter and "Customize Context Menus" in Chapter 4.
- The structure of *.ini* files is similar to that of registry patches (see Example 3-2). Sections are specified in brackets, and individual settings in those sections are listed thereafter.

Search all your INI files for a setting

1. Select **Find** and then **Files or Folders** from the Start Menu.
2. Type `*.ini` in the **Named** field, and in the **Containing Text** field, type the text for which you want to search.

   This has essentially the same effect as searching through the Registry for a setting, in that *.ini* files generally contain only string values. It may be necessary to do this if you're tracking down an annoyance or a particular setting, which otherwise couldn't be found in the Registry.

System.ini and Win.ini

- The settings for previous versions of Windows were stored in *System.ini* and *Win.ini*. While these files are no longer used in Windows 95/98 to the extent they were in Windows 3.x, they are kept somewhat up to date to maintain compatibility with older applications that expect to find or store certain settings in them. There are, however, several settings that have yet to be duplicated elsewhere, such as the `Shell=` line, which make these files still important.
- In the `[Windows]` section at the top of the *Win.ini* file are two lines, labeled `Load=` and `Run=`. These lines were used to list any programs to run when Windows was started, and there may still be something there. Try checking these out to see if something is being loaded of which you're not aware, and remove any unwanted items. The preferred method in Windows 95/98 is to use either the Startup folder in the Start Menu, or the `Run`, `RunOnce`, `RunServices`, and `RunServicesOnce` keys in the Registry (see Chapter 6).

  Clearing out unneeded or outdated information from either of these files will marginally speed up Windows boot time, as well as reduce the likelihood of many conflicts. If you try to clean these out, do so with caution, and be sure to keep backup copies.

Registry Tools

The Registry Editor is included in Windows for viewing and changing the contents of the Registry. Unfortunately, this utility is quite limited, especially when compared with some of the other tools available. The following is a list of available software utilities for use with the Registry, some good and some bad. You may want to take the precaution of backing up your Registry before using any of them. See Appendix F for more information on any of the following utilities, unless otherwise specified:

Registry Search and Replace
: This is a full-featured tool used to make a global search and replace in the Registry much easier and quicker.

Norton Utilities for Windows 98
: This commercial package comes with an enhanced Registry Editor, as well as many other tools. While not available on the Internet, it can be purchased at most computer stores. The Norton Registry Editor is similar to the Windows Registry Editor, but comes with a utility that tracks changes in the Registry, a search-and-replace utility, and other useful features that Microsoft left out.

Open With
: This component of *O'Reilly Utilities—Quick Solutions for Windows 98 Annoyances* is a replacement for Windows' feeble Open With dialog, which allows you to create context menu items on the fly.

TweakUI
: This utility was released on Microsoft's web site soon after the release of Windows 95 in an effort to keep users from messing around with the Registry. It provides access to many settings that would otherwise need to be changed through the Registry. The Windows 98 version of TweakUI is included on the Windows 98 CD. See Appendix A for more information.

RegClean
: This is a freely available Microsoft product designed for Visual Basic developers to correct problems with certain OLE entries in the Registry. Due to many reported problems with this utility, it is recommended that it be avoided.

In this chapter:
- Cleaning Up the Desktop
- Fixing the Start Menu
- Files and Folders
- Making Windows Your Own

4

Tinkering Techniques

Once you get over the initial excitement of double-clicking on files, moving a window from one side of the screen to the other, and maybe winning a game of FreeCell, you may be ready for some serious tinkering.

Why would we want to tinker with the operating system? Well, if you were perfectly happy with Windows 98 right out of the box, odds are you wouldn't be reading this book. We tinker with Windows to make it better: to improve the interface, to reduce the amount of work required to complete a task, to make it run more smoothly and efficiently, and most of all, to make it less annoying (you saw that one coming).

The most important part of software design is the interface. The interface is the only link we humans have with the machines we use—the better the interface, the better the link, and the more useful the machine will be. Since Windows 98 has already been written, the most we can hope to do is to tinker with it so that it works more like we think it should.

The unfortunate methodology behind the design of the Windows 98 interface is that it is supposed to be usable by the lowest common denominator—the person who has never seen Windows before. The problem with this approach is that no user is a beginner forever. An interface should be intuitively designed and easy to use, but it seems as though in some aspects, each successive version of Windows is more dumbed down than the last, which can cause frustration with more advanced users.

One of Windows' strong points is its flexibility: the fact that you can reprogram almost any system object on the desktop to serve a different function, for example, is one of the main reasons that Windows enjoys such a large market share. While the variety of solutions presented here are a testimony to the power and flexibility of Windows 98, I'd also like to note the need for such solutions in the first place.

This chapter takes advantage of basic topics covered in Chapter 2, *Customizing the Interface*—shortcuts, system objects, and some of Windows' more obscure settings—as well as usage of the Registry, discussed in Chapter 3, *The Registry*, to customize Windows far beyond Microsoft's intentions. We'll start by clearing some of the clutter caused by the installation of Windows, and move on to customizing whatever is left over to suit your needs. While most of these solutions target specific annoyances in the operating system, each one can be used to illustrate a broader concept.

Now, I certainly don't expect every user to feel compelled to take all the advice in this book; not everyone is going to want to turn off the **Documents** menu in the Start Menu or remove certain system objects from the desktop, for example. However, by excavating into the Registry and many of the more obscure dialog boxes, you should see other things along the way that will assist you in resolving your own annoyances.

If you haven't reviewed Chapter 3, I suggest you do it at this point. It covers the Windows Registry and the Registry Editor, which are used extensively in many of the solutions in this chapter and later in the book. Many solutions require that you change a setting in the Registry, and then restart Windows for the change to take effect—you'll learn from these examples how this whole system works, and hopefully, how to solve problems that aren't covered by the material here.

Cleaning Up the Desktop

The default configuration of Windows 98—including the way the desktop and Start Menu are configured and which Windows components are included—was decided by Microsoft not with ease of use in mind, but with a view to which configuration would best showcase the features included in the new operating system. While this criterion may be great for the marketing department at Microsoft, it doesn't make for a very pleasant experience for the user.

The best place to start when customizing an interface is to throw out all the stuff you don't want, which will make much more room for the stuff you want. By not being forced to wade through dozens of icons to find the one you want, you can complete your work more easily and with less aggravation.

Clear the Desktop of Unwanted Icons

When Windows 98 is first installed, the desktop is littered with icons, some of which can be removed easily and some of which cannot. While the Recycle Bin is intended as a means by which objects throughout Windows can be deleted by dragging and dropping them into it, many items cannot be deleted this way. This inconsistency is partly due to Microsoft's concern that users will irreparably damage the operating system, and partly due to sloppy software design.

There are two types of objects that reside on the desktop (not including the Taskbar or Start Menu). Those objects which are physical files or shortcuts to files are stored in your Desktop folder (usually *C:\Windows\Desktop*); these items can be deleted or moved as easily as any other file on your hard disk. All other objects are *virtual objects*; they don't represent actual files on the hard disk. Virtual objects include My Computer, the Recycle Bin, and the Network Neighborhood. What follows should help you remove any unwanted icons from your desktop.

Network Neighborhood

If you've installed Dial-Up Networking or any other networking components, you'll see the Network Neighborhood icon on your desktop, regardless of whether your system is connected to a local area network, and regardless of its use to you. If you're connected to one or more other computers on a local area network (see Chapter 7, *Networking*), this icon provides access to the shared files and other resources of those computers. However, if you've only installed Dial-Up Networking for use with, say, an Internet connection, this icon is probably of no use, and can be removed.

Solution 1

1. Open the System Policy Editor (see Appendix A, *Setting Locator*) and select **Open Registry** from the **File** menu.
2. Double-click on the **Local User** icon, and expand the branches to `Local User\Windows 98 System\Shell\Restrictions`.
3. Turn on the **Hide Network Neighborhood** option. Another option here, **No 'Entire Network' in Network Neighborhood**, is useful if you decide to keep Network Neighborhood, but don't need the scope **Entire Network** provides. See Figure 4-3 later in this chapter.

4. Click **OK**, select **Save** from the **File** menu, and close the System Policy Editor. You'll have to refresh the desktop (see Chapter 2, *Customizing the Interface*) for this change to take effect.

Solution 2

1. Double-click on the **TweakUI** icon in Control Panel, and choose the **Desktop** tab.
2. Remove the checkmark from the **Network Neighborhood** item.

Notes and other issues

See "Hide All Icons on the Desktop" later in this section for another solution.

The **Desktop** tab of TweakUI provides a simple means of removing nearly every other desktop icon, with the exception of the My Computer icon.

A consequence of hiding the Network Neighborhood is that any resources previously available through the Network Neighborhood will be unavailable unless mapped to a drive letter (see "Setting Up a Workgroup" in Chapter 7 for more information). Since shell support for the Universal Naming Convention (UNC) notation is handled by the Network Neighborhood, hiding the Network Neighborhood icon will prevent Explorer from accessing resources via UNC names.* If you don't use browsing features on your network, you won't have any use for this icon. Since it's just as easy to bring back the icon as it is to remove it, you can always bring it back if you find that you need it later on. For example, hiding this icon will make it impossible to explore the shared drives and folders of other computers attached over a network or the *Direct-Cable Connection* utility. See Chapter 7 for more information on networks and browsing shared resources.

Undo. To get the Network Neighborhood icon back, follow the above instructions again, but uncheck **Hide Network Neighborhood** in System Policy Editor or check **Network Neighborhood** in TweakUI.

MSN (Microsoft Network)

This one's relatively easy to delete, but is annoying enough to deserve its own entry. Even if you specifically chose that MSN not be installed with

* UNC paths and filenames allow you to access folders and files without first "mapping" driver letters to network resources. An example of a UNC is *\\server\c\windows\desktop*, which specifies the *C:\Windows\Desktop* folder on a machine known as "server." For more information on accessing, sharing, and mapping network resources, see Chapter 7.

Windows 98, the icon still appears on the desktop. This would be considered an unfair advantage for Microsoft, except it didn't work for them in Windows 95—the MSN service was not a success. Here's how you delete this icon:

- If dragging the **MSN** icon into the Recycle Bin doesn't work, right-click on the **MSN** icon on the desktop, and select **Delete**.

Notes and other issues

This should also work on other default icons, like **The Internet**, **Outlook Express**, and **My Briefcase**.

See "Hide All Icons on the Desktop" later in this section for another solution.

Undo. To get the MSN icon back, open **TweakUI** from the Control Panel, choose the **Desktop** tab, and check the **MSN** entry.

Recycle Bin

Having the Recycle Bin icon on your desktop can be convenient, but since there are other ways to delete items (such as right-clicking on them and selecting **Delete**, or selecting an item and pressing the **Del** key), it really isn't necessary. Furthermore, there's a *Recycled* folder on every drive (it's hidden, so you'll have to configure Explorer to show all files), which works just like the main Recycle Bin icon. As described above for some of the other icons, you can delete the Recycle Bin using TweakUI, as follows:

Solution 1

1. Double-click on the **TweakUI** icon in Control Panel, and choose the **Desktop** tab.
2. Remove the checkmark from the **Recycle Bin** item.

Solution 2

There's a more interesting solution, one that may provide a little insight into the Registry and Windows system objects. We can add a **Delete** option to the Recycle Bin's context menu, which may be useful, for example, if you're setting up one or more computers for someone else and want to give them the option of removing the Recycle Bin easily. Figure 4-1 shows the altered context menu.

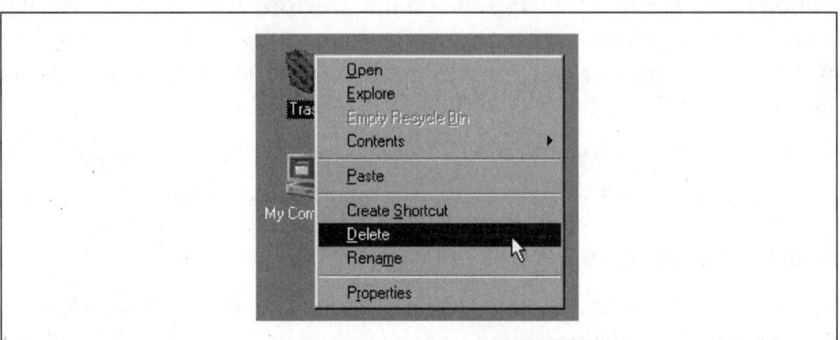

Figure 4-1: Add the Delete option to the Recycle Bin's context menu

1. Open the Registry Editor (if you're not familiar with the Registry Editor, see Chapter 3).
2. Expand the branches to `HKEY_CLASSES_ROOT\CLSID\{645FF040-5081-101B-9F08-00AA002F954E}\ShellFolder\`.
3. Double-click on the `Attributes` value, and replace the contents with `70 01 00 20`. Note that this is a binary value, and the input box may not behave like a normal textbox. If you mess up, just hit **Cancel** and try again.
4. Close the Registry Editor—the change should take effect immediately.
5. You now have the option of deleting the Recycle Bin at any time by right-clicking on it and selecting **Delete**.

Notes and other issues

See "Hide All Icons on the Desktop" later in this chapter for another solution.

Solution 2 will also add the **Rename** option to the Recycle Bin's context menu. See "Customize the Recycle Bin Icon" later in this chapter for more information.

When searching through the Registry for the key in Solution 2, it might be easier to search for the first few characters of the Class ID, or for the text, "Recycle Bin."

Undo (Solution 1). Use TweakUI and recheck the Recycle Bin option to show it on your desktop again.

Undo (Solution 2). To restore your Recycle Bin to its default, removing the **Rename** and **Delete** options from its context menu, start by following the above instructions for the Registry in Solution 2. Instead of the value specified in step 3, however, change it to `40 01 00 20`. Note that this won't restore the Recycle Bin's original name if it has been changed—you'll have to restore it manually.

My Computer

The My Computer icon provides access to all of your drives, Control Panel, your printers, and Dial-Up Networking. Since these resources are also accessible through Explorer and the Start Menu, the My Computer icon isn't strictly required. While there isn't a perfect solution for getting rid of this icon without clearing all the icons from the desktop, the following option should satisfy many of you:

1. Double-click on the **Display** icon in Control Panel, and choose the **Effects** tab. See Figure 4-2.
2. Select the **My Computer** icon in the **Desktop icons** box, and click **Change Icon**.
3. Choose a blank, transparent icon to replace the one that's there. Don't look for one included with Windows; you'll probably have to create it using your favorite icon editor. Press **OK** when you're done.
4. Right-click on the **My Computer** icon, select **Rename**, and replace the title with a single space.

Now, this process doesn't actually remove the icon from the desktop, but renders it invisible, while still allowing access if you know where to look.

Notes and other issues

See "Hide All Icons on the Desktop" later in this chapter for another solution.

Really stubborn icons

Once in a while, you'll encounter an icon on your desktop that you just can't get rid of. Whether it's from another Microsoft upgrade or some other application, the information is usually stored in the same place. Here's a last resort for getting rid of stubborn icons:

1. Open the Registry Editor. (If you're not familiar with the Registry Editor, see Chapter 3.)
2. Expand the branches to `HKEY_LOCAL_MACHINE\SOFTWARE\Microsoft\Windows\CurrentVersion\explorer\Desktop\NameSpace\`.
3. While the key itself will most likely be devoid of values, it should have a few subkeys, which will be named something like

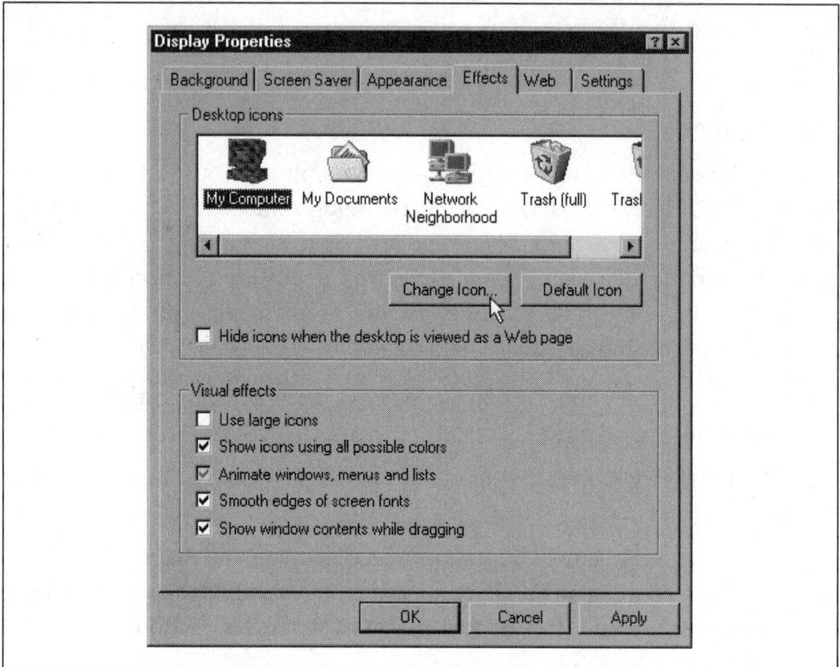

Figure 4-2: Use Display Properties to change the icon of My Computer

`{645FF040-5081-101B-9F08-00AA002F954E}`. These codes are called Class IDs and point to other parts of the Registry that contain more information about them. Class IDs are stored in the `HKEY_CLASSES_ROOT\CLSID` branch.

4. Start by clicking on a key, and look at the `(Default)` value to the right. It *should* contain a description of the item. If it doesn't, you can still find out what it is by right-clicking on the key name in the left pane, selecting **Rename**, then right-clicking on the text itself, and selecting **Copy**. This will copy the key name to the Clipboard. Then move to the top of the Registry tree (select **My Computer** at the root) and select **Find** from the **Edit** menu. Right-click on the **Find What** field, and select **Paste**. Click **Find Next** to search through the Registry for that key. When you find it, do a little digging in that key and its subkeys to find out what it's really for.

5. If one of the keys under the ...`Namespace` branch turns out to match the item you're trying to get rid of, you can go ahead and delete it. Deleting an item here is a little like deleting a shortcut in Explorer—it doesn't actually delete the information from your Registry, it only removes the pointer to the information from your desktop. If you're worried that you might want it back some day, highlight the key and

select **Export Registry File** from the **Registry** menu to create a registry patch. See Chapter 3 for more information on registry patches.

6. When you're done making changes, close the Registry Editor and refresh the desktop. See "Refresh the Desktop Without Restarting Windows" in Chapter 2 for more information.

Notes and other issues

For a list of common Class IDs for desktop items, see Appendix D, *Class IDs of System Objects.*

See "Hide All Icons on the Desktop" later in this section for another solution.

See "Automate the Deletion of Registry Items" in Chapter 3 for a way to write a script that removes icons from the desktop.

Hide All Icons on the Desktop

The following solution will disable all icons on the desktop, including any files in your Desktop folder as well as the virtual icons discussed in the previous sections:

1. Open the System Policy Editor (see Appendix A) and select **Open Registry** from the **File** menu.
2. Double-click on the **Local User** icon, and expand the branches to `Local User\Windows 98 System\Shell\Restrictions` (see Figure 4-3).
3. Turn on the **Hide all items on the desktop** option, and then click **OK**. Select **Save** from the **File** menu when you're finished.
4. Click on an empty area of the desktop and press the **F5** key for this change to take effect.

Notes and other issues

This setting can also be controlled with the Desktop Control Center and HideIt utilities; see Appendix F, *Software to Solve Annoyances*, for more information. If you're using HideIt, configure it to hide Program Manager; this will hide all desktop icons, yet keep the Taskbar intact.

Refer to the earlier topics in this chapter for information on removing individual icons from the desktop.

Undo. To restore your desktop icons, repeat the instructions above, but uncheck the **Hide all items on the desktop** option.

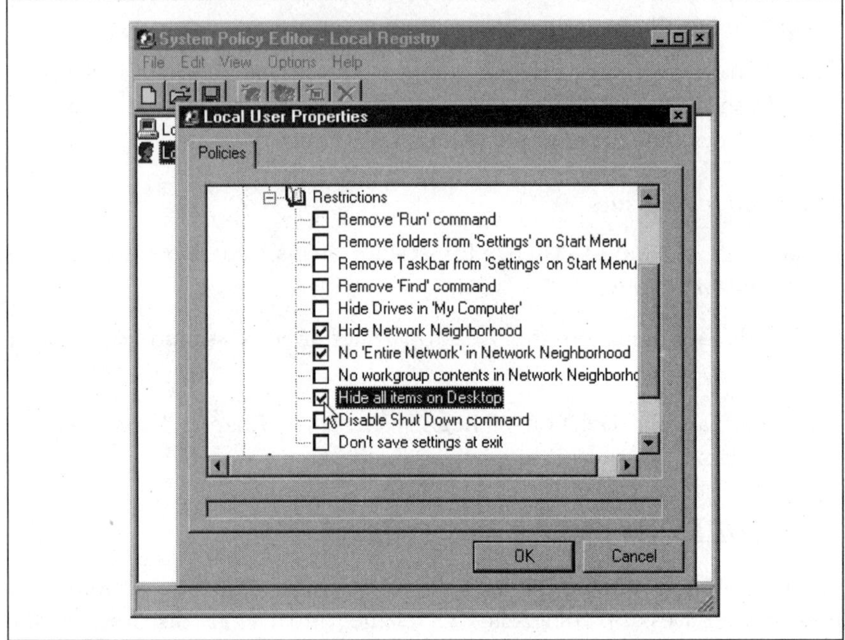

Figure 4-3: Use the Policy Editor to hide all desktop icons

Customize My Computer

Aside from the Start Menu, the My Computer window is the gateway to all the resources on your computer, including all your drives, folders, and files, the Control Panel, the Printers folder, Dial-Up Networking, and the Scheduled Tasks folder. There are many ways to customize My Computer, including adding and removing items from the window and changing the look and behavior of the icon.

Redirect the Desktop icon

Since all of My Computer's default resources are also available in Explorer and the Start Menu, you may prefer to connect another program to the My Computer icon. For example, if you prefer Explorer's hierarchical tree view to My Computer's Macintosh-style navigation, you can configure My Computer to launch Explorer:

1. Open the Registry Editor (if you're not familiar with the Registry Editor, see Chapter 3).
2. Expand the branches to `HKEY_CLASSES_ROOT\CLSID\{20D04FE0-3AEA-1069-A2D8-08002B30309D}`.

3. Right-click on the **Shell** key, select **New** and then **Key**. Type **Open** and press **Enter**.
4. Right-click on the new **Open** key, select **New** again and then **Key**. Type **Command** and press **Enter**.
5. Click once on the new **Command** key, double-click on the `(Default)` value in the right pane, type `explorer.exe` in the box, and press **Enter**. Your Registry Editor window should resemble Figure 4-4. You can, of course, replace `explorer.exe` with the full path and filename of any other program you'd rather use.

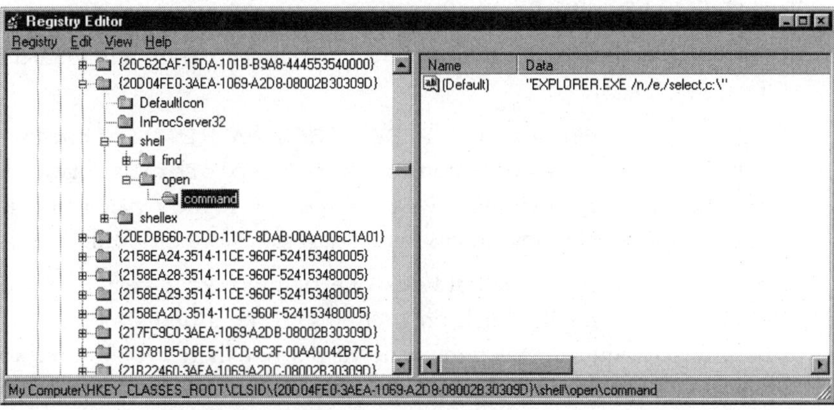

Figure 4-4: Use the Registry Editor to customize the My Computer icon

6. Close the Registry Editor when you're finished. Click on an empty area of the desktop, and press **F5** to refresh the desktop so that this change will take effect.

Now, right-clicking on the **My Computer** icon will display a context menu with two separate **Open** commands: one bold and one normal. The bold item will launch the customized action, and the normal one will open the traditional My Computer window.

Using this method, you can also add additional entries to My Computer's context menu.

Rename My Computer

- To rename the **My Computer** icon, right-click on it and select **Rename**.

Change the My Computer icon

1. Double-click on the **Display** icon in **Control Panel**, and choose the **Effects** tab.
2. Select the **My Computer** icon in the **Desktop icons** box, and click **Change Icon**.

Add entries to the My Computer window

The My Computer window, by default, contains links to several system objects. To add more system objects to the My Computer window, and consequently to Explorer, follow these steps:

1. Open the Registry Editor (if you're not familiar with the Registry Editor, see Chapter 3).
2. Expand the branches to `HKEY_LOCAL_MACHINE\Software\Microsoft\Windows\CurrentVersion\explorer\MyComputer\NameSpace`. You might want to create a registry patch of this branch before continuing, in case you want to restore the default.
3. Under this branch, you should see one or more keys—each named for a different Class ID. Click on each key to see a description in the `(Default)` value in the right pane. If it's not there, you'll have to refer to Appendix D or search the Registry for other occurrences of the Class ID, which may provide a clue to what it's for.
4. At this time, you can also remove any unwanted keys from this branch. Note that there are some items, such as the Control Panel, that don't have corresponding keys here, and therefore can't be removed.
5. To add a new key, right-click on the **NameSpace** key, select **New** and then **Key**. You can then enter any Class ID for the name of the key. (See Appendix D for a table of Class IDs, or copy and paste a Class ID from elsewhere in the Registry.)
6. Refresh the My Computer window to see your changes by pressing the **F5** key.

Remove unwanted entries from the My Computer window

There are two ways to remove icons from the My Computer window. The first is to follow the instructions for "Add entries to the My Computer window," above, and simply delete any keys for unwanted objects. The second is as follows:

1. Double-click on the **TweakUI** icon in Control Panel, and choose the **My Computer** tab.
2. Uncheck any drives you wish to be hidden from My Computer, and consequently from Explorer.

Notes and other issues

The "Add entries to the My Computer window" solution above does not work as you might expect for all system objects. For example, you should be able to add the Network Neighborhood icon, but when you try to double-click on it, it will just open the **Find Computer** dialog.

You can add and remove system objects from other containers, as shown in the "Add entries to the My Computer window" solution above. Some other registry branches (in the same location of the Registry) that work in this way include `Desktop\NameSpace`, `NetworkNeighborhood\NameSpace`, and `Internet\NameSpace`.

To make the contents of My Computer more accessible (for example, while an application is covering the desktop), you can create a folder inside your Start Menu, and drag shortcuts for all of the desired items into the new folder. See "Make Control Panel Applets More Accessible" in Chapter 2 for more information on that and other solutions.

Like the Start Menu and the **Send To** menu, you can add items to the Network Neighborhood window by adding shortcuts to the *\Windows\Nethood* folder, should that appeal to you.

To customize the icons of the drives in the My Computer window, see "Customize Drive Icons" in Chapter 2.

Undo. Remove the new keys added above in the Registry Editor to restore it to its default operation.

Customize the Recycle Bin Icon

Although you can rename any file or folder on your hard disk, as well as almost any system object (including My Computer and Network Neighborhood), Windows won't allow you to rename the Recycle Bin—at least, not easily. To rename the Recycle Bin to something more compelling, such as "Garbage," "Trash," or "Road to Nowhere," follow either of the following procedures.

Add the Rename option to the Recycle Bin's context menu

1. Open the Registry Editor (if you're not familiar with the Registry Editor, see Chapter 3).
2. Expand the branches to `HKEY_CLASSES_ROOT\CLSID\{645FF040-5081-101B-9F08-00AA002F954E}\ShellFolder\`.
3. Double-click on the `Attributes` value, and replace the contents with `50 01 00 20`. Note that this is a binary value, and the input box may not behave like a normal textbox. If you mess up, just hit **Cancel** and try again.
4. Close the Registry Editor. The change should take effect immediately.
5. You now have the option of renaming the Recycle Bin at any time by right-clicking on it and selecting **Rename**.

Manually rename the Recycle Bin

1. Open the Registry Editor (if you're not familiar with the Registry Editor, see Chapter 3).
2. Expand the branches to `HKEY_CLASSES_ROOT\CLSID\{645FF040-5081-101B-9F08-00AA002F954E}`.
3. Double-click on the `(Default)` value in the right pane and replace the text `Recycle Bin` with any new name you wish.
4. Press **OK** and then close the Registry Editor.
5. Click on an empty area of the desktop and press **F5** to refresh the desktop so that this change will take effect.

Change the Recycle Bin icon

1. Double-click on the **Display** icon in Control Panel and choose the **Effects** tab.
2. Select the **Recycle Bin** icon (either full or empty) in the **Desktop icons** box and click **Change Icon**.

Notes and other issues

When searching through the Registry for the Recycle Bin's CLSID key, it might be easier to search for the first few characters of the Class ID, or for the text "Recycle Bin."

A process similar to the "Add the Rename option to the Recycle Bin's context menu" solution above adds the **Delete** option to the Recycle Bin's context menu. See the Recycle Bin entry in "Clear the Desktop of Unwanted Icons" earlier in this chapter for more information.

If you have Norton Utilities for Windows 98, right-click on the **Recycle Bin**, select **Properties**, and choose the **Desktop Item** tab to rename the Recycle Bin.

Undo (Rename in context menu). To restore your Recycle Bin to its default, and remove the **Rename** option from its context menu, start by following the above instructions for the Registry. Instead of the value specified, however, change it to `40 01 00 20`.

Undo (Manual rename). Repeat the process, and manually type `Recycle Bin` for the name.

Change the Icons of System Objects

Although direct support isn't built into Windows for changing the icons used for the various system objects, such as the Control Panel, Dial-Up Networking, and the generic folder, it can be done. The icons discussed here are referred to as *shell icons* and are standard Windows icons used for Windows' *virtual objects*; that is, objects other than drives, folders, files, and shortcuts. There are two ways to change the icons of system objects.

Solution 1: Basic system objects

1. Double-click on the **Display** icon in Control Panel, and choose the **Effects** tab.
2. The **Desktop icons** section lists, by default, five icons: **My Computer**, **My Documents**, **Network Neighborhood**, **Recycle Bin (full)**, and **Recycle Bin (empty)**. Select any icon here and click **Change Icon** to choose a new one.

Solution 2: All system objects

1. Open the Registry Editor (if you're not familiar with the Registry Editor, see Chapter 3).
2. Expand the branches to `HKEY_CLASSES_ROOT\CLSID\{class id}\DefaultIcon`, where *`{class id}`* is one of the Class IDs listed in Appendix D. If the Class ID for the object you want to change is not listed there, do a search in the `HKEY_CLASSES_ROOT\CLSID\` branch for the name of the object. You can back up this entry before you change it by creating a registry patch at this point.
3. Double-click on the `(Default)` value in the right pane.

Tinkering Techniques

4. By default, most system objects will have the `(Default)` value set to something like `shell32.dll,17`, which means that Windows will use the eighteenth icon in the file *Shell32.dll* (0 being the first icon, 1 being the second, and so on).
5. You can specify any existing *.dll*, *.ico*, or *.exe* file here. If the file is not in your system path (see Chapter 6, *Troubleshooting*), you'll need to specify the full pathname (i.e., *c:\icons\ugly.ico*). If the file only contains one icon, or if you want to use the first icon in the file, you can omit the trailing comma and number.
6. If a file contains more than one icon, the easiest way to find out which number corresponds to the icon you want is to browse the file in Windows. To browse an icon file, take any existing Windows shortcut (or create a new one), right-click on it, and select **Properties**. Choose the **Shortcut** tab, click **Change Icon**, type the desired filename, and count from the left—zero (0) is the first, one (1) is the second, and so on.
7. This change should take effect the next time you refresh the folder containing the object you've just customized. For example, press the **F5** key while the desktop is active to refresh any desktop icons.

Notes and other issues

Many system icons can be changed with the Microangelo Engineer utility (see Appendix F).

Although you can change the single icon used for all folders, you can't change folder icons individually. To specify an icon for a specific folder on your hard disk, you can create a shortcut to that folder, and then change the icon of the shortcut.

To change the icons for drives in My Computer, see "Customize Drive Icons" in Chapter 2.

You can't change the icons for applications, but you can change the icons for shortcuts to those applications, such as those used in the Start Menu and on the desktop. Just right-click on the desired shortcut, click **Properties**, choose the **Shortcut** tab, and click **Change Icon**. You can also change the default icon used for application documents (e.g., the icon used for all files with the *.txt* extension). See "Customize Context Menus" later in this chapter for more information.

Undo (Solution 1). The default icons for the items listed in the **Desktop icons** list are as follows (where 0 is always the first icon): My Computer: *cool.dll,16*; My Documents: *mdocs.dll,0*; Network Neighborhood:

cool.dll,17; Recycle Bin (full): *shell32.dll,32*; and Recycle Bin (empty): *shell32.dll,31*.

Undo (Solution 2). If you've backed up any changed entries by creating a registry patch (see Chapter 3), you can apply the patch to restore the setting.

Turn Off the Bouncing "Click Here to Begin" Arrow

The little yellow Click Here to Begin arrow that bounces off the Start Menu when you first start Windows was irritating right off the bat. I suppose it's useful for those folks who can't figure out what Start means, but for the rest of us, it's easy to get rid of.

Solution 1: Using TweakUI

1. Double-click on the **TweakUI** icon in Control Panel, and choose the **Explorer** tab.
2. Turn off the **Animated "Click here to begin" (if room)** option, and click **OK**.

Solution 2: Using the Registry Editor

1. Open the Registry Editor (if you're not familiar with the Registry Editor, see Chapter 3).
2. Expand the branches to `HKEY_CURRENT_USER\Software\Microsoft\Windows\CurrentVersion\Policies\Explorer`.
3. If it's not there, create a binary value called `NoStartBanner`. To do this, right-click on the `Explorer` key, select **New** and then **Binary Value**. Type `NoStartBanner` for the name.
4. Double-click on the `NoStartBanner` value, enter the value `01 00 00 00`, and press **OK**. Note that this type of value is not a text value—you won't be able to erase the numbers. Instead, either highlight a digit with the mouse cursor and type over it, or type and then erase so that there are still four pairs of digits. This may take a little practice.

Notes and other issues

If you don't see the Click Here to Begin arrow, it's likely that a Taskbar button for an open window is blocking it. When Windows first starts, this arrow appears on the Taskbar to the right of the Start Menu button, unless a window is open; having any window appear when Windows first starts is another solution to this problem.

Undo (Solution 1). Repeat the steps in Solution 1, but turn on the **Animated "Click here to begin" (if room)** option to reverse the change.

Undo (Solution 2). Repeat the steps in Solution 2, but change the value in step 4 to `00 00 00 00` to restore the default.

Fixing the Start Menu

As is Microsoft's intention, the Start Menu is the container for most of the basic functionality of Windows 98. It would seem reasonable, then, that one should not only be able to customize this menu with the most commonly used features, but should be able to rid the Start Menu of the items that aren't used.

You probably already know that you can add, remove, and rearrange most of the items in your Start Menu by dragging and dropping, a process explained in greater detail in Appendix E, *Interface Terminology and the Basics.* However, there are certain intrinsic, unmovable entries, such as the **Documents** and **Favorites** menus, that not only get in the way if they're not used, but can make it easier for "prying eyes" to do their prying.

This section deals with the customization of this miniscule interface element, including the button itself, as well as its components. For more information on the Control Panel aspect of the Start Menu, see "Make Control Panel Applets More Accessible" in Chapter 2.

Customize the Start Menu Button

The button on the Taskbar used to open the **Start Menu** consists of a small Windows logo and the word **Start**. The **Start Menu** button was a tough nut to crack—there is no built-in method for customizing the text or the icon that appears here. However, advanced users with the correct tools will be able to accomplish this in only a few minutes. Figure 4-5, for instance, shows a **Start Menu** button that's been customized. Note that anyone not familiar with a hex editor should not attempt this procedure. If you're smart, you'll make sure to back up all files before editing them. Here's how to edit the various aspects of the **Start Menu** button.

Figure 4-5: The Start Menu button after some slight alterations

Change the word "Start" (requires a hex editor)

You'll need a good hex editor to complete the following. The example assumes you're using UltraEdit-32 (available at *http://www.ultraedit.com*), a text editor that can also be used to edit binary files, which makes it a suitable hex editor.

If this is done incorrectly, it can damage the application. If you back up any files before altering them, you eliminate the possibility of permanent damage.

1. Make two duplicates of the file *Explorer.exe* (it's in your *\Windows* folder). Put one in a safe place, and put the other somewhere convenient, such as on your desktop. The copy in the safe place is your backup in case the operation is not successful.
2. Open the conveniently placed copy of *Explorer.exe* in your hex editor. (Not only would it be foolish to try to edit the original *Explorer.exe*, but Windows won't allow it, since it's currently in use.) UltraEdit-32 should automatically switch to hex mode once the file is opened.
3. Select **Find** from the **Search** menu, and type `53 00 74 00 61 00 72 00 74` in the **Find What** field. These numbers are Unicode values in hex and represent the word "Start," where each letter is separated by a null character (#00). You should find several occurrences of this, but if you look at the "translation" on the right, you'll notice that each one of them is just part of the phrase "Start Menu"—except for one. In the original release of Windows 98, it's the last occurrence of **Start**, located towards the end of the file. Your screen should look something like Figure 4-6.
4. Close the **Find** window when you've found the correct occurrence of this value.
5. You can replace any of the five characters here, *but do not change the null characters* (represented by dots). You can replace a character either by clicking on it on the right side and typing directly, or by clicking on its corresponding hex code on the left side and typing a new code (see the following "Notes and other issues" for a listing of hex codes).

   Although you can't specify a word longer than five characters, you can have a shorter word by including spaces (#20) for the remaining characters.

   If you make a mistake, it is usually easier and safer to simply close the file and reopen rather than trying to repair the damage.

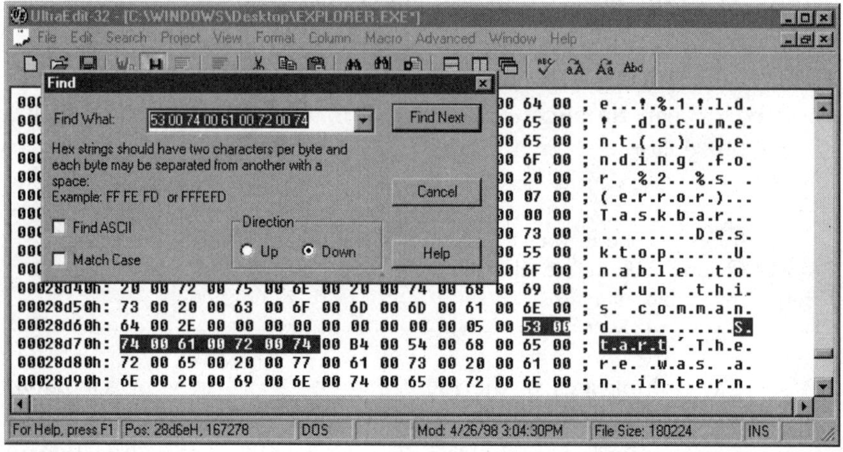

Figure 4-6: Use a hex editor like the one shown to search for the word Start in Explorer.exe

6. When you're done, select **Save** from the **File** menu, and close the hex editor.
7. The next step is to put the altered file in place of the existing one. Assuming you've made *two* duplicates of *Explorer.exe* as recommended above, this will be no problem, although you won't be able to do it while Windows is running. Select **Shut Down** from the Start Menu, choose **Restart in MS-DOS mode**, and click **OK**.
8. Assuming the *altered* file was saved on your desktop, you would type the following:

   ```
   copy c:\windows\desktop\explorer.exe c:\windows
   ```

   Replace `c:\windows` with the actual location of your copy of Windows, if different.
9. Type `exit` to return to Windows. The **Start Menu** button should now reflect your changes.

Change the icon (requires an icon editor)

1. Make two duplicates of the file *User.exe* (it's in your *Windows\System* folder). Put one in a safe place, and put the other somewhere convenient, such as on your desktop.
2. Open the conveniently placed copy of *User.exe* with an icon editor that can read *.dll* and *.exe* files, such as the Microangelo Librarian utility.
3. Explorer uses the flag logo, the very first icon in *User.exe*, for the Start Menu button. What you need to be aware of is that there are several

versions of this icon in the file, each of a different size. Depending on the screen fonts you've chosen (in particular, the "Active Title Bar" setting in the **Appearance** tab in **Display Properties**), Windows may be using the 10×10, 12×12, 14×14, 16×16, 22×22, or 32×32 variations. Your best bet is to update them all.

4. When you're done, save your changes and close the icon editor.
5. The next step is to put the altered file in place of the existing one. Assuming you've made *two* duplicates of *User.exe* as recommended above, this will be no problem, although you won't be able to do it while Windows is running. Select **Shut Down** from the **Start Menu**, choose **Restart in MS-DOS mode**, and click **OK**.
6. Assuming the *altered* file was saved on your desktop, you would type the following:

   ```
   copy c:\windows\desktop\user.exe c:\windows\system
   ```

   Replace `c:\windows` with the actual location of your copy of Windows, if different.
7. Type `exit` to return to Windows. The **Start Menu** button should now reflect your changes.

Notes and other issues

The hex codes for upper- and lowercase letters and for numbers 0–9 used to change the word "Start" in the Start Menu are as follows:

A=41	H=48	O=4F	V=56	c=63	j=6A	q=71	x=78	4=34
B=42	I=49	P=50	W=57	d=64	k=6B	r=72	y=79	5=35
C=43	J=4A	Q=51	X=58	e=65	l=6C	s=73	z=7A	6=36
D=44	K=4B	R=52	Y=59	f=66	m=6D	t=74	0=30	7=37
E=45	L=4C	S=53	Z=5A	g=67	n=6E	u=75	1=31	8=38
F=46	M=4D	T=54	a=61	h=68	o=6F	v=76	2=32	9=39
G=47	N=4E	U=55	b=62	i=69	p=70	w=77	3=33	

You can permanently disable Windows if you don't know what you're doing. Make sure to back up the original versions of any files you alter in a safe place before proceeding. If something does go wrong, and you can't get back into Windows, and you can't restore your backup, you'll need to reinstall Windows.

To change or remove any of the standard components of the Start Menu itself, see "Customize Start Menu Components" later in this chapter.

Undo (either solution). Overwrite the changed file with the backup you saved in a safe place. You did make a backup, didn't you?

Customize Start Menu Components

We know that the contents of the **Programs** portion of the Start Menu is just a folder on your hard disk, and that you can customize most of the items in the **Programs** menu by simply moving, renaming, creating, or deleting shortcuts in that folder. However, what about the items that can't be changed, such as **Help** and **Find**? Some of these intrinsic items can be hidden, and all can be renamed.

Hiding certain intrinsic Start Menu components can be desirable for many reasons: if you never use them, if space in the Start Menu is limited (especially on small screens), for security reasons, or if you frequently find yourself selecting the wrong item.

On the more obscure end of the spectrum, it's possible to rename each of the intrinsic Start Menu components, using the same process as in the previous solution, "Customize the Start Menu Button." Some knowledge of using a hex editor is required—if you have a lot of time on your hands, it's a good way to make Windows a little more distinctive. If you're smart, you'll make sure to back up all files before editing them.

Remove unwanted Start Menu components

The following intrinsic items can be safely removed from the Start Menu (for more information on TweakUI or the System Policy Editor, see Appendix A):

Documents
: Double-click on the **TweakUI** icon in Control Panel, choose the **IE4** tab, and turn off the **Show Documents on Start Menu** option.

Favorites
: Double-click on the **TweakUI** icon in Control Panel, choose the **IE4** tab, and turn off the **Show Favorites on Start Menu** option.

Find
: Open the System Policy Editor and select **Open Registry** from the **File** menu. Double-click on **Local User**, expand the branches to `\Windows 98 System\Shell\Restrictions`, and turn on the **Remove 'Find' command** option.

Run
: Open the System Policy Editor and select **Open Registry** from the **File** menu. Double-click on **Local User**, expand the branches to `\Windows 98 System\Shell\Restrictions`, and turn on the **Remove 'Run' command** option.

Folder Options (in Settings)

Open the System Policy Editor and select **Open Registry** from the **File** menu. Double-click on **Local User**, expand the branches to `\Windows 98 System\Shell\Restrictions`, and turn on the **Remove folders from 'Settings' on Start Menu** option.

Shut Down (disable only)

Open the System Policy Editor and select **Open Registry** from the **File** menu. Double-click on **Local User**, expand the branches to `\Windows 98 System\Shell\Restrictions`, and turn on the **Disable Shut Down command** option.

Taskbar & Start Menu (in Settings)

Open the System Policy Editor, and select **Open Registry** from the **File** menu. Double-click on **Local User**, expand the branches to `\Windows 98 System\Shell\Restrictions`, and turn on the **Remove Taskbar from 'Settings' on Start Menu** option.

Customize the Start Menu item labels (requires a hex editor)

You'll need a good hex editor to complete the following. The example assumes you're using UltraEdit-32 (available at *http://www.ultra-edit.com*). It's a text editor that can also be used to edit binary files, thereby making it a suitable hex editor.

If this is done incorrectly, it can damage the application. If you back up any files before altering them, you eliminate the possibility of permanent damage.

1. Make two duplicates of the file *Explorer.exe* (it's in your Windows folder). Put one in a safe place, and put the other somewhere convenient, such as on your desktop. The copy in the safe place is your backup in case the operation is not successful.
2. Open the conveniently placed copy of *Explorer.exe* in your hex editor. (Not only would it be foolish to try to edit the original *Explorer.exe*, but Windows won't allow it, since it's currently in use.) UltraEdit-32 should automatically switch to hex mode once the file is opened.
3. Select **Find** from the **Search** menu, and type `50 00 72 00 6F 00 67 00 72 00 61 00 6D 00 73` in the **Find What** field. These are Unicode numbers in hex, representing the word "Programs," where each letter is separated by a null character (#00). See the "translation" on the right side of the UltraEdit-32 window to make sure you have it right.

4. The other Start Menu items (**Documents**, **Settings**, **Find**, **Help**, **Run**, and **Shut Down**) are also stored in this way. Just do a search for the corresponding hex code to find a specific entry. See "Customize the Start Menu Button" earlier in this chapter for a hex code key.

   You can replace any of the characters in the word, *but do not change the null characters* (represented by dots). You can replace a character either by clicking on it on the right side and typing directly, or by clicking on its corresponding hex code left side, and typing a new code.

   Whatever word you choose, it cannot be longer than the word it is replacing; for example, your substitute for **Programs** must be 8 letters or fewer. To use a word shorter than 8 letters, replace the remaining characters with spaces (hex code 20).

   If you make a mistake, it is usually easier and safer to close the file and reopen rather than trying to repair the damage.

5. When you're done, select **Save** from the **File** menu, and close the hex editor.
6. The next step is to put the altered file in place of the existing one. Assuming you've made *two* duplicates of *Explorer.exe* as recommended above, this will be no problem, although you won't be able to do it while Windows is running. Select **Shut Down** from the Start Menu, choose **Restart in MS-DOS mode**, and click **OK**.
7. Assuming the *altered* file was saved on your desktop, you would type the following:

   ```
   copy c:\windows\desktop\explorer.exe c:\windows
   ```

   Replace *c:\windows* with the actual location of your copy of Windows, if different.

8. Type `exit` to return to Windows. The Start Menu button should now reflect your changes.

Notes and other issues

You can permanently disable Windows if you don't know what you're doing when using a hex editor to alter system files. Make sure to back up any files in a safe place before proceeding.

To change the look of the Start Menu button itself, see "Customize the Start Menu Button" earlier in this chapter.

There's a utility called Start Menu Changer which provides a graphical interface for making many of the changes described above; see Appendix F for more information.

One of the nice consequences of hiding the Documents menu (see "Remove unwanted Start Menu components," earlier in this chapter) is that the shortcuts that are normally created and stored in the *\Windows\Recent* folder will no longer be created. This means there's one less thing that can slow down your computer, twelve fewer items that will take up disk space and show up in search results, and one less security concern. Note that if you remove the Documents menu, however, any items currently in the *\Windows\Recent* folder won't be automatically deleted.

To clear the Documents menu without disabling it, right-click on an empty portion of the **Taskbar** and select **Properties** from the menu that appears, or select **Settings** and then **Taskbar** from the Start Menu. Choose the **Start Menu Programs** tab, and then click **Clear** to clean out the menu.

To have Windows clear the Documents menu every time you start your computer, double-click on the **TweakUI** icon in Control Panel, choose the **Paranoia** tab, and turn on the **Clear Document history at logon**.

Undo (Remove components). Simply change back any options that you have changed.

Undo (Customize components). Overwrite the changed file with the "safe place" backup you made. You did make a backup, didn't you?

Get Find to Look Where You Want

The Find feature included with Windows is quite handy for finding files on your hard disk or network. The problem is that when you access Find from the Start Menu, it defaults to looking only in the folder that was last searched, meaning that in most cases, you'll have to specify a new location manually.

If you don't know where an object might be hiding, it can be helpful to search across all your drive letters in one swoop; conversely, it can be time consuming to search your entire system when you know that what you're looking for is in a particular branch.

Now, Windows 98 does add a few helpful top-level locations that weren't available in Windows 95, such as **Desktop** and **My Documents**. And if you have more than one hard drive, you can select **Local Hard Drives**. While you can manually point to one of these locations or type one of your own in the **Find** command in the Start Menu, there's no obvious way to set the default search location to be used every time. There are, however, workarounds to this limitation, as well as other ways to use the Find feature.

Solution 1: Open Find from where you want to search

Instead of changing the way the main **Find** command works, sometimes it's easier to use one of the less obvious instances:

- Open any folder in which you want to search, and press **F3** or **Ctrl-F** to search that folder and all folders beneath it. **F3** also works on the desktop, although **Ctrl-F** does not.
- If you're using the Explorer tree view, you can also select **Find** from the **Tools** menu to search from the current folder. For some reason, this menu is not available in single-folder windows.
- If the folder in which you want to search is not currently open, you can right-click on it (even in the tree view) and select **Find**. This also works for the My Computer icon on the desktop, which is, incidentally, a quick way to get **Find** to look through all your drives.
- You can also right-click on the **Start** button and choose **Find**, but this will result in a search rooted in your Start Menu folder (just as **Explore** and **Open** go to that folder). However, it's a quick way to open the window, from which you can manually change the search root.

Solution 2: Change the Find command in context menus

As described in Solution 1, one of the ways to access the **Find** command is to right-click on a folder, and select **Find**. The search root for this command can be customized by editing the Registry:

1. Open the Registry Editor (if you're not familiar with the Registry Editor, see Chapter 3), and expand the branches to `HKEY_CLASSES_ROOT\Directory\shell\find\ddeexec`.
2. Double-click on the `(Default)` value; you'll see the following:

   ```
   [FindFolder("%I", %I)]
   ```

   where `%I` is where Windows inserts the name of the folder from which **Find** was launched. You can replace it with any folder name, such as *C:* (actually, you only need to replace the second instance).
3. The next time you right-click on a folder and select **Find**, it will default to the folder you've specified. The most interesting use of this change is that the context menu for the **Start** button is also changed, which makes a convenient launch point for **Find**.
4. Close the Registry Editor when you're finished. The change should take effect immediately.

You can also change the Find root for all drive icons (`HKEY_CLASSES_ROOT\Drive\shell\find\ddeexec`), the My Computer icon (`HKEY_`

CLASSES_ROOT\CLSID\{20D04FE0-3AEA-1069-A2D8-08002B30309D}\shell\find\ddeexec), and the Network Neighborhood icon (HKEY_CLASSES_ROOT\CLSID\{208D2C60-3AEA-1069-A2D7-08002B30309D}\shell\find\ddeexec).

Solution 3: Make a new icon with your favorite search root

1. Open the **Find** window in any of the usual ways (as described in Solution 1), and choose the desired find location and any additional search options. Leave the **Named** field blank if you want to search for all filenames.
2. Click **Find Now** to perform at least one search with these settings, even if you don't want to do a search right now—otherwise, your settings won't be saved.
3. Choose **Save Search** from the **File** menu. This will put a file with the *.fnd* extension on your desktop (e.g., *All Files.fnd*).
4. Next, obtain and install the Microsoft Find... Extensions utility (one of Microsoft's Powertoys; see Appendix F), which will allow you to add new entries to the **Find** menu that appears in the Start Menu as well as the **Tools** menu in Explorer by simply creating shortcuts.
5. Move the *.fnd* file you created to any out-of-the-way folder, such as your Windows folder. Then, create a shortcut to the *.fnd* file in the *\Windows\Start Menu\Find* folder (don't just move it there). Rename the shortcut to something that reminds you what you're searching; for example, if your custom search is rooted at My Computer, you might call it **Find in all drives**. You can also change the icon to something more distinctive than the default white pieces of paper.
6. The next time you want to perform a search with your custom criteria, choose **Find in all drives** (or whatever you've named your custom search) instead of the standard **Files or Folders**. You can create as many custom searches in this way as you want, as long as each one has a different *.fnd* filename.

Solution 4: Remove unwanted Find menu items

As long as we're on the subject:

1. Open the Registry Editor (if you're not familiar with the Registry Editor, see Chapter 3).
2. Expand the branches to HKEY_LOCAL_MACHINE\Software\Microsoft\Windows\CurrentVersion\explorer\FindExtensions.

3. The subkeys in this branch are extra Find menu items that either came with Windows or were added later by other applications. All of them should contain class IDs that point to registered applications elsewhere in the Registry. If it isn't clear what a particular key is for, just do a Registry search for the respective class ID.
4. It's safe to delete any keys from this branch, although it's advisable to first back them up by creating a registry patch (see Chapter 3). You might, for example, want to get rid of the **On the Internet** entry (located in `...\static\InetFind`) and the **People** entry (located in `...\static\WabFind`).
5. You can also add any entries quite easily, but not by creating keys here; see Solution 3 for an example.

Files and Folders

Probably the most important customization of files and folders is discussed in the section "Customize Context Menus" later in this chapter, where you'll learn about one of the best features of the pseudo-object-oriented interface design in Windows 98.* While Windows doesn't necessarily exhibit the best in modern user-interface design, the concept of context menus is quite useful. Read these topics to learn more, and hopefully improve your working experience with Windows.

One of the new features in Windows 98 is the Web View, love it or hate it. While the Web View primarily allows you to customize the superficial look of your folders, it can be put to good use. See Chapter 8, *Taking Control of Web Integration*, for more information.

Clean Up and Customize System Folders

The default Windows 98 installation occupies tons of hard disk space with a myriad of files scattered in over 160 different directories. While the sheer number and size of these files aren't necessarily problems with today's large, cheap hard drives, the amount of clutter that results can make finding documents, resolving conflicts, and performing other housekeeping very difficult.

---

* True object-oriented design dictates that objects (in this case, files and folders) be aware of their own traits. This design is only mimicked in Windows 98. Instead of each file knowing which application is used to edit it, Windows determines how to handle a file based solely on the filename extension. This design has advantages and disadvantages, but Microsoft's misguided decision to hide filename extensions, the basis for file associations, only makes the whole system more difficult to understand and master.

One of my personal pet peeves about Windows is that sometimes there are a dozen or so folders that all accomplish the same thing. For example, *Program Files*, *Common Files*, *Microsoft Shared*, *Application Data*, *Downloaded Program Files*, *Accessories*, and *MSApps* all contain installed applications and their components. The *My Documents*, *Favorites*, *Personal*, *Received Files*, and *My Files* folders are all designated places to store documents and other personal files. Most users have enough trouble keeping track of documents without having to worry about all these extraneous folders. So, why do we have a dozen places to put things when two or three would do?

As Windows has evolved, Microsoft designers have repeatedly changed their minds about what these "system" folders have been called, and what they should contain. Essentially, Microsoft has not been very careful about conforming to their own standards and keeping their users' sanity in mind when making these decisions. The result has been confusion and irritation among developers and users alike, but the good news is that you can do something to help clean up the mess left by Microsoft.

The following solutions allow you to reassign most of Windows' system folders; of course, which folders you wish to customize, and where you wish to move them is entirely up to you. Solutions 1 and 2 show how to move or rename some folders only. To effectively delete a folder, you must consolidate it with another, as described in Solution 3.

Solution 1

1. Double-click on the **TweakUI** icon (see Appendix A) in Control Panel and choose the **General** tab.
2. Choose the folder you wish to change from the **Special Folders** section, and click **Change Location**. Note that you'll have to open up Explorer first and create any folders you wish to use if they don't already exist, since TweakUI won't let you do it.

The drawback to this solution is that TweakUI only lets you configure a few folders. If the one you want to change is not listed, you'll have to use one of the other solutions.

Solution 2

1. Open Explorer and navigate to the folder you wish to rename or move.
2. Drag the folder to relocate or rename it, just as you would any other folder. If you rename or move *most* system folders, Windows will keep track of them, changing registry settings on the fly. It is usually

obvious that a folder change is being tracked because of the slight delay and increased disk access immediately following the change.

The drawback to this solution is that it doesn't work for all system folders, and in the cases where it does work, it occasionally is not complete. After making a change, it is best to search the Registry for the old folder name or location, and manually change any references to the neglected entries. See Solution 3 for more information.

Solution 3

1. Open the Registry Editor (if you're not familiar with the Registry Editor, see Chapter 3).
2. Most of the system folders are stored in one or more (depending on the folder) of the following registry paths:

```
HKEY_CURRENT_USER\Software\Microsoft\Windows\CurrentVersion\
    Explorer\Shell Folders
HKEY_CURRENT_USER\Software\Microsoft\Windows\CurrentVersion\
    Explorer\User Shell Folders
HKEY_LOCAL_MACHINE\Software\Microsoft\Windows\CurrentVersion\
    Explorer\Shell Folders
HKEY_LOCAL_MACHINE\Software\Microsoft\Windows\CurrentVersion\
    Explorer\User Shell Folders
```

   Supposedly, those folders that are specific to a particular user (assuming there's more than one, which is uncommon) would be specified in the `HKEY_CURRENT_USER` branch, while the rest are specified in the `HKEY_LOCAL_MACHINE` branch. Additionally, those folders that have been customized after installation are listed in the `User Shell Folders` subkey. In practice, the folders seem randomly scattered throughout all locations, sometimes appearing in more than one place, and sometimes not appearing at all.*

   The *Program Files* and *Common Files* folders are both defined in the `HKEY_LOCAL_MACHINE\SOFTWARE\Microsoft\Windows\CurrentVersion` key. For *Program Files*, you'll need to change both the `ProgramFilesDir` and `ProgramFilesPath` values; for *Common Files,*† just change the `CommonFilesDir` value.

---

* While being able to move system folders at all is a testament to the flexibility of Windows, the gross inconsistencies, a Microsoft trademark, can make this a tricky exercise. At least it's better than in Windows 95, where there were even more subkeys, with names like `Shell Folders` and `ShellFolders` (the second occurrence having no space).

† *Common Files* is a subfolder under *Program Files*, which contains more application-specific folders. In fact, you may see some duplication in the contents of *Program Files* and *Common Files*; consolidating these folders may free some disk space and reduce the possibility of version conflicts.

The *Application Data* folder is defined by the `DefaultDir` value in `HKEY_CURRENT_USER\Software\Microsoft\Windows\CurrentVersion\ProfileReconciliation\AppData`.

3. To change a folder location, you must first find the respective entry in any of the registry keys listed above. Then, double-click the value and edit the entry as you please. If there is more than one occurrence of the item you wish to change, you must change them all.
4. In some cases, this is sufficient to make the desired change. However, in the majority of cases, you'll need to take additional steps. For example, you may notice that after changing a value in one of the Shell Folders subkeys and restarting Windows, the value reverts back to its previous state. If this happens, you'll need to not only reenter the change, but make an exact duplicate of it in the corresponding `User Shell Folders` subkey.
5. Odds are that there are references to either the folder itself or files within the folder elsewhere in the Registry; to make the change complete, you must change all references in the entire Registry to reflect the change. Since there can be hundreds of references to some of these folders, especially *Program Files* and *Common Files*, you'll probably need a program like Registry Search and Replace (see Appendix F). Another killer is that some references may contain the short filename version of a folder, while others may contain the long filename version (i.e., *C:\PROGRA~1* for *c:\Program Files*). Make sure to get them all.
6. Make changes to any desired folders, and close the Registry Editor when finished.
7. If you redirect the location of a folder like *Program Files* or *Common Files*, make sure you move the actual files located in these folders to the new locations as well. Otherwise, several programs that rely on these folders won't be able to find their files.

   Also, in some cases, if you've relocated a folder in the Registry without creating it in Explorer, Windows will do it for you. However, it's good practice to make sure that any folders specified in the Registry also exist on your hard disk.
8. You'll need to restart Windows for most of these changes to take effect.

To effectively *remove* a system folder, the best thing to do is to simply consolidate it with another system folder. The benefits of doing this are substantial. For example, Windows 98 comes with the too cutely named *My Documents* folder, which helps to enforce a valuable strategy for keeping track of personal documents by providing a single root for all documents, regardless of the application that created them. This allows you, for example, to sort your documents by project rather than by program. However, this design is seriously undermined by the existence of other system folders with similar uses, such as *Favorites*, *Personal*, *Received Files*, and *My Files*.* Consolidating all of these system folders so that they point to the same place, such as *c:\Documents* or *c:\Projects*, causes a couple of positive things to happen. It provides a common root for all personal documents, making your stuff much easier to keep track of, and it also allows you to open any document quickly using the Favorites menu in the Start Menu.

Special case: The Temp folder

Nearly all applications in Windows use the *Temp* folder to store working files, which are created temporarily while an application is running and are deleted when the application closes. By default, this folder is located in *c:\Windows\Temp*, but it can be easily and safely moved to a different location.

There are several reasons you might want to do this. As any experienced Windows user knows, crashing is, unfortunately, a daily experience. When an application crashes, it doesn't get a chance to delete any temporary files it had created, which means that the *Temp* folder can quickly fill up with hundreds of files that look something like *~DF13F4.TMP*. Not only can this consume lots of disk space, but if any files are open when the application that created them crashes, they become corrupted, which can degrade system performance and cause other problems. If you have more than one hard disk or hard disk partition, it can be beneficial to relocate the *Temp* folder to a drive other than the one on which Windows is installed.

The *Temp* folder isn't specified in the Registry like the others. Instead, it's an *environment* variable. Unlike Windows NT, Windows 98 has no clean way of defining environment variables (such as the system path). Here's how to change the location of your *Temp* folder:

---

* *My Files* is the counterpart to *My Documents* that is used by some versions of WordPerfect and other non-Microsoft application suites. The *Personal* folder was used by Office 95, but not enforced in subsequent releases. Depending on which programs you are using, or have used in the past, these folders may or may not appear on your system.

1. Open a text editor, such as Notepad, and open *C:\Autoexec.bat*. You can create the file if it's not there. Then, add (or change) the following lines:

```
SET TEMP=D:\TEMP
SET TMP=D:\TEMP
```

   where `D:\Temp` is the new desired location of your *Temp* folder. These commands set the values of two variables, both of which are needed.

2. The next time you restart your computer, Windows will use the new folder to store the temporary files. However, Windows will still insist on creating the original *c:\Windows\Temp* folder, even if it's not used.

3. Another line you may wish to add to your *Autoexec.bat* file is the following:

```
DEL D:\TEMP\*.TMP
```

   where `D:\Temp` should match the folder name specified above. This simply deletes all *.tmp* files whenever you boot Windows, which not only creates more disk space, but erases any possibly corrupted files, which can cause Windows not to boot. Most of the time, files in the *Temp* directory are of little use, and can be removed when inactive (the bootup process is a good time to remove them). Of course, if you're worried about deleting possibly valuable data, don't do this.

Notes and other issues

Undo (Solutions 1 and 2, and Special case: the Temp folder). To reverse the change, simply reverse the process.

Undo (Solution 3). As with any changes to the Registry, you can easily restore the original settings if you take the precaution of creating registry patches of any keys before you change them. However, since some of these changes can require that you change dozens or even hundreds of settings, it's better to simply create a backup of the Registry as a whole. Your best defense, of course, is to back up your entire hard disk before making any potentially hazardous changes.

Customize Context Menus

Introduced in Windows 95, and unchanged in Windows 98, is the nearly global functionality of *context menus*. A context menu is what you see when you use the right mouse button to click on a file, folder, application title bar, or nearly any other object on the screen. Most of the time, this menu includes a list of *actions* appropriate to the object on which you've clicked. In other words, the options available depend on the *context*.

The context menu for file icons, the most commonly used and customized context menu, depends upon the type of file selected, which is determined by the file's extension. For example, all text files (with the *.txt* extension) will have the same context menu, regardless of what they contain or which application was used to create them. In addition to common context menu items such as **Copy**, **Paste**, **Delete**, **Rename**, and **Properties**, you'll see **Open** (which is bolded, meaning it's the *default*—the action used when you double-click on a *.txt* file)—as well as **Print** and **Print To**.

The most common example of where the default action can go wrong occurs when one arrogant application snatches a file type on your system. Say you started by installing Netscape Navigator in Windows 95, so that Navigator automatically made itself the default application for all files with the *.html* extension (used by web page documents). Then, when upgrading to Windows 98, Internet Explorer made itself the default application for all *.html* files.* These events in and of themselves wouldn't necessarily be a problem, unless you like to be able to predict what happens when you double-click on *.html* files.

While the most obvious reason to customize is to control the default action, what makes context menus so powerful is that you can assign several menu items to each file type. In the case of *.html* files, for example, you can add as many custom actions as suits your needs: an **Edit** action for your favorite text editor, a **View with Netscape** action, and a **View with Internet Explorer** action.

In nearly all circumstances, it's possible to add, remove, or customize these context menu items. The File Types window is the only dedicated tool provided by Microsoft to manage File Types in Windows. However, despite the importance of file associations, the File Types dialog box isn't designed with efficiency and power in mind. For example, in order to accomplish the simplest of tasks, you'll need to open up to five nearly incomprehensible dialog boxes. For the most flexibility when customizing context menus, you'll want to see "Understanding File Types" in Chapter 3.

---

* The main problem with this is that Internet Explorer automatically becomes the default web browser for anyone who has upgraded to Windows 98, even though it was never explicitly installed. The choice is made without the user's consent, and regardless of whether or not any other programs used this file type before Windows 98 was installed. This behavior has not only sparked a volatile debate between the Department of Justice and Microsoft regarding illegal monopolistic control, but has frustrated millions of users who want nothing more than to be able to easily choose what happens when they double-click on a document on the hard disk.

Use file types to add, remove, and edit context menus

1. Select **Folder Options** from the **View** menu in a single-folder window or in Explorer, and click the **File Types** tab.
2. Select the desired file type from the list and click **Edit**, or click **New Type** to create a new one and claim an unused file extension. Note that the names for most file types are not intuitive; for example, "Microsoft Excel Spreadsheet" is the type name for *.xls* files, which means that, alphabetically, the files are found under "M" instead of "E" for Excel or "X" for *.xls*. If you don't remember the type name associated with a particular file extension, just find a folder containing a file of that type in Explorer, and look at the **Type** column in the **Details** view.
3. In the Edit File Type or Add New File Type dialog, you can specify a new name for this file type, as well as the icon used for files of this type. The Actions list box contains a list of the customizable context menu items. The bold item is the default (the action carried out when you double-click on a file of this type), which also appears in bold at the top of the context menu.
4. You can check the **Enable QuickView** option (available only if the QuickView component is installed) to show the **QuickView** action in the context menu.
5. Click **New** to add new actions, or **Edit** to change any existing actions, and **Remove** to get rid of unwanted actions here. Clicking **Make Default** will bold the currently selected action, making it the default, and will change the icon for the file type (for better or for worse) to reflect the change.

   When editing or creating actions, don't worry about the **Use DDE** option and related settings, as they aren't used except in a few circumstances. If they're used by a particular action, however, it's best to leave them alone. Dynamic Data Exchange (DDE) is a set of poorly documented commands used by Windows to communicate with applications that are already open; for example, when using the **Print** context menu command for *.doc* (Microsoft Word) files, Windows simply communicates with Word and tells it to open the file.
6. Press **OK** and then **Close** twice when finished. The changes should take effect immediately, and any open single-folder or Explorer windows should automatically refresh to reflect your changes.

Add custom context menu actions on the fly

After double-clicking on a file with an extension that has not yet been registered, you might have seen the **Open With** dialog, with a list of applications that happen to be associated with other file types. From this list, you can select an application, type a name for the new type, and continue. However, the two problems with this approach are that you'll never see this box for files that already have at least one association, and that you can't register an action without making it the default. Here's an alternative:

1. Obtain and install the Open With utility, part of *O'Reilly Utilities—Quick Solutions for Windows 98 Annoyances* (see Appendix F).
2. Right-click on any file, associated or not, and select **Open With**.
3. On the left, you'll see a list of associated applications, although unlike in the traditional Open With dialog, only usable Windows programs are listed. You can select an application with which to open the document this once, or click **Make new context menu action** to configure Windows to use the chosen application for a new, more permanent menu item. The new context menu item will be named for the application you've chosen, such as **Open with Notepad**, although you can change the caption to whatever suits you—type `Open` or the name of some other existing action to replace that action.
4. Turn on the **Make Default** option to make the newly added action the default. Any current default action will cease to be the default, but will otherwise remain intact.

The beauty of this is that you don't have to interrupt your work flow when you want to associate a new program with the files you use.

Customize context menus for folders and desktop icons

1. Open the Registry Editor (if you're not familiar with the Registry Editor, see Chapter 3).
2. For folder context menus, expand the branches to `HKEY_CLASSES_ROOT\Directory\shell\`. For the context menus of any system objects, such as **Network Neighborhood**, expand the branches to `HKEY_CLASSES_ROOT\CLSID\{class id}\shell\`, where *`{class id}`* matches one of the codes listed in Appendix D, including the braces.
3. Select **New** from the **Edit** menu, select **Key**, type the name of the new item you want added to the list, such as `Open` or `Edit`, and press **Enter**.

4. Highlight the new key, select **New** from the **Edit** menu, and then select **Key** again.
5. Type `command` for the name of this new key, and press **Enter**.
6. Double-click on the `(Default)` value in the right pane, and type the full path and filename of the application you want associated with this entry.
7. Close the Registry Editor when finished. These basic registry keys are created when you edit file types with either of the previous solutions, although since there's no built-in provision for customizing the context menus of folders or system objects, we must do it the hard way. Your changes should take effect immediately.

Notes and other issues

For other examples where this functionality is put to more specific use, see "Clear Unwanted Entries from Explorer's New Menu," "Customize My Computer," "Print Out a Directory Listing," "Use QuickView with Any File," and "Protect Your File Types," all in this chapter.

Although the traditional Open With dialog won't appear by default for registered files, you can still access it by holding the **Shift** key, right-clicking on the file, and selecting **Open With**. If you install the Open With replacement utility described above, it will replace all occurrences of the traditional dialog.

You can also make the traditional Open With command available for all files, and without having to hold the **Shift** key. Open the Registry Editor (if you're not familiar with the Registry Editor, see Chapter 3), and expand the branches to `HKEY_CLASSES_ROOT/*/shell/openas/command` (create any keys that don't exist). Double-click on the `(Default)` value, and type `rundll32.exe shell32.dll,OpenAs_RunDLL %1`. Press **OK** and close the Registry Editor when you're finished.

See "Understanding File Types" in Chapter 3 for a detailed examination of how file types are stored in the Registry.

See "Use QuickView with Any File" later in this chapter for several solutions to creating context menu items that appear in all files on your system.

Undo. Use the File Types dialog to delete any added context menu items. If you're worried about overwriting certain file types, the best way to back them up is to create registry patches; see "Understanding File Types" in Chapter 3 for more information. If you wish to restore a certain file type's default functionality, you may need to reinstall the application that created the file type (such as Excel for the *.xls* file type), which in some cases may be Windows itself.

Protect Your File Types

One of the most irritating aspects of using Windows is when the settings you've spent time customizing are overwritten by some application, usually due to the carelessness or arrogance of the programmers. A common practice employed by some companies is to jerryrig an application so that it overwrites your file associations, either when it's installed, or even worse, every time the program is run. That way, their program becomes the default.

For some proprietary file types, such as Excel Files (*.xls*), this isn't much of a problem, since there aren't any other programs that use these files. The impact is on more general file types, such as the large quantity of graphics formats (*.gif*, *.jpg*, *.tif*, *.bmp*, and *.png*), which can be used by a dozen different programs. Only you should be in the position to decide which program you use for each task.

There are two motivations for this practice of overwriting existing file extensions without warning or notification, neither of which is of much benefit to the user in the long run. First, it's essentially a marketing scheme, whereby the application that forces itself on users becomes more well known and more frequently used. Second, and probably more important, it's a way for companies to reduce technical support calls; designers feel that Microsoft's File Types window is too convoluted for most users, and instead of taking the time to resolve the issue,* they simply steamroll the user.

The main problem is that the overwriting of file types, or for that matter, any registry setting, is nearly impossible to prevent. Microsoft has failed to provide a way to *write-protect* registry settings, and until application developers learn to respect their users' preferences, there is no perfect solution. Perhaps new standards will be set in the industry soon; for instance, applications that wished to register a file type could do so by

* A good compromise between respect for users and the need to allow users to easily choose their defaults is the way that both Netscape Navigator and Internet Explorer ask before making themselves the default browser. If IE, for example, detects that any of its file types have changed when it is started, you'll see a message like, "Internet Explorer is no longer the default browser. Would you like to make it the default?" This came about after complaints from users like me about file types being overwritten. However, Microsoft has yet to succumb to users' wishes regarding overwriting during installation (of both Win98 and updates to IE). Netscape Navigator, luckily, does ask before overwriting file types during installation.

nondestructively creating additional context menu actions (such as **View with Internet Explorer** or **Open with Photoshop**) rather than by overwriting existing actions.

The following solutions are the best workarounds available to help combat this problem.

Solution 1: Save portions of your Registry

Probably the most effective protection against overwritten file types is to back up the portions of the Registry that are at risk. This is accomplished with registry patches, which can easily be applied to the Registry at any time to restore your customizations. If you're not familiar with the way file types are stored in the Registry, I highly recommend reviewing "Understanding File Types" in Chapter 3 before continuing. For more information on registry patches, see "Using Registry Patches," also in Chapter 3.

This would be a good procedure to follow, for example, before installing an application you believe might overwrite an existing file type. Repeat these steps for each file type you wish to protect:

1. Open the Registry Editor (if you're not familiar with the Registry Editor or registry patches, see Chapter 3).
2. Expand the branches to `HKEY_CLASSES_ROOT\` and select a key that you wish to protect.

   Any given file type is stored as one or more extension keys and a file type key. For example, the extensions *.txt* and *.log* may both be linked with the `txtfile` file type. So, to save the entire file type, you'll need to save `HKEY_CLASSES_ROOT\.txt`, `HKEY_CLASSES_ROOT\.log`, and `HKEY_CLASSES_ROOT\txtfile`. If you only save the extensions, the context menu actions might be lost. Likewise, if you only save the file type key, the extension keys may be reassociated with a different file type key. Since you can only select one key at a time, start with one and repeat the following step for each remaining key.
3. When you've highlighted a registry key you want to export, select **Export** from the **Registry** menu, and specify a filename for the patch. If you're exporting more than one patch, don't worry too much about the name just yet. Make sure not to export two branches to the same file, however; instead of combining the two keys as you might expect, the file will simply be overwritten. Also, don't try to export the entire `HKEY_CLASSES_ROOT` branch, as it contains more information than we need for this purpose, and reapplying it may have undesirable effects.

4. While you'll usually want to save specific extensions rather than an entire file type, you can get a list of all the extensions linked to a specific file type by selecting **Folder Options** from Explorer's **View** menu, and then choosing the **File Types** tab. Then select any file type from the list and look in the **File Type Details** box for a list of active extensions.
5. Once you've exported all the keys you're interested in, close the Registry Editor.
6. Most likely, you'll have a few registry patches from this exercise. Since they're just plain text files, you can easily merge them together into a single patch with Notepad. Choose one file to be the *main* patch, and then cut and paste the contents of the other patches into it. The only editing you'll have to do is to remove the `REGEDIT4` line from all but the main patch.
7. Save your changes to the main patch, and then delete all the other patches. If you're exporting multiple file types, you might want a separate registry patch for each file type, where each patch would contain the file type information and all the extensions.
8. Whenever a particular file type that you've backed up is overwritten by an errant application, just double-click on the patch you made to restore it.

   In most cases, when you apply a registry patch, it will simply overwrite the information that's there with whatever is in the patch. However, in some circumstances, there may be leftover context menu items from any newly installed applications.
9. To apply the patch automatically whenever you start Windows, create a new shortcut in the *\Windows\Start Menu\Programs\Startup* folder (which may be different on your system). When asked for the shortcut's command line, enter the following:

   ```
   regedit /s c:\filetypes\text.reg
   ```

   where *`c:\filetypes\text.reg`* is the full path and filename of the registry patch you wish to apply. Note the `/s` switch, which runs the Registry Editor in *silent* mode, skipping the two prompts that normally appear when registry patches are applied.

Solution 2: Make room for more actions

There's only so much you can do to prevent your file types from being overwritten. A good alternative to worrying about which program is the default for a particular file type is to simply construct a context menu item for each program you wish to use. Here's an easy way to accomplish this on the fly:

1. Obtain and install the Open With utility, part of *O'Reilly Utilities—Quick Solutions for Windows 98 Annoyances* (see Appendix F).
2. Right-click on any file and select **Open With**. Here, you have the choice of opening the file just once with the program you choose, or adding a new context menu item. The good thing about this is that the **Make New Context Menu Action** is nondestructive; instead of replacing existing actions, it creates new actions, such as **Open with Notepad**. You can, of course, edit the action to read Open or Edit, which will then replace any existing actions by that name. See "Customize Context Menus" earlier in this chapter for more information.

   If you don't have *O'Reilly Utilities—Quick Solutions for Windows 98 Annoyances*, you can still right-click on any file while holding the **Shift** key, and then select **Open With** to create new associations (if you don't hold **Shift**, it's only available to unassociated files). However, this more simplistic dialog will only allow you to choose a default action, which is nearly always destructive in that any other associations will be replaced.

Special case: DDE configuration

One sticking point you may encounter when trying to reconfigure file types is that some actions use Dynamic Data Exchange (DDE). DDE is a method of communication between applications, and is sometimes used by Windows to communicate with the applications it launches.

For example, when you right-click on a *.doc* file and select **Print**, Windows opens the file in Wordpad (or Word, if installed), and then sends a DDE message to the application to print the document. This is more efficient than using command-line parameters to print documents, especially when multiple documents are being printed. Rather than opening a separate copy of Wordpad or Word for each document being printed, Windows simply instructs an open instance of the program to perform the task of printing.

The problem with DDE is that it is not only poorly documented, but also different for every application, and therefore not practical for the average user to configure by hand. You can view the current DDE settings for a given file type with the File Types window:

1. Select **Folder Options** from Explorer's **View** menu, and then choose the **File Types** tab.

2. Select a file type from the list (Word, Wordperfect, Excel, and *.html* documents all use DDE by default), and click **Edit**.
3. Choose an item from the **Actions** list (such as **Print** or **Open**), and click **Edit**. If the **Use DDE** option is *not* checked, click **OK** and choose another action.

   If the **Use DDE** option is checked, the four fields in the **Use DDE** section will contain various commands appropriate to the file type and associated application. It's important to realize that while these solutions allow you to reassociate file types with different applications, they don't accommodate these types of DDE commands.

   If a particular file type for an application stops working for some reason, it could be that the DDE information has changed or been erased altogether. If this is the case, you'll usually have to reinstall the application to restore the DDE-enabled file types. However, in most cases (and especially if you never use the **Print** context menu action), it won't make too much difference whether it's there or not.

Special case: Web browser file types

As I've mentioned several times throughout this text, today's web browsers are among the nastiest to deal with when it comes to file types. Not only are there the associations for *.html* and *.htm* files, but for the various URLs (*http://*, *https://*, *ftp://*, *mailto:*, etc.) as well. While these associations aren't much different than the ones described above and in "Understanding File Types" in Chapter 3, there is an easier way to configure them:

1. Obtain and install the Web Browser Delegate, part of *O'Reilly Utilities for Windows 98 Annoyances* (see Appendix F).
2. To change an association, choose an item in the list of methods (such as the Web Browser or Email Client) and select one of the programs to the right. Red stars show which browsers and other applications are in use and which associations have been changed.
3. Once you've made the desired changes, you can save the new settings in a registry patch. The next Internet Explorer update or Netscape Navigator version you install will probably overwrite every setting in some way, and having the patch handy will save you time spent reconfiguring, letting you restore the optimal configuration in a single step.

Notes and other issues

When using the Windows File Types dialog, you may notice that certain file types can't be changed or removed. However, there's a way around this, and you don't have to mess around with the Registry. Start up the old **File Manager** (*winfile.exe*), select **File → Associate** and enter the file extension in the **Files with Extension** text box. You can then associate the extension with an item in the list or select the **(None)** entry to remove it.

A similar problem which plagues Explorer's **New** menu—and relies on registry settings as well—is documented in "Clear Unwanted Entries from Explorer's New Menu" later in this chapter.

Use QuickView with Any File

There are essentially three types of items in any file's context menus: the custom actions that are different for each file type (see "Customize Context Menus" earlier in this chapter), the intrinsic commands (such as Copy, Paste, Delete, Rename, and Properties), and the *context menu handlers*. Context menu handlers are programs that are registered for some or all file types and extend the functionality of context menus, but are too complex for non-programmers to implement. One of the context menu handlers that comes with Windows is the QuickView utility.

QuickView is a relatively handy, albeit limited, tool that comes with Windows. Once installed, it allows you to right-click on certain files and select QuickView to open a window that displays the contents of the selected files. The problem is that, by default, QuickView is only available for a small number of file types, such as *.txt* and *.bmp* files. There are several ways to get QuickView to work with more, or even all, of the files on your system.

Solution 1: Enable QuickView for all files

1. Open the Registry Editor (if you're not familiar with the Registry Editor, see Chapter 3).
2. Expand the branches to `HKEY_CLASSES_ROOT\`, and look for a key labeled simply "`*`" (without the quotation marks), which should appear at the top of the branch.
3. Select the `*` key, and add a new key called `QuickView`.
4. Double-click the `(Default)` value in this new key and type `*`, click **OK**, and close the Registry Editor.
5. You should now see the QuickView option available for every file on your system.

Solution 2: Enable QuickView selectively

1. Select **Folder Options** from Explorer's **View** menu, choose the **File Types** tab, and select the file type with which you want to use QuickView from the list (for more information on this dialog box, see "Customize Context Menus" earlier in this chapter).
2. Click **Edit**, turn on the **Enable Quick View** option, click **OK**, and **OK** again. Note that the **Enable QuickView** option may not be available for some file types. This is due to the fact that Windows has been warned that QuickView doesn't support some file formats. You can override this by using one of the other solutions here.
3. If the type of file with which you want to use QuickView is not listed, click **New Type** to add the extension of the desired file to the list, and then follow the steps listed above.

You'll have to do this for every file type with which you want to use QuickView.

Solution 3: Put QuickView in the Send To menu

- Probably the easiest and most benign solution here is to create a shortcut to *Quikview.exe* (located in your *\Windows\System\Viewers* folder) in your *\Windows\SendTo* folder.

  QuickView will then be accessible from the **Send To** submenu when you right-click on any file.

Solution 4: Use a desktop receptacle

- Create a shortcut on your Desktop for *Quikview.exe*, allowing you to drag any files onto it to be viewed.

Notes and other issues

If you don't have the QuickView option, it's likely that QuickView wasn't installed; double-click on **Add/Remove Programs** in Control Panel, select the **Windows Setup** tab, and turn on the QuickView option to install it.

QuickView has built-in viewing capabilities for most types of data files. You'll be able to view any plain text file (*.txt*, *.log*, *.ini*, *.reg*), any bitmap-encoded graphics file, any Microsoft Word file, most WordPerfect files, most spreadsheets, and even *.exe* and *.dll* files. Despite Microsoft's insistence that Windows 98 is more web-centric, however, QuickView does not support *.gif* or *.jpg* files, the formats used for web page graphics. You'll have to open Internet Explorer to do that!

QuickView may not have a filter for every file you view, but sometimes viewing the raw data is better than nothing at all. There are a few exceptions, however, as some files may simply cause an error with QuickView, meaning that you'll see neither a preview nor a raw data dump.

For those of you who are familiar with the procedure in Solution 1 when used in Windows 95, you know that there was a bug that caused any additions to the * file type to show up only in files with extensions, rather than in all files. This bug has been fixed in Windows 98.

There's also a commercial version of the QuickView utility that supports many more file types and has additional features. You can download a free trial of the software from the Internet (see Appendix F). I haven't found the commercial version to be substantially better than the free one that comes with Windows, but it may be worth it to you, depending on the types of files you frequently view. For graphics files (e.g., *.gif*, *.jpg*, *.bmp*, *.tif*, etc.), you're probably better off with a dedicated graphics viewer that can also display thumbnails, such as Acdsee-32 (see Appendix F).

Undo. Simply remove any registry keys or shortcuts that were created, or turn off any options that were enabled in the above solutions.

Print Out a Directory Listing

What would seem a basic function of Windows, the ability to print out a list of files in any given directory, has been strangely omitted from the operating system. However, there are a few ways, using folders' context menus, to add this functionality to Windows.

Solution 1: Use a DOS batch file

One of the nice things about context menus (which is also one of their limitations) is that they are implemented in a way compatible with how DOS programs have worked for nearly twenty years. For example, if you right-click on a *.txt* file and select **Open**, and the **Open** action is associated with Notepad, Windows simply launches Notepad with the text file specified in the command line, like this:

```
C:\windows\notepad.exe somefile.txt
```

Using this simple syntax, we can add an action associated with a simple DOS batch file to the context menus for folders:

1. Open a text editor, such as Notepad, and type the following two lines into a new document:

   ```
   CD %1
   DIR >LPT1
   ```

This assumes the printer you wish to use is connected to printer port #1; change `LPT1` to `LPT2` if necessary.

2. Save the two-line file into your *Windows\Command* folder, and call it *Printdir.bat.*
3. Right-click on the file in Explorer, select **Properties**, and choose the **Program** tab. Turn on the **Close on Exit** option, choose **Minimized** from the **Run** list box, and click **OK**.
4. Next, open the Registry Editor (if you're not familiar with the Registry Editor, see Chapter 3).
5. Expand the branches to `HKEY_CLASSES_ROOT\Directory\shell`.
6. Select **New** from the **Edit** menu and then select **Key**.
7. Type `Print Contents` for the name of this new key, and press **Enter**.
8. Highlight the new **Print Contents** key, select **New** from the **Edit** menu, and then select **Key** again.
9. Type `command` for the name of this new key, and press **Enter**.
10. Double-click on the `(Default)` value in the right pane, and type the following:

    ```
    C:\Windows\Command\PRINTDIR.BAT
    ```

    assuming that `C:\Windows\` is your Windows folder.
11. To use the new feature, just right-click on any folder icon, and select the **Print Contents** option to print its contents.

Solution 2: Use the Clipboard

1. Obtain and install the Send To Extensions (part of Microsoft's Power-Toys; see Appendix F).
2. Open the folder whose contents you wish to print and select all the files by pressing **Ctrl-A**. Right-click on one of them, select **Send To**, and then select **Clipboard as Filename**.
3. Then, open a plain text editor or your favorite word processor and select **Paste** from the **Edit** menu. If you want, take this time to format, sort, or otherwise clean up the directory listing, and then print it out.

Notes and other issues

The batch file in Solution 1 uses the `DIR` command to display the contents of the selected directory, which is then redirected to the printer with the > character. You can use any of the `DIR` command's options to further customize this feature. To specify the desired sort order, change the line above to the following:

```
DIR /O:xxx >LPT1
```

where `xxx` can be any or all of the following letters, in order by preference: `N` to sort by name, `E` for extension, `S` for size, `D` for date, `G` to group directories first, `A` by last access date (earliest first). Precede any letter with a minus sign (–) to reverse the order. Some examples include `/O:EN` to sort first by extension and then by name, `/O:-D` to sort by reverse date (from latest to earliest), and `/O:SAG` to sort by size and last access date, grouping directories first. Also, try the `/B` switch to display bare filenames without all the extra information, and the `/W` switch to condense the filenames into multiple columns. Type `DIR /?` at the command prompt to see all the possible options. See Appendix C, *Contents of the MSDOS.SYS File* in *MSDOS.SYS*, for information on setting the default sort order for the `DIR` command.

This functionality is also available in *O'Reilly Utilities—Quick Solutions for Windows 98 Annoyances* (see Appendix F for more information).

Turn File Icons into Thumbnail Previews

Windows tries hard to be as graphical as possible, which can sometimes be its downfall. Case in point: when was the last time you found the icon for an application or associated document to be the least bit helpful in determining what was inside?

In Explorer, when you view a folder containing icons (*.ico* files), cursors (*.cur* files), or animated cursors (*.ani* files), their file icons are *previews* of their contents instead of simply generic icons for the application with which they're associated. Now, Windows has the capability to generate these types of thumbnail previews for other kinds of files as well, and a new feature in Windows 98 takes this even further.

Solution 1: Icon previews for bitmap files

The advantage to this solution is that, once the change has been made, it will be automatically enabled for all folders on your system. The disadvantages are that this solution works only for *.bmp* files, and the thumbnail previews will never be larger than the rest of your system icons (usually 32×32 pixels):

1. Open the Registry Editor. (If you're not familiar with the Registry Editor, see Chapter 3.)

2. Expand the branches to HKEY_CLASSES_ROOT\Paint.Picture\DefaultIcon, and change the (Default) value to %1. Note that if the *.bmp* file type is no longer associated with MS Paint, the correct registry location will be somewhere other than in Paint.Picture. Try looking in the (Default) value of HKEY_CLASSES_ROOT\.BMP for the current file type (see "Understanding File Types" in Chapter 3 for more information).
3. Close the Registry Editor and press **F5** to refresh any open windows to re-read the icons for bitmap files. You might have to log out and then log back in for the change to take effect.

Solution 2: Use built-in icon previews for all graphics

The advantages of this solution are that it works for more file types, including *.bmp*, *.jpg*, and *.gif* files, and that the previews can be larger than normal icons. The disadvantages are that the option needs to be enabled for each folder you view (you wouldn't want to set it as the default), and that there's no way to see graphical previews in the Find results window. Also, it's not very well implemented: there's no way to change the size of the previews, and any image files that it doesn't understand are shown with their standard file icons rather than hidden. If you are viewing a folder with more than just a few images in it, the display is quite unattractive and inefficient. As though that weren't enough, this option isn't even available if you have Internet Explorer integration disabled (see Chapter 8):

1. Locate any folder that contains at least one *.jpg*, *.gif*, or *.bmp* file, right-click on its icon (if it's already open, right-click on the control box), and select **Properties**.
2. Check the **Enable thumbnail view** option in the **General** tab of the Properties dialog.
3. Open the folder and select **Thumbnails** from the **View** menu. If the option isn't there, you've probably disabled one of the components of the Internet Explorer integration (see Chapter 8).
4. Select one of the other view modes, such as **Details** or **Large Icons**, to restore the display to normal.

Notes and other issues

In case you've accidentally disabled iconic previews for *.ico* files, *.cur* files, and *.ani* files, the process in Solution 1 can also be used to restore them.

If your bitmap previews seemed to be dithered to 16 colors, and your display mode is set to 65,000 colors (16-bit) or higher, you'll need to enable true-color icons. Double-click on the **Display** icon in Control Panel, choose the **Effects** tab, and turn on the **Show icons using all possible colors** option.

If you wish to have larger icons with Solution 1, double-click on the **Display** icon in Control Panel and choose the **Appearance** tab. Select **Icon** from the **Item** menu, and type in a larger value for the size, such as `48` or `64`. Note that this will enlarge all icons on your system, both on the desktop and in the **Large Icons** display in Explorer.

If you use Solution 2, and have hidden files displayed, you'll notice two new files in any folder you view: *Thumbs.db* (which contains the thumbnail data) and *Desktop.ini* (which contains the settings). *Thumbs.db* can be deleted safely, but *Desktop.ini* may be storing other settings, and therefore should be left alone.

If you need the functionality of the larger previews, but find Solution 2 too limiting, the Acdsee-32 utility (see Appendix F) not only has a superior thumbnail viewer, but is a much better and faster image viewer than Internet Explorer (the only thing Microsoft provides for viewing *.jpg* and *.gif* files).

Undo (Solution 1). Select **Options** from Explorer's **View** menu, click on the **File Types** tab, find the **bitmap** file type in the list, click **Edit**, and then **Change Icon**. Once you've chosen a new generic icon, press **OK** and then **OK** again.

Undo (Solution 2). If you want to turn off thumbnails for any folder, you need to use each folder's Properties sheet. There's no way to globally disable thumbnails in all folders, unless you disable Internet Explorer integration, as described in Chapter 8.

Clear Unwanted Entries from Explorer's New Menu

If you right-click on the desktop or an open folder (or open Explorer's **File** menu) and choose **New**, you will be presented with a special list of registered file types that can be created on the spot. Basically, Explorer will just create a new, empty file (sometimes with a special template) with the appropriate extension in that location. This list is maintained by certain registry entries, and since most of us will not need to create new Ami Pro documents on the fly, there is a way to remove these unwanted entries. While having an extra entry here and there is not necessarily a big deal, it can be quite frustrating if you're forced to wade through a long list of file types every time you want to create a new file. The following solutions should allow you to overcome this annoyance.

Solution 1

1. Double-click on the **TweakUI** icon (see Appendix A) in Control Panel, and choose the **New** tab.
2. Uncheck any unwanted items, or click **Remove** for those items you know you'll never want again.

Note that this doesn't prevent applications from adding subsequent items, either when they're installed, or the next time they're run.

Solution 2

1. Open the Registry Editor (if you're not familiar with the Registry Editor, see Chapter 3).
2. Select **Find** from the **Edit** menu, type `ShellNew`, and press **OK**.
3. Every **ShellNew** key that is found will be a branch of a particular key named for a file extension (see "Understanding File Types" in Chapter 3). If you don't want that file type in your **New** menu, delete the entire **ShellNew** branch.
4. Repeat this for every unwanted file type, and close the Registry Editor when finished. The changes will take effect immediately.

Solution 3 (advanced users only)

If either of the solutions above are ineffective for removing a particularly stubborn entry, you have a last resort. For example, some applications actually replace this entry every time they're started, completely ignoring your preferences. Two popular programs known for this annoying behavior are Adobe Photoshop v4.0 and v5.0 (*http://www.adobe.com*) and JASC's Paint Shop Pro v4.0 (*http://www.jasc.com*). The following solution works on both applications, and should work on any other program that does this as well.

You'll need a good hex editor, such as UltraEdit-32 (*http://www.ultraedit.com*), which we'll use to actually change the program executable.

If this is done incorrectly, it can damage an application. If you back up any files before altering them, you eliminate this possibility.

The following example assumes you're using UltraEdit-32 v5.0 to fix this problem in Paint Shop Pro v4.0. (Evaluation versions of both of these applications are available for download on the Internet.) While the specifics may change for a different editor and "patient," the technique is the same:

1. First, follow the instructions in either Solution 1 or Solution 2 above to get rid of any existing entries.
2. Since Paint Shop Pro automatically adds the **ShellNew** branch (explained in Solution 2, above) every time it starts, we'll start by assuming that this happens in the main executable. Make sure that Paint Shop Pro is not running before you start messing around with the files.
3. Make a backup of the *Psp.exe* file in the Paint Shop Pro installation directory—see "Make a Duplicate of a File or Folder" in Chapter 2 for more information.
4. In UltraEdit-32, select **File** and then **Open**, and select *Psp.exe* from the **Paint Shop Pro** installation directory.
5. Since this editor is used to edit ASCII (plain text) files as well as binary (hex mode) files, make sure it's in hex mode (make sure the **Hex Edit** option is checked in the **Edit** menu).
6. Select **Find** from the **Search** menu, type `shellnew` in the **Find What** field, check the **Find ASCII** option, and click **Find Next**. When UltraEdit-32 finds the first occurrence of **ShellNew**, close the **Find** box, and change `ShellNew` to `ShellNix`. A change this small isn't likely to disrupt anything in the program, but it's big enough that Explorer won't include the entry in the **New** menu.
7. Repeat the process for all additional occurrences of **ShellNew**. When you're finished, select **Save** from the **File** menu and close UltraEdit-32. The change should take effect the next time you start Paint Shop Pro.
8. If you can't find the **ShellNew** text in the application you're editing, or replacing it as described above doesn't do the trick, there are other places to look. For example, many programs have several *.dll* files in the same directory. Use Explorer's **Find** feature to look through all the files in the application's directory for the text **ShellNew**. Repeat the above steps for any file in which it's found.

Notes and other issues

If you use Solution 1 and then look in the Registry, you'll see that TweakUI has simply renamed the **ShellNew** branch as **ShellNew-** for those branches you've chosen to disable. Only if you click **Remove** in **TweakUI** are the branches actually removed.

Admittedly, Solution 3 is extreme, but sometimes the programmers have been so stubborn that it's your last resort. Also, if you get a hankering for some tinkering, learning this type of customization can come in very handy.

Photoshop and Paint Shop Pro are both mentioned in Solution 3 for example only. While they both exhibit this design flaw, they are otherwise good programs. In fact, the figures in this book were created with both programs.

This functionality is also available in *O'Reilly Utilities—Quick Solutions for Windows 98 Annoyances* (see Appendix F for more information).

Undo (Solution 1). If you want to get the entry back into the **New** menu, just put a check next to the item you want in **TweakUI**.

Undo (Solution 2). If you've removed a **ShellNew** branch from an entry and want it back, you'll need to recreate it by finding the extension key in the Registry Editor, selecting **New** and then **Key** from the **Edit** menu, and typing **ShellNew**.

Undo (Solution 3). If you've made backup copies of any files you've edited, all you need to do is replace the changed files with their original counterparts. If that doesn't work, you'll need to reinstall the application you've changed.

Choose Your Short Filenames

One of the trickiest tasks a programmer faces is the addition of new functionality to an application that needs to be backward compatible. In the case of support for long filenames (rather than the old 8.3 DOS standard, where a filename consisted of a rootname with a maximum of eight characters and an extension with a maximum of three characters), which was added in Windows 95, Microsoft had to implement the functionality without making the new files inaccessible to older 16-bit Windows and DOS programs.

The solution was that every long filename has a short counterpart. That is, a file named *A Big Blob.txt* will appear as *ABIGBL~1.TXT*. This makes it possible to open a file with a long filename in a program that doesn't support long filenames, and also makes it clear which filenames have long counterparts.

If you find yourself using the short versions of long filenames often, for example, if you rely on what's called a *legacy* application (written before long filename support), you'll want to have more control of how short filenames are chosen.

Solution 1 (less permanent, more benign)

1. Using any application (either a legacy 16-bit application, or a 32-bit application that doesn't support long filenames), create a document with a short filename, such as *ABIGBLOB.TXT*.
2. Then, in Explorer, rename the file to *A Big Blob that ate Manhattan.txt*, or something like that.
3. Go back to the 16-bit application, and instead of *ABIGBL~1.TXT*, you'll see the same, original DOS 8.3 filename. This is because the long and the short versions are so similar, and the short version was created *first*. If the long filename is too different, this won't work. Now, this is not the most repeatable or reliable solution, but it's pretty benign, and if you get good at it, can be fairly useful.

Solution 2 (more permanent, more dangerous)

Several users have reported unpleasant side-effects with Solution 2, so use it with only with extreme caution (back up your system first), and only if totally necessary.

1. Open the Registry Editor. (If you're not familiar with the Registry Editor, see Chapter 3.)
2. Expand the branches to `HKEY_LOCAL_MACHINE\System\CurrentControlSet\control\FileSystem`.
3. Select **New** from the **Edit** menu, and then select **Binary Value**.
4. Type `NameNumericTail` for the name of the new value and press **Enter**.
5. Double-click on the new value, enter `0` (zero), and click **OK**.
6. Close the Registry Editor when you're finished. From now on, most short filenames will not be created with the *~1* suffix, although additional long filenames that happen to share the *same* short name will continue to be created with the numeric suffix. That is, only the first short filename will be called *ABIGBLOB.TXT*; another long filename in the same directory, such as *A Big Blob that ate Brooklyn.txt*, will have a short filename of *ABIGBL~1.TXT*.

Notes and other issues

Using Solution 2 will only change the way that new short filenames are created; any existing short filenames, which are already stored in your hard disk's file allocation table, will remain unchanged. To reassign the short filename of an existing long filename, simply rename the object to something else. For example, rename *Dog and Pony.wpd* to *Dog and Poodle.wpd*, and then back again, which will change the corresponding short name from *DOGAND~1.WPD* to *DOGANDPO.WPD.*

Making Windows Your Own

The toolbars in applications, the icons on the Windows desktop, the various splash screens that appear, and the entries in the Start Menu are all designed to appear a certain way when first installed. Unfortunately, the criteria used to make those decisions are often based more on showcasing various aspects of the software than on actually making the application easier to use. So why settle for the defaults?

While much of the rest of this chapter falls loosely under the category of customizing, the following topics deal specifically with changing defaults to make Windows easier to live with.

Change Installation Defaults

During the installation of Windows, you are asked to enter your name and company name, as well as the CD key on the back of your CD jacket. Throughout the rest of the installation, other settings are written to the Registry that have repercussions long after installation is completed. Fortunately, it's easy to change those values and others written during the installation process. All of these values are stored in the Registry, so go ahead and fire up the Registry Editor and follow these steps.

Registered user

Your name and company name entered during setup are used not only in Windows' various About boxes, but inserted as the default name and company name for installation of countless third-party applications. While there's the possibility that you may have misspelled your own name during installation, it's more likely that your computer came with Windows preinstalled, so the registered user is something like "Compaq Customer." Whether you've bought your computer from someone else, switched employers, or simply decided to drop your middle initial, you shouldn't be stuck with those old defaults:

1. Expand the branches to `HKEY_LOCAL_MACHINE\Software\Microsoft\Windows\CurrentVersion`.
2. To the right, among a myriad of settings, are the three settings in which we're interested. You can change **RegisteredOwner** (your name) and **RegisteredOrganization** (your company) to anything you want simply by double-clicking on them and typing.

CD key

Why would you want to change the CD key? Well, subsequent installations of Windows (not including newer versions) will require that you enter the CD key again. However, setup checks the current installation, and if what you enter doesn't match the registry value, it fails. Think of how easy it is to enter a series of ones, compared to copying the entire 25-digit code on the back of the CD jacket—especially if you should lose the code number altogether. Here's how to change the CD key:

1. Expand the branches to `HKEY_LOCAL_MACHINE\Software\Microsoft\Windows\CurrentVersion`.
2. The `ProductId` value contains the CD key used during the last installation of Windows. Make sure to replace it with the full 25 digits, since the setup dialog will allow no fewer and no more than 25 digits.

Installation drive

If you installed from a CD, and your CD drive was known as drive *D*:, *d:\win98* will be the default path used to look for the Windows 98 distribution files whenever you add a Windows component or device driver. However, it's likely that an upgrade or other configuration change may change the drive letter of your CD drive, and therefore change the location of the Windows 98 installation files.

My recommendation is to abandon the CD and copy all the files to the hard disk. That way, whenever you add or remove a Windows component, or add any new drivers, the files will be read right off the hard disk, quickly and without any prompts. If you have the space (it requires a little over 100MB, which many of you probably won't be able to spare), you can just copy the contents of the *\win98* folder on your CD into a directory on your hard disk (*\windows\install* is a good place). Don't bother copying any of the other folders, including the subfolders of *\win98*.

At any rate, to change the default installation directory, follow these steps:

1. Expand the branches to `HKEY_LOCAL_MACHINE\Software\Microsoft\Windows\CurrentVersion\Setup`.

2. In this key, you'll see most installation directories used for things like the temporary install directory,* the location of the *\Windows\System* directory (don't change this), and, of course, the location of the setup files. Double-click on the `SourcePath` value to change it. If you're specifying a new location of the CD, type `d:\win98\`, where `d:` is the drive letter of your CD drive.

Notes and other issues

Changing the registered user as described above changes the registered user information for Windows only, not for applications installed on your system that may have stored user information separately from Windows. However, any newer applications that use the current user name and organization as defaults during their installation will reflect the change.

If you've changed the location for Windows' setup files, Windows will simply prompt you for the correct location when it needs them. There's no danger of not being able to install drivers if you specify the wrong location for the `SourcePath` value.

If, for some strange reason, you installed Windows 98 from floppies, you may want to change the installation drive as well—even if you don't plan on copying the files to your hard disk. This will prevent Windows setup from polling your floppy drive every time it looks for new drivers. If it asks for a Windows distribution disk, you can still always pop it in and specify *a:* for the source.

Another good place to direct the install path is the *\Windows\System* folder. Often Windows will ask you to insert the CD to install drivers that have already been installed. Unless you want to make sure to use the drivers from the CD (if you're diagnosing a problem, for example), you can just point to the *\Windows\System* folder, and it will read the files there. Even if you don't change the `SourcePath` value to reflect this, you can still point to the *\Windows\System* folder, as well as *\Windows*, *\Windows\INF*, and *\Windows\System\Iosubsys* whenever prompted.

Add New Folder Options

At first glance, the **Advanced settings** list in Explorer's Folder Options window (accessible by selecting **Folder Options** from Explorer's **View** menu, and choosing the **View** tab) is presented in a somewhat awkward

* The temporary install path (specified in the `SetupTempDir` value) is the directory that Windows setup will use to store about 80 megabytes of data when you install. If you're running low on disk space, and have another drive or partition with more space, you can redirect this folder so that subsequent installations of Windows will have the room they need to complete.

list format, apparently to accommodate the large number of options. However, the less-than-ideal presentation is designed to allow customization, permitting you to add or remove items from the list. See Figure 4-7 for an example of a customized version of this window.

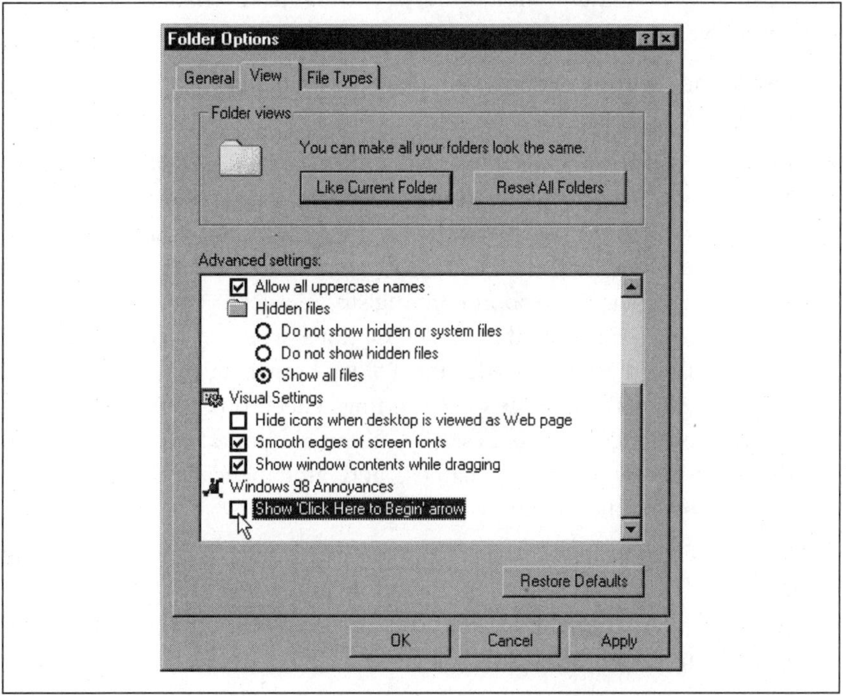

Figure 4-7: The advanced Folder Options dialog is a flexible, customizable list of registry settings

While this process isn't necessarily intended for you to extend or change any particular features of *Explorer*, it does allow you to provide a fairly clean interface for virtually any registry setting, including those that might affect Explorer. The idea is that you link up a checkbox or radio button to a value—any value you choose—in your Registry. This would, for example, allow you to make certain registry changes accessible to other users (for example, members of a workgroup you administer), reducing the need for them to mess around with the Registry. You can also remove unwanted options that you don't want others changing.

The format is actually quite remarkable, because you don't have to be a programmer to utilize this feature. You can add new options to a certain portion of the Registry, and then tie those options to other registry settings. The downside is that the syntax requires that numerous parameters be typed, which can be time consuming. One thing that may be confusing is the way that these settings require that you split up any target registry paths. Instead of `HKEY_LOCAL_MACHINE\Software\Microsoft`, you'll have to specify the path as `Software\Microsoft` and the root as `80000002` (which points to the `HKEY_LOCAL_MACHINE` root).

The following procedure should allow you to make changes to existing settings as well as add your own settings fairly easily:

1. Open the Registry Editor (if you're not familiar with the Registry Editor, see Chapter 3).
2. Expand the branches to `HKEY_LOCAL_MACHINE\Software\Microsoft\Windows\CurrentVersion\explorer\Advanced`. Notice that the actual hierarchy in the Folder Options window is reproduced here in the Registry (although items appear in a different order than their corresponding registry entries). For example, the **Hidden files** section in the Folder Options window is mirrored as a branch labeled **Hidden** under the **Folder** branch in the Registry. And the **Remember each folder's view settings** check box is mirrored as the **ClassicViewState** branch. Basically, items are sorted alphabetically in the Registry by their key names, and alphabetically in the Folder Options list by their captions.
3. Take this opportunity to back up the entire branch by highlighting the **Advanced** key and selecting **Export Registry File** from the **Registry** menu. This way, you'll be able to easily get back the defaults without having to reinstall Windows.
4. You can remove any subkeys from this branch to get rid of the respective unwanted entries in Folder Options. To add a new item, just create a new key and call it anything you want (something descriptive is always helpful, though).
5. The values inside each key determine the key's properties. To add a property to the key, create a new value named for one of the properties listed below. Then, double-click on it and type the contents for the value, as described in Tables 4-1 and 4-2.
6. The value type (String, Binary, `DWORD`) of the `CheckedValue`, `UnCheckedValue`, and `DefaultValue` parameters all depend on what the resulting value requires. For example, if the option you're setting is a `DWORD` value, then these three parameters must also be `DWORD` values.
7. After you've created keys and entered the appropriate property values, your Registry should look something like Figure 4-8, and the resulting Folder Options window should look like Figure 4-7. Close the Registry Editor when you're finished.

Table 4-1: Visual Properties of Folder Options Items

Name	Data Type	Description
`Type`	String	This can be either `group`, `checkbox`, or `radio`, representing a folder, checkbox, or radio button, respectively. Checkboxes are square options, and can each be either on or off. Radio buttons are round options, and are linked to other radio buttons in the same folder, in that only one at a time can be selected (you can have multiple groups of radio buttons). And folders, of course, are used to organize the various other options. This parameter is required by all items.
`Text`	String	The actual caption of the option as it will appear in the dialog. This can be as long as you want (better too descriptive than too vague), but the paradigm dictates that only the first word is capitalized and that there is no period. This parameter is required by all items.
`Bitmap`	String	The icon used for a folder item, which has no meaning for checkboxes or radio buttons. By default, it's a rather ugly bent arrow. The syntax *`filename, index`* is the same as for the DefaultIcon property for file types, as documented in "Understanding File Types" in Chapter 3. You can leave out *`filename`*, and instead specify only a number (the comma is still required), but the icons provided are limited and quite ugly. For example, you can use `,207` for the default folder icon, but it'll be black-and-white instead of yellow. This parameter is required for all folders.
`HelpID`	String	The filename and optionally the help context ID of the help documentation for this item. If the user selects the item and presses the **F1** key, this is what will appear. The syntax is *`filename#id`*, where *`filename`* is the name of a *.hlp* or *.chm* file, and `id` is the help context id of the topic you want to display. This parameter is optional.

Table 4-2: Registry Properties of Folder Options Items

Name	Data Type	Description
`HKeyRoot`	DWORD	A number representing the root of the registry path containing the actual setting data to be stored. Use the hexadecimal number `80000000` for `HKEY_CLASSES_ROOT`, `80000001` for `HKEY_CURRENT_USER`, `80000002` for `HKEY_LOCAL_MACHINE`, `80000003` for `HKEY_USERS`, `80000004` for `HKEY_PERFORMANCE_DATA`, `80000005` for `HKEY_CURRENT_CONFIG`, and `80000006` for `HKEY_DYN_DATA`. For some reason, it must be separated from the rest of the registry path, specified in `RegPath`. This parameter is required for all checkbox and radio items.

Tinkering Techniques

Table 4-2: Registry Properties of Folder Options Items (continued)

Name	Data Type	Description
`RegPath`	String	The path of the registry location in which to store the setting, not including the root (see `HKeyRoot`, above). For example, for `HKEY_CURRENT_USER\Software\Microsoft\Windows\CurrentVersion`, you would only enter `Software\Microsoft\Windows\Current Version` here. This parameter is required for all checkbox and radio items.
`ValueName`	String	The name of the actual registry value in which the setting data is stored. The value is located in the registry location specified in the `RegPath` parameter. This parameter is required by all checkbox and radio items.
`CheckedValue`	Data type varies	The value stored in the registry value specified by the `RegPath` and `ValueName` parameters above, when the option is turned *on*. If you're configuring this option for use with both Windows 95/98 and Windows NT 4/5, use both the `CheckedValueW95` and `CheckedValueNT` parameters instead. This parameter is required by all checkbox and radio items.
`UnCheckedValue`	Data type varies	The value stored in the registry value specified by the `RegPath` and `ValueName` parameters above, when the option is turned *off*. This value is optional; if omitted, it is assumed to be `0`.
`DefaultValue`	Data type varies	The default value, used if the registry value (specified by the `RegPath` and `ValueName` parameters above) does not exist. As soon as the option is turned on or off in the Folder Options window, the value is set to either `CheckedValue` or `UnCheckedValue`. This value is optional; if omitted, it is assumed to be `0`.

8. When the Folder Options dialog is displayed, each option is set according to the value of the setting specified by `ValueName`; the value is simply compared with `CheckedValue` and `UnCheckedValue`, and then set accordingly. When the **OK** button is pressed in Folder Options, the settings in the Registry are then written using the same criteria.

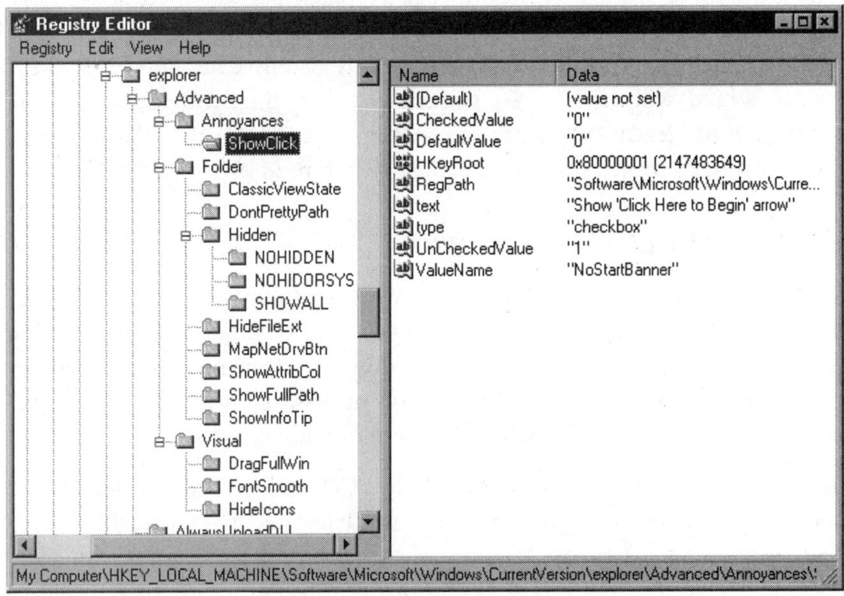

Figure 4-8: Advanced Folder Options settings are configured in the Registry

Notes and other issues

Note that in the example given in Figures 4-7 and 4-8, the `Checked-Value` parameter is equal to `0`, while the `UnCheckedValue` parameter is `1`—the opposite of their default values, and possibly counterintuitive. This is because the *on* state of the option is to show the "Click Here to Begin" arrow, while the *on* state of the registry value is to hide it.

See Chapter 3 for more information on using registry patches, which is a good way to reproduce your customization on any number of computers. Note, however, that since registry patches can't be used to remove registry keys, you'll have to use Windows Scripting Host (WSH) scripts if you want to automate the removal of items from advanced Folder Options settings (see "Automate the Deletion of Registry Items" in Chapter 3 for more information).

To reproduce a setting elsewhere in the Windows interface or the interface of a third-party application, you'll first need to find the respective registry setting—see "Finding the Right Registry Key" in Chapter 3 for more information.

If you try to add a setting using the above procedure and it doesn't show up in Folder Options, maybe something's missing. Make sure you include all the required property values for the item in question.

Undo. Assuming you've created a registry patch as described above, you can simply apply the patch to restore the default options. However, since registry patches are simply merged with existing data, any new keys you've added will remain. To get around this, simply delete the entire `HKEY_LOCAL_MACHINE\Software\Microsoft\Windows\CurrentVersion\explorer\Advanced` branch before applying the patch.

Configure CD-ROM Autorun

Windows 95 introduced the concept of CD autorun, a specification that automatically runs a specified program on a CD when an autorun-enabled CD is inserted into a CD drive. While this is a convenient feature, especially for beginner-level users who don't necessarily know how to install software, it can be an irritant for anyone more advanced.

The Autorun feature works by polling the CD drive every few seconds to see if a CD has been inserted. If Windows detects a CD that wasn't there a few seconds ago, it reads the label of the disc and looks for a file called *Autorun.inf* in the root directory. *Autorun.inf* usually contains two pieces of information: a pointer to an icon file (for display in My Computer and Explorer) and a pointer to the autorun program, if any. If an autorun program is specified, Windows then runs the program, which is usually a brightly-colored banner with links to the application's setup program and documentation as well as an exit button. If, instead, Windows detects an audio CD, the configured CD player is opened and the first track starts playing.

Another annoying consequence of this feature is that double-clicking on the CD icon in the My Computer window will launch the autorun program for autorun-aware CDs, instead of showing a standard folder window like it does for non-autorun CDs and all other drives. In order to open or explore the disc, you must either right-click on the CD icon and select **Open** or **Explore**, respectively, or switch to the Explorer window.

Suffice it to say that Microsoft has provided no obvious way to configure or even disable this feature. With the following instructions, you can customize Autorun.

Disable Autorun

This solution allows you to easily turn off Autorun for CD-ROMs and audio CDs, without loosing Explorer's ability to automatically identify a disc.

1. Double-click on the **TweakUI** icon (see Appendix A) in Control Panel, and choose the **Paranoia** tab. (Does that moniker make sense here?)
2. Uncheck either or both of the **Play audio CDs automatically** and **Play data CDs automatically** options, and click **OK**. The change should take effect immediately.

Disable CD polling

While the TweakUI solution above disables the Autorun feature, it doesn't turn off the repetitive polling (reading) of the CD drive. The problem with the polling feature is that inserting a disc can cause Explorer to refresh itself, which can be frustratingly slow. Also, if you're using a CD writer, you'll need to turn this off so that it can't interrupt the CD recording process. Note that turning off the polling feature will not only disable the Autorun functionality, but will prevent Explorer from updating an Explorer window with the contents of a newly inserted CD:

1. Double-click on the System icon in Control Panel, and choose the **Device Manager** tab.
2. Expand the **CD-ROM** branch, and select the entry for your CD-ROM drive. If you have more than one CD drive, or have a CD changer, you'll have to repeat this for every CD drive letter.
3. Click **Properties**, and then choose the **Settings** tab.
4. Turn off the **Auto insert notification** option.
5. Click **OK**, and then **OK** again. You'll have to restart Windows for this change to take effect. From now on, your system won't know when you've inserted a CD, and definitely won't run it right away.

Configure Autorun for audio CDs

Unlike for data CDs, the Autorun feature for audio CDs can be configured to work with any program. Note that this solution requires that Autorun for audio CDs be enabled, and that the **Auto insert notification** option (mentioned in the preceding section) be turned on:

1. Select **Folder Options** from Explorer's **View** menu, and choose the **File Types** tab.
2. Select **AudioCD** from the list of file types, and click **Edit**.
3. You can choose a new CD player to be launched automatically for all audio CDs by double-clicking on the **Play** action, clicking **Browse**, and selecting the desired program executable. (Note that for the *Cdplayer.exe* program included with Windows 98, you'll need to include the `/play` command-line parameter to have the program

begin playing as soon as it's opened.) However, you may not want the CD to be played right away.

4. Click **New**, and then type `Open` in the **Action** field and `explorer.exe` in the **Application used to perform action** field. Click **OK** when you're finished.
5. Next, highlight the new **Open** entry in the **Action** list and click **Set Default** so the word **Open** now appears bold.
6. Click **OK** when you're finished. The change should take effect immediately. Assuming you've made the **Open** action the default, you should see a folder window with an icon for each track when you insert an audio CD. You can then double-click a specific track to play it, drag it to make a shortcut, or insert it into your CD recording software to copy the track.

Notes and other issues

Even after disabling Autorun completely, clicking on a CD's icon in My Computer will still bring up the Autorun program. However, this will never happen automatically, and you can still explore the contents of the CD by using Explorer, or by right-clicking on it and selecting **Open** or **Explore**.

If you disable the Autorun feature for data CDs, the Autorun program on any given CD will obviously not run. However, this doesn't mean you can't still use the software on a CD; you just have to run or install it yourself. To do this, open Explorer and select your CD drive. In the root directory of most CDs containing software, you'll see *Setup.exe* or *Autorun.exe*. You can simply run this program to install the software, which is probably what would happen automatically if Autorun were installed. Sometimes, however, the program used for Autorun is not obvious; in this case, double-click on the *Autorun.inf* file, and look for a line that begins with `open=`. This is what instructs Windows which program to run automatically; it should point to a program on the CD, which you can just run manually. If you don't see an *Autorun.inf* file in the root directory of the CD, it doesn't support Autorun.

If you turn off the polling of the CD drive, and then insert a CD and want Explorer to reflect the change, simply press the **F5** key in any open Explorer window to force Windows to re-read the disc.

Using the Autorun functionality, you can create custom icons for use with the other drives in your system—see "Customize Drive Icons" in Chapter 2 for more information.

Get Rid of Irritating Splash Screens

It's a sickness: it seems that each subsequent version of any given application gets larger, more complex, and slower. One trick that's used for large (and sometimes even small) programs is to display a splash screen, a large graphical banner with the application's title and logo while the program loads. This device is used to improve the *perceived* startup time, but often has the side effect of making the program load even more slowly.

What's even worse is that some add-on utilities that load with Windows display their splash screens as Windows is starting, which is of little use to anyone. What follows are some tips for disabling these screens, as well as a list of a few common applications' splash screens, and how to disable them.

A general solution

While there's no such thing as a standard splash screen or a standard way to disable it, there are a few tricks you can try to get rid of one:

- First of all, don't underestimate the documentation. Search the help file for the words "splash screen," "startup logo," or whatever else comes to you. Also, look for a readme file in the application directory and on the distribution disks for any other hints.
- Many applications have a settings window, often with plenty of tabbed pages, and some of them are kind enough to let you turn off the splash screen, although the setting is often hard to find.
- Look in the Registry for any suspicious values; open up the branch for the application, usually in `HKEY_CURRENT_USER\Software\`*`Manufacturer`*`\`*`Program Name`*. Naturally, be careful not to screw up any more critical settings.
- Look in the application's folder (and its subfolders) for any *.bmp* files; sometimes deleting or renaming the bitmap used for the splash screen is enough to prevent it from being displayed. Double-click on any *.bmp* files you find to view them.
- Lastly, some applications (see Norton Utilities below) come with registry patches for disabling the splash screens. Look in the application directory and on the distribution disks for any suspicious *.reg* files.

Symantec's Norton Utilities, Navigator, and Antivirus

1. Look in your various Norton directories and on the distribution disks for your software for any registry patches (*.reg* files). For Norton Utilities and Norton Navigator, the patches to turn off the splash screens

are called *Nusplash.reg* and *Nnsplash.reg*, respectively. For Norton Antivirus, the patch filename is *Logo_off.reg*.

2. Double-click on each file to remove the respective splash screen.

Eudora Mail (Pro and Light versions)

1. Make sure Eudora isn't running, and open *Eudora.ini* in the *Eudora* directory with a text editor, such as Notepad.
2. In the `[Settings]` section, add the line `NoSplashScreen=1`. Save the file when finished, and start up Eudora. To Qualcomm's credit, this is also mentioned in the accompanying documentation.

Corel WordPerfect (Versions 6 through 8)

1. Right-click on the shortcut to WordPerfect and select **Properties**.
2. Choose the **Shortcut** tab and add a space and then a colon (`:`) after the text in the **Target** field. Click **OK** when you're finished.

WS_FTP

1. Right-click on the shortcut to WS_FTP, and select **Properties**.
2. Choose the **Shortcut** tab, add a space and then type `-quiet` after the text in the Target field. Click **OK** when you're finished.

Notes and other issues

Note that the solutions above for specific application apply to releases of the software available at the time of this writing, and may change in subsequent versions. If enough people complain, a company might make the setting more readily accessible, or even disable the splash screen altogether.

In this chapter:
- *Fine-Tuning Your Components*
- *Fixing Software Bottlenecks*
- *Upgrading Your System*

5 Maximizing Performance

The real-world performance of a computer depends less on its raw processing power than on its ability to respond immediately, start programs quickly, and display graphics and animation smoothly, allowing us to complete our work with less waiting.

There are two general strategies you can use to improve the performance of a computer: configuring what you've got to work better, and knowing what and when to upgrade.

The primary focus of configuring your system's hardware and software is removing bottlenecks. For example, the way Windows uses the swap file (also called virtual memory) is inefficient, and dealing with this bottleneck can result in performance increases all across the system. You should approach these problems with the attitude that your computer has a certain theoretical top speed, and you need to fix whatever is slowing it down so that you can get closer to that speed.

Upgrading, however, is a different story. Aim to raise the theoretical top speed, after you've done as much bottleneck-reducing configuration as is practical. Start by asking yourself where your money is best spent, which isn't always obvious. For instance, there are always faster processors available, but usually just adding more memory can have a bigger impact on performance.

Now, I'm the last to condone throwing money at any problem. Even if money were no object, and we could simply buy a new computer or component whenever the proverbial ashtray gets full, we'd still have to take the time to install and troubleshoot new hardware, and reconfigure all the software. So, upgrading is not always the best choice, either to resolve a problem or to improve performance. Spending a little time fine-tuning your hardware and software, and spending a little money replacing certain components, *can* make a difference.

However, there is a certain point past which your computer is going to turn into a money pit. The older your system is, the less you should be inclined to keep it alive. It's easy to calculate the point of diminishing returns; just compare the estimated cost of an upgrade (include *your* time here as well) with the cost of a new system (minus what you'd get for selling or donating your old system). I stress this a great deal, as I've seen it happen all too often: people end up spending too much and getting too little in return. A simple hardware upgrade ends up taking days of troubleshooting and configuring, and then one finds out that yet something *else* needs to be replaced. Taking into account that the final result will need to be upgraded soon, it can be more cost effective to replace the entire system, and either sell or donate the old parts.

Fine-Tuning Your Components

You'll be amazed at how significantly just a few adjustments can improve a computer's performance. Hopefully, you won't have the chance to be amazed at how easily you can screw up a computer, however; make sure to write down any settings before you change them. For example, if you're changing jumpers on a card, be sure to make a note of where they were, just in case you need to "undo" your changes. For the same reason, you should back up any configuration files before making changes that may adversely affect your system.

What follows is a collection of tips, hints, and tweaks that can really make a difference in the hardware you've already got. Interspersed with hardware tweaks, however, are discussions of subjects like the right viewing angle for your monitor and some tips on pointing devices. The importance of these shouldn't be underestimated; making your computer more comfortable to use is remarkably effective in improving the overall experience:

Monitors

Good use of your monitor is important, especially if you use your computer for long periods of time. First of all, you shouldn't be looking up or down at a monitor; it shouldn't be tilted at all, and should be placed directly at eye level. If you're too high or low for this, you can either raise the monitor or use an adjustable chair. Using a monitor at eye level is more comfortable and also decreases the risk of back and neck injury.

If you keep the glass clean, your images will be sharper; spray some window cleaner on a paper towel, not on the monitor directly, to clean it. If you wear glasses, consult your optometrist about eyewear made especially for computer screens. Reading or driving glasses simply don't have the proper focal length for this purpose. Lastly, the contrast and brightness should be set so that black appears dark black and not washed-out gray (try adjusting these settings with a full-screen DOS session), and so that text is bright and high-contrast. Try turning the contrast control all the way up, and the brightness control slightly above its minimum setting.

Note that everything appearing on the monitor was put there by the video card—see the next topic for more information on improving the display.

Video cards (also known as display adapters)

First, you should configure your display adapter to show the highest color depth it will support. Windows 98's default color depth is a measly 256 colors (which is at least better than Windows 3.x's 16 colors). 256 colors may seem like a lot, but it's not; the real problem is the difference between the way that Windows handles colors in 8-bit (256-color) mode and 16-bit (65,536-color) mode.

Have you ever noticed that all the colors on your screen become distorted for a split-second whenever you view certain web pages? Do the photographic images you view appear spotty or excessively grainy? Do you notice ugly bands or streaks where a smooth sky or gradient should appear in a picture? Do you find that Windows won't display 256-color icons or animated cursors?

All these problems are symptoms of an *adaptive palette*. When your display is set to 256 colors, it means that there can never be more than 256 individual colors in use at any given time. Since 256 isn't nearly enough to encompass all the colors in the spectrum, Windows simply chooses the best 256 colors each time you display something on your screen, such as an image or a web page. If you have multiple images showing at the same time, they all must share the same group of colors, or palette. Windows must choose colors most common to all the images; more images results in poorer matches for each image. Furthermore, if you have multiple application windows open, each trying to use 256 colors, Windows will calculate the palette based on the needs of the active window, and then display all the other inactive windows based on the active window's palette. This can look absolutely horrendous in some circumstances.

However, since 65,536 colors (16-bit mode, or 2^{16} colors; sometimes called *High Color*) is sufficient to display photographic images, the palette is fixed, and does not have to *adapt* to what is on the screen. This gives us a richer, faster display; web pages, games, and photos look better, and you don't have to put up with the bother of a constantly changing palette. Sixteen million colors (24-bit mode; sometimes called *True Color*) works similarly to 16-bit mode, except that it provides more color depth for even better image quality.

To set the color depth, double-click on the **Display** icon in Control Panel and choose the **Settings** tab. To the left is a drop-down list labeled **Colors**, with all of the color depth settings your video card supports. Select **High Color** (16-bit) or **True Color** (24-bit) from the list.

There are two limitations of your video card that may affect the settings here. First, the amount of memory on your video card dictates the maximum color depth and resolution you can use. The memory required by a particular setting is calculated by multiplying the *horizontal size* times the *vertical size* times the *bytes per pixel*. If you're in 16-bit color mode, then each pixel will require 16 bits, or 2 bytes (since there are 8 bits/byte). At a resolution of 1024×768, that's 1024×768×2 bytes/pixel, or about 1.57 megabytes. Therefore, a video card with 2 megabytes of memory will be able to handle the display setting, but a card with only 1 megabyte will not.

As you adjust your color depth, Windows may automatically adjust other settings depending on your card's capabilities. If you increase your color depth, your resolution might automatically decrease; likewise, if you raise the resolution, your color depth might go down. See "Upgrading Your System" later in this chapter for information on upgrading the memory on your video card, as well as upgrading your video card.

The other limitation that may affect your available settings is the refresh rate that your card will be able to generate. While the maximum refresh rate is not dependent on the amount of your card's memory, you may have to lower your resolution to achieve the desired rate. Windows should automatically adjust your refresh rate to the highest setting your card supports, although this is not always the case.

If you notice that your display appears to be flickering, especially under fluorescent lights, you'll need to raise your refresh rate, either by adjusting the refresh rate setting directly, or by lowering your resolution or color depth. Consequently, if you hear a slight *whine* from your monitor, it means your refresh rate is too *high*. The minimum refresh rate you should tolerate is 72Hz. People with corrective lenses seem to be more sensitive and might require a higher setting to be comfortable. Since most cards available today support refresh rates of 75Hz and higher, this is usually not a problem.

Double-click on the **Display** icon in Control Panel, and choose the **Settings** tab. Click **Advanced** and then choose the **Adapter** tab. If your display driver supports it, you can adjust your refresh rate with the **Refresh Rate** setting. If the setting is not there, you'll either need to obtain a more recent video driver, or reduce your resolution or color depth.

In many circumstances, you can *significantly* improve your video card's performance by getting newer drivers from the manufacturer (see Chapter 6, *Troubleshooting*). Drivers optimized for your video card can increase speed, offer higher resolutions with more colors, give you more control over the refresh rate, and offer better stability than the plain vanilla drivers that come with Windows.

Motherboards and the system BIOS

The settings available in a computer's BIOS setup screen will vary significantly from one system to another, but some settings are common throughout all systems. The BIOS setup is usually accessed by pressing a key—such as **Delete** or **Esc**—immediately after powering on your system and before the initial beep.

Make sure all settings you understand are correct: the configuration of your hard disk, floppy drives, keyboard, and ports should all match your system. Make sure your BIOS correctly reports the amount of memory in your system; it's possible that the system is not using all the installed memory.

If your motherboard has I/O ports (serial and parallel) built in, you can usually configure them in the BIOS setup as well. If, however, your mouse or printer is plugged into a separate card, this may not be the case. You should disable any ports that aren't being used, and make sure there aren't any conflicts here with other devices in your system. Some computers can configure their ports automatically; you should turn this feature off if you don't need it, since it doesn't always work correctly. See the discussion of modems in "Fixing Device-Specific Problems" in Chapter 6 for more information.

If your BIOS has built-in antivirus support, disable it immediately. This feature causes compatibility problems with Windows, and can slow down your system. Additionally, antivirus software does a much better job of this, as it can be updated to support the newest viruses.

Many systems have advanced BIOS settings that can improve performance as well. A little investigation can yield some good results, but be very careful not to change any settings you don't understand. Your motherboard or system manual should explain each setting. It's a good idea to write down any settings here before you change them.

Floppy diskette drives

Floppy drives have undergone almost no substantial development in the past decade (other than the lingering demise of the 5.25" floppy). The only thing you can really do to a floppy drive is keep it clean; dust can slow down the drive and can even make the disk unreadable. Also, don't use floppies that have errors on them. For faster, larger, and more reliable floppy formats, see "Better floppy formats" in Chapter 6.

Hard disks

As far as your physical hard drive is concerned, the best thing you can do is make sure your drive is securely fastened to your computer case; it shouldn't wobble or rattle at all. Air should flow past the drive easily, as it should throughout the entire case.

More important, however, is how you take care of the *inside* of your hard drive; namely the data stored on it. There are several things that you can do maximize the performance, capacity, and reliability of your drive, and all involve manipulating your files.

The best way to ensure maximum performance from your drive is to defragment it regularly (weekly). Figure 5-1 shows how frequent use can cause files to become fragmented, which can slow access and retrieval of all data on the drive, and increase the likelihood of lost data.

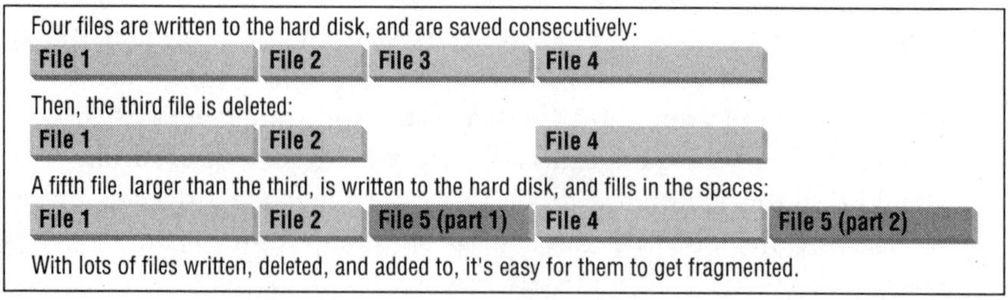

Four files are written to the hard disk, and are saved consecutively:

File 1 | File 2 | File 3 | File 4

Then, the third file is deleted:

File 1 | File 2 | | File 4

A fifth file, larger than the third, is written to the hard disk, and fills in the spaces:

File 1 | File 2 | File 5 (part 1) | File 4 | File 5 (part 2)

With lots of files written, deleted, and added to, it's easy for them to get fragmented.

Figure 5-1: File fragmentation on your hard disk can slow performance and decrease reliability

To defragment your drive, run the Disk Defragmenter (*Defrag.exe*), which rearranges the files on your hard disk so that they are no longer fragmented. It also defragments the free space, and optionally places the files you access more frequently (like programs and recently modified documents) at the start of the drive and less frequently accessed files at the back of the drive. You can launch it from the Start Menu by selecting **Programs → Accessories → System Tools → Disk Defragmenter**.

In addition to defragmenting your drive, you can adjust a few Windows settings to optimize your hard disk performance to suit your needs. Double-click on the **System** icon in Control Panel, and choose the **Performance** tab. Click **File System** and choose the **Hard Disk** tab to display the hard disk performance settings for your machine. The disk cache is configured by selecting one of three options for the **Typical role of this computer**. Experiment with each of these to achieve the best results, although most users will benefit most by keeping it at **Desktop computer** here. If you choose **Network Server**, Windows will devote more memory to the disk cache; while this should result in better disk performance, it will reduce the memory available for other applications. If you have plenty of memory to spare (64MB or more), you should try it. Make sure **Read-ahead optimization** is all the way to the right, and click **OK** when you're finished.

You can maximize the capacity of your drive by setting up FAT32 if it's not already being used, and by clearing unused files from your system. See "Convert Your Drives to FAT32" and "What to Throw Away" later in this chapter for more information.

Lastly (and I'll beat this one to death), make sure all your data is backed up all the time. See "Preventative Maintenance and Data Recovery" in Chapter 6 for more information.

Hard disk controllers

Most hard disk controllers don't have any settings (SCSI controllers are the major exception). However, some older, high-end controllers, usually on 486s, have caching or local-bus capabilities. These types of controllers generally require special drivers, some of which aren't available for Windows, and they usually don't achieve any better performance than the cheap controllers built into most new motherboards.

If your controller has memory on it, the RAM will be put to much better use on your motherboard (if it's the right type); you'd then be able to replace the controller with a $10 generic controller. More system RAM will mean more memory for applications, reducing the need for excessive disk access, and yielding better overall performance than if you left the memory on the controller card.

SCSI controllers

Each SCSI device attached to your SCSI controller may have different requirements. If your controller supports it, make sure settings like data rate and synch-negotiation are properly matched to *each* of your SCSI devices.

Check to see if your SCSI bus is properly terminated; active terminators, while more expensive than their passive counterparts, usually do a better job.

Lastly, you should be using native 32-bit drivers made especially for your adapter; any lines in *Config.sys* or *Autoexec.bat* are just slowing things down. See "Do I Still Need Config.sys and Autoexec.bat?" in Chapter 6 for more information.

CD drives

As with many other devices here, you should make sure the driver for your CD drive is a native, 32-bit driver made especially for Windows 95/98. Any lines in *Config.sys* or *Autoexec.bat* are just slowing things down. See "Do I Still Need Config.sys and Autoexec.bat?" in Chapter 6 for more information.

If the drivers are all correct, double-click on the **System** icon in Control Panel, and choose the **Performance** tab. Click **File System** and choose the **CD-ROM** tab to display the CD drive performance settings for your machine. Adjust the **Supplemental cache size** to your liking; the resulting memory required is displayed below. The more memory you use here, the better; if you have 32MB of RAM or more, move the slider all the way to the right. If you have under 32MB of RAM, make it smaller by moving to around 30% of the maximum; the memory you save will be better spent elsewhere. If you don't use your CD-ROM much, move this slider more to the left to leave more memory available for other applications.

Lastly, match the setting of **Optimize access pattern for** to the speed of your drive. Click **OK** when you're finished.

Modems

The most common cause for slow connection speeds is noisy phone lines. Noise can cause data corruption. If your modem gets corrupted data, it must request that the data be sent again. If 15% of the data needs to be resent, your modem will be 15% slower than it should be.

Start by connecting a telephone handset to the phone line or to the jack labeled "phone" on the back of your modem, and make a normal call. If you hear any crackling, it means the line is very noisy (you may not be able to hear low-to-moderate noise, however). If you suspect line noise, try replacing the wall jack and the phone cord connecting the modem to the wall. Note that the phone cord shouldn't be any longer than is absolutely necessary.

Also, make sure there isn't anything else on the line between the computer and the wall. That is, any answering machines, fax machines, and telephones should be plugged into the back of your modem (the jack labeled "phone"), and your modem should be plugged *directly* into the wall. These devices can interfere with transmission, especially if the signal must pass through them in order to reach your computer.

On the software side, make sure you have a driver made especially for your modem. While a generic modem driver may work with your modem, a new driver supplied by the manufacturer of your modem might enable higher connect speeds (such as 33.6k and 56k), as well as compression and better error correction.

If you have an external modem, make sure it's connected to a high-speed serial port, equipped with a 16550A chip or better. Otherwise, your serial port may be a bandwidth bottleneck.

If you have an external ISDN modem connected through a serial port, your serial port is most likely a bandwidth bottleneck. Even the high-speed 16550A-based serial ports only allow up to 112kbps, although ISDN can go up to 128kbps (or 230kbps with compression)—that's a minimum loss of 16kbps, or 12%. Look into a high-end serial port based on the 16650 or 16750 chips. For internal ISDN adapters, see "Network cards," later in this list. For more general information on ISDN, see "Installing Dial-Up Networking" in Chapter 7, *Networking*.

Printers

Old printer cables commonly cause problems, such as lost data and slow printing. Your printer cable should be new and securely fastened at both ends. While long printer cables can be convenient, shorter ones are more reliable and may provide faster printing—don't use a longer cable than is necessary. Longer cables may even simply not work with some printers, yielding only gibberish or even nothing at all. Make sure you have a bidirectional cable, which allows communication in both directions. Many newer printers also require the more expensive IEEE-1284 cables for best performance and reliability.

Some computers have more than one printer port, although they may not all have the same capabilities. If you experience slow printing, you should test printing with each one to see which is fastest.

If your parallel port is built into your motherboard (as most are), you should go to your system BIOS setup screen (see "Motherboards and the system BIOS," earlier in this list) to make sure your parallel port is configured for its optimal setting. Refer to your motherboard or system manual for details.

Remove any switching boxes, printer-sharing devices, and extraneous connectors unless they are absolutely necessary.

If your printer is shared by two or more computers over a workgroup, the printer should be connected to the computer that uses the printer the most. If you are experiencing slow printing over a network, you should look into a print server solution; this is often just an expansion card installed in your printer, allowing you to connect it *directly* to your network instead of just to one of the computers on your network. This usually results in faster, more reliable, more convenient printing. See "Network cards" below for more tips.

As far as the software goes, most of the drivers included with Windows should work fine. In fact, many new printers come with special software that allows you to control the printer on-screen, but usually requires lots of memory and disk space. If Windows supports your printer *without* this special software, use the Windows driver instead for the fastest printing.

Network cards

Network cards and their drivers usually come with lots of settings, which are usually configured out of the box for compatibility rather than performance. For example, the default setting for the bidirectional feature (allowing data to be transmitted in both directions simultaneously) on most network cards is disabled, since some types of configurations don't support it. As long as all network cards in your workgroup support it, and you're using 10-baseT cabling instead of the older 10-base2 (most cards support both connectors), you should enable bidirectional communication.

Since longer cables can contribute to slower transmission and even lost data, you shouldn't use cabling longer than is necessary.

Obviously, you should be using the most recent drivers for all of your network adapters for the best performance. Windows will always perform best over a network if it's using its own native 32-bit drivers, and not older drivers loaded in *Autoexec.bat* or *Config.sys*; see "Do I

Still Need Config.sys and Autoexec.bat?" in Chapter 6 for more information. Furthermore, Windows has a tendency to install more drivers than are truly necessary for the type of connection you're using. Extra drivers not only waste memory, but slow network communications as well. See Chapter 7 for more information on the drivers required for your connection, and try removing all unnecessary ones.

Sound cards

Many sound cards come with DOS drivers and other DOS configuration software. While these drivers may be necessary for DOS games, they are almost never needed in Windows. These drivers not only take up valuable memory and slow system startup, but may cause slowdowns when you try to use sound in Windows. See "Do I Still Need Config.sys and Autoexec.bat?" in Chapter 6 for more information on removing these drivers. See "Getting DOS Games to Work," also in Chapter 6, for more information on sound card drivers in DOS.

Make sure to obtain the most recent native Windows 32-bit drivers from the manufacturer of your sound card; newer drivers may add new features, such as full duplex, used for Internet communication programs, and advanced mixer and sound recording utilities.

If you find that your system slows down whenever it plays sound, which it shouldn't do, check for DMA conflicts; see Chapter 6 for additional information.

Mice and other pointing devices

If you have any software that came with your mouse, it's probably unnecessary and just taking up memory and disk space. Unless you need it for some advanced features, such as programming the third mouse button, you should remove the software, as Windows supports nearly all mice out of the box. Now, this doesn't include any specialized mouse drivers which may be required by your hardware, but rather the "utilities" package (such as "Intellipoint" for Microsoft mice, or "Mouseware" for Logitech mice) that may have come with your mouse. Other than that, keep the ball clean and use a clean mouse pad for best performance.

Double-click on the **Mouse** icon in **Control Panel** to adjust the sensitivity of your mouse. You can also adjust the double-click speed, and turn on "pointer-trails" to increase visibility on laptop displays. Since the mouse is a primary method of input, fine-tuning these settings can go a long way toward improving your relationship with your mouse.

Speak to your mouse occasionally; don't let it become lonely or feel abused.

Keyboards

Double-click on the Keyboard icon in Control Panel to adjust the various settings of your keyboard. Moving the **Repeat Rate** slider all the way to the right will actually make your computer seem faster, especially when scrolling through a long document or moving the cursor through a lot of text. The **Repeat Delay** is different, though; adjust this to your liking, and test the setting in the Keyboard Properties dialog's **Click here and hold down a key to test repeat rate** text box.

Sticky or dirty keys can slow things down as well; you can pull your keys off one-by-one and remove whatever is caught underneath. Some people have actually been successful cleaning the entire keyboard by immersing it in plain water (unplugged, of course), and then waiting for it to dry. Since keyboards are quite inexpensive, though, you might as well replace it if it's not in top condition.

Keep in mind that most keyboards haven't been effectively designed for use with the human hand (no matter what Microsoft tells you in trying to market their "Natural" keyboard). Your best defense in reducing hand and back strain is to position your keyboard (and yourself, if you have an adjustable chair) so that your elbows are at the same level as your hands, and your arms are well supported. And if your chair tilts forward, it may induce a more comfortable sitting and typing position.

Another way to increase typing performance is to not use your keyboard as much. Look into the new wave of natural-speech dictation programs available.

Everything else

Keep it clean, keep it cool, and make sure you have the latest drivers.

Fixing Software Bottlenecks

In some ways, Windows 98 takes good advantage of your hardware, a liberating change from the stifling experience of Windows 3.x. In other ways, however, Windows itself can be a bottleneck, causing frustration and wasted time. Since all the software you run is dependent upon the operating system, tweaking Windows for better performance should cause performance gains across the board—to a point.

First, there's one easy thing you can do to make Windows substantially more responsive than when you first install it. Windows 98 adds animation to almost every visual component in the operating system, something that can make your new Pentium II seem like a 386. Fortunately, it's easy to turn off some or even all of this animation. See "Taming Mindless Animation" in Chapter 2, *Customizing the Interface*, for more information.

Another easy thing you can do is to speed up the display of menus. Rather than waiting for the standard half-second or so delay before menus are opened, you can reduce this value so that menus are opened more quickly. Double-click on the **TweakUI** icon in Control Panel (see Appendix A, *Setting Locator*) and choose the **Mouse** tab. Move the slider for **Menu speed** all the way to the left and click **OK**. See also "Stop Menus from Following the Mouse" in Chapter 2 for yet another tweak.

The following are a few additional things you can do to configure Windows, which by default is not set up for optimal performance. These tips, combined with those in the previous section on fine-tuning your hardware, should help you get the most out of the Windows platform.

Convert Your Drives to FAT32

Now that multi-gigabyte hard disks are affordable and common, more users are being faced with the problem of large cluster sizes. Clusters are the smallest units into which a hard disk's space can be divided. A hard disk formatted with the traditional file allocation table (FAT) system found in Windows 95 and all previous versions of Windows and DOS can have no more than 65,536 clusters on each drive or partition.* This means that the larger the hard disk, the larger the size of each cluster. For example, a 1.2GB drive will have a cluster size of 32K.

The problem with large clusters is that they result in a lot of wasted disk space. Each cluster can store no more than a single file (or a part of a single file); if a file does not consume an entire cluster, the remaining space is wasted.

So, a 1K file on a disk with a 32K cluster size will consume 32K of disk space; a 33K file on the same drive will consume 64K of space. The extra 31 kilobytes left over from the 33K file is called slack space, and can't be used by any other files. With thousands of files (especially those tiny shortcuts littered throughout a Windows installation), the amount of wasted slack space on a standard 2GB drive can add up to over a hundred megabytes.

The FAT32 system included in Windows 98 can handle more than 4 billion clusters, resulting in much smaller cluster sizes. The same 1GB

---

* A single hard disk can be divided into two or more smaller logical drives (*C:*, *D:*, and so on) called partitions. See "Designate Drive Letters" in Chapter 6 for more information on multiple partitions.

drive formatted with FAT32 will have only a 4K cluster size. Figure 5-2 compares four files stored on a traditional FAT system with the same files on a new FAT32 disk.

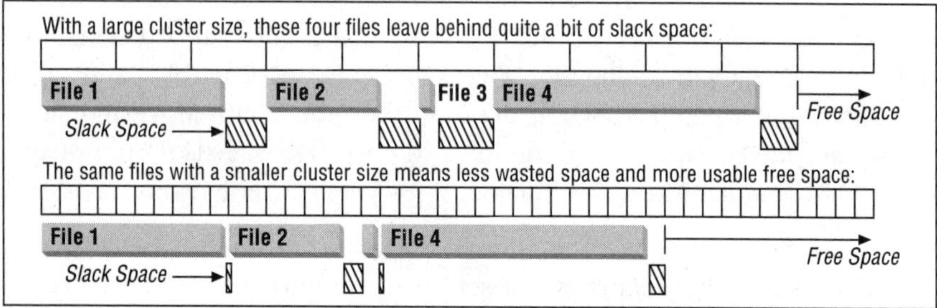

Figure 5-2: FAT 32 stores files more efficiently by allowing smaller cluster sizes

You can see how much space is wasted by any given file by right-clicking on it, selecting **Properties**, and comparing the **Size** with the **bytes used**. You can also see the space wasted by all the files in a directory by typing `dir /v` at the command prompt (see Appendix B, *DOS Lives*). To find out how much slack space is on an entire drive, go to the root directory of the drive in Explorer and press **Ctrl-A** to select all the contents of the drive (you must have hidden files visible for this to work). Press **Alt-Enter** to display the properties of the selection, which will contain the sizes of all the files and the amount of space they take up.

The other advantage of FAT32 is that it supports larger partitions. Where traditional FAT wouldn't allow you to have a partition larger than 2 gigabytes (larger drives would have to be divided up), FAT32 supports partitions up to 2 terabytes (2,048 gigabytes, or over 2 trillion bytes).

To find out if a hard disk is formatted as FAT32, right-click on its icon in Explorer or My Computer, and click **Properties**.

There are three ways to convert a drive to FAT32. If you're setting up a new drive for the first time, *Fdisk* will give you the option of enabling FAT32 for any drives larger than 540MB (traditional FAT will be used for all smaller drives).

Of course, repartitioning and reformatting is simply not a practical option for those of us that already have data on our drives. Windows 98 comes with the FAT32 Drive Converter (*Cvt1.exe*), which walks you through the process of converting one or more drives. Just run this program and follow the instructions on-screen.

Lastly, for the most control, PartitionMagic (3.0 or later), a commercial program from PowerQuest, allows you to resize and move disk partitions around *without* reformatting, as well as to convert existing drives to FAT32 and create new FAT32 drives. If you had your hard disk divided into several partitions because of the 2GB limit with traditional FAT, you may want to take this opportunity to consolidate your drives into one large partition. This is the only solution that allows you to do this without reformatting.

For the most part, FAT32 is safe, and I recommend using it. However, there are some minor drawbacks that warrant attention. First of all, once you convert a drive to FAT32, you can't convert it back to traditional FAT without a program like PartitionMagic. Also, FAT32 is not compatible with Windows NT 4.0 and earlier (if you have a dual-boot setup, NT won't recognize any FAT32 drives), although Windows NT 5.0 includes support for FAT32.

Lastly, FAT32 has a bug that sometimes causes the amount of free space on your drive to be calculated incorrectly. This bug shouldn't result in any lost data or reduced performance, but it can fool Windows into thinking that you're out of space when you're really not. This most often happens when Windows doesn't shut down correctly, such as after a crash. To fix the problem, just run Scandisk (*Scandskw.exe* in Windows, *Scandisk.exe* in DOS); if there is a discrepancy between the reported free space and the actual free space, it will be fixed. Note that this will only resolve the temporary discrepancy; it won't eradicate the bug.

Have Windows Power Down Your Computer Automatically

You may have noticed that some computers—especially laptops—are able to shut themselves off when you choose **Shut Down** from the Start Menu, rather than displaying the "It's now safe to turn off your computer" screen. This is convenient, and makes for faster shutdowns.

In order to configure your computer to behave this way, you'll need the following: If you're using a desktop as opposed to a portable computer, you must have an ATX-compliant case and motherboard. You can tell an ATX system from the power button; if it's a momentary pushbutton that doesn't stay in when you press it, you probably have an ATX case. The difference is that power switches in ATX systems send a "shut down" command to the motherboard, rather than simply cutting power.

Secondly, you must have Power Management (APM) enabled in your system BIOS. Enter your system BIOS setup screen when first starting your computer (usually by pressing the **Del** key), and make sure any options labeled **Advanced Power Management**, **APM**, or **APM-aware OS** are enabled. Refer to your motherboard or system manual for details. If APM is correctly enabled, you should see an icon labeled **Power** or **Power Management** in the Control Panel. If you don't, either your system doesn't fully support APM or Windows hasn't recognized it. To force Windows to recognize APM, run the Add New Hardware wizard (in Control Panel) and have it automatically detect any new hardware.

If these two conditions are met, Windows 98 should automatically power down your system the next time you shut down.

Resurrecting the Floppy Diskette

Although you can right-click on a floppy drive icon in Explorer or My Computer and select **Format** to format it, there are a couple of better alternatives:

- Use the command prompt to format floppies; see "Better floppy formats" in Chapter 6 for more information.
- Don't use floppies to store information for a long period of time, but just to transfer files from one computer to another.
- Use *.zip* files not only to fit more information on each floppy, but also to make files otherwise too large to fit on floppies. The native Windows WinZip program is easy to use and powerful, but the PKZIP DOS utility has the `-&` parameter, which allows you to span really large files over multiple floppies. See Chapter 5, *Maximizing Performance*, for details.
- Windows and DOS only allow you to format floppies to their standard 1.44 megabyte capacity, but it's possible to squeeze more space out of them with distribution media format (DMF). In fact, those Microsoft products still shipped on floppies come on DMF-formatted diskettes. The DMF format can hold about 1.7 megabytes, but a special utility is required to format DMF diskettes. Programs capable of performing DMF formats include WinImage 2.2 (see Appendix F) and Norton Navigator for Windows 95/98 (commercially available).

Speed Up System Startup

There are several factors that can impact the amount of time it takes for your computer to load Windows. As you install software and add devices, Windows will naturally be somewhat bogged down. There's not a whole lot you can do about that, short of removing programs or formatting and reinstalling from scratch. However, you should systematically check out all of the following factors, trimming and cleaning up where you can:

- You should have a minimum of 32 megabytes of RAM, but 64MB or even 128MB is better. Since memory prices have fallen so dramatically, it's remarkably inexpensive to add more RAM to your system, and doing so will *significantly* improve performance across the board.
- A slow hard disk can slow down the bootup process. Make sure you defragment often (see "Fine-Tuning Your Components" earlier in this chapter). If you're using an older hard disk, you might consider upgrading, which will not only get you more disk space, but will improve disk performance as well. See "Upgrading Your System" later in this chapter for details.
- Make sure you have sufficient free disk space for your swap file. Windows uses part of your hard disk to store portions of memory; the more disk space you devote to your swap file, the easier it will be for Windows to store data there. See "Stop Windows from Wildly Accessing Your Hard Disk" later in this chapter for more information.
- Sometimes having too many files in your *\Windows\Temp* folder can not only slow Windows startup, but can prevent Windows from loading at all. Windows and your applications use this folder to temporarily store data while you're working with documents. When those applications and documents are closed, they sometimes leave the temporary files behind. Add the line `del c:\temp\*.tmp >nul` to your *Autoexec.bat* file to automatically delete these files every time you start your computer.

  Note that some programs, such as Microsoft Word, can be configured to use the *Temp* directory to store *autorecovery* files—files that are used to recover data that wasn't saved and otherwise would be lost in the event of a system crash or power outage. You should make sure your programs are configured to store these files not in the *Temp* folder, but in another location, such as a subdirectory of the *Temp* folder.
- If you have over 600 fonts installed on your system, it may add several seconds to the boot process. If you can survive without all those fonts, try removing several hundred of them. If you periodically need a lot of fonts, you might want to invest in font management software, such as Adobe Type Manager, which can remove and reinstall fonts in groups at the click of a button.
- Network drivers for your network card and Dial-Up Networking (see Chapter 7) will always take a little while to load, initialize the hard-

ware, and log onto the network. Try disabling any drivers and networking options such as drive letter mapping that you don't need.

- If you're using Windows, there's a timed delay when you first turn on your computer that you can eliminate. Using a plain text editor, such as Notepad, edit your *Msdos.sys* file in the root directory of your boot drive (usually *C:*). Add the line `BootDelay=0` to the `[Options]` section of the file, or edit the line if it exists already, and save the file. For more information on the *Msdos.sys* file, see Appendix C, *Contents of the MSDOS.SYS File.*
- You may have noticed that Scandisk is sometimes run when Windows is starting, usually if the system was not shut down properly. This is generally a good idea; however, it's easy to disable if you find that it's happening more often than is reasonable. Double-click on the **TweakUI** icon in Control Panel, choose the **Boot** tab, and change the **Autorun Scandisk** option to suit your needs.
- If you're not using the DriveSpace (or the older DoubleSpace) feature, the disk compression utility that comes with Windows, its drivers may still be taking up valuable memory and slowing system startup. Simply delete *Drvspace.bin* and *Dblspace.bin* from the root directory of your boot drive (usually *C:*) and from your *Windows\Command* folder. Note: Don't do this if you are currently using DriveSpace or DoubleSpace to compress your hard disk!
- Some system vendors (Compaq and NEC, to name a couple) sometimes install their own proprietary shell interfaces on top of Explorer (the default shell). These interfaces are usually designed to hide the default Windows desktop and show a "friendlier" startup screen. Not only does this just make it more confusing for those who may have used Windows previously, but it takes longer to load. Open *System.ini* in a text editor, such as Notepad, and look for the line that begins with `shell=`. If the line is there, and *Explorer.exe* is not specified on the right side of the equals sign, remove the line entirely, and save. If you know your system is using such a shell, but you can't find it specified here, see the next paragraph. See Chapter 3, *The Registry*, for more information on *.ini* files.
- Probably the most common thing that can slow down the loading of Windows is the number of programs configured to load at boot time. These programs are specified in several places. Look carefully in each location, and feel free to remove anything you don't want running. The "Errors during startup" topic in Chapter 6 describes in more detail the various ways that programs are configured to load at Windows startup.

- Antivirus programs are commonly configured to run whenever you turn on your computer. These programs are always in memory, scanning programs as you open them and files as you download them. In most cases, this is overkill. For most users, getting a computer virus is about as likely as getting struck by lightning. I wouldn't necessarily recommend getting rid of all antivirus programs; just restrict their use to manually scanning your system when you want, and disable the automatic feature. You'll notice a faster startup for Windows and applications.
- Run the System Information utility (*Msinfo32.exe*) and highlight **\Software Environment\Running Tasks** from the tree.* Look at each entry to the right for any programs that may be running. Each program that runs is taking up memory, taking time to load, and possibly causing conflicts. Note that this list may be intimidating, and most of the components are simply necessary Windows processes. However, it can be a useful tool for finding an elusive program. Naturally, it's best not to delete something because you see it here, but rather to use it to gain more understanding of the system. See "Errors during startup" in Chapter 6 for details on disabling background programs.
- Lastly, much of speeding up your computer involves cleaning out files you don't need anymore. It's best to back up your system before deleting anything, or at least to rename or move files to see if they're being used before you get rid of them.

Stop Windows from Wildly Accessing Your Hard Disk

Many users who have installed Windows without taking time to customize the way it uses the hard disk are disappointed to find that it frequently seizes up for up to a minute with random, pointless disk activity. This is due to the way that Windows handles disk caching and virtual memory.

Normally, Windows loads drivers and applications into memory until it's full, then starts to use part of your hard disk to "swap" out information, freeing up more memory for high-priority tasks. The file that Windows

* There's a bug in Office 97 setup which actually overwrites the system information utility included with Windows 98. This is caused by the fact that the two versions are installed to different directories; a Microsoft oversight. For the most part, the Office 97 version is more complete, although the Windows 98 version has an additional **Tools** menu, which provides access to other Windows components. If you're using the Office 97 version of System Information, look in the **Applications Running** branch of the tree.

uses for this type of "virtual memory" is the swap file, which is usually called *Win386.swp*, and is located in your Windows folder.

Virtual memory can slow down performance if it's not configured correctly, and the slowdown can be significant. Although Windows instructs you to "let Windows handle disk cache settings" for best results, this obviously does not yield the best results. Here's how to eliminate random disk activity and improve system performance.

Part One: Virtual Memory

One of the reasons why the default settings yield such poor performance is that the swap file grows and shrinks with use, and quickly becomes very fragmented. Once you've set the swap file size to be constant, however, you won't have to worry about this:

1. Right-click on the **My Computer** icon, select **Properties**, and choose the **Performance** tab.
2. Click **Virtual Memory**, and then select **Let me specify my own virtual memory settings**.
3. The location and size of your swap file are now displayed in front of you. If you want to choose a different drive (assuming you have more than one) for your swap file, run **Disk Defragmenter** on that drive first, and then specify the drive here.
4. Specify the same value for the **Minimum size** and the **Maximum size**, so Windows won't spend so much time resizing the file. A good size is roughly two and one-half times the amount of installed RAM; so, for example, you should create a 40 megabyte swap file if you have 16 megabytes of RAM.
5. Press **OK**, and then **OK** again, and confirm that you want to restart your computer.

Part Two: Defragmenting the swap file

While Part One will eliminate the possibility of your swap file becoming fragmented, it won't defragment an already fragmented swap file. You'll need to defragment it at least once for it to remain that way in the future.

- If you have Norton Utilities for Windows 95/8, you'll be able to optimize the swap file without moving it using the Speedisk utility.
- If you don't have such a utility, and you have the time to do it right, you can defragment the swap file manually. If you have more than one partition or hard disk in your system, you can defragment the swap file by moving it from partition to partition. First, run Disk

Defragmenter on a partition other than the one containing the swap file. Next, move the swap file to that partition, keeping its size constant. Then defragment the original drive, and move the swap file back.

- If you don't have multiple partitions, you can try temporarily disabling your swap file. This can be dangerous, as Windows may not be able to boot if it doesn't have enough memory. You should be all right, however, if you have 32MB of RAM or more. Once you've disabled your swap file, you can delete the file (*Win386.swp*), defragment your hard disk, and then re-enable it.

Part Three: Virtual Cache

Windows has a Virtual Cache feature which improves disk performance. However, its default configuration is similar to that of the swap file; it grows depending on your use. The problem is that it can grow too large, filling up all your memory, which causes Windows to start filling up your swap file. This can cause your hard disk to seize up for up to a minute:

1. Open the *System.ini* file in a plain text editor, such as Notepad. (See Chapter 3 for more information on *.ini* files.)
2. Add the following two lines to the `[vcache]` section (add the section if it's not there):

   ```
   MinFileCache=0
   MaxFileCache=4096
   ```

   These values, in kilobytes, regulate the size of the Virtual Cache. The 4096 (4 megabytes) is a good value if you have 16 megabytes of RAM or more. If you have 48 megabytes of RAM, you should increase the value to 8192. If you have fewer than 16 megabytes of RAM, you should not use this value, but run out instantly and upgrade your memory.

Part Four: RAM

You may have thought that I overlooked the obvious solution—add more RAM! The more memory you have, the less frequently Windows will use your hard disk, and the better your system performance will be.

Since Windows isn't very efficient or compact by any stretch of the imagination, you'll need to feed it as much memory as you can afford. 16 megabytes is the absolute minimum, but 32 megabytes is much better. Many new computers are coming with 64 or even 128 megabytes, which should be plenty to hold you for quite a while.

When Windows 3.x was first released, 32 megabytes of RAM cost around a thousand dollars. The same quantity of memory (a faster variety) at the release of Windows 98 cost around 35 dollars. See "Upgrading Your System" later in this chapter for more information.

What to Throw Away

By erasing unneeded files and folders on your hard disk, you'll not only get more space, but make your drive more responsive and reliable. Additionally, removing drivers and applications that are no longer used will clear more memory for your other applications, which can substantially improve overall system performance.

When you first install Windows, your hard disk is littered with files you don't need. The standard installation of Windows 98 puts about 3,000 files in over 160 folders, consuming over 300 megabytes of disk space.

Now, whether or not you need a particular file can be subjective, so the 3 megabytes of *.wav* files that one person wants to get rid of as soon as possible might be deemed extremely important by someone else.

Be careful, however—removing files that are still needed can cause some applications, or even Windows itself, to stop functioning. It's always good practice to move any files in question to a different directory or drive, or rename them, before deleting them entirely. Again, backing up your entire hard disk is very important. What follows is a list of some files that can be deleted for sure.

In your Windows folder and all its subdirectories

Do a search by selecting **Find** and then **Files or Folders** from the Start Menu for any of the following files. Double-click on any suspicious files to see what's inside, and delete them if desired. If double-clicking on a file displays the Open With dialog (such as for *.001* files), click **Cancel**, and then drag the file into Notepad to see what's inside.

Files with the following extensions are all candidates for deletion:

- Anything with the extensions **.log*, **.old*, **.- - -*, **.bak*, and **.000*, **.001*, **.002*, (and so on . . .).
- Any files with the extensions **.bmp* (bitmap files), **.wav* (sound clips), and **.avi* (video clips). These can take up a great deal of space, and are usually superfluous.
- In the Windows directory only, the many **.txt* (text) files, which are essentially *Readme* files.

- Almost any files with the following dates, since they belong to old versions of Windows:

  03/10/92 (Windows 3.1)
  09/30/92 (Windows for Workgroups 3.1)
  11/01/93 (Windows for Workgroups 3.11)
  12/31/93 (Windows 3.11)
  07/11/95 (Windows 95)
  08/10/96 (Windows 95 OSR2)

- The entire *WIN32S* directory in your *Windows\System* directory, if it exists. The *WIN32S* directory is used only in Windows 3.x to allow certain 32-bit applications to run, but some older applications incorrectly install it in Windows, or it may be around if you upgraded from an earlier version of Windows. If you remove this directory, make sure to remove any references to it in your *System.ini* file, and restart Windows.

In your Temp directory (usually Windows\Temp)

- Ideally, all files in this directory are placed there temporarily by open applications, and automatically deleted when not in use. Therefore, you should never try to delete any files that may be in use. However, many applications forget to delete these files. If you find files in your *Temp* directory that have a date or time *earlier* than the last time you started your computer, you can delete them. Additionally, if you exit Windows, you can safely delete any files in that directory, as none of them will be in use when Windows isn't running.

In the root directory of your boot drive (usually C:\)

- Any files with the extensions **.txt*, **.prv*, **.log*, **.old*, **.- - -*, and **.dos* may be deleted, except for *Bootsect.dos* (see "Files NOT to delete," later in this list). If your *Autoexec.bat* or *Config.sys* files are empty, they can be deleted. See "Do I Still Need Config.sys and Autoexec.bat?" in Chapter 6 for tips on emptying these files so that they can be removed.

Anywhere else on your system

- Other files that may be deleted include *Mscreate.dir*, an absolutely useless, empty, hidden file created by all of Microsoft's installation programs, and placed in every folder used by every Microsoft application. There may be hundreds of these empty files on your hard disk (see the discussion of slack space in "Convert Your Drives to FAT32" earlier in this chapter).

- Any directory named *~Mssetup.t* is a temporary directory created during the installation of a Microsoft program, and can be freely deleted if it still exists after the installation of an application is complete.
- If you're trying to create more disk space, you may want to delete **.hlp* (help) files for applications that don't need them (see the "Notes and other issues" at the end of this topic). Also, many applications include bitmaps (**.bmp*), sound clips (**.wav*), and video clips (**.avi*), which take up enormous amounts of disk space for virtually no reason.
- For some reason, some programs (including the tutorial that comes with Windows) insist on installing video clips (**.avi*, **.mov*, and **.mpg*) to your hard drive. These files can be quite large, each one eating up to several megabytes of disk space. To see what the video contains before deleting it, double-click on it to open the appropriate video player. These files can almost always be deleted without detriment to the program that put them there (other than the obvious disabling of sounds by deleting the sound files).

Specific programs you can delete

- Most Windows components can be removed by double-clicking on the **Add/Remove Programs** icon in Control Panel, choosing the **Windows Setup** tab, and unchecking any unwanted components. This is better than simply deleting unwanted files, as links to the programs will also be cleared.
- The Internet Connection Wizard, which is located in *\Program Files\ICW–Internet Connection Wizard* (as well as *\Program Files\Internet Explorer\ICW*), takes up 0.75 megabytes, and can be safely deleted. Windows runs this program once—the first time you try to access the Internet after installing Windows 98—regardless of whether or not you already have a Dial-Up Networking connection configured.
- The folder called *Online Services* (included to encourage competition with MSN) contains the setup files for several online services. Even if you choose not to install MSN or any of the other Online Services, the files will be copied anyway. It's perfectly safe to delete them. If you want to get them back, they're in the *\Win98\OLS* folder on the Windows 98 CD.

Files NOT to delete

- Never delete any files from your *Sysbckup* directory—these files are used to store backups of important system files that may become corrupted or overwritten by older applications, as well as backups of your registry files.

- Your registry files, *System.dat* and *User.dat* (as well as *System.1st,* in the root directory of your boot drive), should always be left alone.
- Any files in your root directory, as well as those \ *Windows* and \ *Windows\System* folders not specifically mentioned above, should be left alone. This includes *Bootsect.dos, Boot.ini, Ntldr,* and *Ntdetect.com,* which are used if you've set up a dual-boot system with Windows NT. And this especially includes *Io.sys, Msdos.sys,* and *Command.com,* which comprise DOS.
- Any files and folders in your *\Program Files* or \ *Windows\MSAPPS* directories that have names like *Microsoft Shared* and *Common Files* should not be touched. These files can be used by several applications simultaneously, which is why they haven't been placed in the folders of the applications that put them there.

If in doubt

- If you're not sure if something should be deleted, but want to try anyway, move it to another directory first to see if everything works without it for a day or so.
- Check the file's **Last Accessed** date (right-click on it and select **Properties**). If it's recent, most likely it's still being used. For information on removing a particular application, contact the manufacturer of that application, or refer to the application's documentation.

Special consideration: Hidden files

- Some files on your hard disk are hidden files; files that, by default, can't be seen in Explorer. To configure Explorer to show hidden files, select **Folder Options** from Explorer's **View** menu, and choose the **View** tab. Turn on the **Show all files** option, and press **OK**. Any hidden files will be visible, but their icons will be somewhat transparent.

  Most hidden files have been made hidden in order to protect them from deletion. If you see a hidden file, think twice before deleting it for this reason.
- To make another file hidden (to protect it, or whatever), right-click on it and select **Properties**. Check **Hidden**, and press **OK**.
- If you're trying to delete or alter a hidden file in DOS, use the `ATTRIB` command (see Appendix B).

Notes and other issues

See "Clean Up and Customize System Folders" in Chapter 4, *Tinkering Techniques*, for more information on all the extra empty folders that Windows won't let you delete.

See "Coping with Loss: Using the New Windows Help System" in Chapter 2 for more information on the several files that may be created on the fly for use with help files, and on which ones may be deleted.

Getting Into and Out of DOS

Windows 98 is a graphical operating system based on DOS, even though Microsoft has gone to great lengths to obscure that fact. Those who still rely on DOS programs or play a lot of DOS games may want to make access to DOS easier.

Boot directly into DOS

This essentially makes Windows 98 behave more like Windows 3.x, where the system boots directly into DOS, giving you the opportunity to load Windows by simply typing `win` at the command prompt:

1. Double-click on the **TweakUI** icon in Control Panel (see Appendix A, *Setting Locator*) and choose the **Boot** tab.
2. Turn off the **Start GUI automatically** option and press **OK**.

How to exit to DOS

Normally, selecting **Shut Down** from the Start Menu and choosing **Restart in MSDOS mode** will exit to DOS with no fuss. However, doing this causes a small piece of Windows to remain in memory, which can cause compatibility problems with some DOS programs. There are two ways to configure Windows so that you can exit to DOS completely:

- If you delete the shut-down logos (*Logos.sys* and *Logow.sys*) from your Windows directory, you will be returned to the DOS prompt whenever you choose "Shut down your computer." See "Replace the Startup and Shutdown Screens" in Chapter 2 for information on these files.
- Assuming you've followed the instructions in the previous item, "Boot directly into DOS," you should be able to type `MODE CO80` and press the **Enter** key at the "It is now safe to turn off your system" screen* to exit to DOS.

* That's the letters C and O followed by the number 80. Note that you won't see the text you type until you press **Enter**.

Better command prompt shortcuts

There are a few things you can do to improve command prompt shortcuts, the primary means for getting to DOS without leaving Windows:

1. Right-click on *Dosprmpt.pif* (in your Windows folder) and select **Properties**.
2. Choose the **Program** tab, and enter `DOSKEY` in the field labeled **Batch File**. Doskey (*Doskey.exe*) is a little toy that comes with Windows as well as previous versions of DOS and keeps a memory of all the commands you enter in DOS. When in the command prompt, you'll be able to use the Up and Down cursor keys to cycle through commands you've typed before, as well as use the left and right arrow keys to edit what you've typed.
3. Also in the **Program** tab is the **Working** field, which specifies the initial directory when you first open the command prompt. My preference is to specify the desktop folder (usually *C:\Windows\Desktop*), which helps set the context of the folder as the working directory.

Notes and other issues

See "Create a Startup Menu and "Getting DOS Games to Work," both in Chapter 6, for useful applications of these solutions.

The "Boot Directly into DOS" option essentially changes the line `BootGUI=1` to `BootGUI=0` in the *Msdos.sys* file (see Appendix C, *Contents of the MSDOS.SYS File*).

To successfully exit to DOS, you may have to disable the "Fast Shutdown" feature. If the solution above doesn't work, run the System Configuration Utility (*msconfig.exe*). Choose the **General** tab, click **Advanced**, and turn on the **Disable fast shutdown** option. Click **OK** twice when you're done.

You can configure certain drivers to be loaded when you exit Windows, but you must use a special shortcut to do so. See "Do I Still Need Config.sys and Autoexec.bat?" in Chapter 6 for more information.

Transfer Windows onto Another Hard Disk

With the release of an operating system as large as Windows 98, it's quite reasonable that many of you may need to upgrade your hard disks. While you can simply reinstall Windows and all of your applications on the new drive, this obviously isn't a very attractive solution. However, it's not that easy to transfer Windows, either.

There are several ways to transfer the data from one drive to another. Each of these solutions works under the following assumptions:

- First, both the old drive and the new drive should have only a single partition; installing two drives with multiple partitions can cause the drive letters to go haywire, meaning that you may not be able to start Windows (see "Designate Drive Letters" in Chapter 6 for more information). The solution given in "Transferring data manually: SCSI drives," later in this chapter, shows a way around this, although it only works if your new drive is connected to a SCSI controller.
- Second, these solutions assume that you've correctly connected and prepared your new drive according to the instructions included with your drive.

Using a backup program

If you've got a tape drive, or some other backup device, your best bet is to back up your system and restore it onto the new hard drive. This is the safest method, and requires the least technical expertise. However, you may have to reinstall Windows in order to restore your backup. See "Restoring Windows After a Crash" in Chapter 6 for more information.

Using a disk transfer utility

Due to the difficulty of this procedure, and the all too common need to upgrade, a few companies have released commercial utilities designed to copy all the data quickly and painlessly from one drive to another, duplicating any partition information. This works so well that you can then unplug your old drive, replace it with the new one, and boot up normally.

Programs that do this include DriveImage by PowerQuest (the makers of PartitionMagic) and DiskClone by Quarterdeck.

Transferring data manually: IDE drives

1. Connect both hard disks to your computer at once, configuring the new one as the *slave* and the old one as the *master*.
2. Turn on your computer and load Windows normally. The new drive will probably show up in Explorer as drive *D:*.
3. From within Windows, open a command prompt window, and type `FORMAT d: /U /S`, where *d:* is the drive letter of your new disk. This will format the drive, preparing it for use and testing it for errors. The `/S` option makes it bootable, and the `/U` forces an unconditional format (which is faster and more reliable). Close the command prompt window when it's finished.

4. Open Explorer and navigate to the root directory of drive *C:*. Select **Folder Options** from Explorer's **View** menu, and choose the **View** tab. Turn on the **Show all files** option and click **OK**.
5. Select all the files by pressing **Ctrl-A** and drag them *all* into the root directory of drive *D:*. This will begin what is likely to be a rather length copy process. If Windows complains about copying any particular files (such as *Win386.swp*, your swap file), you may be forced to cancel and then continue by copying individual folders.
6. When copying is finished, shut down Windows. Disconnect the old drive and put the new one in its place, configuring it now as the *master* drive. Turn on your computer, and Windows should boot normally.

Transferring data manually: SCSI drives

SCSI controllers have the unique ability to allow you to connect a hard disk without having it controlled by the BIOS. This means that you can easily copy the contents of a multipartition IDE or SCSI drive to a new drive (SCSI only) without having to worry about the drive letters changing. This will only work for either SCSI controllers without a BIOS, or SCSI controllers with a BIOS and the ability to disable it for certain devices. Consult your SCSI controller's manual for details.

If you're copying only a single partition to a SCSI drive, follow the instructions for IDE drives, above. Otherwise, follow these steps:

1. Connect the new SCSI drive to your SCSI controller. You'll probably have to make the SCSI ID for the new drive higher than that for the old drive.
2. Configure your controller (if it has a built-in BIOS) to disable the BIOS for the new drive, so that Windows has control over the drive letters. See "Designate Drive Letters" in Chapter 6 for the difference between BIOS-controlled drives and Windows-controlled drives.
3. Copy your files from each of your old drive's partitions to the corresponding new partitions, following the instructions for IDE drives, above.
4. When you're done, shut down Windows, reconfigure your new drive so that it is controlled by the BIOS, and restart.

Notes and other issues

If, for whatever reason, you need to copy the files in DOS, use the XCOPY32 utility, which will preserve your long filenames. Use the undocumented /h parameter to copy hidden files, although system files will still be ignored. See Appendix B for more information on DOS commands.

If you use one of the disk transfer utilities mentioned above with a multi-partition hard disk, it will automatically scale the new partitions relative to the old ones. For example, if your old 1GB drive has two 500MB partitions, and you're installing a new 3GB drive, the utilities will create two 1.5GB partitions. You can then use a program like PartitionMagic to resize the partitions, if desired.

Upgrading Your System

When asked which component is the most important in a system, the answer is both easy and impossible. On one hand, all of the components work together to form a complete system, and therefore are equally important to a well-tuned computer. On the other hand, the quality and speed of certain components can affect overall system performance and efficiency more than that of other components. Additionally, certain parts, while important to some users, may be insignificant or even unnecessary to others. One thing for sure is that a single component *can* be a significant bottleneck, hindering the performance of the rest of the system.

Another factor is the cost of the various components. For example, memory is quite cheap and effective at increasing performance, while faster CPUs are more expensive and result in less of a performance gain. So, if funds are limited, more memory is usually the better choice.

Computers are designed to be completely modular, in that nearly all the parts in one computer are upgradable and interchangeable with those found in other computers. Upgrading single components rather than replacing the entire system is usually much less expensive, and allows you to spread out the cost of a new computer over a long period of time. If many components in your system need upgrading, however, you may be better off buying an entirely new system. That way, you'll have two working computers rather than one machine and a pile of obsolete parts. If you're upgrading several computers, you may be lucky enough to combine the left-over parts into an entirely new system.

When purchasing a new, prebuilt system, you should be aware that the quality of the components is often below what you'd get if you bought the components separately. Computer system vendors make more money by including substandard, generic parts in their systems rather than brand-name, top-of-the-line components. If you know how to build a computer from scratch and have the time, you're usually better off doing so, and you'll probably save money. Most companies allow you to customize your system with various components, though, so make sure you demand the best. Some companies, especially the larger mail-order firms, tend to include a long list of top-of-the-line components for one low price, so shop around. The moral when buying a new system is to look at more than just the CPU speed and the sticker price.

Name brand components are important in that they're more likely to be supported by their manufacturers in the years to come. Many users were disappointed to find out, for example, that they were unable to get appropriate drivers for their no-name video cards when Windows was released, and were forced either to use generic drivers or to replace the cards altogether. A good test for a hardware manufacturer is to see if they still support products they stopped making years ago. Check the technical support area of a company's Internet site to see if they have drivers and troubleshooting information for their old products. If they support yesterday's products today, they're likely to support today's products tomorrow. If a company doesn't have some kind of support on the Internet, it's time to choose a different company. In short, do your research now before you spend a dime.

Choosing New Components

Since a computer is ultimately the sum of its parts, you can improve an existing system, or know what to look for in a new system, by being able to choose the components effectively. There are some general considerations to keep in mind when choosing new components. For example, if you buy something you know is going to be obsolete in six months, such as the CPU, don't buy the top of the line, as the extra money will be getting you close to nothing in the long run. However, spending a lot on a good monitor that will last for years is smart, and will pay off in the long run.

Monitors

The monitor is arguably the most important single component in a computer system, and next to the printer, usually the most expensive. Your monitor is what you spend the most time looking at; your eyes will thank you for choosing wisely, especially if you wear corrective lenses or are prone to headaches. The monitor is the component least likely to become obsolete; a good monitor will probably outlast every other component in your system, so it's the best place to put your money. My advice to those looking for a new computer is that it's best to take some money out of the budget for the computer and spend it on the monitor. *Don't skimp here!*

A large, clear monitor makes your computer more pleasing to use. Don't settle for anything less than a 15-inch display; even 17-inch displays are becoming more affordable. If you can afford it, invest in a bigger, better quality monitor, and postpone that CPU upgrade for a while.

Look for a flat, square screen surface—bulging, round screens are obsolete and distort images. You'll want lots of controls to adjust not only brightness and contrast, but image size and position, color temperature (the saturation, or "warmth" of brighter colors), rotation, and the "pincushion" effect. *Insist* on digital push buttons controls; analog dial controls don't have memory, so you'll need to adjust the controls every time you change the video mode, which happens more frequently than you may think. Don't waste your money on built-in speakers unless you have limited desk space or can afford the novelty; separate speakers will provide better sound and save you some money.

Go to one of those big computer stores and carefully compare all of the available monitors in your budget range. It's important to get one you like, and don't be afraid to ask who makes the picture tube inside.

You may also be interested in one of the newer flat-screen desktop monitors available. These monitors are usually only about an inch thick and use the same technology as the better laptop screens available. Flat screens certainly look cool, and they take up a very small amount of desk space. Combined with Windows 98's ability to support multiple monitors, the potential of a couple of flat monitors hanging on the wall side-by-side, with the Windows desktop spanned between them, is intriguing, to say the least.

However, flat screens have three disadvantages (for now): fixed resolution, inferior quality, and higher price. Flat screens have a fixed number of horizontal and vertical pixels, which means that if you try to display a resolution lower than the screen's native resolution, it will either appear choppy and distorted, or just very small. And flat screens commonly have resolutions of 800×600 and 1024×768, so if you want a higher resolution, you're out of luck. Also, the picture quality and color depth of flat screens still isn't as good as the better full-size monitors, and combined with their higher price, it can make for a hard sell.

The same positive and negative things that apply to flat screens also apply to laptops, with the exception that the cheaper, poorer-quality passive-matrix screens (sometimes called dual-scan or fast-scan) are still being used. While these are cheaper, they produce much poorer image quality, and usually aren't worth it—especially if you can afford an active matrix (TFT) screen.

Video cards (also known as display adapters)

The video card is what puts the image on your monitor, so a faster video card will mean a faster display. The video card is responsible for the resolution, the color depth, and the refresh rate. The resolution (the number of pixels on the screen) and the color depth (the maximum number of colors that can be displayed simultaneously) are both dependent on the amount of memory on the card. The more memory on a video card, the better; more memory means higher resolutions and more colors, which means better picture quality. The refresh rate is *not* the speed at which your video card can draw things on the screen, but rather how many times per second the image on the screen is *redrawn*—if your screen flickers, the refresh rate isn't high enough. Make sure your video card supports a resolution of 1024×768, a color depth of 65,536 colors, and a refresh rate of at least 72Hz. For more information on these settings, see the discussion of video cards in "Fine-Tuning Your Components," earlier in this chapter.

One of the many things to look for on a video card is the amount and type of video memory on the card. You'll probably be able to find cards with any one of the following types: DRAM (the slowest and cheapest), VRAM, WRAM, and SGRAM (the fastest and most expensive). DRAM is probably sufficient for most uses, although faster types may be worth the extra money if you play a lot of games or work with graphics. Look for cards with at least 4MB of on-board memory; 8MB is better. Some cards allow you to upgrade the amount of memory, although the cost of upgrades (say, from 4MB to 8MB) is usually much higher than the price difference between the upgradable and fully equipped models.

Nearly all video cards on the market today are accelerated, meaning that they can do certain calculations so that your CPU doesn't have to. Faster video cards produce smoother animation, better quality video, and faster scrolling text in your word processor, while reducing the load on your processor. The graphics acceleration is controlled by a controller chip on the card; if your video card has a common controller chip rather than a proprietary one, your card is more likely to be supported by the software you wish to run.

Some cards also have 3D acceleration, which not only means faster 3D in games, but better quality rendering with more colors. The downside is that, in some circumstances, the software you run must specifically support the 3D controller chip on your card. Look for newer 3D cards that support the OpenGL standard and that are compatible with Direct3D (Microsoft's standard 3D drivers).

Don't pay any attention to benchmarks. Bar graphs and charts that compare the performance of various cards are just devices used by magazine editors to sell more magazines. Benchmarks generally measure arbitrary quantities, such as data throughput and characters per second, rather than more important things like build quality, driver reliability, and the availability of extended features. While the speed of a video card may be of mild importance to someone who plays a lot of graphics-intensive video games, it's really not of much interest to most Windows users. Resist the temptation to allow an advertised benchmark to influence your purchase decisions.

There are now four different kinds of video cards; the type you get must match the slots on your motherboard (see the following section, "Motherboards"). Nearly all video cards are peripheral computer interconnect (PCI) cards, which require the PCI slots found in all Pentium-based systems. If you have an older system, you might have to get a vesa local-bus (VLB) or industry-standard architecture (ISA) card, although these should be avoided. Accelerated graphics port (AGP) is a relatively new variant of PCI that supports much higher data speeds for 3D accelerated cards. If your system has an AGP port, you should get an AGP card, which shouldn't cost any more than a comparable PCI card. If you're currently using a 486 with VLB slots, and are looking for a new video card, you might consider upgrading the motherboard as well so you can instead invest in a PCI card.

It's important to have a brand-name video card, as no-name or clone video cards aren't widely supported, and may be difficult to get to work down the road.

Motherboards

The motherboard is what holds the CPU chip (see the next section), the memory, and all the expansion cards. Different motherboards have different features, but you should choose a motherboard that matches the type of CPU you wish to use. For example, you'll need a Pentium II class motherboard to use a Pentium II chip. Most motherboards support a wide range of CPU speeds, so it's best to choose a motherboard that will accommodate faster chips later on. Look also for the newer motherboard designs. For example, a Pentium-based motherboard will not support the newer Pentium II chips, and is rather a dead end when it comes time to upgrade.

Since the motherboard also connects all of your expansion cards, you'll need one that has lots of the right kind of slots. Most cards plug into the basic type, ISA, which has been around for 15 years. EISA and VLB are essentially obsolete enhancements of this architecture, and should be avoided. Look for motherboards with at least 3 ISA slots, 4 PCI slots, and an AGP slot (see the previous section). Some stingier motherboard manufacturers include fewer slots; while you may think that you'll probably never need that many, there's no reason to limit yourself. Insist on as many as you can get.

A good motherboard has built-in serial and parallel ports, as well as a built-in hard disk controller, lots of slots for additional memory (4 is the norm, but 6 or 8 is better), and a large secondary cache (512k or larger). Many new boards also have the option of a built-in ultra-wide SCSI controller for much less than a standalone controller would cost—a worthwhile investment.

A motherboard with many jumpers and switches can be difficult to configure, so look for boards with only a few, well-labeled jumpers. In fact, make sure all of the connectors are clearly labeled in English on the board, and not simply numbered.

CPU

The processor does all the work, but also becomes obsolete the fastest. Don't settle for anything less than a Pentium or a Pentium II chip, but you don't necessarily need to get the fastest one. The faster the processor speed (measured in megahertz), the faster your computer will be able to perform calculations. Note that this is just one of several factors on which overall system speed depends; jumping from 200MHz to 400MHz will *not* double the speed of the computer.

Do some math before deciding on a CPU. Divide the processor speed by the price to get the megahertz-per-dollar of each chip. You'll find that the fastest chips are rarely the best deal. True, a faster chip will last slightly longer before it needs to be upgraded, but the extra money (which can be substantial) to get the top-of-the-line today won't matter so much when it's time to upgrade later on. Your best bet is to buy one or two steps below the top-of-the-line, if you can afford it. If money is tight, go for a slower processor. You can always upgrade later if you have a motherboard that supports faster chips. In fact, the *combined* price of buying the slower CPU now and the faster CPU later will often be *lower* than buying the faster CPU now.

Note that your motherboard must support the chip you put into it, so it's a good idea to compare the price of a new chip with that of a new motherboard *and* chip. For example, replacing your 486-66 processor with a 486-100 processor won't require a new motherboard, but also won't yield the performance increase of a new Pentium motherboard and chip. Additionally, if you plan on getting a new video card, your money is better spent on a PCI card than on a VLB card, meaning that this would be a good time to upgrade that old 486 to a Pentium.

Remember to get a fan to mount on that chip as well; a well-cooled processor will last longer and perform better.

Memory

There are no two ways about it: the more memory, the better. When Windows 3.x was first released, 32 megabytes of RAM cost around a thousand dollars. The same quantity of memory (a faster variety) at the release of Windows 98 cost around 35 dollars.

Today there are many different kinds of single inline memory modules (SIMMs), small circuit boards holding a varying number of memory chips. You must choose the type of SIMM that your computer requires, including the number of pins (168, 72, or 30), the access speed (ranging from 10 to 60 nanoseconds), and the bus speed (66 or 100 MHz). Faster memory usually doesn't cost much more than slower memory, but is a much better investment.

Adding more memory to a computer will almost always result in better performance. Windows loads drivers, applications, and documents into memory until it's full; once there's no more memory available, Windows starts storing chunks of memory in the swap file on your hard disk to make room in memory for more information. Since your hard disk is substantially slower than memory, this "swapping" noticeably slows down your system. The more memory you have, the less often Windows will use your hard disk in this way, and the faster your system will be.

While Windows 98 requires a minimum of 16 megabytes of RAM, you probably won't find a new computer with less than 32MB these days, and you'd probably be better off with 64MB. If you use high-end graphics programs, such as Adobe Photoshop, you'll benefit from even more memory.

Computer case

The computer case doesn't directly affect performance, but there are differences in design that warrant attention. Look for a case with several fans for better cooling, plenty of drive bays for future expansion, and easy access. A well-designed case won't have sharp edges inside, and won't require you to dismantle the entire computer to accomplish something as simple as adding more memory. Some newer cases can be opened without need for a screwdriver, making that task just a little easier.

It's remarkably difficult to find a well-made computer case these days; most manufacturers want them cheap and small. Bigger cases do have room for more drives and usually have better power supplies, but anything larger than a midsize case is usually unnecessary. Make sure you get at least a 230-watt power supply, although 300 watts is better; insufficient power can cause your drives to fail.

Here's a tip if you're looking for a good high-end case; rack-mount cases, which are usually black with two large handles in front, are generally of much higher quality than the standard gun-metal gray cases you'll find in most computer stores.

Hard disks

A hard disk should be fast, capacious, and reliable. Look for a solid brand rather than a close-out deal. Get the largest capacity you can afford, because you'll use it. Besides, hard drive costs are plummeting, and it's not unusual for one drive to cost only 25 dollars more than another with half the capacity.

Probably the most important feature, however, is the speed. The speed of a hard disk is measured in two quantities, access time and transfer rate. The access time, measured in milliseconds, is the average length of time required to find information, and the transfer rate, measured in megabytes per second, is the speed at which the drive can transfer data to your system. While the access time (look for 11ms or smaller) is almost always quoted alongside the capacity of a drive, the transfer rate isn't always publicized. However, if you're looking for maximum performance, it's a good thing to look for. Lower access times and higher transfer rates are better.

Hard disks today come in two primary flavors: SCSI and IDE. IDE drives plug into an IDE controller, which is often built into the motherboard. SCSI drives require an expensive adapter (see "SCSI controllers" later in this chapter), but if you already have one, it's not an issue. Many new motherboards come with SCSI controllers built in. IDE drives are generally cheaper, and are almost as fast as SCSI drives; installation is relatively easy, too. SCSI drives, while more expensive, offer benefits such as larger available capacities, faster transfer rates and access times, and easier and more flexible installation. SCSI hard disks, like other SCSI devices, can also be external, a handy feature if you don't have any free space in your case, or just want to share the drive between multiple computers.

The last thing to look for is the cache size, especially for SCSI drives. High-end wide-SCSI drives will have a megabyte cache; you'll be hard-pressed to find an IDE drive with more than 256KB of cache memory.

If you're seriously considering either technology, refer to the discussions of the respective controllers below.

Hard disk controllers

The hard disk controller is what your hard disk and floppy drives plug into. With the exception of Small Computer System Interface (SCSI) controllers, the discussion of hard disk controllers is limited to the Integrated Drive Electronics (IDE) variety. IDE is a very inexpensive solution; the controller is almost always built into the motherboard, or available on a very cheap expansion card. If your controller is built into your motherboard (a good thing to look for in a new motherboard), you won't need a new one. Otherwise, look for the cheapest one you can find; they're all the same. Most include parallel and serial ports for printers and mice, respectively. Look for a card where the jumpers or switches are labeled in English *on the card.* There are more expensive IDE controllers available, but unless you really need the advanced options they offer, don't bother.

An IDE controller can support up to two drives. Some motherboards and expansion cards include two IDE controllers, bringing the total up to four. You can plug IDE hard disks and IDE CD-ROM drives into an IDE controller, but once you've hit the limit, that's it. See the next section, "SCSI controllers," for a comparison.

SCSI controllers

SCSI adapters can be used with any SCSI devices, including hard disks, CD-ROM drives, scanners, tape drives, removable cartridge drives, optical drives, and CD recorders. There are several varieties of SCSI, including SCSI-1, SCSI-2, Fast SCSI-2, SCSI-3, Ultra-SCSI, Wide-SCSI, and Ultra-Wide SCSI. For most users, SCSI-2 is sufficient, but you should check the requirements of all of the devices you intend to use with it to see what you'll need.

A good SCSI controller will have its own BIOS, so you can boot off a SCSI hard disk. Look for a Plug-and-Play PCI SCSI adapter for best performance. Controllers with bus-mastering offer better performance than those without, as well as being less of a burden on the rest of the system while in use. It's very important to get a solid brand-name SCSI controller to ensure compatibility with any SCSI devices you intend to use, as well as to make obtaining the latest drivers for any version of Windows easy.

The two most common devices used with a SCSI controller are hard disks and CD-ROM drives. Since these two drives are also available as IDE (see the previous section "Hard disk controllers"), there's usually a choice to be made between the two technologies when purchasing the drives. Since you can mix and match devices (you can have an IDE CD-ROM drive and a SCSI hard disk, or vice versa), you'll never be entirely committed to your decision. The primary advantage to IDE is that IDE controllers are cheap, and IDE devices are usually less expensive than their SCSI counterparts. SCSI devices, especially Ultra-Wide SCSI, offer better performance than IDE devices, and the higher-end SCSI controllers don't burden the system as IDE controllers can. While most IDE controllers support only two devices, SCSI adapters support up to seven. SCSI is flexible, supporting many different kinds of devices, while IDE controllers support only hard disks, CD-ROM drives, and some tape and Zip drives. A SCSI device can be internal (mounted inside your computer), or external (in its own case, connected with a cable to your computer). IDE devices can only be internal.

If you don't plan on using other SCSI devices, such as a scanner or CD recorder, you probably don't need to spend the extra money for a SCSI controller. But, those who want the performance and slickness of SCSI won't find a better alternative. Refer to the previous section, "Hard disk controllers," and the next section, "CD drives," for more details.

CD drives

A CD drive should do two things well. It should be fast, and it should recognize all of the different types of CDs you want to use: CD-ROMs, multisession CDs, recordable CDs, Audio-CDs, PhotoCDs, and Multi-mode CDs containing both data and music.

The speed of a CD drive is measured by how much faster it is than a normal audio-CD player; an eight-speed drive is eight times faster. The two numbers to look for in your CD drive are access time and transfer rate. The access time, measured in milliseconds, is the average length of time required to find information, and the transfer rate, measured in kilobytes per second, is the speed at which the drive can transfer data to your system. CD-ROM drives are much slower than hard disks, so access times will be in the range of 120ms to 300ms, as opposed to 8ms to 14ms for hard disks—look for an access time of 200ms or smaller. The transfer rate is about 150 kilobytes per second times the speed of the drive; an eight-speed CD drive should have a transfer rate of about 1.2MB per second. Lower access times and higher transfer rates are better.

The brand of CD drive you purchase isn't that important; Windows should support nearly anything you throw at it. In fact, CD drives are getting to be as common as floppy drives, so as long as the drive is fast and supports all of the different types of CDs, it should be all right; the more expensive drives aren't necessarily any better than the cheap ones. (They may, however, be sturdier or better-looking.) The only choices worth mentioning are the loading mechanism, and whether the drive is IDE or SCSI.

There are three types of loading mechanisms: motorized tray, caddy, and slot. The caddy is a plastic cartridge that holds the CD, and helps keep dust out of the drive and away from the CD. Drives with motorized trays are less expensive, more common, and don't require caddies—just place the CD on a tray that extends out of the drive, and close it. The problem with motorized trays is that nearly all of them are very flimsy and easily breakable; look for a sturdy drive, if nothing else. The third, less common variety is the slot drive, named for the fact that you simply insert the CD into a slot; no caddies and no flimsy trays. These types of drives are far superior, but hard to find. CD changers often use this type of loading mechanism.

The choice between IDE and SCSI is the same as for hard disks, discussed previously. If you're seriously considering either technology, refer to the previous discussions of the respective controllers.

Modems

A modem allows your computer to communicate with other computers over standard telephone lines. Modems need to support dozens of different protocols, or languages, but nearly all modems available today support all the protocols you'll need. The primary considerations are speed and price. Faster modems are more expensive, but since many online services, including the phone company, charge you for connect time, you shouldn't skimp here. Don't settle for less than 33,600bps; some modems go up to 56K, but aren't widely supported, and in the real world, aren't all that much faster than their 33,600bps predecessors. Look for a brand name, as you want to be sure not only that your software supports the modem, but that it will be supported in the future.

ISDN adapters, while technically not modems, basically perform the same task. If you are able to get an ISDN phone line into your home or office and can afford the extra expense of the adapter and service, this will offer much better performance than any modem.

Before investing in a new modem, do some research into the various alternatives available in your area. DSL, cable modems, and wireless services are all much faster than telephone-based Internet access and not much more expensive. The advantage to standard modems is that they can be used almost anywhere.

Sound cards

A good sound card is Sound Blaster compatible; it's that simple. Look for lots of features, however, such as 16-bit sound, wavetable, a CD-ROM connector (so you don't need another controller), 32-voices, Plug-and-Play support, and a MIDI connector. Some sound cards support 3D sound, although the benefits of this feature aren't readily apparent. Don't bother getting the CD connectors available with some sound cards; they're likely to cause more trouble (in the form of hardware conflicts) than they're worth.

Get yourself a fairly good set of speakers (cheap ones are often flimsy and sound very tinny), but don't spend too much; your computer isn't able to produce sound of high enough quality to take advantage of any speakers costing over $100.

Network cards

The most important feature of a network card is compatibility. Make sure the card you choose is able to communicate with the rest of your network and comes with drivers for your version of Windows. Buying a name brand will help ensure that you'll always be able to find drivers. Look for a Plug-and-Play, PCI network card.

The type of network card you get usually depends on the kind of network to which you're connecting. For example, if you have a 10baseT network, you must get a network card that has a 10baseT connector (the most common). However, if you're using the older 10base2 connectors (coaxial cable), your best bet is to get a "combo" card which supports both. That way, you can upgrade later on.

If you're considering a new network, 10baseT is generally better than 10base2, although 10baseT requires a hub if you want to connect more than two computers. To connect only two computers with 10baseT, get a category-5 crossover cable rather than a standard category-5 patch cable.

See Chapter 7 for more information on setting up a local network.

Printers

There's such a wide range of printers available, it's impossible to cover all of the choices. The decision is usually based upon your budget and your needs. Get a solid brand-name printer; a good printer should be a workhorse, lasting for years. The choice most people make is usually between inkjet and laser printers. Simply put, laser printers are more expensive, faster, and have better print quality than inkjet printers. Inkjet printers are less expensive, take up less space, yet often print color.

A laser printer should have a resolution of at least 600 dots per inch (dpi) and should print at least six pages per minute; some printers print up to 16 pages per minute and support resolutions of up to 1200 dpi. Check the price of a new toner cartridge for each printer you're considering, since this can be an expensive maintenance consideration.

Inkjet printers are also available in 600 dpi, and commonly print 3–5 pages per minute, or 1–2 pages per minute for color. Some printers advertise higher resolutions than 600 dpi, but those figures aren't very realistic. Get one that supports color, even if you don't think you'll need it. If you do get a color printer, make sure it has at least two cartridges; one for black printing, and one for color. Some older color printers require you to swap cartridges whether you're printing black text or color, meaning that you can't do both at the same time.

If you plan to use a printer over a network, make sure the one you get is networkable. This doesn't necessarily mean that it can connect directly to your network (although some can with a print server expansion card), but rather that its drivers support being used from any computer on the network to which the printer is connected.

Mice

Cheap mice are usually alright, but don't last long. Try lots of different kinds in the store, and choose one that's sturdy, comfortable, and not too ugly. Make sure the ball is placed under your fingers instead of under your palm for greater control. It should have a long cord and a plug with thumb screws so you don't need a screwdriver.

Most mice have two buttons, and some have three. Windows uses only two, but a third button can be programmed to take over other operations, such as double-clicking or pasting text. Three buttons isn't necessarily better than two, however—just different.

Personally, I hate mice. I use a pressure sensitive, cordless, battery-less stylus, or pen, which draws on a tablet. The pen is more comfortable, more precise, more natural, more fun, and more flexible than any mouse. My advice: try a tablet before you invest in another rodent.

Other alternatives to consider include trackballs, touch-pads, and track-points, like the ones that come with newer laptop computers. These often take up less desk space, require less movement of your hands (which can reduce hand fatigue), and don't require cleaning.

Before subscribing to the mouse mantra, do a little footwork and see if you can find something you like better.

Keyboards

Get yourself a solid keyboard; the brand doesn't matter (although, in my opinion, IBM still makes the best keyboards). Just make sure it has a nice long cord and isn't too hideous. Too many keyboards are flimsy and cheap. Shop around to find one with a solid feel and good quality keys; your fingers will thank you. Some people like soft-touch (mushy) keyboards, while others like tactile (clicky) keyboards; get one that suits your taste and won't hinder your work.

Compact keyboards not only take up less disk space but require less movement of your hands, which can reduce hand fatigue. Larger keyboards usually feel more solid, though, and may be more comfortable for those with larger hands.

True ergonomic keyboards are now getting more affordable and more popular. Some of the more radical designs have split, adjustable keyboards, curved to fit the motion and shape of your hands. Try these before buying, as they aren't for everyone.

Carefully scrutinize the so-called "Natural" keyboards from Microsoft and other manufacturers, which mimic the more carefully designed, higher-quality ergonomic keyboards. These devices usually aren't any better for your hands than standard flat keyboards, and can actually do more damage than good. If you're worried about hand injury, see a doctor.

Lastly, some keyboards have a few extra keys made especially for Windows, providing quick access to the Start Menu and other things. Don't spend any extra money for this type of keyboard, but some people like the convenience.

Look into some type of wrist or arm supports, too. I like those soft, gel-filled wrist rests, but if you're susceptible to wrist pain, it's better not to put pressure on them with any kind of wrist rest. Look for a chair with adjustable armrests, or even the free-moving forearm supports that clamp to your desk.

Lastly, question hand entry altogether. Companies like Dragon Systems and IBM have released what they call "natural-speech" dictation systems, which allow you to speak comfortably into a microphone and dictate as you would to a secretary. These can be quite effective, but they aren't for everyone.

Tape drives, removable cartridge drives, and CD recorders

These types of drives allow you to store a lot of data on special media. However, each system has its own set of advantages and disadvantages, and its own intended purpose.

For backing up your system in the case of an emergency, you'll be hard-pressed to beat a tape drive. Their reliability, speed, low media cost, and backup software make them ideal backup devices.

CD recorders are becoming very attractive solutions for archiving data as well as for sharing data with others. Blank CDs are extremely cheap, costing only one or two dollars per 650-megabyte disk, and are compact and extremely reliable. The best part is that almost anyone will be able to read the disks, which means you won't have to spend the money on a second drive.

Some CD writers also support rewritable CDs (CD-RW), which can be erased and rerecorded repeatedly. While these disks are convenient, they have both advantages and drawbacks. They're quite effective when used in conjunction with packet-writing software (like Adaptec's DirectCD), which allows you to write to a CD as though it were just another drive in Explorer (no "mastering" software required). The fact that they're rewritable means that you can turn a CD-RW drive into a 600MB removable cartridge drive. The downside is that the disks can't be read in most normal CD readers, and cost around $25 each; compared with normal CD-ROMs costing not much more than floppies, CD-RW may not be such a great deal.

For repeatedly transferring large quantities of data from one place to another, though, removable hard disks are the answer. Syquest and IOmega both make removable hard-disk drives that store a gigabyte or more on each cartridge. The cartridges are much more expensive than either blank CDs or tapes, but they're very fast, fairly reliable, and require no special backup software to use, since they show up as another drive letter in Explorer. In many cases, it's much faster to transfer extremely large files with a removable cartridge drive than with an Ethernet network connection.

See "Preventative Maintenance and Data Recovery" in Chapter 6 for a comparison of different types of backup devices.

Also, research the cost of the *cartridges* before investing in a particular technology. A drive that seems like a good deal in the store may turn out to be a money pit when you take into account the expensive media. Try comparing your cost to store, say, one gigabyte (which isn't as much as it sounds) using each type of drive, including both the cost of the drive and the cost of the media. Other things to consider include speed, reliability, and availability of the media. Don't forget portability—how likely is it that others will be able to read these cartridges?

6

Troubleshooting

In this chapter:
- *General Troubleshooting Techniques*
- *Error Messages*
- *Preventative Maintenance and Data Recovery*
- *Hardware Configuration*
- *DOS to the Rescue*

Often it's the entire Windows experience, rather than just Windows itself, that can really drive you nuts. In fact, Windows 98 goes farther than any previous version to help solve and even prevent problems, although it tends to cause many of the problems it alleviates.

Due to the sheer number of components that make up a modern computer system, it can be difficult to isolate the cause of a given problem. Hardware conflicts, buggy drivers, and poorly written software all contribute to any number of different problems. You may be experiencing frequent lock-ups, error messages, malfunctioning hardware, or data loss. These problems can be distilled into two basic forms: hardware or software malfunctions, and data loss due to these malfunctions.

While it's possible and even fun to blame Windows, it's not always productive. To deal with malfunctioning hardware or software, you need to first isolate the problem, and then take steps to solve whatever trouble you've uncovered. Unfortunately, isolating the problem is often the hardest part; a computer is a system of hundreds of different components all working together, and the symptoms aren't always obviously related to the problem.

Most hardware and software problems are caused by incompatibilities or conflicts, where two or more components don't work together—even though each may work perfectly well on its own. Faulty or out-of-date drivers frequently cause hardware problems, while incompatible *.dll*s can cause a myriad of software troubles. For example, one of the most common difficulties is trying to get a modem to work with a newly installed motherboard. The obvious tactics are to blame the modem or computer manufacturer, but there may be a conflict with the way the mouse port is configured in the system BIOS. If you don't know how to use the diagnostic components in Windows, finding problems like these can be ridiculously difficult.

While most Windows users will agree that these types of problems are annoying, nothing compares to trying to convince a technical support representative that the problem you're experiencing is *not* someone else's fault. Since most problems (even those that are hard to isolate) are easily fixed, it's always a good idea to do a little investigating before packaging the problem item up and bringing it back to the mega-super store where it was purchased.

On the other end of the spectrum is data loss, which I think is nicely summed up by the following haiku:

> Your file is missing?
> It might've been important,
> But now it is gone.

Coping with data loss requires two strategies: preventative maintenance and data recovery. Assuming you've isolated and solved the source of the data loss (usually one of the problems discussed above), there are several methods you can employ to make sure your work is safe, and to recover it when it isn't.

Regardless of the type of problem, there's no substitute for a full system backup. Even if your computer equipment is insured with Lloyds of London, once your data is gone, it's gone.

General Troubleshooting Techniques

Just a few words of advice before we begin: if it ain't broke, don't fix it. Many problems are actually caused by people looking for problems to solve. For example, installing a new device driver just for the sake of having the newest drivers on your system may introduce new incompatibilities. While the material presented here is intended to aid in general troubleshooting and data recovery, some of the solutions can cause other problems, so it is strongly recommended that you back up your entire hard disk before continuing.

Drivers and Installing Hardware

A driver is a piece of software that allows your computer to communicate with the various devices attached to it. For example, your printer has a driver that contains all the capabilities of your printer, such as paper sizes and print resolution. The beauty of this design is that an application like your word processor can simply send your document to Windows with the instruction "print," and Windows will take care of the rest. This way, each application doesn't need to know anything specific about your printer, or, for that matter, the specifics of any of your hardware.

Problems arise when a driver is either defective or outdated. Drivers designed either for a previous version of Windows or for a previous version of the device can create problems. Additionally, manufacturers must continually update their drivers to fix incompatibilities and bugs that emerge after the product is released. It's usually a good idea to make sure you have the latest drivers installed in your system when troubleshooting a problem. Newer drivers usually offer improved performance, added features and settings, better stability and reliability, and better compatibility with other drivers in your system.

Also, be aware that some drivers may not be the correct ones for your system. For example, when Windows is installed, it may incorrectly identify your video card or monitor and hence install the wrong driver, or even a *generic* driver. A common symptom for this is Windows not allowing you to display as many colors or use as high a resolution as the card supports. Make sure that Device Manager lists the actual devices you have installed on your system (double-click on the **System** icon in Control Panel, and click the **Device Manager** tab).

Device drivers worth investigating include those for your video card, monitor, sound card, modem, printer, network adapter, scanner, SCSI controller, tape drive, and any other drives or cards you may have. If you're not sure of the exact manufacturer or model number of a device, take off the cover of your computer and look, or refer to the invoice or documentation that came with your system. Most hard disks, floppy drives, CD drives, keyboards, mice, power supplies, memory, and CPU chips don't need special drivers (except in special circumstances).

Windows 98 comes with a significant number of drivers for hardware available at the time of its release, but as time passes, more third-party devices will require their own drivers.

It's possible to find out if Windows comes with a driver for a specific piece of hardware before you even install it. Double-click on the **Add New Hardware** icon in Control Panel. Click **Next**, and then **Next** again. Windows will take a few seconds (you won't see a progress bar here) to poll all of your Plug-and-Play devices. You'll then be given the option of having Windows search for your new hardware; since we're only looking for a driver, choose **No** and then click **Next**. Choose the type of hardware from the list shown that most closely matches what you're looking for, then click **Next** to display a list of manufacturers and their products (see Figure 6-1).

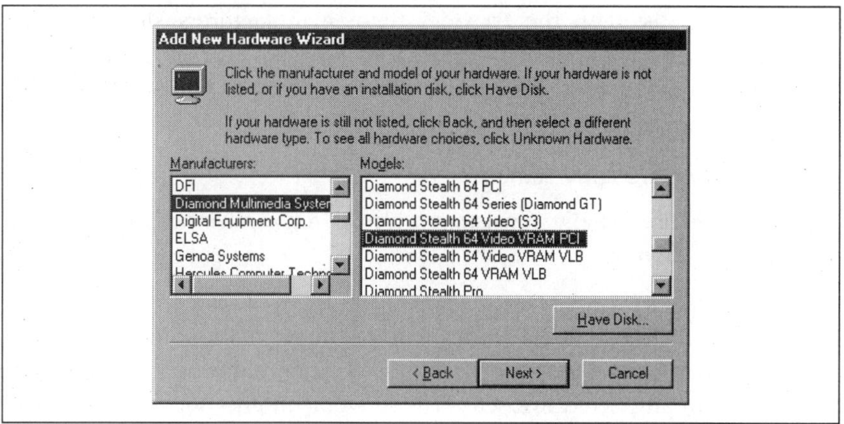

Figure 6-1: List the devices supported by Windows by using the Add New Hardware wizard

If you actually want to go ahead and install the device, or if the device is already physically installed in your computer, it's better to choose **Yes** to have Windows automatically search for the device. It may seem to take longer, but it's more reliable, since Windows will automatically detect the particular configuration settings as well (otherwise you have to configure them). The downside is that you don't get the list shown above.

Note that not all devices need to be installed in this way. Many devices, such as hard disks and CD drives, are automatically detected and configured when Windows starts; you should see their icons in the My Computer window without any fuss. Some other devices are detected by Windows during startup, but require that you answer a series of questions and sometimes insert a driver disk before you can use them. It all depends on the type of device and how well (if at all) the manufacturer has followed the Plug-and-Play specification. If you're in doubt, consult the documentation to see what the manufacturer recommends.

On the other hand, if a device is already installed and the driver has already been chosen, there are two ways to figure out if the correct driver is being used. First of all, the name used to identify the device in Device Manager is a good clue. For example, if, under the Display Adapter category, your video card is listed as a *Diamond Viper V330*, then that's the driver that's being used, even if that's not really the video card you're using.

However, there's more to the driver than just the name; to find the date and revision number of the driver, double-click on the device in Device Manager and choose the **Driver** tab. While Windows does come with plenty of drivers, very few of them are actually written by Microsoft even if Microsoft is listed in the **Provider** field; manufacturers simply submit their drivers for inclusion in the package. You can usually assume three things about the drivers included on the Windows CD versus those that come with your devices:

- The drivers are fairly stable.
- The dates are usually consistent with the release history of the manufacturer's drivers.
- Any special features or extras present in the manufacturer's version of the drivers have been left out. For example, many after-market display drivers include support for more colors, higher resolutions, hotkeys, panning windows, etc. The drivers on the Windows CD will usually not have any of these.

An easy but not foolproof way to tell if you're using the driver that came with Windows is to look at the driver date—it should be 5-11-98, if you're using the initial release of Windows 98. If the date is different, the driver probably came from another source, such as a driver disk, the Web, or a previous installation of Windows. Drivers with newer dates are usually—but not always—more recent. (Note that the **Driver File Details** button rarely has any useful information.) If you're trying to solve a problem, or take better advantage of your hardware, your best bet is to visit the home page of the device's manufacturer and download their latest and greatest driver.

To change the driver for the selected device, either by installing a newer version or by replacing it with a driver for a different device, click **Update Driver.*** You'll then see yet another wizard that allows you to show Windows where to get the new driver. Click **Next**, select **Display a list of all the drivers**, and click **Next** again. You can also use the **Search for a better driver** option, although it's usually more of a pain to do it this way.

At this stage, you'll see a list of "Compatible Hardware," which usually consists of the one currently installed driver. Any additional drivers listed

* Note that some drivers have their own installation programs, while other drivers must be installed when the corresponding device is automatically detected at Windows startup. If the driver has no install program, and you aren't asked to locate the driver when you first start Windows, you can almost always update the driver in this way. If in doubt, check the driver's documentation (usually in a *readme.txt* file). Not many manufacturers follow the standards closely, which can be very frustrating.

here are those that Windows identifies as supporting the *same device* as the currently installed driver; if the currently installed driver is wrong, the other items in this list may also be wrong. Click **Show all hardware** to view all the devices in the current category; you'll see a window similar to Figure 6-1. Note that you can't change the category of the device; if it's a video card, you can't choose a driver for a SCSI adapter.

Even if your device is listed, your manufacturer may have a newer driver.* The nice thing about the **Show all hardware** window is that it shows all the installed drivers along with their dates. If you install a third-party driver, and then return to this window, you'll see the new driver alongside the driver that comes with Windows (if applicable).

You can also click **Have Disk** at this point to browse your hard disk for another driver. A common scenario involves downloading a zipped driver from the Web, unzipping it to a directory (see Appendix E, *Interface Terminology and the Basics*), and then using this dialog to instruct Windows to load the driver. Windows will accept any folder containing a valid driver, which is detected by the presence of an *.inf* file. Actually, all the drivers already installed on your system have a corresponding *.inf* file in the *\Windows\INF* folder. It's possible, however, that an installed driver won't show up in the Driver List window; in this case, you can sometimes use **Have Disk** and point Windows to the *\Windows\INF* folder to select the right driver.

The *.inf* file is the heart of each Windows driver. Sometimes it contains all the necessary device information; for example, most modems require only this single file. At other times, the *.inf* file contains information and links to *.dll* and *.vxd* files, which do the actual work of the driver. Unfortunately, each device is different—don't expect a set of tricks that worked for one driver to necessarily work on another driver.

The evolution of drivers

It's important that any drivers you use with Windows 98 be designed *especially* for the Windows 95/98 platform. Using drivers made for older versions of Windows or DOS may cause problems ranging from poor performance to crashes to the device not working at all. Newer 32-bit drivers offer much better performance and stability, as well as extra features like support for Plug-and-Play, and compatibility with other devices in your system.

* Nearly all companies today make all their drivers freely available for download—don't let a company charge you for something that other companies offer their customers for free. Refer to the instructions that come with the new drivers for the particular installation procedure.

The Win32 driver model, a specification introduced in Windows 98, is a new type of driver that is compatible with both Windows 98 and Windows NT 5.0. This type of driver is always preferable but is often (at the time of this writing) not available. Some manufacturers might even have both standard 32-bit drivers (for Win95 and Win98) and Win32 drivers (for Win98 and NT 5 only). Ideally, all drivers should offer the same functionality, stability, and performance, but more than likely, there will be a tradeoff somewhere along the way. You might even consider installing and trying out all driver varieties for your device so that you can be sure to have the best one.

If a new, 32-bit driver isn't yet available, you should be able to use an older Windows driver (designed for Windows 3.x), although this isn't recommended if you can avoid it. If you are loading DOS drivers in your *Config.sys* or *Autoexec.bat* files, you may be preventing Windows from installing proper 32-bit drivers—see "Do I Still Need Config.sys and Autoexec.bat?" later in this chapter for more information.

Some users may be disappointed to discover that a manufacturer of a discontinued product has stopped supporting the product, or that the company has gone out of business. If this happens, you may be out of luck and forced to replace the device if it isn't supported in your version of Windows; see Chapter 5, *Maximizing Performance*, for more information on upgrading your system. There is a way out, however. Many products, such as video cards, modems, and SCSI controllers, use similar components that are widely supported by the industry. For example, many varieties of S3's video card chips are used commonly in video cards today. By looking at your video card, you should be able to determine which variety of *chipset* it uses: look for the brand and model number. Even if the manufacturer of your video card has gone out of business, there may be other video cards that use the same chipset, and therefore may use the same driver.

Misbehaving drivers

Never install more than one new driver at a time. By upgrading one driver at a time, you can easily isolate any potential new problems and recognize when an existing problem has been solved. Wait for Windows to restart and try starting a program or two. If you install several new drivers at once, you'll have a hell of a time trying to find where you went wrong.

When you install a driver, Windows first copies the various driver files to as many as five different folders. Then the Registry is configured with the driver filenames, the specific resources used by the device (IRQs, I/O addresses, etc., all of which are discussed later in this chapter), and any special settings. A common problem is that the special settings can be incorrect, and no amount of fiddling with them can straighten out a misbehaving device.

This often happens with network cards and SCSI adapters, where the device doesn't function at all, or Windows doesn't recognize the device's resources correctly, or an attempt to use the device hangs the system. The solution is simply to reinstall the driver. The best way to go about this is to locate and select the device in Device Manager and click **Remove**, then close Device Manager and restart your computer. During Windows startup, you should then see a message to the effect that Windows is installing a new device, at which time it may ask for the driver disk. You can either point it to the appropriate location, such as your floppy drive or a folder on your desktop, or point it to your *Windows\System* folder, which forces it to use the old drivers. Windows then reinitializes the device and resets all its special settings, which, in many cases, will solve the problem.

More drastic measures include removing all the actual driver files from the hard disk before allowing Windows to install new ones. Since all drivers are different, there are no standard files to remove. Conscientious developers provide an uninstall utility for their drivers, or at least a list of the supported files so you can find them easily. If in doubt, contact tech support and ask them how to *completely* remove their driver.

My last piece of advice is to copy the latest drivers for all of your devices onto floppy disks for easy access the next time you need them. You'll be glad you did this when you realize that you can't download the right driver for your modem if your modem has stopped working.

Resolving Conflicts and Other General Problems

The most common type of hardware problem is a *conflict.* A conflict occurs when two devices try to use the same resource, such as an interrupt request line (IRQ) or memory address. The telltale signs of a conflict include one or more devices not working, one or more devices not showing up in Device Manager, or your system crashing every time one or more devices is used. The first step in diagnosing a conflict is to check the drivers (see "Drivers and Installing Hardware" earlier in this chapter).

Each installed device can use one, several, or even no resources. Usually, an expansion card, such as a sound card or modem, uses a single IRQ, a single I/O address range, and sometimes a direct memory access (DMA) address. Other devices can consume more than one of these resources, as well as other resources: memory addresses, SCSI IDs, IDE channels, and serial and parallel ports.

If two or more devices try to use the same resource, problems ranging from slow performance to system crashes can occur. Most older devices (called *legacy* devices) allow you to configure which resources they use by setting appropriate jumpers or switches on the devices themselves. Newer devices allow their settings to be changed with software. The newest Plug-and-Play products work with your Plug-and-Play BIOS to automatically configure themselves to work with other Plug-and-Play and legacy devices, theoretically avoiding all conflicts.

Note that some devices that connect to your computer's external ports, such as printers, don't technically use any resources of their own; however, the port to which they're connected does use resources. You can usually change the resources used by any given device (ports included). The trick is to configure all your devices to use different resources so that no conflicts occur. All devices are different; refer to the documentation included with the device, or contact the manufacturer for specific configuration instructions.

To determine which resources are still available in your system, as well as which devices are using the remaining resources, open the Device Manager by double-clicking on the **System** icon in Control Panel and choosing the **Device Manager** tab. Select **Computer** from the top of the list, and click **Properties** to display the Computer Properties dialog, as shown in Figure 6-2.

By choosing any of the four types of resources (IRQ, I/O, DMA, or Memory), you'll see how each is used by the various devices in your system. Any gaps in the numbers represent available system resources, which you should be able to assign to new devices. Most resource conflicts are shown here as well: if you see two cards assigned to IRQ 10, it's a safe bet that that's part of the problem.

Be aware that some devices *can* share resources. For example, your communication ports share IRQs (COM1 and COM3 both use IRQ 4, and COM2 and COM4 both use IRQ 3). Sometimes this is benign, such as having a mouse on COM1 and another pointing device (such as a graphics tablet) on COM3. However, most modems will complain (system hangs, slow performance, and other malfunctions) if they share resources with any other devices. If you have three or more devices connected to COM ports, you may have to either juggle them around or install configurable COM ports that can be configured more flexibly.

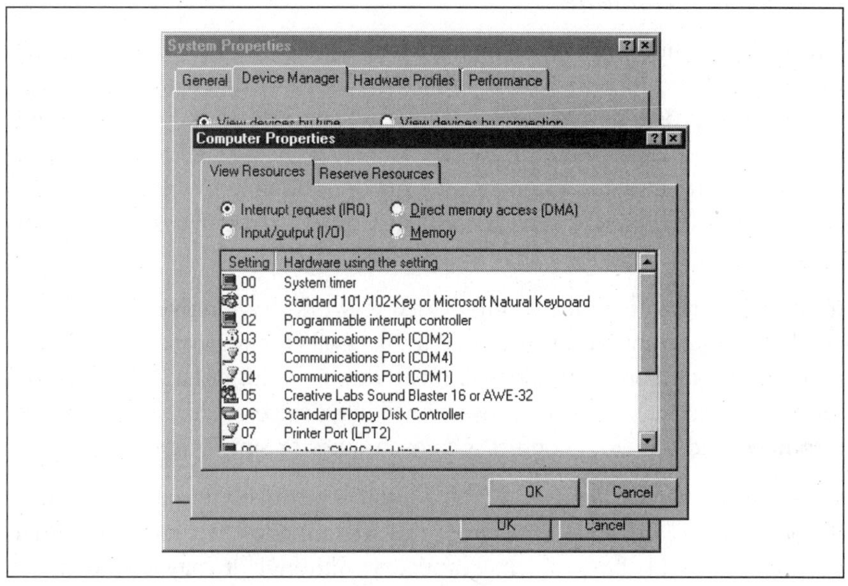

Figure 6-2: You can determine which resources are being used by looking at the Computer Properties in Windows's Device Manager

If you find some other type of conflict, start by either removing or reconfiguring one of the devices involved. You may be required to reconfigure several devices, literally shuffling resources around until all the conflicts are resolved. Again, the method used to change the resources used by a particular device depends upon the device itself. You should be able to see all the resources used by a given device by selecting it in Device Manager, clicking **Properties**, and choosing the **Resources** tab.

Note that the information presented in Device Manager may not necessarily reflect the current state of your system. If your computer was made before about the middle of 1995 and doesn't support Plug-and-Play entirely (or at all), you may have devices installed that don't show up, as well as devices displayed that aren't actually installed. The **Refresh** button is used to reread the devices in your system, but it won't detect anything more than is normally seen when Windows starts. **Refresh** is used primarily to detect devices attached to or disconnected from your system after Windows has started without having to restart. To force Windows to re-detect the hardware attached to your computer, use the **Add New Hardware** icon in Control Panel, and confirm that you want it to search for new hardware when asked.

Installing new hardware

If you're installing more than one device, do so one at a time; it's much easier to isolate problems when you know which device has caused them. You should expect installation of Plug-and-Play devices to be quick, automatic, and painless, at least in theory. However, many devices, while able to configure themselves automatically, may not be able to adapt entirely to your system. Be prepared to reconfigure or even remove some of your existing devices to make room for new ones.

If you're trying to get an existing device to work, try removing one of the conflicting pieces of hardware to see if the conflict is resolved. Just because two devices are conflicting doesn't mean that they are at fault. It's possible for a third, errant device to cause two other devices to occupy improper resources, and therefore conflict with each other or simply not function.

If removing a device solves a problem, you've probably found the conflict. If not, try removing all devices from the system, and then reconnect them one by one until the problem reappears. Although it may sound like a pain in the neck to remove all the devices from your system, it really is the easiest and most sure-fire way to find the cause of a conflict. Since there are so many different combinations of resource settings, it can be a laborious task to resolve conflicts. Some devices come with special software designed for this task; the software can either advise you of proper settings, or in some cases, even make the changes for you. Make sure to review the documentation for any mention of such a utility.

Firmware

User-upgradable firmware is a feature found in many new devices. Firmware is software stored in the device itself, and is used to control most hardware functions. While it's not possible to, say, increase a hard disk's capacity by upgrading its firmware, it is possible to improve performance slightly, as well as to solve any compatibility problems that may have been discovered after the product shipped.

The beauty of firmware is that if you purchase a peripheral, and the manufacturer subsequently improves the product, you can simply update the firmware to upgrade the product. While user-upgradable firmware can increase the initial cost of a product slightly, such an increase is dramatically outweighed by the money the manufacturer can save by not having users send in equipment to be updated. Naturally, user-upgradable firmware is also a boon to the end user, who can make simple updates in a matter of minutes, without having to send in the product or even open up the computer.

To find out the firmware version for a particular device, select the device in Device Manager, click **Properties**, choose the **Settings** tab if it's present, and look at the **Firmware Revision** field. If you're experiencing problems with a certain device, check with the manufacturer of the product for a newer firmware revision. In many cases, you'll be able to download a simple software "patch" that will update the firmware to the newest version, possibly fixing problems and even adding new features.

Devices that commonly have user-upgradable firmware include modems, CD drives, CD recorders, removable drives, removable and tape drives, motherboards (in the form of an upgradable BIOS), SCSI controllers, and network adapters, hubs, and routers.

Some older devices allow you to change the firmware by upgrading a chip. It's not as convenient as software-upgradable firmware, but it's better than nothing.

Plug-and-Play

Most new internal peripherals, such as cards and drives, and some external devices, such as printers and scanners, will be automatically detected when Windows boots up. Ideally, Windows should notify you that the new device has been identified, and give you the option of using the driver that comes with Windows, if available, or providing the driver on your own, either with a diskette or a folder on your hard disk. Windows should then load the driver, configure the device, and restart with no ill effects.

Problems arise when the new device either doesn't work or causes something else to stop working. Even the newest Plug-and-Play devices can sometimes cause conflicts, although with the passage of time, the PnP compliance of most new devices has generally improved. To aide in troubleshooting conflicts where PnP devices are involved, it's important to first realize exactly what Plug-and-Play technology is. PnP-compliant devices must have the following characteristics:

- The device must have a "signature" that is returned when Windows asks for it. Windows then looks up this signature in its driver database, and either finds a driver that matches it or asks you to insert a disk with a compatible driver. If a compatible driver is not found, no driver will be loaded for the device.
- All configurable resources of the device must be software-adjustable; that is, it is not necessary to physically set jumpers or switches on the hardware to reconfigure it. This doesn't mean, however, that the

device can't come with jumpers; some cards let you disable their Plug-and-Play features and set resources manually, a very handy feature.

- The driver, if supplied, must be capable of instructing Windows which resources the device can occupy, and must be able to receive instructions from Windows and reconfigure the card accordingly. That way, Windows can read all the possible configurations from all the drivers, and then reconfigure each one so that there are no conflicts.

You can see, then, how dependent PnP devices are on their drivers, and why a buggy driver can cause problems with the entire system. One common bug in some drivers is that they are unable to reliably configure the corresponding device. For example, say a sound card can occupy IRQs 5, 7, 9, 10, and 11, but the driver is incorrectly programmed to also accept IRQ 13. When Windows attempts to shuffle all the devices around, it may then ask the sound card to occupy IRQ 13; since this is impossible, it will remain at its previous setting (or at no setting at all), and most likely cause a conflict with another device, say, a modem or parallel port. In this scenario, a tiny bug in a single driver has caused two separate devices to stop functioning.

Now, it's also possible that Windows will be *unable* to find a mutually agreeable configuration for all installed devices—even if one does exist—which means that Windows will simply boot with one or more conflicts. In most cases, Windows won't even tell you that PnP has failed. This is where you have to take matters into your own hands: learn to recognize the symptoms, which include crashing, hanging, and slow performance, and know how to look for conflicts. See the beginning of this section for details.

One of the loopholes that you can take advantage of is the way that Plug-and-Play systems assign resources, particularly IRQs, to PCI devices. Your BIOS will assign a different IRQ to each *slot*, rather than having each device try to grab an IRQ for its own; this ensures that PCI cards don't conflict. The funny thing about PnP BIOSes and Windows 98 is that sometimes some IRQs are neglected. If you have a full system and find yourself running out of IRQs, this can be a real problem. The good news is that you can enter your system's BIOS setup (see the next section) and manually assign an IRQ to each slot, often even specifying previously ignored IRQs, such as IRQ 12, 14, and 15.* This will then leave spaces open

* Note that IRQs 12, 14, and 15 aren't always available, and sometimes can be occupied by other motherboard components or non-PCI devices. In most cases, trial and error is the best approach to take.

(usually lower IRQs), which other devices in your system can then occupy.

Finally, a common problem with Plug-and-Play is its propensity to detect devices that have been already configured. For example, after you've hooked up a printer, installed the drivers, and even used it successfully, Windows may inform you the next time you boot that it has detected a newly attached device, namely, your printer. This is almost always caused by an incorrect initial installation; for example, you may have connected your printer after Windows had started. The best course of action is to remove the drivers for the device (usually through Device Manager), reboot, and allow Windows to detect and setup the printer automatically. Naturally, you should check the printer's documentation for any abnormalities of the installation process.

Windows won't start

An all too common problem is that Windows simply won't start. This is an extremely broad problem, usually occurring without an error message or any obvious way to resolve it. Most of the many causes of this problem deal with hardware drivers, conflicts, or file corruption, all of which are discussed elsewhere in this chapter.

However, one solution that is fairly easy to implement is the following, which deals specifically with file corruption. Often by simply deleting your swap file and temporary files, you can allow Windows to load without incident.

Don't do this if you suspect that your hard disk has crashed, since it may make matters worse. See "Disk crash" in "Preventative Maintenance and Data Recovery" later in this chapter for more information. If you're worried about deleting potentially valuable temporary files that may contain data from previously open documents, try skipping step 4.

1. If you find that Windows either doesn't complete its startup process, or does something weird like rebooting before it's finished loading, restart your computer by pressing the **Reset** button or the **Ctrl-Alt-Del** keys. Then press the **F8** key immediately after the beep and the small message in black-and-white, "Starting Windows 98," appears.
2. You'll then see the Windows startup menu, as described in "Create a Startup Menu" later in this chapter. Press **Shift-F5** at this point to exit to the command prompt.

3. The Windows 98 swap file (*Win386.swp*) is usually located in your *Windows* directory, although your system may be different. Change to your Windows directory using the `CD` command (usually `cd \windows`), and then type the following:

```
attrib -r -s -h win386.swp
del win386.swp
```

4. Then change to your temp directory using the CD command (usually `cd \windows\temp`) and type the following:

```
attrib -r -h *.tmp
del *.tmp
```

5. The last step is to run Scandisk by typing `scandisk` at the prompt.
6. When Scandisk is finished, restart your computer, and allow Windows to boot normally. If you see the Windows startup menu, make sure to choose the first option, **1. Normal**, and then be patient as Windows loads.

Fixing Device-Specific Problems

For most components in the system, the number one rule for getting things to work is to make sure you have the latest and correct driver from the manufacturer, although this isn't always as easy as one would like. In many circumstances, obtaining the correct driver may be impossible, or simply not applicable. The next step in getting most hardware to work in Windows is to eliminate any hardware conflicts, which is discussed in "Resolving Conflicts and Other General Problems" earlier in this chapter.

But more often than not, problems are unique to a particular type of component. For example, modems often suffer the same types of problems, which don't necessarily affect any other types of hardware. The following guidelines should help you solve most component-specific problems, as opposed to general lockups or application error messages.

And don't forget that a nonfunctioning component can be a great excuse for an upgrade (see Chapter 5).

Video cards (also known as display adapters)

Even without the correct video driver installed, you should probably be able to use Windows at a resolution of 640×480 with 256 colors; this is a standard mode supported by nearly all VGA cards, and is Windows' default display mode. Most video card problems are caused by faulty or incorrect video drivers, however, so it's best to check with the card's manufacturer first.

Now, if you don't have a VGA-compatible card, you're much better off simply purchasing a new card (good ones can go for as low as $50), which will be much easier and less of a hassle than trying to get that old obsolete display adapter to work properly.

Most modern video cards are based upon a certain chipset, usually identifiable by the large, square chip in the center of the card. If the chip is covered with a sticker, remove the sticker to see what's printed on the chip surface. In fact, Windows may be able to detect the type of chip, even if it can't determine the make and model of the card. Common chipset manufacturers include S3, Cirrus Logic, ATI, Tseng, and Western Digital; each of these comes in several varieties as well. If you can determine the type of chipset your video card uses, you should be able to use either a generic video driver made for that chipset, or a driver for another card that uses the same chipset.

If you know you are using the correct video driver, but can't use all of the resolutions it supports, make sure Windows is identifying your monitor correctly.

If you're trying to use Windows 98's support of multiple monitors, there are a few things to be aware of. Your system BIOS chooses which video card is your *primary* adapter and which card is your secondary adapter. To switch their priority, either to resolve a problem or for personal preference, you'll have to swap their physical positions in your computer. Since your primary video card does *not* need to explicitly support multiple adapters, but the secondary card does, you may have to swap them to get multiple monitor support to work at all. One problem you may encounter is trying to negotiate one PCI card and one AGP card; since most BIOSes initiate PCI before AGP, your AGP card will never be the primary card. In this case, you'll either have to make do with what you've got or install two PCI cards.

Monitors

If Windows knows what type of monitor you're using, it can determine which resolutions and color depths it supports. In Windows 95/98, monitors have drivers, although they do little more than inform Windows of the monitor's capabilities. Newer Plug-and-Play monitors allow Windows to automatically identify your monitor, although a driver may still be required. To see if your monitor is specified correctly, double-click on the **Display** icon in Control Panel. Choose the **Settings** tab, click **Advanced**, and then choose the **Monitor** tab in the new window.

It's possible for your video card to generate video signals that your monitor isn't able to display, especially if your resolution, color depth, or refresh rate are set too high. While a video card and a monitor don't have to be matched precisely to work, it's worth investigating whether or not your monitor can support all of your video card's modes.

You may be able to use a higher resolution or color depth with your monitor by lowering your video card's refresh rate. You should also lower the refresh rate if you hear your monitor whistling, and raise the refresh rate if the display flickers.

For problems using multiple monitors, see "Video cards (also known as display adapters)" earlier in this chapter.

Hard disks and floppy diskette drives

These drives almost never need special drivers, unless they use a proprietary interface such as your parallel port. Windows will support virtually all integrated drive electronics (IDE) drives right out of the box, as well as many SCSI controllers and devices.

Most hard disks, with the notable exception of SCSI, require that you specify their parameters (number of heads, cylinders, sectors per track) in your computer's *BIOS setup*, usually accessible by pressing some key just after you first turn on your system. Newer systems with a Plug-and-Play BIOS can autodetect most drives.

If Windows does not recognize your floppy or hard disk, you'll need to obtain a driver specific to the controller to which it's connected. If you continue to have trouble accessing the drive, make sure the jumpers are set appropriately and the cables are connected correctly.

Hard disk controllers

Most hard drives available today are the IDE type. Since new IDE controllers can be purchased for around $10 these days, you should simply throw out your existing IDE controller if it needs a driver, or if it takes more than five minutes to get working.

Proprietary IDE controllers, such as caching controllers, usually perform worse and cause more problems than the standard controllers built into nearly all new motherboards. You're better off taking the extra memory from the controller and installing it on the motherboard, throwing away the proprietary controller, and using the one on the motherboard.

Windows comes with drivers for most types of hard disk controllers, including IDE, RLL, ESDI, and SCSI. If Windows doesn't support your controller, and you can't get a driver from the manufacturer, you're out of luck.

SCSI controllers

Most SCSI controllers are either supported by Windows out of the box, or have 32-bit drivers you can use that come with the SCSI card or are available from the manufacturer. For the most part, all SCSI controllers are fairly well supported, with recent drivers nearly always available. If you're having a SCSI problem, you should first check to see if newer drivers for your card are available.

If you're unable to find drivers for your SCSI card, you may still be able to use it in Windows if you can find a driver for *another* card that uses the same SCSI controller chip, sometimes called a miniport driver. Common miniport manufacturers include Adaptec, BusLogic, Future Domain, NCR, and Trantor. For example, you may have a sound card that has a built-in SCSI controller intended for your CD drive. If that SCSI controller just happens to be made by Adaptec, for example, you should be able to use a driver for the corresponding Adaptec product that runs off the same chip.

Next to drivers, the two most common problems with SCSI controllers and the devices that attach to them are bad cables and incorrect termination. When diagnosing any SCSI problems, it's best to have replacements for all the cables, so you can easily swap them to help isolate the problem. The use of improper or non-SCSI adapters and connectors is also a common culprit.

As for termination, a SCSI chain (the long string of devices connected by cables) won't work properly unless it's correctly terminated. Make sure that each end of the chain, but nothing in the middle, is terminated, either by using the built-in termination on your SCSI controller and SCSI devices, or by attaching stand-alone terminators (active terminators are best). You should never have more than two terminators unless you have more than one controller. The SCSI card itself should be terminated, unless you have internal and external devices, in which case the devices at the end of each side should be terminated.

For problems with specific devices connected to SCSI controllers, such as CD drives, hard disks, and removable drives, refer to the corresponding topic elsewhere in this section.

CD-ROM drives

Most CD drives don't need special drivers. In fact, if you plug in a CD drive and then start up Windows, it should automatically detect the drive and display an icon for it in My Computer. If your drive isn't detected, first check the controller. Most CD-ROMs connect to your IDE or SCSI controller; if your drive isn't recognized, most likely the controller isn't working or you don't have the right drivers for your controller installed. Some older CD drives connect to proprietary controllers or sound cards. For these, you also may need a driver made especially for your controller/ drive combination; check the documentation for details.

Tape drives

Most tape devices don't require general-purpose drivers of their own, mostly because there is no standard for them. Any backup program compatible with your drive will come with its own drivers, which work with the installed drivers for the controller to which your drive is attached. So, if you have a SCSI tape drive, you'll need to first make sure the drivers for the SCSI controller are working. The backup program you use will come with generic drivers for SCSI tape drives, as does the backup software that comes with Windows 98.

Most tape devices come with their own backup software, which is usually guaranteed to work with the drive. If the manufacturer of your tape drive does not supply software, or if the supplied software is not a 32-bit application made *especially* for Windows 95/98, you'll need to use a different program, such as third-party commercial backup software or Microsoft Backup.

If you're trying to get Microsoft Backup or another backup program to recognize your drive, you should consider comparing the price of new backup software with the price of a whole new tape drive that includes its own 32-bit backup software.

If you must use old backup software with Windows 98, either because of monetary limitations or to maintain compatibility with other computers running older versions of Windows or DOS, you can still back up your long filenames with a separate utility. See "Restoring Windows After a Crash" later in this chapter for more information.

Note that you'll never see a drive letter for your tape drive in My Computer, unless you install a special utility designed for that purpose, such as Seagate Direct Tape Access. I've never found these utilities to work very well, however.

Removable, optical, and recordable CD drives

Removable cartridge drives, such as magneto-optical, Syquest, and IOmega drives, as well as CD recorders, traditionally connect to SCSI controllers. Therefore, as long your SCSI controller is functioning and the SCSI drivers are installed, you should be able to connect any SCSI device, make sure the chain is terminated, and it should work without a fuss, and without any special drivers.*

If you're having trouble getting a SCSI device like this to work, newer SCSI drivers or an update to the SCSI BIOS (contact the manufacturer) should solve the problem.

Some devices attach to IDE controllers via parallel ports. While these connections may seem more convenient or less expensive than SCSI, they're generally slower, less reliable, and more finicky. Additionally, parallel-port-connected devices usually require drivers provided by the manufacturer, which, of course, must be intended specifically for use with Windows 95/98.

Problems with external devices (SCSI and parallel-port connections) usually involve bad cabling. Make sure all cables are correct and seated firmly in their connectors, and that all thumbscrews are tightened.

Modems

If your modem is 9600bps or slower, it's not worth the time to get it to work. You can get a 56kbps modem for less money than it would cost in long-distance support calls to find drivers for the old one.

While choosing the appropriate driver is important, you can usually get by with one of the standard modem drivers included with Windows. In fact, Windows might simply call your modem a standard modem if it can't autodetect the make and model, even though a driver for your modem may be included with Windows. While a driver made especially for your modem will usually yield better performance and reliability, you can sometimes use a driver for another product by the same manufacturer, as long as it's the same speed.

Essentially, the only piece of configuration information Windows really needs to use your modem is knowledge of its maximum speed and its *initialization string*. This is a long string of seemingly nonsensical characters, beginning with AT, used to send commands to your modem to prepare it for dialing.

* Recordable CD drives require special recording (mastering) software in addition to an appropriate driver.

If Windows recognizes your modem, but you can't seem to get it to work, or simply can't find the appropriate driver, try entering your modem's initialization string into Windows. To obtain your modem's initialization string, either contact the manufacturer of your modem or refer to the documentation. If you currently have older software that works with your modem, a good trick is to snoop around the configuration section of the software to find the configuration string it's using.

Double-click on the **Modems** icon in Control Panel, select your modem from the list, click **Properties**, and choose the **Connection** tab. Click **Advanced**, and type your initialization string into the field labeled **Extra settings**.

If you can't find your modem in the list, double-click on **Add New Hardware** in Control Panel, and confirm that you want to it to search your system for newly attached devices. If Windows doesn't identify your modem, or it identifies it as an "unknown device," there are two possible causes of this problem. Either your modem is a proprietary model, such as some built-in modems found in portable computers, or the serial port to which it's connected is not functioning.

If yours is a proprietary modem (always something to avoid), you won't be able to use it without a proper driver from the manufacturer.

Serial port conflicts and misconfiguration are the most common causes of modem recognition problems. External modems are connected to serial ports, which usually are just cables that plug into the motherboard (see "Motherboards and CPUs," later in this chapter, for more information on serial ports).

Enter your computer's BIOS setup to verify that the serial port to which your modem is connected is *enabled* and configured correctly. Most likely you'll have two ports, one connected to your mouse, and the other to your modem (see Figure 6-3). Consult the documentation that came with your computer or motherboard for details.

Internal modems, on the other hand, are expansion cards that contain their own serial ports. Enter your computer's BIOS setup, and make sure any serial ports on your motherboard that you're not using are *disabled*, as they could otherwise conflict with your modem.* Commonly, only one serial port is used by the mouse (see Figure 6-3), but both are enabled on all new systems and motherboards by default.

* See "Stop Windows from Detecting Devices" later in this chapter for an additional solution.

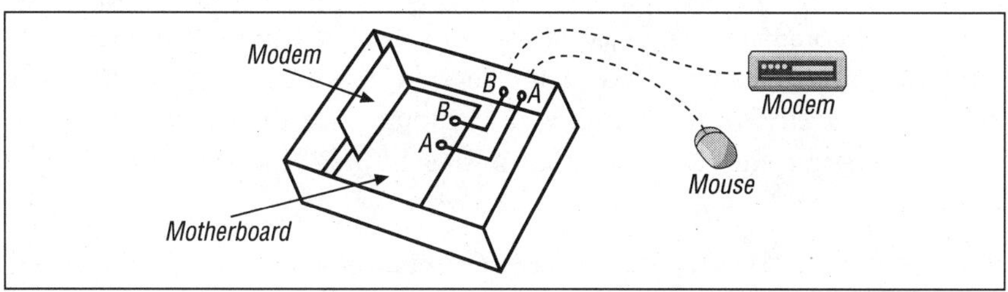

Figure 6-3: Common connections for serial ports; disable port B if you have an internal modem, enable B if you have an external modem

If Windows recognizes your modem correctly or as the generic "standard modem," the next step in resolving the problem is to verify communication with the device. Start by running HyperTerminal (use **Add/Remove Programs → Windows Setup** if you don't have it installed) to communicate with the modem. When prompted, type anything for the **Name**, and press **OK**. In the Connect To box that follows, choose **Direct to ComX** from the **Connect using** listbox, where **ComX** is the port to which your modem is connected, usually COM1 or COM2. Press **OK**; if your choice is correct, you'll be sent straight to HyperTerminal's main window.

Type `ATZ`, a simple reset command, and press **Enter**. If you receive an "Ok" after the successful completion of this reset, it means communication between your computer and your modem is working, and the problem is probably an incorrect driver or configuration program in your software.* If you don't receive an "Ok," there's probably a hardware conflict, as described above.

If you know the software is installed and configured correctly, there are external factors that can either prevent modems from working or slow modem performance. Start by removing all other electronic devices from the phone line, including answering machines, fax machines, autodialers, and standard telephone handsets. Any of these can actually interfere with the modem, preventing it from detecting the dial tone, or causing it to hang up prematurely. Other factors include bad phone cables and wall sockets. Try replacing your old phone cord with a brand new one just long enough to reach the wall jack.

Occasionally, a functioning modem can stop working temporarily. Since modems are constantly receiving commands from your computer, it's

* The software I'm referring to is the communications program you're using, which may be HyperTerminal, Dial-Up Networking (see Chapter 7, *Networking*), or some other Internet access program. If you're experiencing a problem with your software, consult the documentation that came with the software.

possible for the modem to become confused if it is sent a garbled or incomplete command. The easiest way to correct a confused modem is to turn it off and then on again. If the modem is an internal model, you'll need to *completely* power down your computer and then turn it on again; simply pressing the **Reset** button or restarting Windows may not be sufficient.

If you have an ISDN modem, these techniques won't necessarily apply. However, most external ISDN adapters connect through serial ports, which can suffer conflicts as described previously. Internal ISDN modems are treated by Windows as network adapters (see Chapter 7) rather than as modems.

As with any modem, make sure you have the latest drivers and, if applicable, the latest firmware.

Printers

Common printer problems involve bad cabling as well as bad drivers. Solving cabling problems is easy; just replace your parallel cable with a new one. IEEE 1284–compliant cables are the best, and are usually required for newer inkjet and laser printers. Some printers won't function if they're too far away from your computer, so try a shorter cable. See "Motherboards and CPUs" later in this chapter for more information on parallel ports.

As with most other peripherals, getting the right drivers is essential, though Windows can print plain text without fonts or graphics on nearly any printer without knowing what kind of printer you have. If you don't have a driver made especially for your model, you still may be able to use your printer with Windows by installing the Generic/Text Only driver included with Windows, although this will only enable very limited output. To use fonts or print graphics on your printer (only for printers that are capable of printing graphics, of course), you may be able to substitute another printer's driver. Try installing a driver for a similar printer made by the same manufacturer; look for a similar model number. For example, if you have a Hewlett-Packard 600 series inkjet printer, you might be able to get it to work with drivers for HP's 500 series.

Also, since many printers are compatible with Hewlett-Packard's PCL printer control language (PCL3, PCL5, etc.), you may be able to use the driver for the Hewlett-Packard Laserjet Series II for laser printers, or the Hewlett-Packard Deskjet driver for inkjet printers. If you have a Postscript laser printer, you should be able to use the driver for one of the Apple Laserwriter varieties.

Aside from drivers and cabling, common printer problems involve incorrect paper: use laser paper for laser printers, and inkjet paper for inkjet printers—none of this multipurpose junk.

Scanners and cameras

Scanners require not only the appropriate drivers to function in Windows, but special scanning software as well; as with tape drives, the two usually come together. If you can't find drivers or software that specifically supports your scanner, you're probably out of luck. However, since many companies simply repackage scanners made by other manufacturers, you may be able to obtain a driver from the original manufacturer (OEM) of the stuff under the hood.

As for cameras, since there are so many different kinds, probably the only productive discussion involves how they connect to your computer. Typically, this is through the parallel port.

Scanners commonly are connected through SCSI ports, but can also plug into parallel ports as well as proprietary controller cards. Getting scanners to work almost always involves getting the controller cards to work. See the previous discussion of SCSI cards for more information. See "Motherboards and CPUs," later in this chapter, for more information on ports.

Sound cards

Any sound card worth its weight is compatible with the Sound Blaster sound card by Creative Technology, originally called Creative Labs. If you can't find a driver for your sound card, try a driver for one of Creative's models.

If your sound card is older and doesn't support digitized sound (prerecorded sound effects and speech), it may still support MIDI synthesis (cheesy synthesizer music), and should be compatible with the driver for the Ad Lib card.

Windows should be able to detect your sound card, as well as the resources it uses. If your system crashes while trying to play sound on your sound card, and you know the correct driver is installed, try changing the resources used by the card; see "Resolving Conflicts and Other General Problems" earlier in this chapter for more information. If you can't get your sound card to work at all, and can't contact the manufacturer for the latest 32-bit drivers, you're probably going to have to replace the card.

Network cards

Windows should be able to detect your network adapter and install the correct drivers for it automatically. However, there are so many different types and manufacturers of network cards, and so many of those are proprietary, that you may be out of luck if you can't obtain drivers made specifically for your version of Windows. Note that due to the nature of Windows, you will have several drivers installed for any given network adapter, including the dial-up adapter, which isn't a network card at all (see Chapter 7 for more information). Since there are no "generic" or "standard" network drivers, if you can't find a driver for your network adapter, your only hope, other than replacing the card, is to use a driver for another card.

Memory

Bad memory can manifest itself in anything from frequent error messages and crashes to your system simply not starting. Errors in your computer's memory (RAM) aren't always consistent, either; they can be intermittent, and can get worse over time.

Nearly all newer computers, at least those capable of running Windows, use single inline memory modules (SIMMs), which are easy to install and remove. Most motherboards have about four SIMM slots, which should be clearly numbered on the motherboard. You'll either see something like slot 0, slot 1, slot 2, and slot 3, or bank 0 and bank 1. A *bank* is simply a pair of slots; some types of SIMMs must be installed in groups of two. All SIMMs must be installed in the lowest numbered slots first. You can't have a SIMM in slot 3 without having SIMMs in slots 0, 1, and 2.

The first thing you should do is pull out each SIMM, and make sure there isn't any dust or other obstruction between the pins and your motherboard. Use a dry tissue or lens cleaning paper; don't use any liquids or solvents. Look for broken or bent pins, broken SIMM holders, metal filings or other obstructions, and of course, any burn marks. Make sure all your SIMMs are seated properly; they should snap into place, and should be level and firm (don't break them while testing their firmness).

If all that is in order, there are three ways to determine if your RAM is actually faulty. The first way is to use a software testing program that is capable of checking RAM, such as CheckIt for DOS, a commercial package. Use the program to run a continual test of your RAM; have it repeat the test many times, perhaps overnight. The downside of testing your RAM by using any type of software is that this testing is not 100% reliable. Also, once you've found a problem, you need to follow the next method *anyway* to find and replace the faulty SIMM.

The second method requires a friendly, patient, helpful person at a small computer store—a rare commodity these days, especially with the popularity of large, faceless mega-super computer marts filled with inexperienced technicians. Look for a local mom-and-pop type store, and see if they have a memory testing device. These devices are too expensive for the average user, but almost anyone who sells RAM will have one. Take all your SIMMs in and ask the salesperson to check them for you. Not only is this test very reliable, but the person doing the testing will instantly be able to match whatever memory you need. Don't let them charge you for this service—they have enough to gain by selling you replacement memory if any of your SIMMs turn out to be faulty.

The third method of finding and replacing bad RAM is to go to your local computer store and just buy more RAM—it's only necessary to buy one SIMM, as most likely only one SIMM in your system is faulty. Make sure you get the right kind (32-pin, 70-pin, 168-pin, etc.), and the right capacity.

Systematically replace each SIMM in your computer with the one you've just acquired, and test the system by turning it on. If the problem seems to be resolved, you've found the culprit—throw it out immediately. If the system still crashes, try replacing the *next* SIMM with the new one, and repeat the process. If you replace all the memory in your system and the problem persists, it may be a bad CPU or motherboard. To eliminate the possibility that the problem is caused by a device other than the RAM, remove all unnecessary devices from your system before testing your RAM in this way.

You can, of course, also take this opportunity to add more memory to your system; at the time of this writing, memory costs a little over a dollar per megabyte, down from about $45 per megabyte at the release of Windows 95.

Motherboards and CPUs

There's really nothing you can do to diagnose a bad CPU chip (recognizable by frequent system crashes, or your machine not booting up at all), other than to simply replace it. Your best bet is to take your motherboard, complete with CPU and memory, into your local computer store, ask them to test it for you, and replace any components that need replacing.

Motherboards can also be finicky, but a problem may be caused only by a misconfiguration in the motherboard's BIOS setup. Consult the documentation for information on how to enter the BIOS setup; this usually involves pressing **Del** or **Ctrl-Alt-Enter** just after you turn the system on and memory is counted.

Also, check with the manufacturer of the motherboard to see if newer firmware (see "Firmware" earlier in this chapter) for your motherboard is available; newer motherboards allow you to update the BIOS by simply downloading and running a small program.

Lastly, even the newest motherboards come with jumpers (tsk, tsk). It's best to go through the entire manual and verify that each jumper is set correctly.

Error Messages

Error messages rarely describe a problem accurately, essentially because developers rarely put any thought into them. Usually, the computer will report that a program has crashed or isn't able to load, but the problem may be something completely unrelated to what the message is reporting. There are many different kinds of error messages, but only the more "popular" ones displayed by Windows are discussed here. If you're looking for a list of all possible error messages or codes, you're out of luck, since it doesn't exist.

If only one specific application displays a particular error message, your best bet is to contact the manufacturer of the application for technical support with their product. Many companies now have troubleshooting, updates and patches, and frequently asked questions (FAQs) on their web sites.

Common error messages usually tell you that a file is missing or corrupted, an error has occurred, or a specific device isn't working or turned on. Error messages telling you that *you've* done something wrong, such as trying to drag-drop a file onto your CD drive or trying to use quotes in a filename, don't really apply here, for obvious reasons.

Errors during startup

You may have seen a strange message when Windows is loading, either during the display of the Windows logo screen or after the Taskbar appears. This can be caused by many different things, but there are a few common culprits:

A driver won't load.

When Windows is starting up, it loads all of the installed drivers into memory. A driver may refuse to load if the device for which it's designed isn't functioning or turned on, or if the driver itself isn't installed properly. If you remove a device, make sure to take out the driver files as well—even if it isn't generating an error message, it could be taking up memory. Driver errors may also be caused by hardware problems. Refer to the "Hardware Configuration" section later in this chapter for more information.

A program can't be found.

After Windows loads itself and all of the drivers, it loads any programs configured to load at startup. These include screen savers, scheduling utilities, all the icons that appear in your tray, and any other programs you may have placed in your *Startup* folder or that may be configured in the system Registry to load automatically. If you remove an application, for example, and Windows continues to attempt to load it at startup, you'll have to remove the reference manually, as discussed under "Please wait while Windows updates your configuration files," later in this list.

A corrupt Registry.

See Chapter 3, *The Registry*, for any errors regarding your Registry.

A corrupt or missing file.

If one of Windows' own files won't load, and you're sure it isn't because of a third-party driver or application, you may actually have to reinstall Windows to alleviate the problem. I'll take this opportunity to remind you to back up frequently.

An error message of this sort usually includes a filename. To isolate the problem, you must search your hard disk for the reported file, and look in several places in Windows for the *reference* to the file. If you don't know what exactly the error means, you should definitely do both; a lot can be learned by finding how and where Windows is trying to load a program. However, if you know that the file or files are no longer on your system, you can proceed to simply remove the reference. Conversely, if you know the file *is* still on your system, and you want to get it working again, you'll probably need to reinstall whichever component or application it came with to fix the problem.

Please wait while Windows updates your configuration files.

While this isn't an error, it is a message you may see occasionally when Windows is starting. It simply means that Windows is copying files, such as those required by software installed the last time you used Windows, that it wasn't able to copy while running. For example, if a program you install needs to replace an old *.dll* in your *\Windows\System* folder with a newer version, but the *.dll* is in use and can't be overwritten, the program's setup utility will simply instruct Windows to overwrite it automatically the next time it's restarted.

The following locations are places that files or drivers can be specified to load when Windows starts. Often simply removing the reference to the file solves the problem. At the very least, locating the driver will help determine the culprit:

- Search your hard disk for the file (right-click on the **My Computer** icon, select **Find**, and type the filename). If you find a *.dll*, *.exe*, or *.vxd* file, but you're still not sure what it is or how it got there, right-click on it and select **Properties**. Click on the **Version** tab to view the various information presented. Software developers will often place the name of the application or manufacturer associated with the file here. If the version tab isn't there, neither is the information. You can also QuickView the file, if you have QuickView installed, to see other, more cryptic information that may be of help.
- Look in your *Startup* folder (usually found in your *Start Menu* folder—*\Windows\Start Menu\Startup*, by default) for outdated or unwanted shortcuts. A previously installed application may have placed a shortcut here for some reason. If you have moved or deleted the application, the shortcut may still be there, irritating you every time you turn on the system. Right-click on any shortcut and select **Properties** to learn more about it.
- Older programs might still install themselves in your *Win.ini* file (anywhere on the line that starts with `LOAD=` or `RUN=`). Use a text editor such as Notepad to edit this file. You may want to back it up before proceeding. Also, some older drivers are specified throughout your *System.ini* file, but can be hard to isolate. See Chapter 3 for more information on *.ini* files.
- Search your Registry for the filename in the message. If you don't know the name of the file, try looking in any of the following registry keys for other programs and drivers loaded at Windows startup:
  - `HKEY_LOCAL_MACHINE\SOFTWARE\Microsoft\Windows\CurrentVersion\Run`
  - `HKEY_LOCAL_MACHINE\SOFTWARE\Microsoft\Windows\CurrentVersion\RunOnce`
  - `HKEY_LOCAL_MACHINE\SOFTWARE\Microsoft\Windows\CurrentVersion\RunOnceEx`
  - `HKEY_LOCAL_MACHINE\SOFTWARE\Microsoft\Windows\CurrentVersion\RunServices`

- `HKEY_LOCAL_MACHINE\SOFTWARE\Microsoft\Windows\CurrentVersion\RunServicesOnce`
- `HKEY_CURRENT_USER\SOFTWARE\Microsoft\Windows\CurrentVersion\Run`
- `HKEY_CURRENT_USER\SOFTWARE\Microsoft\Windows\CurrentVersion\RunOnce`

Note that in any of these keys, you may see a reference to a file without any description, such as *Wfxctl32.exe*. Obviously, the filename alone is not self-evident. However, a quick search on the hard drive will reveal that the file is located in the *\Program Files\WinFax* folder, evidence that the file belongs to the WinFax application.

Programs notorious for putting things in these places include backup utilities that automatically load their useless scheduler programs, antivirus utilities, fax programs, and the software that comes with older versions of Microsoft mice and keyboards. If in doubt, throw it out.

Page fault, Illegal operation, and Fatal exception

These errors are usually caused by a bug in software, where an application or driver tries to use part of your memory that's currently being used by another program. You should expect this to happen occasionally, due to the complexity of today's software, but if it happens more frequently than once a day, it could be the sign of a more serious problem. When software crashes, it can either cause one of these error messages to be displayed, or can cause your system to hang or even restart.

Often these error messages are accompanied by lists of numbers (accessible by clicking **Details**). Now, one would expect the **Details** option to present pertinent, useful information: what happened, why it happened, and how to keep it from happening in the future. Unfortunately, Microsoft generally doesn't like to bother with descriptive or helpful error messages, so we're stuck with this useless box. The information in the **Details** view is of absolutely no use to end users,* unless, for example, you're specifically asked to relay this information to someone in technical support. Otherwise, don't even bother with the **Details**; swallow your pride and click the **OK** button, knowing full well that it's not okay, and it never will be.

The first step is to see if you can reliably reproduce the problem. If it seems to be application- or device-specific, where the same action in a

* Don't be fooled: the **Details** view often lists a specific executable, blaming it for the protection fault. However, this doesn't necessarily mean that the program listed actually caused the problem; it only means that it was the first running application to encounter the problem.

program or the repeated use of a certain device causes the crash, then you've found the culprit. This is the most common cause of crashes, especially today with companies shortening application testing periods to get their products to market faster. In the same way, buggy drivers can often cause crashes. For example, if your system crashes every time you try to use your scanner, the first thing to check is the scanner driver. It's then only a matter of fixing the problem. See "Drivers and Installing Hardware" earlier in this chapter for more information.

If the occurrences appear to be random and are not associated with any piece of hardware or software, there are some remaining possibilities. Errors in your system's memory and on your hard disk can cause these problems as well. To diagnose and repair any problems on your hard disk, use the Scandisk utility included with Windows, or one of the more-powerful third-party utilities available. While there are programs that can test system memory, a quicker and more reliable method is to replace your computer's memory, one SIMM at a time, until the problem is solved—see the section "Memory" earlier in this chapter for more information.

Crash and burn

If an application crashes and *doesn't* display an error message, it usually has just frozen. Depending on the severity of the crash, the application may not be responding to the mouse or keyboard, may not be updating its display, or may have turned the screen completely black. In most situations, you can press **Ctrl-Alt-Del** to display the Close Program box, as shown in Figure 6-4.

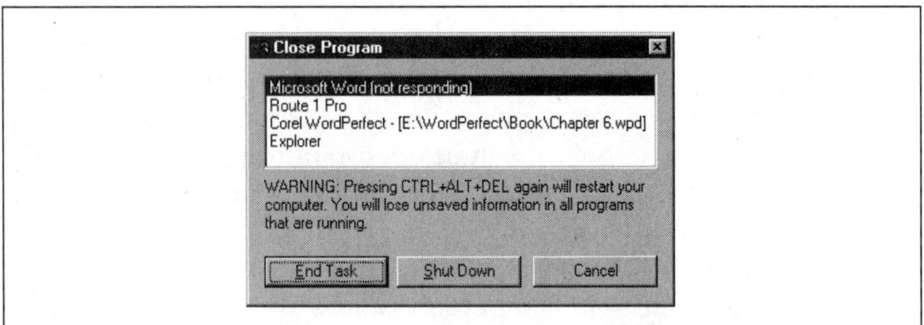

Figure 6-4: Pressing Ctrl-Alt-Del displays the Close Program box, allowing you to close a hung application

You are now fortunate to have the option of closing a misbehaving program, or shutting down Windows completely. You can close any running program here by selecting it from the list and clicking **End Task**, whether it has crashed or not. In fact, this is a good way to close programs that don't have windows, such as screen savers and other background programs. (Note that 16-bit applications closed in this way may behave unpredictably.) If an application has stopped responding, you'll notice that "not responding" appears next to the application's name. A program doesn't have to be misbehaving in order for you to have access to this window, however.

Applications that aren't responding don't always allow themselves to be shut down. Conversely, it's possible that an application reported as not responding may be doing so only temporarily; some programs, such as those that access certain devices, may appear to hang during normal operation. For this reason, it's best to have patience and give all hung applications a few minutes to correct themselves. Additionally, once you've used **End Task** on a hung application, it may take a little while for Windows to close it.

Another thing to be aware of is that many applications are made up of several components. It's possible for one of those components to crash and leave the rest of the program in operation. It's also possible for a program to crash and leave one or more of its components in memory. This can cause problems, although it certainly varies with the program. Try pressing **Ctrl-Alt-Del** again to see if the program is still running after it's been closed.

Since any crashed program can cause systemwide instability in Windows, it's good practice, though aggravating, to restart Windows every time a crash occurs. The following programs are part of Windows, and commonly appear in the Close Program window. Closing them with the method just discussed can solve some problems temporarily, but may not stop many other problems from reoccurring.

Msgsrv32 (not responding)

This program is one of Windows' components that runs invisibly in the background. It performs several necessary functions, including the following (this information is taken from Microsoft's knowledge base):

— Mediates Plug-and-Play messages among various parts of the operating system.

— Coordinates automatic responses to setup programs. This includes checking whether a setup program has improperly overwritten Windows files, and optionally restoring the Windows versions of those files—see "Your Sysbckup folder" later in this chapter.

— Displays the initial logon dialog box if multiple users are configured, or in some circumstances, if networking is enabled.

— Plays the system startup and shutdown sounds.

— Loads installable Windows drivers at startup and unloads them at shutdown.

— Runs the shell program (usually *Explorer.exe*) and reruns the shell if it closes or fails to respond.

Because of the varied nature of this program, almost anything can cause it to crash. If it does, you can end its task. If this happens more than once, it's best to restart Windows immediately.

Rundll32.dll

This program is used by some applications to run parts of other applications, and therefore doesn't necessarily correspond with any particular error. However, the following two circumstances relate to this file:

— If you see the message "Rundll32 - This program has caused an illegal operation and will be shut down," it could be caused by a missing entry in your *System.ini* file. Using a text editor such as Notepad to edit the file, look for the line that starts with `drivers=` in the `[boot]` section. If *mmsystem.dll* isn't specified on the right side of the equals sign, add it. If you continue getting this error, try removing all other drivers from the line until *mmsystem.dll* is alone. Make sure to make a backup of *System.ini* before editing it.

— If the Close Program window reports "Rundll32.dll (not responding)," end the task, and try whatever it was you were doing again. This has been known to happen when a modem fails while trying to connect to another computer using Dial-Up Networking (see Chapter 7 for more information).

Explorer

Explorer is the default Windows shell; it handles the desktop, the Taskbar, the Start Menu, the My Computer window, the Control Panel, Dial-Up Networking, and all single-folder and exploring windows. Unless a different application is configured as the shell (listed in the `shell=` line in *System.ini*), *Explorer.exe* is loaded automatically when you log in.

Explorer can crash for no apparent reason, and at any time. In most situations, if Explorer crashes or is terminated, it will be automatically restarted by *Msgsrv32.exe* (explained previously). However, if Explorer doesn't automatically restart—for example, following the "Abnormal Program Termination" error—you'll have to restart it manually. Since Explorer isn't running, pressing **Ctrl-Esc** or double-clicking on the desktop will launch the Task Manager (*Taskman.exe*). Select **Run Application** from the **File** menu, type `explorer`, and press **Enter**. This should restart Explorer, which will load the desktop and Taskbar. If it doesn't, press **Ctrl-Alt-Del** to display the Close Program box, and then click **Shut Down**.

Under most circumstances, Explorer crashing and restarting shouldn't adversely affect any other running applications, although you may find that the mouse isn't behaving or has even disappeared, drag-drop no longer works properly, the tray has vanished, or other minor and not so minor symptoms appear. As with other crashes, you should save any open documents and restart Windows at your earliest convenience.

Missing files

Files can simply vanish from your hard disk, because of user error or file corruption, or because another program has removed or renamed the file. There's not much you can do about this, other than to keep backups of files that tend to disappear, making it easy to replace them when necessary. If you discover that a file that came with Windows or another application is missing, you usually need to reinstall the application to restore the file. Note that if a file is missing, it's likely that other files are missing as well, and reinstalling insures not only that all necessary files are present, but that any associations between the files are correct.

If you know that a single file is missing, you can usually retrieve it from the distribution disks. To save distribution costs, companies often compress their files, thereby reducing the number of disks required to store the application as well as the amount of time required to install it. If you're trying to retrieve a file from a newer Microsoft application (including Windows), the files are stored in *cabinet files* (see "Using the Windows Registry Checker" in Chapter 3 for more information). Otherwise, the company may be using the industry standard ZIP format (see Appendix E), or Microsoft's old Compress/Expand utility; if the names of the distribution files look like *Ctl3d.dl_*, you should be able to restore them to their usable state by typing `expand ctl3d.dl_ ctl3d.dll` in DOS.

Shutdown problems

If you've ever tried to shut down Windows, and have watched it simply hang at the "Please Wait" screen, or even reboot rather than shutting down, you've encountered a common problem with Windows 98.

This problem was even worse in Windows 95, which tried to unload all device drivers from memory before shutting down. If a particular driver did not allow itself to be unloaded, the system hung, and you were forced to turn it off or reboot manually.

Windows 98 theoretically solves the problem by no longer trying to unload drivers, although it still may hang at the shutdown screen for no apparent reason. If Windows 98 often hangs at the shutdown screen, you should try disabling Windows' "fast shutdown" feature. Run the System Configuration Utility (*msconfig.exe*) and choose the **General** tab. Click **Advanced**, turn on the **Disable fast shutdown** option, and click **OK** twice when you're done.

Another cause of shutdown hanging may be corrupted shutdown bitmaps (see "Replace the Startup and Shutdown Screens" in Chapter 2, *Customizing the Interface*).

Regardless of the cause, there should be no adverse effects if you manually shut off your computer whenever it hangs at the shutdown screen, but wait for the hard drive light to go out, as the drive may be saving important data to your disk.

Version control

Here's a tough one: many different programs share files, called Dynamic Link Libraries (DLLs), with one another. These files provide functionality that many applications share, such as the "File Open" box. In fact, Windows is primarily a collection of *.dll* files used by the various applications that run in the operating system.

The problem arises when an errant application overwrites a newer version of a *.dll* with an older or different version. This problem has been addressed with something called *Version Control*, where each file contains specific version information. For example, when you install a new application, the setup program will test every file it copies to your hard disk against any files it's replacing. If it detects that a file on your hard disk is newer than the one that came with the application, it will skip the file. Using a file's version information is more reliable than simply counting on file dates, which can be easily changed. For example, all files released with Windows 98 have the same 5-11-98 date, regardless of their version.

In theory, this works quite well. However, older applications don't always follow the rules, and newer applications sometimes come with shared files that introduce new bugs. Since the *.dll* files that come with Windows are used by the majority of applications, as opposed to *.dll* files used by only a single program, Microsoft DLLs are under the most scrutiny. Microsoft is notorious for replacing files shared by many different programs with new, buggy versions that either cause problems, or change some basic interface components to suit their own products. While this practice of Microsoft's is frowned upon, their monopolistic position in the industry pretty much insures that they can do what they want, and let other manufacturers clean up the mess.

To determine the version of any file, right-click on it in Explorer, and click **Properties**. You should see a **Version** tab; if not, the file you've chosen doesn't contain any version information. This tab displays the version of the file, some copyright information, usually the name of the manufacturer, and a short description of the file. Shuffle through the items in the **Item name** list to see the various clues.

You may find that a more effective solution is to use VersionTracker, part of *O'Reilly Utilities—Quick Solutions for Windows 98 Annoyances* (see Appendix F, *Software to Solve Annoyances*), which allows you to simply type in the name of a file to see the latest version. Not only is this faster than having to find the file, but if there's more than one copy of the file on your system, VersionTracker will tell you in no uncertain terms *which* copy is being used.

File types that usually contain version information include *.dll* files, *.exe* files, *.drv* files, *.vxd* files, and *.ocx* files.

Newer versions of *.dll* files usually serve the same purpose as the original version, but add more functionality, include bug fixes, or improve performance. In some isolated situations, a certain *.dll* file can be replaced with a completely different file, with which it shares only the filename. This is rare, with the possible exceptions of *Winsock.dll* and *Mapi32.dll*.

Occasionally, a program will complain that a *.dll* or other shared file cannot be found. For some reason, this happens quite often; files that were initially installed with an application simply vanish. While reinstalling the program usually solves the problem, you may be able to resolve the problem more quickly by looking on the application's distribution disk or CD for the file. If you find it, try copying it to the application's installation folder, or if that doesn't work, to your *\Windows\System* directory.

Now, there are more *.dll* files that can be listed in any one place, let alone in this book. Many come with Windows, and many more are installed on your system by the thousands of applications and drivers currently available. What follows is a list of a few common troublemakers, and how to cope with them. This should in no way be considered a comprehensive guide to resolving conflicts between all applications, but rather should be viewed as an exercise in dealing with several isolated problems. Essentially, the solution to any problem is to make sure you have the *correct* file for your system, not necessarily the newest one.

Wsock32.dll

This file and its 16-bit counterpart, *Winsock.dll*, are used by most, if not all, Internet applications, and the version on your hard disk depends on which Internet dialer you're using. If you're using Dial-Up Networking, which comes with Windows 98 (see Chapter 7), the file should be dated 5-11-98, although it may have been replaced by Microsoft with a more recent file. Updates to Internet Explorer may come with a newer version of *Wsock32.dll*.

The problem occurs when another Internet dialer, such as Trumpet Winsock, AOL, or an older version of Netscape Navigator, replaces the file on your hard disk with its own version. Since the various creators of this file have included entirely different functionality in each version, it is *not* necessarily advantageous to have the *latest* version of the file. If your Internet applications stop working, check this file. You may need to replace it with the one appropriate to your dialer. See "The path less traveled," later in this chapter, for an important consideration.

Mapi32.dll

Mail Application Programming Interface (MAPI) is the specification that allows any application to email a file or block of text using the installed email program. However, since Microsoft neglected to include the necessary customization hooks in the file, each email program you install must overwrite the file in your *\Windows\System* folder with its own version.

This causes substantial problems. For example, Eudora (a very popular email program and, in my opinion, the best available) includes its own version of the file. If you install Eudora and enable its MAPI feature, it will rename any existing *Mapi32.dll* file to *Mapi32.000* and put its own version in its place. If you happen to have Microsoft Office 97 installed, this action will entirely disable Outlook 97,* which relies heavily on Microsoft's version of the *Mapi32.dll* file. To resolve the problem in this case, you'll need to first disable the MAPI feature in Eudora, and then restore Microsoft's version of the file.

* Outlook 98 somewhat resolves this problem, in that it is only dependent on MAPI if it's not installed in Internet-only mode.

Ctl3d32.dll

This file and its cousins, *Ctl3d.dll* and *Ctl3dv2.dll*, seem to cause lots of problems. They're used by older applications to display certain 3-D effects, wherein the controls in some dialog boxes have the "carved" look that has become the Windows standard. Software designed especially for Windows 95/98 already contains this functionality, but older applications rely on this file for basic operation. Although the newer versions usually are preferred, some applications will display an error if you use anything but the specific version that came with the product. You guessed it: bad programming. As of this writing, the most benign version of each of these files is as follows: for *Ctl3d32.dll*, Version 2.31; for *Ctl3d.dll*, Version 2.05; and for *Ctl3dv2.dll*, Version 2.31.

If you don't have these versions, don't panic, and don't waste time trying to obtain them. This is just a guideline if you are having trouble with any of these files, or find that you have several versions floating around. Make a habit of backing up these files so that you can easily restore them if they become overwritten.

Threed.vbx

This is a custom control used by some applications written in the Visual Basic programming language. Custom controls like 16-bit *.vbx* files and 16- and 32-bit *.ocx* files are special *.dll* files that add modular functionality to programs. *Threed.vbx* is just one of these, and is mentioned because of its popularity. The problem of incompatible versions actually exists with all *.vbx* and *.ocx* files, now called ActiveX controls, just as with all *.dll* files. Be aware that these files have version information as well, and that newer versions of these files can be overwritten with older versions.

The path less traveled

While it isn't emphasized now as much as it was in the heyday of DOS and Windows 3.x, the system path is still an important setting in Windows 98. It can be helpful or detrimental, depending on how it's used.

The system path, a listing of folder names that is initialized when Windows boots, is an *environment variable* that is kept in memory until you shut down. If a folder name is listed in your system path, you'll be able to run a program contained in that folder *without* having to specify its location. For example, the MOVE utility, located in your *\Windows\Command* folder, can be executed from any directory in DOS, without having to specify the path, and without having to change the directory to the containing folder. (See Appendix B, *DOS Lives*, for more information on DOS commands.) Likewise, in Windows, if you select **Run** from the Start Menu, type

`Notepad`, and press **Enter**, Notepad will be run, even though you didn't specify the full path of the executable (as in `c:\windows\notepad.exe`). Both of these are possible because both the *\Windows\command* and *\Windows* folders by default are included in the system path.

You may not think this applies to you, but it may. The same rules that apply to program executables also apply to shared files, such as *.dll* and *.vbx* files. If you have multiple versions of a file floating around in different directories specified in your system path, any of the available versions of the file may be in use—not necessarily the latest one. For example, say you have the appropriate version of the file *Winsock.dll* in your *\Windows\System* directory, but you have another, older copy of *Winsock.dll* in your *c:\AOL* directory. It's entirely possible that some programs might mistakenly use the older version, just because they found it in a directory in the path.

How do you escape this trap? First of all, remove any unnecessary directories from your path, which is configured in your *Autoexec.bat* file. If you have a custom path configured, it will look something like this:

```
PATH=c:\norton;c:\;c:\aol;c:\progra~1\micros~1
```

Each entry is separated by a semicolon, and any long filenames are shortened to their short filename counterparts: *c:\Program Files\Microsoft Office 95* will appear as *c:\progra~1\micros~1*. If you don't have a custom path configured, there will be no **PATH=** line present, and you can move on. By default, *\Windows*, *\Windows\Command*, and *\Windows\System* are all in your path, although they are built into the operating system, and won't show up here.

If the path ends up leading nowhere, there's another scenario that might be causing a file conflict. As an example, take the *Ctl3d32.dll* file discussed earlier in this chapter. Say you have the latest version of this file in your *\Windows\System* folder, where it should be. All applications that use this file will look for it there first, unless there happens to be a copy of the file in the application's *own* directory. If the file is not already in memory (it's loaded only once, no matter how many programs are using it), the application will load the first version it finds. If there's a copy of the file in the application directory, it will be loaded, even if it's older.

What's worse is that any subsequent programs that also use this file will simply use the one in memory, even if it's not the one in the *\Windows\System* folder.

Luckily, this is easy to solve, albeit somewhat difficult to isolate. Simply search your entire hard disk for the file; select **Find** and then **Files or Folders** from the Start Menu, and choose **My Computer** in the **Look in** list. If you see more than one copy of the file in the search results window, it could be causing a potential conflict.

You might want to make backups of all the found files before continuing.

Widen the **In Folder** column in the search results window so you can see where each file is located. If one of them is in *\Windows\System* (or in any other Windows subdirectories, for that matter), then it most likely belongs there. Compare the versions of the files by right-clicking, selecting **Properties**, and clicking on the **Version** tabs (see "Version control," earlier in this chapter). Now, you want to end up with only the newest file on your system, so what you can do at this point is simply delete all but the newest file, and move it to the *\Windows\System* folder if it's not already there.

Note that this solution by no means applies to all *.dll* files, which is why it's smart to back up any files before continuing. Some files have identical names only by coincidence, although this is rare. Of course, deleting a file just because there's another around by the same name is not a good idea unless you know that the files serve the same purpose. One way to make sure is to look through *all* the information in the **Version** tab; if the Company Name and Product Name are the same, you can be pretty sure that the files are duplicates. On the other hand, if the files have vastly different sizes, odds are that one is not a suitable replacement for the other.

Note also that if you've configured Windows to display hidden files, you may also find duplicates of some *.dll* and *.vxd* files in a folder called *Sysbckup* (explained in the following section). It's important that you don't delete any files from this folder unless you update them with newer versions.

Your Sysbckup folder

In Windows, you'll find a hidden folder called *Sysbckup* under your *\Windows* directory. This folder contains copies of some of the more important files used in Windows, kept around in case the originals get overwritten or corrupted. If an application replaces a file in your *\Windows\System* directory that's also in your *Sysbckup* folder, Windows will automatically replace the new file with what it believes is a reliable copy from the *Sysbckup* folder.

You can use this to your advantage by placing copies of any files you wish to protect in this way into the *Sysbckup* folder. Be careful when doing this, however, not to replace any vital files with older versions, and make sure not to delete any files in this directory. For more information, see the reference to the "Msgsrv32 (not responding)" error in the section "Crash and burn" earlier in this chapter.

Preventative Maintenance and Data Recovery

There's no substitute for backing up, and there's no better method of disaster recovery than having a good copy of all your data. Any stolen or damaged hardware is easily replaced, but the data stored on your hard disk is not. Unfortunately, hindsight is 20/20, and if you didn't back up, there's not much you can do about it after the fact. So, we'll begin our discussion with some preventative maintenance before covering any disaster recovery techniques.

Back Up Your Entire System

There are more ways to back up your data than by storing it. The sole purpose of a backup is to have a duplicate of every single piece of data on your hard disk that can be easily retrieved in the event of data loss. Imagine if your computer were stolen, and you had to restore a backup to a brand-new computer. Could you do it? If the answer is no, you're not backed up.

You need to be able to complete a backup easily and often, store the backup in a safe place away from the computer, and retrieve all your data at any time without incident. If it's too difficult or time-consuming, odds are you won't do it—so make it easy for yourself.

The bare minimum backup should entail one or more floppy disks containing your recent, most important documents and data. Floppies are cheap, and all computers have floppy drives; the downside is that floppies are slow, too small to back up large amounts of data, and *very* unreliable. While it's most important to back up your recent documents, it's best to have all your documents as well as Windows and all your applications backed up as well. This will save you time and aggravation when you need to restore your system to full working order. If you only back up some of your files, you'll have to reinstall all your applications, reconfigure their toolbars and other preferences, reconfigure your Dial-Up

Networking connections, and handle a myriad of other overwhelming tasks.

Ideally, you should be able to back up your entire hard disk on a single piece of media. Since floppies aren't suitable for this task, you should invest in a backup solution if your data is at all important to you. The hardware you use should be fully supported by Windows; you can't use 16-bit software to back up long filenames, so make sure you have 32-bit backup software that supports your backup hardware. The backup media (tapes, cartridges, or disks) should be cheap and reliable, and you should be able to use them over and over again.

Which backup solution is appropriate for you depends on your work habits. Tape drives, optical drives, removable cartridges, and recordable CDs are selling like hotcakes these days, and for good reason. While removable cartridge drives (such as Syquest drives, or IOmega Zip and Jaz drives) and recordable CDs are great for quickly archiving data, they still aren't as appropriate as tape drives for backing up entire systems and restoring them in the event of a disaster.

Removable drives and CDs offer random access, meaning that you can open Explorer and read or write to any file immediately. This may be convenient in the short run, but this convenience comes at a price; the media used for these types of backups can be quite expensive, and the backup procedures for random-access drives can be more labor-intensive than for tape drives.

Tape drives are still the most cost-effective, reliable, and appropriate method for backing up and recovering your system after a disaster. The caveat is that tape drives require special backup software,* and tend to be slower than comparably priced removables, especially when restoring single files. However, remember what's important here: you need to easily and painlessly duplicate the contents of your *entire* system on *one* cartridge, and be able to restore some or all of that data just as easily.

While tape backup software may seem awkward on the surface, it's designed to allow you to perform a backup in a single step, and without user intervention. Good backup software will also make restoring easy; the best programs keep catalogs of your backups, allowing you to find a backed-up file easily and to get it back with the least amount of hassle possible.

---

* Windows 98 comes with a scaled-down version of Seagate Backup Exec, which is, in my opinion, the best backup software utility available at the time of this writing. This continues Microsoft's tradition that each successive backup program included with Windows is incompatible with its predecessors; but hopefully, the Seagate package will be in use for years to come.

You need to find the system that works best for you and fits in your budget. Do some research before investing in any one technology, and make sure it truly suits your backup needs. Try this: add the cost of the drive you're considering to the cost of the media required to store the entire contents of your hard drive *twice*, and compare it with other solutions. Table 6-1 shows six example technologies, and the cost for each to back up a 4-gigabyte (4300-megabyte) hard drive.

Table 6-1: These Average Prices for Various Backup Solutions Show That Initial Bargains Are Rarely Good Deals

Technology	Drive Cost	Cartridge Cost	Cartridge Capacity	Cartridges per Backup	Total Cost for 2 Backups
DAT tape	$400	$10	4 GB	1 = $10	$420
800MB tape	$150	$29	800 MB	5 = $145	$440
Rewritable CD	$350	$25	650 MB	7 = $175	$700
1GB removable	$300	$65	1 GB	4 = $260	$820
Zip drive	$150	$10	100 MB	43 = $430	$1,010
Floppies	$30	$0.35	1.4 MB	3,000 = $1,050	$2,130

Naturally, the prices and capabilities of the various technologies will change as quickly as the weather, but the methodology is always the same. Note also that the reference to the use of a recordable CD drive specifies *rewritable* CDs; if you were to do a backup with standard gold CDs, you'd have to buy new disks for each backup. See the next section for the reasoning behind having enough media for *two* backups.

Doing your research will save you time and money in the long run, not to mention the extra peace of mind.

Tips for a better backup

The following tips should help you ensure that you will never be without adequate data protection, whether you've already invested in a backup solution or not:

- The problem with backups is that most people don't do them. A few minutes every two weeks is all it takes, and this can save many, many hours in the future. A good time to do a backup is just before lunch, just before you go home (if the computer is at work), or just before you go to bed (if the computer is at home). You can also schedule your backup to automatically and regularly occur at any time.
- Don't do a backup while you're working on the computer. Your backup program not be able to reliably back up any files that are in

use. Your system will also be slower and more likely to crash if you are doing too many things at once.

- Most backup utilities designed especially for Windows 95/98 give you the option of backing up the Registry. You should always take advantage of this feature, as it is a good safeguard, offering better assurance that you'll be able to restore your Registry, should the need arise. Naturally, backing up the Registry doesn't mean you must restore it along with everything else, but it's nice to have that luxury. Note that without a valid registry backup, all those backed-up applications won't do you any good.
- Run Scandisk, or Norton Disk Doctor, if you have it, before each backup. If your disk or your files are corrupted, so will be your backup.
- Don't back up to floppies if you can avoid it. Floppies are much more likely to fail than your hard disk, although it's better than no backup at all.
- Maintain at least two sets of backups, alternating media each time you back up. If you back up to tape, for example, use one tape for the first backup, the other tape for the second backup, then use the first tape again. That way, if there's a problem with one tape or the backup is fouled up somehow, you'll still have a fairly recent backup. Just imagine if you overwrote a good backup with a bad one and the power went out in the middle; you would then have no backup at all.
- Your backups should not be kept near your computer, especially not *inside* the computer. If your computer is stolen, or if there's a fire, your backups will go with it. Keeping one of the backups in your car or somewhere else off the premises is a good idea. And if you make your living off a computer, you might consider keeping a backup in a safe deposit box.
- Most backup programs allow you to specify a name for the media the first time you use them (or whenever you *initialize*), which allows the cataloging feature to tell you on which tape a certain file resides. Make sure each of your tapes or cartridges has a unique name that matches the tape's handwritten label, which will ensure that your software identifies each tape the same way you do. Call your tapes something like "Backup A" and "Backup B," or "Larry," "Moe," and "Curly." You'll be glad you did when your backup software asks you to insert Moe, for example.
- Make a copy of your backup program on floppies, and keep it somewhere safe. If you can't install your backup software, you won't be

able to access your backups. And if the backup software is on a CD, you won't be able to get at it without installing a CD driver in DOS or reinstalling Windows completely.

- Configure your system for unattended backups. Ideally, you should only have to insert a single cartridge and click "Go" to complete a backup. Don't put up with lower-capacity backup devices that require you to swap cartridges in order to do a single backup. Additionally, most backup software has options to bypass any confirmation screens; by taking advantage of these, you eliminate the possibility of starting a backup before you go home, and coming to work the next day only to see the message, "Overwrite the data on tape?"
- Don't bother with incremental backups. Most backup software allows you to do a full-system backup, and then supplement it with incremental backups which only store the files that have changed since the last backup. While this means that you can back up in less time, it also means that you'll have to restore each of those backups when recovering from a disaster—one full backup and ten incremental backups adds up to 11 restores. More importantly, incremental backups require that the original full backup is intact. If something happens to that one backup, all subsequent incremental backups will be rendered completely useless.
- Lastly, test your system; don't wait until it's too late to find that the restore process doesn't work. Just do a simple trial backup of a single folder or branch. Then, try to retrieve the backup to a different drive or folder. Not until you've successfully and completely retrieved a backup can you consider your data safe.

Better floppy formats

Diskettes are still the standard, despite the fact that they're unreliable, slow, and small. However, everyone has a floppy drive, the disks are cheap, and it's a great way to transport small amounts of data. To avoid a headache, however, always format every floppy diskette before you use it. It'll take an extra couple of minutes, but it may save you hours in the long run.

Floppies are very unreliable. They are highly susceptible to dust, damage, and heat, and can turn on you in an instant.

Use DOS to format your floppies. It's faster and more reliable than using Windows' format feature, it gives you more free space, and it yields better multitasking. Just type `Format a: /u` at the MS-DOS prompt, substituting `a:` with the drive letter you wish to format. The `/u` parameter specifies an *unconditional* format, meaning that it won't use up part of the floppy with the unnecessary "unformat" information that the Windows format includes.

If *any* errors such as bad sectors or sectors not found are reported during the disk format process, throw the disk out *immediately*. Disks cost around 30 cents apiece; if in doubt, throw it out.

Lastly, *never* use floppies to store any information for more than a few hours; that's what your hard disk is for. A floppy disk backup, for example, is much more likely to die than your hard disk. Floppies should only be used to install software and transport data from one computer to another.

See "Resurrecting the floppy diskette" in Chapter 5 for additional floppy tips.

Make a startup disk

You'll never need a boot disk until your system doesn't start, and then you'll wonder why you never took the three minutes required to make one. A boot disk is just a floppy with a few special files on it, enabling you to start your system if something goes wrong with your hard disk. It's easy, quick, and *very* useful.

Windows even has a built-in method for doing this; double-click the **Add/Remove Programs** icon in Control Panel, choose the **Startup Disk** tab, and then click **Create Disk**. If you're a do-it-yourselfer, you can just as easily do this through DOS by typing `Format a: /u/s` (see the previous section, "Better floppy formats," for more information). The `/s` parameter tells your computer to install the special system files on the disk. No, you can't just copy these files manually.

Regardless of how you create a startup disk, however, it won't be complete until you do a few more steps that Microsoft doesn't tell you about. Copy the hidden file *Msdos.sys* from the root directory of your boot drive (usually *C:*, unless you're using DriveSpace or some other disk compression program) onto the floppy, replacing the one that's there. This will enable you to run Windows when you boot from the floppy, a task that otherwise isn't possible. Also, copy *Format.com* and *Sys.com* from your *\Windows\Command* folder onto the floppy; this will help you prepare your hard disk for the reinstallation of Windows, if necessary.

You should also put the DOS drivers for your CD drive on the startup disk. Since you can't access your CD drive outside of Windows without CD drivers installed, you won't be able to reinstall Windows if it becomes necessary. Having the drivers already set up on your startup disk will make this problem trivial. Refer to the instructions that came with your CD-ROM drive for details, as the procedure varies across different types of drives. Make sure you can boot from the floppy and access your CD-ROM drive right away, without any additional steps. Just because your disks and manuals are easy to find now, doesn't mean they will be around in six months. See "Restoring Windows After a Crash," later in this chapter, for more information.

Lastly, label the disk with today's date, write-protect it, and put it in a safe place.

Getting the latest drivers

A good preventative measure is to routinely check the web sites of the manufacturers of the various devices installed on your system. Newer drivers solve problems and incompatibilities that may otherwise damage your system. While it's always a good idea to keep up with the latest drivers, once in a while a new driver may introduce a new problem to the system. An effective way to guard against errant drivers is to routinely back up your Registry. If you encounter a problem, you can just restore the backup, which in many cases will restore your system to its previous state.

Registry backups

Windows 98 comes with a utility that automatically creates a backup of your Registry every time you boot. However, this won't do you much good if you don't know how to retrieve the backups. See "Backing Up the Registry" in Chapter 3 for more information.

Hardware protection

Most of these topics deal with software issues: protecting your data, creating boot disks, etc. However, there are a few things you can do to reduce the likelihood of problems with your hardware.

All hardware is sensitive to heat, light, dust, and shock. Don't block any vents on your computer or your monitor, and routinely vacuum all around to remove dust (too much dust can cause your components to overheat and your disk drives to fail).

Make sure you have a capable fan in your power supply, and one mounted directly on top of your CPU—an extra fan in front won't hurt, either. If you can't hear your computer, odds are it isn't being adequately cooled. Make sure that air can flow freely inside from the front of the computer to the back; look for a mass of cables blocking the passage of air. Overheated components can cause system crashes, slow performance, and data loss.

If your computer and every external peripheral is connected to a surge protector, the possibility of damage by an electrical surge is virtually eliminated. Many surge protectors also allow you to run your phone cord through them, protecting your modem from damaging phone line surges. And if you live in an area susceptible to blackouts, you might consider an uninterruptible power supply (UPS), which eliminates the problem of lost data due to lost power.

Make sure all your cables are tied neatly behind the computer so pins and plugs don't become loose or get broken; pets love to chew on cables, pulling them out and otherwise mangling them. And tighten all those cable thumbscrews.

Clean the ball of your mouse, and use a mousepad, or if you use a graphics tablet, keep the surface clean. Don't spray glass cleaner on your monitor, but on the paper towel instead. Keep floppies, tapes, and other magnetic cartridges away from your monitor and speakers; they're just big magnets which can turn disks into coasters in no time. Straighten up and fly right, too.

Data Recovery

There are certain measures you can take to restore your system *after* a disaster, although your luck will dramatically improve if you've taken the steps outlined in the previous sections. This section covers only software, since recovering hardware (for example, if it were destroyed in an earthquake) requires either ample insurance or a fat checkbook.

It may seem as though even the most sophisticated equipment is quite fragile and easily susceptible to data loss. This is just one of the annoyances of the average Windows experience.

If you've backed up your system, you can make repairs without worrying about losing any more data. For example, to bring a hard disk back to working order, you may be required to format it. If you don't have to worry about recovering data you don't have otherwise backed up, you can proceed to format. However, if you haven't backed up, you'll need to try to recover as much data as possible before repairing the damage. The following list describes several different extremes of damage, each with its own symptoms and solutions:

File corruption
: If you can't access a certain document or start a certain application (or get errors while Windows is booting), but everything else seems to work, the problem is most likely due to one or more corrupted files. This can almost always be fixed with Scandisk (*Scandisk.exe*). Usually, Scandisk will be able to fix the problem by either repairing the damaged file, or marking a small portion of your hard disk as unusable, depending on the severity of the damage.

It's possible, however, for Scandisk to repair the problem without being able to recover the file completely. If this is the case, you'll either need to replace the files or reinstall the application to which the files belong. See earlier topics in this section for more information on Scandisk and replacing missing files.

Registry error
: This is the same thing as the previous item, but it only applies to the files that make up your Registry. See Chapter 3 for more information on backing up and recovering a damaged Registry.

Disk error
: A disk error is a physical defect on your disk, often called a bad sector. This manifests itself by something as benign as the occasional read error, or something as serious as your computer hanging whenever a file or group of files is accessed.

While your hard disk will probably never develop bad sectors, floppies and removable disks are more susceptible to shock, dust, and other sources of physical damage that can lead to bad sectors. Although every new hard disk comes with some bad sectors, all of them are marked as bad before the disk leaves the factory. But if the number of bad sectors continually increases over a short period of time, it usually means the drive needs to be replaced. If a floppy or removable cartridge similarly develops bad sectors, you should not only discard it, but investigate the drive as well for problems.

The Scandisk utility is able to find most bad sectors and mark them as unusable, and if you have Norton Disk Doctor, that's even better. Both of these programs will move any files located on the bad sectors so that they reside on good sectors. Unfortunately, this often means the file has been irreparably damaged, and should be deleted and replaced with an intact copy.

To find out if the problem is permanent or temporary, format the drive completely (after backing up all your data). If the problem doesn't go away, you should replace the drive immediately. Otherwise, you've apparently fixed the problem.

Sector not found, invalid directory entries, or other errors where you see gibberish instead of filenames

This usually means that your hard disk needs to be reformatted, but probably not replaced. Try to back up as many files as you can as quickly as possible; this type of problem tends to grow quickly. Once you've recovered as much as you can, reformat the drive, and start refilling it. If you have Norton Disk Doctor, you may be able to repair the directory structure without reformatting. Note that Scandisk is usually not up to the task of fixing this type of problem, although it may be worth a try.

Disk crash

If your hard disk has crashed, you most likely can't even get it to turn on. A common symptom is that your computer won't boot unless you disconnect the hard disk from the controller. Old hard drives can simply die, another good reason to back up often. There's not much you can do at this point, but the manufacturer of the hard drive, or even professional data recovery businesses (which have a very high success rate), may be able to recover some or all of your data.

Be careful here, since it's possible to make your data nonrecoverable by trying to recover it yourself. If you're concerned about your data, you should shut off the system and remove the drive immediately as soon as you detect a crash. *Don't* start the system again just to see if it boots this time; this may further damage your data, or even make the disk unrecoverable.

Once you've solved whatever caused the problem in the first place, you can proceed to restore your data onto your now functioning hard drive.

Restoring Windows After a Crash

The purpose of backing up is to give you the opportunity to restore your system to its original state if something unforeseen should happen to your hard disk, whether it be theft, fire, malfunction, or just user error. You'd be surprised at how many people back up their systems without having any idea how to restore their files later, should a problem arise. The backup doesn't do you any good if you can't get at your files later, so it's important to take steps to make sure you can restore your system *from scratch* if necessary.

The most important consideration is that the software you use to restore your files must be the same one you used to back them up. That means that if you back up your hard disk using 32-bit backup software made especially for Windows 95/98 (either the included Backup utility or a third-party solution), and your hard disk crashes, you'll have to reinstall Windows as well as your backup software from scratch before you can restore anything else.

Now, reinstalling Windows doesn't necessarily mean that you lose your Windows preferences and must reinstall all your applications. The idea is to reinstall Windows, as well as the drivers for your backup device, if necessary, to a state sufficient to run your backup program. Sometimes, this isn't necessary; it just depends on what your backup software requires.

The following solutions represent general procedures covering a wide range of scenarios, although you should use your best judgement when following any of these, as your situation might be different. It's probably a good idea to familiarize yourself with the following procedure *before* you actually have to use it; that way, you can better prepare yourself and minimize the headache.

Using the Windows Backup utility

Microsoft made a wise choice when it licensed a scaled-down version of Seagate's Backup Exec utility for inclusion in Windows 98. Backup Exec 2.0 is an updated version of Arcada Backup for Windows 95 (which Seagate purchased in 1997). This is an excellent program, which actually has a functional restore; it's surprisingly difficult to restore with many backup programs available today.

You shouldn't rely on this release to be compatible with backups made with any previous release of the so-called "Microsoft Backup," however. So, if you've upgraded from Windows 95, and you haven't done so already, you'll want to make a backup with this new version.

To restore a backup made with Microsoft Backup onto a clean hard disk, follow these directions. You'll probably want to skip the first two steps if you're not installing onto a clean system:

1. If you need to prepare your hard disk for Windows, start by inserting your startup diskette (see "Make a startup disk," earlier in this chapter), and turn on your system. When the DOS prompt appears, type `format c: /u/s`, which will erase your entire hard disk, and make it bootable. If you need to make your hard disk bootable without erasing it, type `sys c:`, instead. You should replace `c:` in

both of these examples with the proper drive letter of your hard disk, if different.*

2. Unfortunately, at this point, you won't be able to access your CD in order to install Windows. You'll need to first install the drivers that came with your CD drive (as well as SCSI drivers, if you're using a SCSI CD drive), as well as *Mscdex.exe*, the Microsoft DOS utility that assigns a drive letter to your CD drive. The particular commands depend on your CD drive—consult the drive's documentation for more information.
3. Once you've enabled access to your CD drive, you'll be able to install Windows. When installing, Windows setup will ask you where to install the files. The default is usually *c:\windows*, but you should specify a different, temporary location, such as *c:\just4now*. That way, you won't have to worry about any conflicts between this temporary installation and the files you're going to restore. If your temporary and permanent Windows installation directories are the same, the restore program won't be able to restore any files that are in use during the restore, which means you won't have a complete restore.
4. Select a **Custom** setup, and make sure to include the **Backup** component.
5. When Windows has been successfully installed, the last step is to load any extra drivers required by your backup device. For example, for SCSI tape drives, you may need special SCSI drivers. Consult the documentation that came with your drive and, if applicable, your controller for the appropriate drivers. Having fun yet?
6. The next step is to fire up Microsoft Backup, select the **Restore** tab, and choose your backup device from the **Restore From** list. If you don't see your tape drive or other device listed here, it means you haven't installed all the proper drivers.
7. If you don't see the contents of your last backup in the lower-left pane after selecting the correct backup device, click **Refresh**. Assuming you want to restore everything, simply check the box next to each drive letter. Checking drive *C:*, for example, will select all of the folders and files on that drive to be restored. Click **Start** when you're finished.
8. If all goes well, your backup utility will completely restore the contents of your drive. If you run out of disk space because of the

* These are only guidelines, and don't replace the experience or extra details necessary to fully prepare a new hard disk for use with Windows. Installing and partitioning hard disk drives is beyond the scope of this book.

extra, temporary installation of Windows, you'll only want to restore some of the files—say, just the true Windows installation and a few essentials. You'll then be able to restart the good version of Windows (see the next step), delete the temporary installation, and proceed to restore the rest of your system.

9. This process should include the *Msdos.sys* file, which must be restored into the root directory of your hard disk (usually *c:*). This file is read by the operating system when Windows first starts, and contains the location of your Windows files. Before the restore, the file should point to your *c:\just4now* directory (or whatever you've called it). After the file has been replaced with the version on tape, it should correctly point to the version of Windows that has been restored as well (usually *c:\windows*). This means that the next time you restart, the permanent version of Windows should automatically load. At this point, you can delete the entire *c:\just4now* branch by dragging it into the Recycle Bin.
10. Your hard disk should be completely restored at this point. You should run Scandisk (*Scandskw.exe*) one last time to check for any residual errors.

Using a third-party solution

There are many reasons you might want to use a backup program other than the one that comes with Windows. Many backup devices require proprietary software, and power users will want the extra features offered by a better product, such as a compare utility, a scheduler, and a cataloging feature. Catalogs keep track of all your backups, allowing you to simply choose a file to be restored and have the program tell you which tape you need.

Some backup programs, such as Seagate Backup Exec 2.0 (the program upon which Microsoft Backup 98 is based), allow you to create recovery diskettes. You'll definitely want to take advantage of this feature. *Recovery diskettes* are intended to make a full system restore easier, but depending on the backup software that created them, their contents and the procedure for creating them will vary. In most cases, recovery diskettes are simply Windows startup disks containing the CD drivers and other drivers required to reinstall Windows and set up the backup software.

For the most part, the emergency recovery procedure for any Windows-based backup program is the same as for Microsoft Backup, the only difference being that you'll have to manually install your backup software before you restore.

Using DOS software

There are three scenarios for using a DOS-based backup utility. While none of these are as common as a Windows-based solution, they each have their advantages and disadvantages.

- If you're using an older DOS backup program, it won't be able to back up your long filenames. While this may not sound very serious, consider that your *\Program Files* folder, which many programs, including Windows, rely on, will appear as *\PROGRA~1*.

  The best solution is to simply switch to a Windows-based program, such as the one that comes with Windows 98 (see the previous topic). If that doesn't work, you should be able to find a Windows version of the DOS program you're using now, or a new Windows program that supports your drive.

  Regardless, there is still a way to use your DOS-based backup program and keep your long filenames (LFNs) intact, although it's recommended as only a temporary solution. Microsoft has included a command-line utility on the Windows CD called *Lfnbk.exe*, located in the *\tools\reskit\file\lfnback* folder. Here's how it works: You use Lfnbk to create a database of all your long filenames, in essence, backing them up separately from the files. You then back up all your files and their short filenames along with the LFN database, using your backup program. When it comes time to restore, you start by restoring your files, and then use the Lfnbk utility to reapply your long filenames to the restored files. Obviously, this means you must use Lfnbk originally in order to later restore your long filenames. If you haven't created a Lfnbk long filename database, this utility will be no use to you.

  Read the included documentation file for more information on the use and limitations of Lfnbk. When restoring the long filenames, make sure you have a copy of Lfnbk on a floppy, as you most likely won't be able to access your CD-ROM without Windows. There's also a similar shareware program called Doslfnbkup (see Appendix F); Version 2.2 or later works with Windows 98.

- Some Windows-based programs come with a DOS counterpart used to restore either your entire system, or enough of it so you can get back into Windows. This is a good feature to look for when researching a new backup solution, since you won't have to reinstall Windows just to restore Windows. Make sure it supports long filenames as well (see the previous topic). Refer to the program's documentation for details.

- The third type of DOS backup utility is an imaging utility. These types of programs simply take a single "snapshot" of your hard disk, which can then be dumped back onto your drive in the event of an emergency. The drawback is that you can't usually do a selective restore, where you choose which files to be restored, but rather must restore the entire drive at once. Also, you'll usually need to restore on top of an empty drive, which means that any new files written since the last image backup will have to be backed up and restored separately. The advantages are that the restore is generally much faster, and you won't have to reinstall Windows, assuming the software has a true DOS-based restore function.

Notes and other issues

If you're diligent, you'll want to back up your Registry frequently and independently of your full system backup—see Chapter 3 for more information.

If you're having trouble getting your tape drive to work with Windows, see "Fixing Device-Specific Problems," earlier in this chapter.

Hardware Configuration

Often, solving a problem with a computer means simply finding the correct configuration. It's not unusual to spend hours shuffling around the various devices in your system in an effort to resolve all the conflicts, or even just to get it all to fit in the box.

Sometimes, if you can't come to an acceptable resolution, you may have to set up multiple configurations, just to get everything to work. Windows supports two kinds of multiple configurations:

Multiple Users

This configuration allows you to reconfigure all your installed software for each user. That is, if you log in as "Jack," the desktop wallpaper, the toolbars in your word processor, and the Internet Explorer favorites will all reflect Jack's preferences. If Jack then logs out, and "Jill" logs in, all these settings will then reflect Jill's preferences.

See Chapter 3 for more information on how multiple users are stored in the Registry, and Chapter 7 for more information on configuring your computer for multiple users.

Hardware Profiles

This configuration allows you to save different sets of Device Manager settings. Say, for example, that you have two different pointing devices and a modem, all of which plug into serial ports. Since most PCs only devote two IRQs to serial ports, it's common that only two serial port devices can be used at any given time. In order to have all three devices connected simultaneously, yet still be without conflicts, you'll have to set up two or more hardware profiles.

Double-click on the **System** icon in Control Panel, and choose the **Hardware Profiles** tab. In most circumstances, you'll only see one entry in the list: "Original Configuration." To create a new profile, click **Copy** (intuitive, huh?), and type the name you wish to give the new profile. Initially, both profiles will be identical. However, any subsequent settings in Device Manager will be applied to only the current profile.

So, in the serial port example, one hardware profile might be configured to support both pointing devices while treating the modem as though it weren't connected. In order to use the modem, you'd switch to another hardware profile that would enable the modem but disable one of the pointing devices. See "Stop Windows from Detecting Devices" later in this chapter for more information.

The other nice thing about hardware profiles is that you only load the drivers for the devices that you're using, which saves memory and boot time. Other uses for hardware profiles include docking stations for portable computers, where one profile would include the peripherals connected to the docking station (external monitor, printer, network), while the other profile would only support the devices inside the machine.

The following solutions cover some of the more common configuration problems, questions, and complaints associated with Windows 98, pertaining both to settings used in hardware profiles and to more general configuration techniques.

Stop Windows from Detecting Devices

One of the problems with Plug-and-Play is its tendency to leave out devices you want to use, or less commonly, detect and load drivers for devices you don't want to use. Much of the rest of this chapter is devoted to getting Windows to detect and support devices that it otherwise ignores. But there may be times when you don't want Windows to load a driver for your modem, say, because it conflicts with your graphics tablet.

Although there is no way to prevent Windows' Plug-and-Play feature from detecting and installing drivers for some devices, you can disable most devices that may be causing conflicts. The best use for this is in conjunction with multiple hardware profiles, where you might want to disable a device in one profile, yet enable it in another. See the discussion of hardware profiles in the previous section.

Windows detects devices automatically on startup, as well as manually when you use **Add New Hardware** in Control Panel. When Windows is starting, you usually can't stop it from identifying and installing drivers for most devices, although you can sometimes trick it into treating a device as unknown. When using the Add New Hardware wizard, though, you must either allow Windows either to configure all the devices it finds, or force it to configure no devices by hitting **Cancel**.

In addition to the obvious way to keep Windows from detecting a device (i.e., by yanking it out of your computer), there is a built-in method for disabling certain devices *after* they've been detected:

1. Double-click on the **System** icon in Control Panel, and choose the **Device Manager** tab.
2. Select the device you wish to disable, and click **Properties**.
3. At the bottom of the General page, you'll usually see a **Device usage** section. This section won't be present for some devices (such as CD drives and hard drives). To disable the device, check the **Disable in this hardware profile** option.

   This will prevent Windows from loading drivers for this device the next time Windows boots. If you have more than one hardware profile, this setting will affect only the current profile. In most cases, and with all Plug-and-Play compliant hardware, disabling a device will completely free its resources (IRQ, DMA, I/O address, etc.), making them available for other hardware in your system. However, some non-Plug-and-Play hardware may still consume resources even if the device is disabled in this way.
4. If you check the **Remove from this hardware profile** option (if it's present), the device will be removed from the profile and, in theory, will *not* automatically be detected the next time you restart Windows. This tends to work well for some devices and not as well for others.
5. If you check the **Exists in all hardware profiles** option, it's supposed to do the opposite of the **Remove from this hardware profile** option, explained above. That is, the currently selected device will then appear in all other profiles, assuming you have more than one. This is a workaround to the problem that once you've removed a device, you will never be able to get it back. For this very reason, it's recom-

mended that you avoid both of these settings unless absolutely necessary, and simply use the **Disable in this hardware profile** option.

6. Click **OK** when you're finished. You'll have to restart Windows for this change to take effect.

Notes and other issues

Part of the problem with this solution is that the availability of these options is inconsistent. Some appear for certain devices and are missing from others. It would, of course, be nice if Microsoft made them available all the time.

Some devices can't be disabled in this way. To see if a device can be disabled with other methods, refer to the documentation that came with the device.

Connect Peripherals Without Restarting Windows

Plug-and-Play, if it works, can be very handy. However, its design limits its usefulness, in that newly attached devices are only automatically detected at Windows startup, with the exception of hot-plugable PCMCIA cards.

One of the great things about SCSI technology, besides the fact that it's Plug-and-Play that actually works (and worked long before Windows 95 was released), is the ability to plug in or turn on a SCSI device and use it without having to restart your computer. The ability to plug and unplug external SCSI devices, such as hard drives, removable cartridge drives, scanners, SCSI printers, and other peripherals, is a great time saver. Other hardware can be *hot-plugged* in this way as well, such as parallel-port devices, printers, cameras, and some PCMCIA devices. However, just because the technology supports it doesn't mean that Windows will automatically recognize newly attached hardware and install the appropriate drivers.

What you need to do is force Windows to re-detect specific hardware without restarting. The Add New Hardware wizard isn't any good for this, since it's designed to detect hardware that hasn't yet been configured. Besides, it takes way too long (rebooting is almost always faster), and usually requires that you restart Windows anyway.

After you've properly connected and turned on the external device (don't try this for internal devices, like expansion cards or drives), follow these instructions. Note that, in most cases, the same process will work for removing devices without restarting.

General-purpose solution

1. Double-click on the **System** icon in Control Panel, and choose the **Device Manager** tab.
2. Click the **View devices by connection** option at the top of the Window, which then reorganizes the tree. Instead of being sorted by category, the devices are arranged by the way they are connected to the motherboard. This, for example, groups all your SCSI devices together (see the next solution).
3. Make sure **Computer** at the top of the list is highlighted, and click **Refresh**. This will take anywhere from 5 to 20 seconds, but when it's done, any newly attached devices should appear in the list. Any newly attached devices should now be visible in the tree, once you expand the appropriate branches to find them. Also, any drives you've attached should automatically appear in the My Computer window; likewise, any devices you've *removed* will disappear from the My Computer window.
4. If, at this time, Windows detects a device that it hasn't seen before, it'll prompt you for drivers and such, which then usually requires you to reboot. However, the beauty of it is that you'll only need to do it once; any subsequent engaging or disengaging from the system will be relatively painless.
5. If you can't find your new device, choose the **View devices by connection** option, find your SCSI card in the list, and expand it out to see all the devices attached to it.
6. Close the Device Manager when you're finished.

Adding and removing SCSI devices

There's a shortcut to the above method that works for nearly all SCSI controllers. It refreshes much faster and is less likely to cause problems with any other hardware in your system. Rather than refreshing the entire tree, all you need to refresh is the SCSI controller itself:

1. Follow the instructions in the previous "General-purpose solution" section, but instead of highlighting **Computer** in the list, highlight your SCSI controller.
2. Locate the entry for your SCSI controller. It can be in any of several different places on the tree, depending on your model. For SCSI controllers with PCI connectors, it will be in the **\Plug and Play BIOS\PCI bus** branch. If you have more than one SCSI controller, click the plus sign next to each controller to see which devices are

connected; this should be enough information. Figure 6-5 shows Device Manager in **View devices by connection** mode, with the first of two SCSI controllers highlighted.

3. Simply highlight your SCSI controller, and then press **Refresh**.

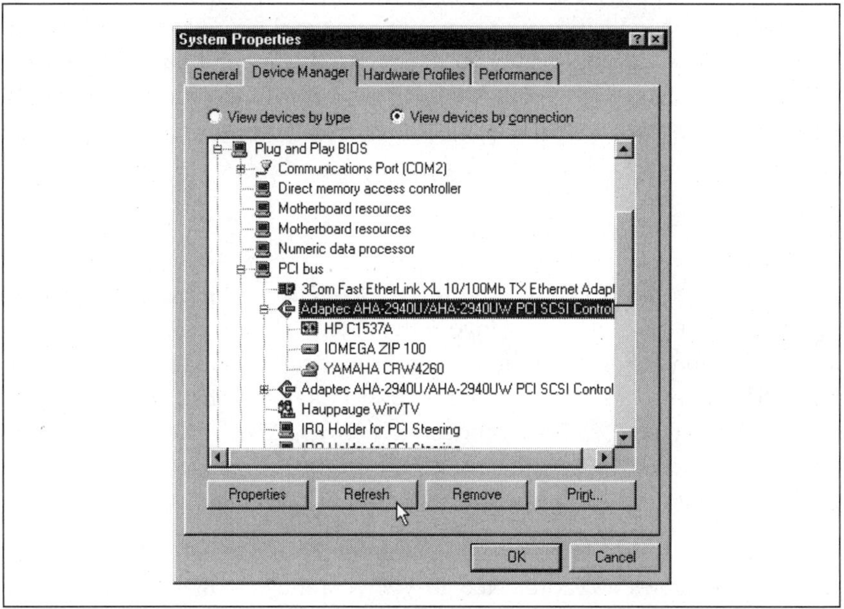

Figure 6-5: Finding your SCSI controller in the tree can significantly reduce the time required to detect new devices, since Windows will only refresh that controller

Notes and other issues

Make sure any external devices are also plugged in and turned on (if applicable); without power, Windows won't be able to see them.

In some circumstances, refreshing Device Manager in this way will cause your system to lock up. If you can't get control back after a minute, you'll most likely have to restart your computer. If you're trying to refresh SCSI devices only, follow the second solution; since it doesn't bother refreshing the entire system, you're less likely to "hit a nerve."

While technically you can attach and remove internal SCSI drives, it's not recommended, as connecting and disconnecting the four-prong drive power cable while the system is on can easily short. For this reason, it's best to power down before connecting or disconnecting any devices internally. Regardless, you'll need to restart your computer when connecting or disconnecting any IDE drives.

There are some SCSI devices for which this will not work; you may still have to restart your system to force Windows to recognize newly attached devices.

If you change the SCSI ID of a device before reconnecting it to your system, one of two things may happen. Either Windows will not recognize the change, which may or may not prevent the device from working, or Windows will think that you're connecting an entirely new device, which is a design flaw in Windows. If Windows thinks you're installing a new device, it'll ask for drivers, and then, depending on the device, may require that you restart.

Designate Drive Letters

Each disk drive on a PC, whether it's a CD-ROM, a floppy, a removable, or a hard disk, has its own drive letter. Some drives are separated into several sections, called partitions, and each partition has its own drive letter. This goes back to the very first IBM PCs, which had only one 5.25" floppy drive (some deluxe models had two). The drives were called simply "A" and "B". Later, the IBM XT's massive 10-megabyte hard drive was called simply "C".

There are two ways that drives are assigned drive letters, both dependent on how the drives are connected to your computer. Those controlled by your BIOS, which don't require any software drivers, usually include your floppy drive and most hard drives, for which drive letters are created when your system is first turned on. Drives controlled solely by software aren't recognized until the software is loaded, usually by Windows. These types of drives include CD drives, removable cartridge drives, network drives, and some SCSI hard disks.

Generally, drive letters are assigned to these drives depending on the order in which they are loaded. Your first floppy drive is always assigned to A:, and the second floppy, if you have one, is assigned to B:. The hard disk drives controlled by your BIOS always start at C:, and go from there. Any software-controlled drives, such as CD and network drives, follow.

For example, assume a computer with three hard disks, two floppies, and a CD drive. Two of the hard disks are IDE drives (drives 1 and 2) and are controlled by the computer's BIOS; drive 3 is a SCSI drive, and is controlled by SCSI drivers* built into Windows. And just for fun, we'll add

* Not all SCSI drives are controlled by drivers. Any SCSI adapter with its own on-board BIOS (a good feature) will load its drives as though they were BIOS drives. If your motherboard comes with a built-in SCSI adapter, it most likely has its own BIOS. Whether IDE or SCSI drives are loaded first depends on how your SCSI BIOS is configured.

a Zip drive and a network-shared drive, and make each hard disk have at least two partitions. In Windows 98, drive letters will be assigned, by default, as follows:

A: Floppy Drive #1

B: Floppy Drive #2

C: Hard Disk #1 (IDE), First Partition

D: Hard Disk #2 (IDE), First Partition

E: Hard Disk #1 (IDE), Second Partition

F: Hard Disk #1 (IDE), Third Partition

G: Hard Disk #2 (IDE), Second Partition

H: Hard Disk #3 (SCSI), First Partition †

I: Hard Disk #3 (SCSI), Second Partition †

J: CD Drive †

K: Zip Drive †

L: Network Drive †

Note that only the first partitions of the two BIOS-controlled drives are listed first. Then, starting back with the first drive, the remaining partitions are listed, followed by the remaining partitions of the second drive. Once all of the partitions of the BIOS-controlled drives are loaded, Windows adds the software-controlled hard disk (#3) and the CD drive.

Only those drive letters marked with a dagger (†), the drives controlled by software, can be changed in Windows. The drive letters for any BIOS-controlled devices can't be reassigned in Windows 98, although Windows NT is able to reassign drive letters for any drive on the system.

While this example shows a bunch of drives, most users will only have a single hard drive with a single partition, probably with a CD-ROM drive, and one or two floppy drives. Here's how to designate drive letters for drives that support it:

1. Double-click on the **System** icon in Control Panel, and click on the **Device Manager** tab.
2. Find the device (CD drive, Zip drive, or other device) that you wish to configure from the list, and highlight it.
3. Click **Properties**, and choose the **Settings** tab.
4. By default, the **Removable** option is turned on for all CD drives and removable cartridge drives, such as Zip drives. For hard disks, this option is turned off by default. In order to change drive letters, you'll need to make sure this option is turned on. Remember that you can only reassign hard disks that are *not* controlled by the BIOS, such as

some SCSI hard disks. If **Removable** is initially turned off, make sure to turn it off once again when you're finished with this procedure.

5. You can now choose a new drive letter for the highlighted drive. In the section entitled **Reserved drive letters**, choose the *same* letter for both the **Start drive letter** and **End drive letter**. The only time you'll want to choose different drive letters for **Start** and **End** is if you're configuring a hard disk with more than one partition (such as Drive #3 in our example). If the letter you choose conflicts with any other drive, and the other drive is not BIOS-controlled, Windows will reassign the other drive to make room for the one you're configuring.
6. Press **OK** and then **OK** again when you're finished. You'll have to restart your computer for this change to take effect.

Notes and other issues

The above solution will only work if Windows has control over the device. This means that if a particular drive is not BIOS-controlled, but rather supported by drivers specified in your *Config.sys* or *Autoexec.bat* files, you'll need to either remove those entries (see "Do I Still Need Config.sys and Autoexec.bat?," later in this chapter) or reconfigure them (refer to the documentation that came with the device).

Network drives connected through a Microsoft Windows network will not show up in Device Manager. You'll need to remap them in order to change their drive letters. See "Setting Up a Workgroup" in Chapter 7 for more information.

I like to name drives something descriptive, such as N: for network drives, S: for Syquest Drives, and Z: for Zip drives. Too bad you can't use C: for CD drives.

For your reference, the drive letter information for all your drives is stored in the Registry (see Chapter 3) under the `CurrentDriveLetterAssignment` and `UserDriveLetterAssignment` values in the following keys:

- For all SCSI devices, and most non-SCSI CD-ROM drives, look in `HKEY_LOCAL_MACHINE\Enum\SCSI`.
- For IDE hard disks, look in `HKEY_LOCAL_MACHINE\Enum\ESDI`.
- For standard floppy drives, look in `HKEY_LOCAL_MACHINE\Enum\FLOP`.

Stop Windows from Randomly Searching the Floppy Drive

A bizarre and annoying quirk, which first appeared in Windows 95, has unfortunately made its way into Windows 98. For some reason, Windows will try to read the floppy drive at any time, and for no apparent reason.

The most likely cause is that a program was launched from the floppy drive at some point, and Windows has now made this the current drive. However, this problem manifests itself even when the system is restarted, meaning that there's something else going on here.

There are many things that can cause this problem, such as references to the floppy drive in certain places, as well as some third-party software. To identify the source of the problem, try the following:

- When refreshing the Start Menu, Explorer may reread the contents of the *\Windows\Recent* folder, which comprise the **Documents** menu. Windows may then poll the floppy drive if any of the shortcuts in that folder contain references to it. Select **Settings** and then **Taskbar** from the Start Menu, choose the **Start Menu Programs** tab, and click **Clear** to empty this list. See "Customize Start Menu Components" in Chapter 4, *Tinkering Techniques*, for more information.
- Clear out the history of the Start Menu's **Run** command. Use TweakUI (see Appendix A, *Setting Locator*), choose the **Paranoia** tab, check the **Clear Run history at logon** option, and then click **Clear Selected Items Now**. You can then turn off the **Clear Run history at logon** if you wish.
- Search your hard disk for all DOS and Windows shortcuts that point to programs on a floppy drive. Select **Find** from the Start Menu, and then **Files or Folders**. Type `*.lnk, *.pif` in the **Named** field, type `a:` (or `b:`, if applicable) in the **Containing text** field, and click **Find Now**. The find results will then list any DOS and Windows shortcuts on your system that reference your floppy drive. In most circumstances, you can delete any files that are found (shortcuts to programs on floppies are rarely useful): if you're unsure, right-click on the shortcut and click **Properties** to find out more about it.
- Search your hard disk for all files with the configuration file extension `*.ini` that contain the text `a:`, using the procedure in the previous item. If one or more files are found, use a text editor such as Notepad to edit the file and remove the reference. See "Using .ini Files" in Chapter 3 for more information if you're not familiar with editing these files.

- Take out the line that reads `LocalLoadHigh=1` from your *Msdos.sys* file, if it's there. See Appendix C, *Contents of the MSDOS.SYS File*, for more information. Note that this line will only be there if you intentionally placed it there in the first place, and is not required to run Windows.
- Search your entire Registry for `a:`, looking for any references to files or programs on your floppy drive. More specifically, the path `HKEY_CLASSES_ROOT\CLSID` may contain references to OCXs or *.dlls* that it may have found on your floppy drive.
- If you have a program like Norton Navigator for Windows that saves the 10 most recently visited folders for each application's File Open and File Save dialogs (otherwise a useful feature), it may have saved a reference to your floppy somewhere along the way. Consult the documentation for this, or any other program you suspect, for more information on clearing the various "history" lists.
- Check for any viruses on your system (some users have reported the *Neuville* virus); you'll need an antivirus utility for this.
- Lastly, check the programs that are loaded automatically; Windows may expect that one of them resides on a floppy drive or, more likely, the program being loaded may be looking for some data or supplementary file on a floppy drive. See "Errors during startup" earlier in this chapter for the different ways programs are configured to run at startup.

Force NumLock to Behave

Ever since IBM introduced their enhanced 101-key keyboard with two sets of cursor keys back in 1984, the **NumLock** key on most keyboards is turned on by default. Since some prefer it turned off while others prefer it on, there are several ways to change the default. However, Windows has a nasty habit of occasionally overriding system settings when it comes to the status of the **NumLock** key. The following are several solutions to choosing the setting you prefer.

Solution 1

- In most modern computers, you can set the default in your CMOS setup. This screen, usually accessible by pressing **Del**, **ESC**, or some other key when your computer first boots up, is where you also define the parameters for your fixed and floppy drives, memory settings, the clock, and other system parameters. Refer to the manual that came with your computer or motherboard for instructions on changing this setting; it's usually something like `Numlock Default: ON / OFF`.

Solution 2

- Include the command `NUMLOCK=OFF` or `NUMLOCK=ON`, depending on your preference, somewhere in your *Config.sys* file (on its own line). See "Do I Still Need Config.sys and Autoexec.bat?" later in this chapter for more information.

Solution 3 (if you have Microsoft's Intellipoint software installed)

1. Open the Registry Editor (if you're not familiar with the Registry Editor, see Chapter 3).
2. Expand the branches to `HKEY_CURRENT_USER\Control Panel\Microsoft Input Devices\Keyboard`. If the `Keyboard` key isn't there, add it.
3. Select **New** from the **Edit** menu, then **String Value**, and type `NumLock` for the name of the new value.
4. Double-click on this new value, and type either `ON` or `OFF` in the box that appears, depending on your preference.

Notes and other issues

If none of these solutions work, look for and remove other third-party keyboard utilities (such as Microsoft's useless Intellipoint software, which comes with their faux-ergonomic *Natural* keyboards).

Adjust Your Printer Timeout

If you've ever printed in Windows 98, your work has undoubtedly been interrupted with the little "Windows will retry in 5 seconds" window shown in Figure 6-6 that appears if your printer is not turned on, is out of paper, or is just warming up.

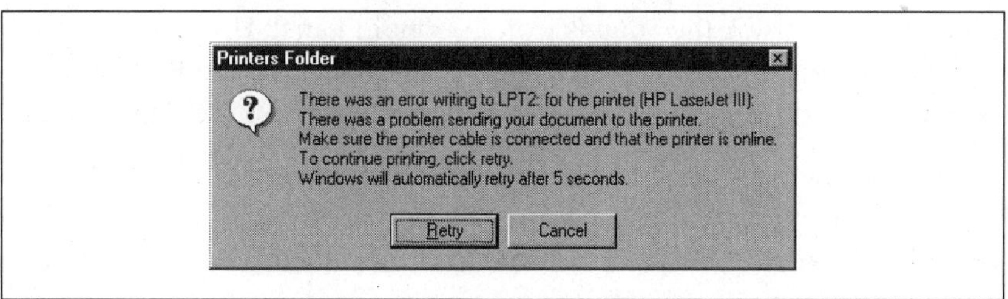

Figure 6-6: The Printer Timeout window, which interrupts your work with no useful information, is just plain irritating

The time that Windows waits before notifying you that the printer isn't ready is called the *timeout*. In Windows 3.x, the timeout was easily changed through Control Panel to suit one's printer and work habits, but this adjustment can be difficult to find in Windows 98. It can be terribly irritating to have to look at this retry window every 5 seconds. Here's how to make it more tolerable:

1. Start by selecting **Printers** from the Start Menu's **Settings** menu. Right-click on the printer you wish to change, click **Properties**, and choose the **Details** tab.
2. In the Timeout settings section, you'll see two options. The counter-intuitive **Not Selected** field is the amount of time Windows waits before telling you the printer won't print. If you find this window appearing too often, change its value to 90 seconds, or whatever value works for you. Conversely, if you want to know right away whenever there's a problem with your printer, shorten the time to something like 5 seconds.
3. Click **OK** when you're finished.

Notes and other issues

This solution won't work for some systems, and the little box will still appear regardless of this setting. Other than obtaining specialized printer drivers from the manufacturer of your printer, there's no other way to change this setting.

You may have noticed that if your printer is not plugged in to your computer, this box does not appear at all. In fact, Windows may never notify you that it can't print in this situation.

Turn Off the PC Speaker

Most of us who are annoyed by the various beeps and sputters of our sound cards and the good old PC speaker have turned off most of the sound "events" using the **Sounds** icon in Control Panel. However, on some computers, turning off all of the sound events will cause the PC speaker to be used instead for the default beep. Very rarely is this a pleasant sound.

For some reason, it isn't possible to permanently remove or disable the **System Speaker** device in Device Manager (see "Stop Windows from Detecting Devices" earlier in this chapter), and there's no other way to disable sounds, even with the Volume Control.*

* Yes, the Volume Control does have an optional **PC Speaker** control, but it has no effect on the system beep. Arrrggghhh!

Luckily, there are three, albeit not very obvious, workarounds to the problem.

Solution 1

- Yank the PC speaker out of your computer. It's almost always obvious once you remove your computer's cover, and is usually connected to the motherboard by a two-conductor wire that can be easily disconnected. You'll find it remarkably liberating.

Solution 2

1. Using the sound recorder (*Sndrec32.exe*), create a small *.wav* file of silence.
2. Double-click on the **Sounds** icon in Control Panel, and choose each of the following from the **Events** list: **Asterisk**, **Default Sound**, and **Exclamation**. For each one, click **Browse**, and select the new, silent *.wav* file you've created. Instead of an annoying *.wav* file or the jarring PC beep, this silent file will be played, allowing you to work in relative peace.

Solution 3

- Double-click on the **TweakUI** icon in Control Panel (see Appendix A). Under the **General** tab, in the **Effects** list, turn off the **Beep on Errors** option. Click **OK** when you're finished.

Notes and other issues

Why did Microsoft make this so difficult for us?

DOS to the Rescue

DOS is our friend, as well as our foe. It had better be our friend, since Windows requires it in order to function. This means that, more or less, Windows is susceptible to the same problems that DOS has had since 1979. Sure, Windows NT abandons DOS altogether, but NT has its own problems.

DOS can be useful as well. It's nice to be able to fix a malfunctioning Windows installation without having to reinstall everything from scratch. It's better than NT's dependence on 3 "emergency recovery diskettes" which are more likely to fail than your hard disk. It's also a whole lot better than the Macintosh's little unhappy face, which you'll see when something is wrong.

I, for one, like being able to turn my computer on, load DOS in *seconds*, and, for example, format a floppy—without having to wait for Windows to load.

Like it or not, DOS is the foundation of the PC, and sometimes you must take advantage of its virtues and limitations in order to get anywhere in the Windows world. *Windows 95 in a Nutshell*, by Tim O'Reilly and Troy Mott (O'Reilly & Associates), has a great discussion of the role of DOS on the Windows platform. See Appendix B of this book for more information on the DOS prompt and the more common DOS commands.

Do I Still Need Config.sys and Autoexec.bat?

Before Windows 95 and Plug-and-Play, some devices in your system required device drivers to be listed in two text files in the root directory of your hard disk, called *Config.sys* and *Autoexec.bat*. While this was necessary back then in order to use Windows 3.x, nearly all the functionality of these two files has now been replaced by Windows 95/98.

However, even if your computer shipped with Windows preinstalled, these files may still be there, loading drivers you don't need. As our recollections of DOS-based computers and Windows 3.x fades, this question is asked less often, but until Microsoft abandons the Windows-on-DOS platform (see Chapter 1, *Making the Most of Windows 98*), it's still something we need to consider.

The problem with these old files is that the drivers they load aren't as efficient or as stable as their 32-bit Windows counterparts. They take up more memory, and slow down boot time as well. Additionally, a device driver specified in one of these files might actually prevent Windows from detecting and using a certain device. Ideally, you should remove these files altogether, but first you need to make sure all of the functions your particular copies provide for you can be completely reproduced in Windows.

If you don't have a *Config.sys* or *Autoexec.bat* file in your *c:* directory, you obviously don't need to continue. However, you might want to take a look at "Create a Startup Menu," later in this chapter, for other uses of these files.

When you turn on your computer, there are several things that happen. After it's through counting memory and identifying hard disks, your system will beep to signify that it's done with its power-on self-test (POST). Then, the basic operating system files (in essence, DOS) are loaded off the hard disk, at which time *Msdos.sys* is read (see Appendix

C). DOS reads *Config.sys* (if it's there) and executes *Autoexec.bat* (if it's there). When *Autoexec.bat* is finished, Windows is loaded.

Drivers specified in *Config.sys* usually have the extension *.sys*, and are called real-mode drivers. Generally, the *Config.sys* file loads drivers for your disk cache (such as Smartdrv), memory manager, CD drive, and sound card, for any removable or optical drives, and for your scanner, as well as a myriad of parameters like `Files=50`, `Buffers=20`, and so on. Windows 98 eliminates the need for all of these. In fact, during Windows setup, most of these types of entries will be automatically taken out, as they can conflict with the corresponding Windows replacements. The goal is to remove this file entirely.

Autoexec.bat is similar to *Config.sys*, although instead of just installing drivers, its primary role is to load programs, set environment variables, and load drivers. *Autoexec.bat* is a DOS batch file run automatically every time your computer is turned on, just before Windows loads. The goal is to clean out as much junk from this file as possible, although the file may be necessary for a few basic functions.

These two files are simply text files that can be edited with a plain text editor, such as Notepad. Windows comes with a DOS text editor as well: type `edit c:\config.sys`, for example, to edit the file in DOS. If you make backups of these files (for example, type `copy config.sys config.bak`) before you start tinkering with them, you'll eliminate the possibility of disabling your system. If anything goes wrong, simply replace the files you've altered with your backups.

Note that some older devices may not work without drivers specified in these two files. If this is the case, you are *strongly* encouraged to seek 32-bit Windows replacements. See the section "Drivers and Installing Hardware" at the beginning of this chapter.

The following are the steps involved in liberating yourself from *Config.sys* and *Autoexec.bat*:

1. Start off by opening *Config.sys* in any plain text editor, and putting the word `rem` in front of *every* line. Save the file and restart your computer when you're done. The `rem` command turns each entry into a remark, essentially a decorative label which is ignored by DOS. This is better than removing the lines completely, because you may have to go back and restore one or more of the entries.
2. As always, when Windows restarts, it automatically scans your computer for any new devices it finds. If you've disabled any old device drivers with the previous step, Windows may suddenly "see"

one or more new devices, and attempt to install a new, native 32-bit driver for each one. Refer to the documentation that came with any specific devices if you encounter problems, and see "Drivers and Installing Hardware" as well as "Fixing Device-Specific Problems," both earlier in this chapter, for details.

The one common problem that arises in this scenario is that Windows may need to retrieve drivers from the Windows 98 CD. If your CD-ROM drive is one of the devices that was previously supported by *Config.sys*, and Windows needs to access the CD to get the necessary drivers,* you may encounter a Catch-22. If this happens, skip all drivers until Windows loads. Then, go back and re-enable the lines in *Config.sys*, and restart again. Take this opportunity to copy the files in the *\Win98* directory on the CD onto your hard drive, and then start the process over. When Windows asks for the CD, simply point it to the directory on your hard disk.

3. Once Windows appears to have loaded all the drivers it intends to, try out all your devices. You may have to run the Add New Hardware wizard in Control Panel to search for any newly added hardware if your system doesn't support Plug-and-Play completely. If a device works, you can remove its driver from *Config.sys* for good. Otherwise, take out the `rem` command you placed in front of the driver to re-enable it.

4. If everything appears to be working properly now that all the statements in the *Config.sys* file have been disabled, you can delete it, and continue with *Autoexec.bat*.

   The same process applies to *Autoexec.bat*, with the exception of the `Path` statement. For some mysterious reason, it never occurred to the folks at Microsoft to include Windows support for this functionality. See "The path less traveled" earlier in this chapter for more information.

Notes and other issues

If you think that keeping these old drivers loaded all the time is a good idea in case you need to reinstall Windows, you are mistaken. You will have better performance and stability if you use the native Windows drivers only. However, I strongly recommend copying all your old CD drivers to a bootable floppy, so they are available in the event of an emer-

* Standard IDE CD drives usually won't experience this problem. However, if your CD drive is connected to a proprietary interface or a SCSI controller for which Windows hasn't previously loaded drivers, you may need the files on that CD.

gency, such as a disk crash. Since Windows does not do this automatically, it's a good idea to do it yourself while it's still fresh in your mind. See "Make a startup disk" earlier in this chapter for more information.

If you still need these DOS drivers when you run a certain DOS application, you can configure Windows to load them automatically when needed, rather then keeping them in memory all the time. First of all, you can move any such *Autoexec.bat* statements into a file called *Dosstart.bat*, placed also in your root directory. This file will be run whenever you restart in MS-DOS mode.

You can also move any statements needed temporarily from your *Config.sys* file to the properties of a DOS shortcut, to be loaded when the shortcut is run. Right click on the *MS-DOS Prompt* shortcut located in your *Windows* directory (or the shortcut for any other DOS application you need to configure), and click **Properties**. Choose the **Program** tab, click **Advanced**, turn on the **MS-DOS mode** option, and select **Specify a new MS-DOS configuration**. You can now enter any desired drivers here as though they were loaded in *Config.sys* or *Autoexec.bat*. Click **OK** and then **OK** again when finished.

See the next section for a reason to keep *Autoexec.bat* and *Config.sys* around.

Create a Startup Menu

Startup menus appear when you first turn on your computer, before Windows loads. There are three varieties, each with different purposes and limitations. They are shown in order of execution; that is, if you were to use all three, they would appear in this order.

Windows NT dual-boot menu

If you've installed Windows NT 4.0 or 5.0 on the same system as Windows 98, the Windows NT installation program will automatically create a dual-boot menu, allowing you to choose which operating system to load every time the computer is started. The dual-boot menu usually gives you the choice of Windows NT, Windows NT with the plain vanilla VGA video driver, or Windows 98, which it may call MS-DOS or Windows, depending on your version of NT.

There are two ways to edit this menu. The first method simply allows you to select a default option and the delay:

1. In Windows NT, double-click on the **System** icon in **Control Panel**, and choose the **Startup/shutdown** tab.

2. Choose the desired option from the **Startup** list, and specify the delay where it says **Show List for xx Seconds**, where **xx** is the number of seconds you choose. Setting the "MS-DOS" option as the default and choosing a delay of 10 seconds means that the menu will be displayed for 10 seconds. After that time, if no selection is made, MS-DOS will be chosen automatically.

The second method requires that you edit a system file, but allows you to change the text and ordering of any of the items:

1. Using a plain text editor, such as Notepad, edit *Boot.ini*, which resides in the root directory of your boot drive (usually *c:*). Since this file has the System attribute set, you'll need to turn it off with the DOS `ATTRIB` command before you can edit it. Refer to Chapter 3 for more information on editing INI files, and Appendix B for more information on the `ATTRIB` command.
2. There are two sections here, `[boot loader]` and `[operating systems]`.

   The `[boot loader]` section contains the `timeout` setting (the delay discussed previously) and the `default` setting (also discussed previously).

   The `[operating systems]` section lists all of the items shown in the menu. By very careful not to change any text not already enclosed in quotation marks. To the left of the equals sign on each line is the drive containing the startup files for the operating system—don't change this. This is also what's used in the `default` setting above. To the right of the equals sign are the label, enclosed in quotation marks, and any settings, such as `/basevideo /sos` for NT's safe mode).

   You can change the labels and reorder the lines, but leave everything else alone.
3. Save the file and reboot when you're finished.

Windows startup menu

This menu is built into Windows, and will appear if Windows didn't load successfully or wasn't shut down completely the last time the computer was used. Its primary purpose is to provide access to the command prompt and Windows safe mode to aid in troubleshooting startup and configuration problem.

You can display this menu manually by pressing the **F8** key during system startup, just after the system beep and before the Windows logo appears. When the menu appears, you have eight choices:

1. **Normal**

   Choose this to load Windows normally as though nothing has happened.

2. **Logged (\BOOTLOG.TXT)**

   This is the same as #1, except that all the steps of the bootup process are recorded in the *Bootlog.txt* file in the root directory of your boot drive. View this file after startup to help determine if any drivers or tasks failed to load.

3. **Safe Mode**

   This loads Windows with the default VGA display driver (640×480 in 20 colors) and no network support, so that you can change settings if you can't get into Windows normally. This is useful, for example, if you've changed your video driver to a new one that doesn't work. The **F5** key instead of the **F8** key above has the same effect as selecting this option.

4. **Safe Mode with Network Support**

   This is the same as #3, except that your network drivers (if any) are loaded as well in case you need network access to effect repairs.

5. **Step-by-step Confirmation**

   This is the same as #1, except that Windows will ask you before loading each and every driver. This is useful in isolating certain problems that may be occurring when you load Windows. If you press **Shift-F8**, it will either turn on or off step-by-step confirmation, so you can use the feature in conjunction with any of the other options here.

6. **Command Prompt Only**

   This will boot you directly into DOS after loading *Config.sys* and *Autoexec.bat*, rather than loading Windows. Press **Shift-F5** either here or when your computer first starts to go into the command prompt without loading *Config.sys* or *Autoexec.bat*. See "Boot directly into DOS" in "Getting Into and Out of DOS" in Chapter 5 to force your computer to use this option every time.

7. **Safe Mode Command Prompt Only**

   This is the same as choice 6, except that *Autoexec.bat* and *Config.sys* are skipped. If you then want to run Windows in safe mode, type `win /d:m` at the command prompt.

8. **Previous Version of MS-DOS**

   If you've installed Windows over an older version of MS-DOS, and have opted to keep DOS on your system, you can load it at this time by selecting this option.

MS-DOS startup menu

The third type of startup menu has been around since MS-DOS 5.0 and is the most flexible of the three. While it doesn't allow you to change operating systems, you can set up any number of different configurations. You can give yourself the option of booting into DOS, loading Windows, loading Windows in safe mode, loading another version of Windows, booting into DOS with special drivers required for your favorite DOS game, or anything else you may need. While most users won't need this menu at all, those of you who still use DOS applications or games will find this menu very useful.

Although the Windows documentation doesn't tell you how to create this menu, or even that it's possible, the old DOS tricks still work, so it's a good idea to get your DOS manual ready. This functionality can be useful for those who use DOS more than just occasionally and who don't want to be forced to wait for Windows to load just to play a DOS game. Note that this procedure can be tricky and requires some basic knowledge of the *Autoexec.bat* and *Config.sys* files; see "Do I Still Need Config.sys and Autoexec.bat?" earlier in this chapter for more information.

The following is an example showing how to create a menu that gives you a choice between DOS and Windows every time you start up. Your actual files may differ substantially, but the methodology will be the same. Remember to back up your existing files before you begin:

1. Configure your computer to boot directly into MS-DOS; see "Getting Into and Out of DOS" in Chapter 5.
2. Use a text editor such as Notepad to open your *Config.sys* file, located in the root directory of your boot drive (usually *C:*). If it's not there, create a new file.
3. Type the text shown in Example 6-1 at the *top* of the file. Make sure that there aren't any commands floating around that aren't part of a particular section. Sections are denoted by `[brackets]`. The text will probably need some adjustments for your system.

Example 6-1. Config.sys File Commands to Create an MS-DOS Startup Menu

```
[Menu]
MenuItem = MS-DOS
MenuItem = Windows
   ... include any additional menu items here
MenuDefault MS-DOS,4
MenuColor 15,1
[MS-DOS]
   ... put all your MS-DOS drivers here
[Windows]
   ... put all the real-mode drivers required for Windows
       here (should be empty for most users)
[etc.]
   ... make a section for each additional menu item, with
       each name matching a new "menuitem" command above
[Common]
   ... put all the stuff you want loaded all the time, no
       matter which menu item is selected
```

4. Now, save *Config.sys*, and open *Autoexec.bat* (create it if it's not there), using the same text editor, and type the lines shown in Example 6-2 at the *top* of the file (this may need some adjustments if you have added more menu items).

   Follow the logic in this file, as you'll probably have to change the `IF` statements to suit your particular choices. The **`%CONFIG%`** variable is set by DOS to whatever menu item is chosen, and the `IF` statement is used to redirect execution depending on the variable. In the example shown, if the user selects **Windows**, the `win` command is issued, and the rest of the file (where it says ". . . put all your DOS autoexec stuff here") is skipped.

Example 6-2: Autoexec.bat Commands to Create an MS-DOS Startup Menu

```
@ECHO OFF
REM * If user selects "Windows" it must be run manually here *
IF "%CONFIG%"=="Windows" win
IF "%CONFIG%"=="Windows" goto skip

    ...put all your DOS autoexec stuff here
:skip
```

5. Save your changes when finished, and restart your computer to test the new menu.

Notes and other issues

The particular drivers required by your system depend on the devices you have installed. There are no "standard" *Config.sys* or *Autoexec.bat* files, other than the two examples given above.

Getting DOS Games to Work

There is almost nothing more frustrating or difficult than to get certain DOS games to work on a Windows system. It seems as though each game needs its own drivers and memory settings installed just to start. Additional problems, such as getting sound to work and using the CD drive when Windows *isn't* running, are even more difficult to resolve.

Luckily, more game designers are releasing native 32-bit Windows games, especially now that Microsoft has improved its DirectX drivers. DirectX allows game designers to write software that can communicate directly with video and sound hardware, which is necessary for high performance gaming. This type of high-speed communication with hardware was previously only available from within DOS, which is why so many game designers continued to release DOS-based games, even after the release of Windows 95. The first version of DirectX, a technology that was originally marketed as a feature of Windows 95, wasn't released until about six months after the operating system was introduced.

In the old days of conventional memory and expanded memory managers, one often spent hours tuning and reconfiguring so that a game would have enough of the right *kind* of memory to run. Ahh, such memories.

Now that Windows has all of the necessary memory managers and device drivers built in, they don't need to be specified in *Autoexec.bat* and *Config.sys*, which means that you need to use the drivers needed by the particular game only when Windows *isn't* loaded. While the situation is infinitely better than it was just a few years ago, there are still problems. Some poorly designed games won't run from within Windows, but require some of the services Windows provides to work at all; avoid products like this at all costs.

The key to solving these types of problems is to engineer an appropriate environment for each DOS-based game you run. This environment is mostly dependent on how you enter DOS, either from within Windows or directly at startup. There are five ways of getting into DOS, each with its own advantages and disadvantages. The different solutions are presented in order of preference, the first being the most convenient and preferred.

Open a Command Prompt from within Windows

Whether you open the Command Prompt from the Start Menu, double-click the game's executable (*.exe* or *.com* file) directly from Explorer, or use a Windows shortcut to launch the DOS game (in most cases), you'll be using the Command Prompt from within Windows. The Command Prompt, also known as a DOS window, enables you to run most DOS programs from within Windows.

The advantages of using the Command Prompt are:

- Most games will actually run in a DOS window with few or no special settings. Since Windows controls the CD drive and sound card, it means that the game can access these devices without any special drivers. Having Windows take care of these drivers means that they won't take up precious DOS memory.
- You don't have to restart your computer or close any of your applications to run a DOS game in this way. Note that DOS games can be unstable, so it's best not to leave Windows applications open with unsaved work if you do this.
- You can create shortcuts in the Start Menu for each of your DOS games, virtually eliminating the typing otherwise involved.
- You can load special settings and drivers, even with DOS games run in Windows. To specify special memory settings, or any *Config.sys* drivers or *Autoexec.bat* commands to load with the game (such as sound card or mouse drivers), first create a Windows shortcut to the game. Right-click on the shortcut and select **Properties**. Choose the **Memory** tab to specify the amount of memory to reserve for the game; refer to the game's documentation for the game's memory requirements. If you choose the **Program** tab, click **Advanced**, and turn on the **MS-DOS mode** option; it's the same as restarting the computer in MS-DOS mode.

The disadvantages of using the Command Prompt are:

- Many games require a great deal of memory, or access your hardware directly, meaning that they won't work, or will run more slowly, while Windows is running in the background.
- If a DOS game only runs from within Windows, you'll have to wait for Windows to load before running the game, which is a bit ironic.

Restart in MS-DOS mode

If a game won't run from within Windows, you can select **Shut Down** from the Start Menu, and choose **Restart in MS-DOS Mode**. This unloads Windows, which will allow you to run nearly all DOS games that don't run in a DOS window.

The advantages of using **Restart in MS-DOS mode** are:

- You can create a Windows shortcut to the game which automatically shuts down to DOS, runs the game, and then reloads Windows. Right-click on the shortcut, click **Properties**, choose the **Program** tab, click **Advanced**, and turn on the **MS-DOS mode** option.
- Furthermore, in the **Advanced Program Settings** dialog of the shortcut properties sheet, you can specify a special *Config.sys* or *Autoexec.bat* file to be used exclusively with the game. Since you're unloading Windows, you may need to load a DOS-based CD driver, a mouse driver, and sound card drivers. Such requirements depend entirely on the game, which is the beauty of this design.
- Since Windows isn't running in the background, the game can run at its full speed.
- Configuring games to run this way doesn't mean that they can't also run with one of the other MS-DOS settings explained hereafter.

The disadvantages of using **Restart in MS-DOS mode** are:

- This method, while sometimes necessary, can take more time and effort to configure. Once you've done it, however, it's a snap to use.
- If you turn on your computer just to run a DOS-based game, you have to wait for Windows to load before you can run the game. Additionally, you have to wait for Windows to reload after the game concludes, unless, of course, you shut the computer off.
- Windows doesn't unload itself entirely from memory with this method, which means that some games may still not run. See the next sections, "Boot directly into DOS" and "Exit to DOS."

Boot directly into DOS

The "Boot directly into DOS" solution in "Getting Into and Out of DOS" in Chapter 5 outlines the steps necessary to make your bootup process more like that of Windows 3.x, where Windows 98 is not automatically loaded when you first turn on your computer. While this requires that you reconfigure your startup procedure somewhat, the advantages can be worth it, especially if you play a lot of DOS games or use a lot of DOS-based applications.

The advantages of booting directly into DOS are:

- You can configure a DOS startup menu (as described earlier in this chapter) to allow you to choose between Windows and any number of DOS games. In fact, if you create a menu item for each game, you can specify separate *Config.sys* and *Autoexec.bat* statements for each game.

- You won't have to wait for Windows to load before running a DOS game. Furthermore, you can start Windows after the game concludes by typing `win` at the command prompt.

The disadvantages of booting directly into DOS are:

- The DOS game you're trying to get working may not be worth the time and effort required to implement this method. Of course, some games are worth it.
- If a game requires a sound card or CD drivers, you'll have to load them when the computer starts, which requires some work. Make sure these drivers are loaded only when you use the DOS game, and not when Windows is running (see "Do I Still Need Config.sys and Autoexec.bat?" earlier in this chapter). Furthermore, these drivers, while required by many games, also take up conventional memory, which may not leave enough over for the actual game to run. It's a lovely Catch-22.

Exit to DOS

This has all of the same advantages and disadvantages of the previous solution, with the following exception: rather than starting in DOS, this method allows you to start your computer in Windows and exit Windows entirely (not the same as restarting in MS-DOS mode) to run your DOS game. See "How to exit to DOS" in "Getting Into and Out of DOS" in Chapter 5 for instructions.

The advantages of exiting to DOS are:

- This method has one important, but not obvious advantage over "Boot directly into DOS," explained previously. Many sound cards come with DOS drivers for *Config.sys* that are required to initialize the sound card settings (especially for Plug-and-Play cards), but that don't need to remain in memory for them to be effective. The drivers take up a considerable amount of memory, and can even conflict with some games, but you may not get sound in some games if you *don't* install them.
- In some circumstances, if you exit to DOS with this method, your sound card may be initialized sufficiently for the game to work, without having to have those pesky drivers loaded in memory. You get the functionality without the memory penalty.

The disadvantage of exiting to DOS is:

- This method may be more trouble than it's worth.

Boot directly into DOS with a boot disk

This has all of the same advantages and disadvantages of the previously discussed "Boot directly into DOS" solution, with the following exceptions.

The advantages of using a DOS boot disk are:

- You can create an alternate configuration for a game without touching your existing Windows installation: no DOS menus, no Windows shortcuts, and no additional configurations that may conflict with any of your Windows applications.
- In many cases, you can use the boot disk on any computer, allowing you to run the game without having to change anything on the hard disk (other than installing the game).
- This also works with Windows NT.

The disadvantage of using a DOS boot disk is:

- Startup diskettes are a pain.

Notes and other issues

Since all DOS games are different, each game you use may require a different method. Try contacting the manufacturer of the game for any suggestions they may have.

See "Do I Still Need Config.sys and Autoexec.bat?" earlier in this chapter for more information on drivers and commands in each of these files.

In this chapter:
- *Setting Up a Workgroup*
- *Installing Dial-Up Networking*
- *Coping with Dial-Up Networking*
- *Mixing and Matching Networks*
- *Security and Multiple Users*

7 *Networking*

A network is the interconnection of two or more computers that facilitates the exchange of information between them. There are several different kinds of networks, each with its own limitations and advantages.

A simple workgroup can comprise merely two computers connected with a single cable (often called a peer-to-peer network). This is ideal in an office or small business setting, where all systems can be linked together with a minimum of hardware and cabling, and configured to *share* resources. A shared directory, for example, is a standard directory residing on a single computer, made accessible to any other computer on the network as though it were actually on each computer's hard disk.

Common in larger organizations is the client/server setup, which differs from a peer-to-peer network less in technology than in the roles the different computers play. For example, one computer on the network, which might be running Unix or Windows NT, takes on the role of the server, and is configured to handle tasks such as email, printing, storage, backup, and administration. This allows configuration and maintenance of the whole network from a single workstation. In addition, servers often handle user authentication, wherein users of client machines (running Windows 98, for instance) could log on to the network and be authenticated by the server.

A different kind of connection, usually involving a telephone line or a more expensive high-speed connection, allows you to access the Internet from either a lone PC or a local network. It can get more complicated if you want to connect a workgroup to the Internet, which involves the combination of several different technologies.

While Windows supports most types of networking out of the box, the actual process involved in setting up networking can be quite confusing, and troubleshooting a network can drive you nuts.

Many of you may be wondering (assuming you've gotten this far) what practical use networking offers to someone who has only one computer or who is not interested in connecting to the Internet. In some cases, networking will be of absolutely no use to you; just move on, or better yet, go outside and get some fresh air. However, networking offers some interesting advantages, often more interesting than an office workgroup configured to share a printer. The capacity to play multiplayer games is enough of a reason to fuss with networking. Or if you have a portable and a desktop computer, networking can be a very fast and convenient method for transferring files and printing. So don't rule out a network just yet.

To start building a network, you should understand the distinction between local and remote resources. A *local resource* (such as a directory or printer) is one that resides on or is physically connected to your own computer. Conversely, a *remote resource* is one that resides on another computer connected to yours over a network. For example, a web page on Microsoft's web server is a remote file, while an HTML file on your own hard disk is a local file. The two files may look the same in your browser, but each has its own unique limitations and capabilities.* Naturally, what's local to you may be remote to someone else on the network.

The type of network connection you establish depends on how you want to access remote resources and on what hardware and software you have to work with. This chapter focuses on two common and easily built types of networks: the peer-to-peer workgroup, and the dial-up Internet connection. In addition, a new technology called Virtual Private Networking, which enables you to simulate a private workgroup across the Internet, is also discussed.

A network is built by installing hardware and configuring various network protocols, most of which are named with cryptic acronyms. By combining different sets of protocols and binding them to the adapter you wish to use, you can enable different kinds of communication. By *binding* a protocol (which is really just a language) to, say, a network card, you're

* One of the problems inherent in the way that Microsoft has integrated their web browser into the operating system is that they've tried to blur the distinction between local and remote information and resources. By making your local folders appear as though they are web pages, rather than making remote resources work as though they were local, they've forced an unfamiliar interface upon something we use every day.

telling Windows that you wish to transmit data in that language over that network card.

A sample network dialog, shown later in this chapter in Figure 7-2, is where all the different protocols and network hardware drivers are specified and configured in Windows 98. Table 7-1 shows several common types of connections and the usual protocol binding required to establish them.

Table 7-1: Common Types of Connections That Require One or More Protocols

For this connection...	bind this protocol...	to this adapter.
Ordinary Dial-Up Networking	TCP/IP	Dial-Up Adapter[a]
Ordinary peer-to-peer Workgroup	IPX/SPX	Your network card
	NetBEUI	Your network card
Virtual Private Networking	NDISWAN	Virtual Private Networking Adapter
	IPX/SPX	Dial-Up Adapter #2 (VPN Support)
	NetBEUI	Dial-Up Adapter #2 (VPN Support)
	TCP/IP	Dial-Up Adapter
Dial-Up Networking through a LAN router	TCP/IP	Your network card
	IPX/SPX	Your network card

[a] The Dial-Up Adapter used in ordinary Dial-Up Networking is really a *virtual* adapter, rather than a piece of hardware. This driver is what enables Windows to send and receive network signals over your modem. Refer to "Installing Dial-Up Networking," later in this chapter, for instructions on setting up this type of connection.

You'll notice that some connections require multiple protocols, and even multiple adapters. Now, it's certainly conceivable that you might use more than one type of networking on a system; in that case, you'd simply install all the necessary adapters and protocols for each one. For example, to use both ordinary Dial-Up Networking and peer-to-peer networking (as shown in Table 7-1), you'd have a total of two adapters and three bound protocols. What's important is that the TCP/IP protocol be bound to the adapter used for Internet connectivity, and the IPX/SPX and NetBEUI protocols be bound to your network card. That way, the protocols can happily be transmitted across the hardware that utilizes them.

What this comes down to is that installing the right protocols and drivers is important to getting your network to function. The problem is that Windows doesn't do this for you. For example, if you chose to install the

Dial-Up Networking component when you set up Windows 98 in the hope that you would be able to connect to the Internet without too much fuss, you'll be annoyed to find out that the necessary protocols are missing. Rather than automatically installing TCP/IP and binding it to the Dial-Up Adapter (which is what we need), Windows gives us the IPX/SPX protocol instead (which is usually used for close-proximity workgroups, such as NetWare and Microsoft networks).

Obviously, there's more to setting up, troubleshooting, and maintaining a network than having the right protocols installed, but it's a good place to start. This book only touches the surface of a much larger topic, but the following information should be enough to get you going with networking.

Setting Up a Workgroup

Connecting two computers to form a basic peer-to-peer workgroup is remarkably easy with Windows 98, as long as you have the proper equipment, drivers, and a few hours. Ideally, you should be able to set up a functioning workgroup in less than ten minutes, but that doesn't include fishing for drivers, resolving hardware conflicts, or finding that your cable is seven inches too short.

Although there are many types of local area networks, network adapters, drivers, and operating systems, we'll be dealing only with the most basic peer-to-peer workgroup, using only the software that came with Windows and some Ethernet hardware.

To set up a workgroup, you'll need the following:

- Two computers, each running some version of Windows. It's possible to network two systems running different versions of Windows, although for the sake of simplicity, we'll assume that you're using Windows 98 on both. The instructions for Windows 95 will be similar, although the screens and driver names may differ somewhat. If one or more of the systems is running Windows 3.x, it's recommended that the system be upgraded to at least Windows for Workgroups 3.11; earlier versions don't have enough network support to make it worthwhile.
- Two network cards, preferably Plug-and-Play. You should be able to find such cards at your local computer store for less than $50 apiece, although better cards will offer better performance and more flexibility. Quality and performance issues aside, the only thing you should be worried about is the type of plugs on the back of each card; they should match one another and the type of cable you're using.

- Lastly, you'll need a network cable long enough to connect both of your computers. There are essentially two different technologies commonly available for inexpensive workgroups: 10base2, which uses cheap, coaxial cable, and 10baseT, which uses slightly more expensive twisted pair (TP) cable that's like a fat phone cord.

  10base2 allows you to connect as many computers as you want by daisy-chaining them together with several segments of cable and small connectors. The downside is that 10base2 doesn't support bidirectional communication, in which signals travel in both directions simultaneously, and its performance and reliability aren't too good. 10baseT offers better performance and reliability, and is visually much tidier than 10base2. 10baseT requires a hub costing $60 or more and a length of category-5 patch cable for each computer. If you plan on connecting only two computers with 10baseT, you can skip the hub and instead use a single category-5 crossover cable. See Figure 7-1 for a visual comparison of these different types of setups to help determine which is best for you.

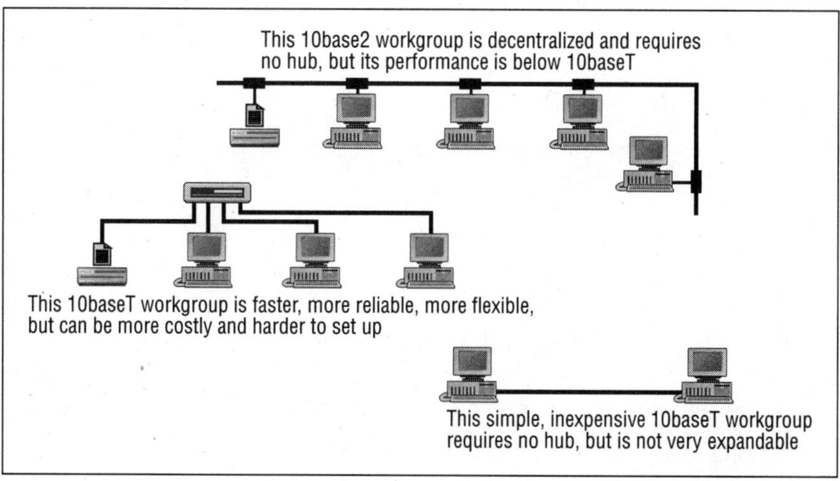

Figure 7-1: Your technical needs and the layout of your computers can help determine which type of cabling to use

Once you have all of the components, take the following steps. Note that network adapters vary significantly, and the particular design of your network cards may require a different procedure.

Part 1: Hardware and drivers

1. Install a network card in each computer. Refer to the documentation included with the cards for specific hardware and software setup.

2. *Before* bothering with the cabling or drivers, run the diagnostic or test software included with the network adapters to verify that each adapter is functioning properly and is not conflicting with any other devices. Most network installation problems are caused by hardware conflicts, and eliminating them now will save hours of work.
3. When installing the drivers in Windows 98, make sure you're using native 32-bit drivers made especially for your version of Windows. Contact the manufacturer of the network cards, or go to their Internet site to acquire the latest software. If the installation program installs drivers in your *Config.sys* or *Autoexec.bat* files, you're not using the latest version of the drivers.
4. Make sure Windows recognizes your network cards in Device Manager and doesn't report any conflicts. Double-click on the **System** icon in Control Panel, choose the **Device Manager** tab, and expand the **Network adapters** branch. If there's a yellow or red smudge over the icon for your network adapter, Windows has either encountered a problem with the driver or a hardware conflict. See "General Troubleshooting Techniques" in Chapter 6, *Troubleshooting*, for more information.

Part 2: Protocols

The next step is to configure Windows with the proper protocols and settings:

1. Double-click on the **Network** icon in Control Panel to view the network settings. Figure 7-2 shows a sample Network Properties window, listing the various clients, adapters, protocols, and services that should be installed. If you don't have the drivers shown, click **Add** and choose the appropriate items from the list. They're usually found by selecting **Microsoft** as the **Manufacturer**.
2. Among the drivers you'll need to have installed for a standard Windows workgroup are Client for Microsoft Networks (a "client") and File and Printer Sharing for Microsoft Networks (a "service"). There are two adapter drivers shown in Figure 7-2, one for Dial-Up Adapter, the *virtual* adapter used by Dial-Up Networking, and one for the physical network card installed in the computer.
3. You'll also notice two protocols: the IPX/SPX-compatible protocol, which is *bound* to the network card (signified by the "->" arrow), and TCP/IP, which is bound to the Dial-Up Adapter. When you first add a protocol, there will automatically be an instance of the protocol for each adapter. For example, TCP/IP will be bound to both the Dial-Up

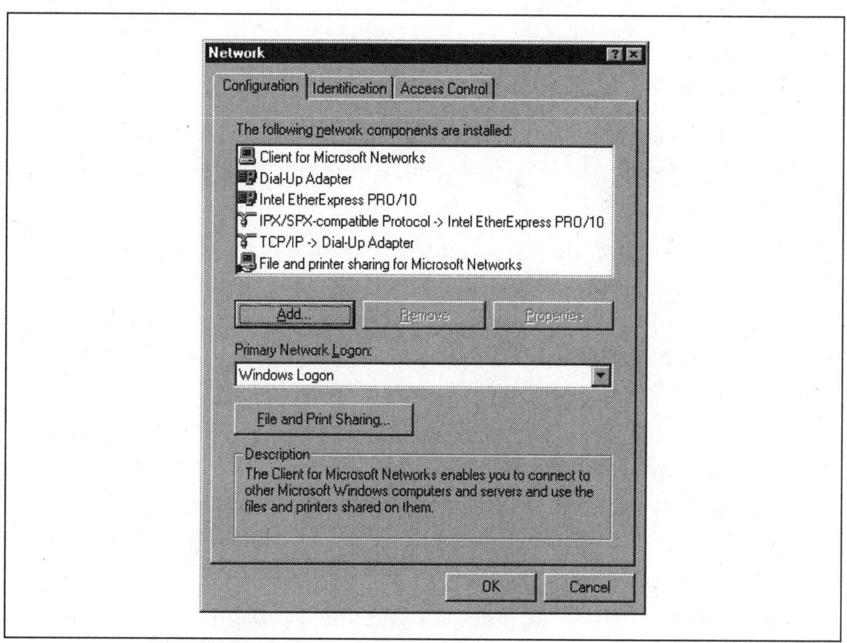

Figure 7-2: The Network dialog is used to configure adapters as well as bind protocols to those adapters

Adapter and your network card. Since TCP/IP is used only for the Dial-Up Adapter, we can remove the instance pointing to the network card (see the discussion at the beginning of this chapter as well as "Installing Dial-Up Networking," later in this chapter, for details on protocols and TCP/IP). Likewise, you can remove the instance of IPX/SPX that points to the Dial-Up Adapter. It's best to have protocols bound only to the devices that actually use them.*

4. In most cases, you won't have to set any properties for any of the drivers listed here, with the possible exception of the network card. If your network cards have more than one type of connector (known as "combo" cards), you'll sometimes need to specify which type you're using. Having the driver automatically detect the connector being used can slow Windows startup and cause other problems. Don't bother with any other settings here unless you are certain you want to change them.

* In some cases, you'll need NetBEUI to remain bound to the Dial-Up Adapter in order to use the Network Neighborhood with the connection, which is useful for certain types of WAN access, as well as Virtual Private Networking (discussed later in this chapter).

Part 3: Options and cabling

Once you're done specifying the various drivers and protocols, there are a few more options to set in the Network Properties window:

1. From the drop-down list labeled **Primary Network Logon**:, choose **Windows Logon**. Then click **File and Print Sharing**, turn on both options, and click **OK**.
2. Next, click on the **Identification** tab. The first field, **Computer name**, is a unique one-word name for the computer; no other computer in your workgroup should have the same name. Next, specify a name in the **Workgroup** field that is common to all the computers in your workgroup.*
3. It's normal (albeit frustrating) for Windows to repeatedly restart after installing any network drivers or changing network settings. It's faster to simply answer "no" every time Windows asks you to restart; when you're done, you'll need to restart only once to have all the changes take effect.
4. It's important to isolate and resolve any problems as they pop up along the way. If you see any error messages, or if your network adapter isn't recognized correctly in Device Manager, it could cause your network not to function. It's infinitely easier to fix the problem now; once everything is connected, any one of a hundred different things can stop your network from working, and finding the problem can be next to impossible.
5. Connect the cables and hub (if applicable). Make sure your hub is powered, and all your connectors are securely fastened. Having extra cables around makes it easy to diagnose a bad cable (which is common). Once you connect the cable, the network should be immediately active.

Part 4: Sharing resources

The primary access to your network is the Network Neighborhood,† accessible through the Desktop icon as well as Explorer (if you've hidden this

---

* The workgroup setting is used to group the various computers on your network. If you only have two or three machines, use the same setting for all of them. On larger networks with multiple workgroups, each computer will only be able to see other computers in their own workgroup in Network Neighborhood, but will have access to all other workgroups in the Entire Network window.

† Network Neighborhood is also used to browse computers connected with the Direct Cable Connection (DCC) component that comes with Windows. Suffice it to say that networking makes DCC virtually obsolete.

icon as described in "Network Neighborhood" in Chapter 4, *Tinkering Techniques*, you'll probably want to get it back). Any computer connected to your workgroup should show up in Network Neighborhood. If it's in your workgroup, it will be in the top level; otherwise, it will be in a branch for its workgroup under the **Entire Network** branch. When you're configuring the network, each branch will be empty, however, until you specify each computer's shared resources:

1. If a computer has a printer, drive, or folder that you want to make available to the other computers in the workgroup, you can do so by right-clicking on its icon in Explorer and selecting **Sharing**. Figure 7-3 shows the standard **Sharing** tab for a drive.

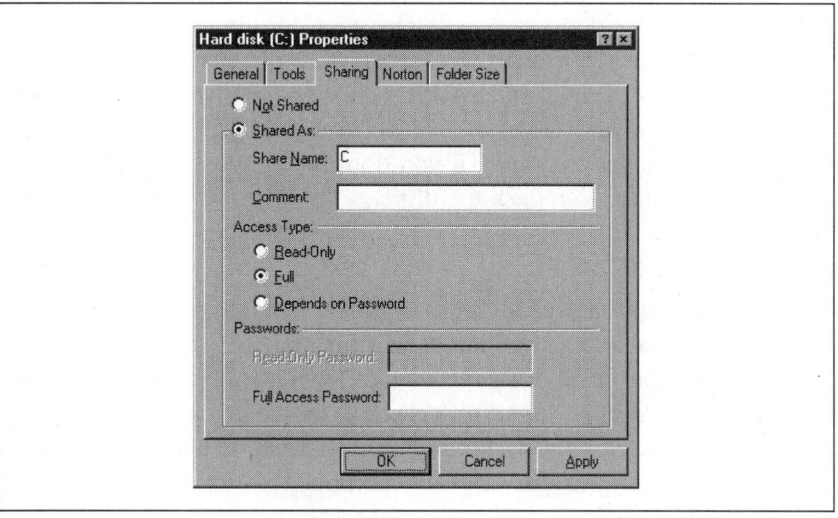

Figure 7-3: Right-click on a drive, folder, or printer, and select Sharing to choose how the resource will be shared in the workgroup

2. To share a device, change the option at the top of the **Sharing** window from **Not Shared** to **Shared As**. The **Share Name** is the name for the resource that will show up in Network Neighborhood on the other computers.

3. For drives and folders, you can choose the **Access Type**; in most cases, you'll probably want **Full**. The default setting, **Read-Only**, won't allow users on remote computers to change or delete any files or folders on the shared drive, but will still allow them to read and copy these files and folders.

   The **Depends on Password** setting allows you to configure up to two levels of password protection to the resource. For example, you could enter a password in the **Full Access Password** field and leave the **Read-only Password** field blank, giving everyone read access, but only privileged users write access to your data.

4. A few seconds after you press **OK**, a small hand will appear over the resource's icon in Explorer, signifying that it is now being shared. You'll probably want to share any printers attached to each computer in the workgroup, as well as most of the drives, and perhaps a few selected folders, such as the desktop folder or some common documents folder. It's up to you, and sharing can be easily disabled or changed at any time.
5. Any shared drives or folders should show up immediately on the other computers in the workgroup. Just open the Network Neighborhood from the desktop or Explorer to view the resources available from each computer in the workgroup. You can even display the local computer's shared resources through Network Neighborhood. The shared folders and drives should behave as though they are actually connected to the computer. If you don't see a newly shared resource, press the **F5** key to refresh the display.

Part 5: Mapping drives

You can also *map* a shared drive or folder on the network so that it appears as just another drive letter on your system.* This allows you to access the remote drive or folder without having to use Network Neighborhood, which may be useful for accessing frequently used drives, and is necessary to provide network access for older DOS or Windows programs that don't recognize the Network Neighborhood:

1. From Explorer's **Tools** menu, choose **Map Network Drive**. You'll see the Map Network Drive dialog shown in Figure 7-4. Unfortunately, Windows 98 doesn't allow you to browse the network for shared devices here, meaning you'll have to type them in manually (although you'll be able to use the Network Neighborhood to view the structure of other systems). For example, assuming a remote computer is called "Blue," and the drive on the computer you want to map is *shared* as "C" (note the absence of the expected colon), you'd type the following in the **Path** field:

   ```
   \\blue\c
   ```

* In some circumstances, Windows 98 will map *only* a full drive, and will refuse to map individual folders on remote computers. This might occur if your network spans multiple versions of Windows.

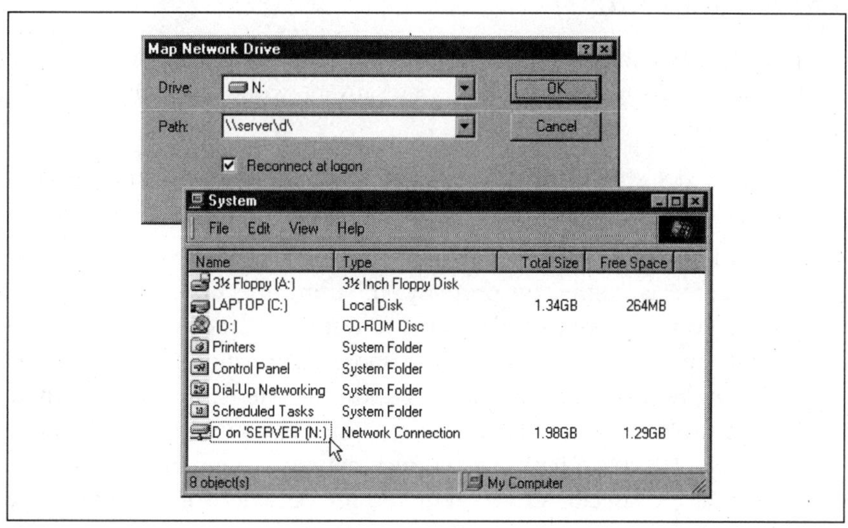

Figure 7-4: Mapping a remote drive to a new drive letter allows you to access remote resources without the Network Neighborhood

Note also the drop-down list which contains a history of the last few mapped network paths.

2. Then, from the **Drive** list, choose the *new* drive letter you want to use on this computer that will *map* to the drive or folder you specified for the Path.

3. Lastly, turn on the **Reconnect at logon** option if you want Windows to map this drive every time you start Windows; otherwise you'll have to do it manually each time (the default is *off* here). Note that having Windows automatically reconnect mapped drives at startup can significantly slow the boot process.

Shared printers, on the other hand, aren't accessible in Network Neighborhood, and can't be mapped in Explorer. To have Windows recognize a shared remote printer, you'll need to install a printer driver on each computer that will be using it. On each computer in the workgroup except for the one directly connected to the printer, double-click on the **Add Printer** icon in the Printers window. When asked, **How is this printer attached to your computer**, select **Network Printer**, and proceed normally, following the directions on-screen. In most cases, Windows will simply copy the printer driver files from the host computer to which the printer is directly connected.

Troubleshooting

There are several things that can cause a network not to work. Try some of the following suggestions to alleviate any network problems you may be experiencing:

- If you're not able to map any network resources, make sure the **Network Neighborhood** icon is visible (see Chapter 4).
- If you know the network cards are functioning properly and the network cable is connected properly, try using the diagnostic software that came with your network cards to test the connection (contact the manufacturer of your adapters for more information). Replacing the cable, or replacing the connectors and terminators, for 10base2, may fix the problem. If the diagnostic software reports no problems, odds are that you don't have the correct network components installed. Note that the specific drivers required for your network adapters may be different.
- If you see any other machines listed in the Network Neighborhood, it means that everything is working properly. If you don't see shared drives or folders, you'll need to turn on sharing for the devices you wish to share; see "Part 4: Sharing resources," earlier in this chapter, for more information. Note that you may need to refresh the Network Neighborhood window (press the **F5** key) to display the most recent connected resources.
- If everything shows up, but the network frequently crashes or exhibits slow performance, make sure you don't have any other network software loaded (such as in *Config.sys* or *Autoexec.bat*) that could be conflicting with the network drivers included in Windows. Contact the manufacturers of your network cards for the most recent drivers, and look for any troubleshooting tips they may have that are specific to their hardware or software.
- Try opening the command prompt (while still in Windows) and typing `net view` to see all of the machines currently logged on to your network. To see the resources offered by a particular machine, include the name of the machine in the command line. For example, assume you typed `net view` and got the following:

```
Servers available in workgroup MY_NETWORK.
Server name              Remark
------------------------------------------
\\BLUE                   Blue Computer
\\RED                    Red Computer
\\GREEN                  Green Computer
The command was completed successfully.
```

You could then type **net view \\red** to list all of the resources shared by the machine known as *Red*. The advantage here is that all resources are listed, instead of just shared disks and folders in Network Neighborhood:

```
Shared resources at \\RED

Sharename    Type         Comment
-------------------------------------------
C            Disk         Red Boot Drive
D            Disk         Red CD Drive
DESKTOP      Disk         Red Desktop Folder
LASERJET     Print        Laserjet printer
The command was completed successfully.
```

Installing Dial-Up Networking

Windows 98 comes with all the software necessary to connect to the Internet, in the form of Dial-Up Networking. Dial-Up Networking uses your modem to simulate a direct connection to the Internet over standard phone lines, making it seem as though you were plugged in with a network card. While there are other ways to connect to the Internet, such as through a commercial online service like AOL or MSN, or via other dial-up software, such as the aging Trumpet Winsock utility, Dial-Up Networking provides the most flexibility and the largest collection of supported software.

The most common application of Dial-Up Networking is to connect a single computer to the Internet for web browsing, email, or any other standard form of Internet communication. However, Dial-Up Networking has other uses that require different drivers and protocols, such as dialing into a corporate intranet, or connecting two computers. The following procedure assumes you're setting up a standard Internet connection, which is supported by most Internet service providers (ISPs). Your needs may be different, depending on your method of connection and your ISP's capabilities.

There are several steps involved in getting Dial-Up Networking to connect to an Internet account. For some reason, simply installing the Dial-Up Networking component that comes with Windows 98 isn't enough; the correct drivers aren't installed, and the settings aren't configured properly. This section outlines the steps needed to install Dial-Up Networking correctly on your system and configure it for optimum performance.

To set up Dial-Up Networking, you'll need the following:

- Any modem with native 32-bit Windows 95/98-compatible drivers. It should be at least 14,400 baud (though 33,600 or faster is preferred), properly installed and functioning. Make sure it's configured correctly by double-clicking on the **Modems** icon in Control Panel.

- A standard phone line. While you don't need a dedicated line for an Internet connection, it may be a good idea if you plan to spend a lot of time online.
- A dial-up account with a local ISP. The account should support standard point-to-point protocol (PPP).

Once you get the account, the ISP should send you the following information:

- Your username and password.
- A local phone number used to make the connection. The number should not be a toll call (ask your operator to confirm), and the modem on the other end should be at least as fast as your modem Ask your ISP if they support your modem's speed and protocol.
- One or two name server IP addresses, each with four numbers separated by periods; e.g., 123.213.132.11
- Any special connection instructions, if your ISP doesn't support standard PPP. Just tell them you're using Windows 98, and they'll tell you whether or not their service is compatible with Dial-Up Networking.

Now, Windows also comes with an Internet Setup Wizard that supposedly does the job for you, but it's really a waste of time, and will not be discussed here. Learning the manual installation of the required components will not only help you cover a wider variety of configurations, but will also aid in diagnosing and solving problems and make for a more efficient setup. Take the following steps to insure you have the proper drivers installed.

Part 1: Networking components

1. Double-click on the **Add/Remove Programs** icon in Control Panel, and choose the **Windows Setup** tab. Highlight **Communications** in the list of components, and click **Details**.
2. Make sure you have a checkmark next to the Dial-Up Networking component. If not, check it now, and press **OK**. You'll be asked to restart your computer at this point; select **No** to postpone this until all your configuration is complete.
3. Double-click on the **Network** icon in Control Panel. You should have the following network components installed: Client for Microsoft Networks, Dial-Up Adapter, and TCP/IP. If one or more of these required components aren't shown in the list, click **Add**, select

Microsoft as the manufacturer, and select the components from the available categories.

4. If you have another adapter installed, such as a network card, you'll see multiple instances of TCP/IP and of any other installed protocols. Each instance is a binding to each installed adapter (see the discussion at the beginning of this chapter). The one we care about, in this case, is `TCP/IP->Dial-Up Adapter`; you may want to remove other instances of TCP/IP you know aren't being used. Also, as shown in Figure 7-5, any non-TCP/IP protocols bound to Dial-Up Adapter should also be removed, unless you know you'll need them.

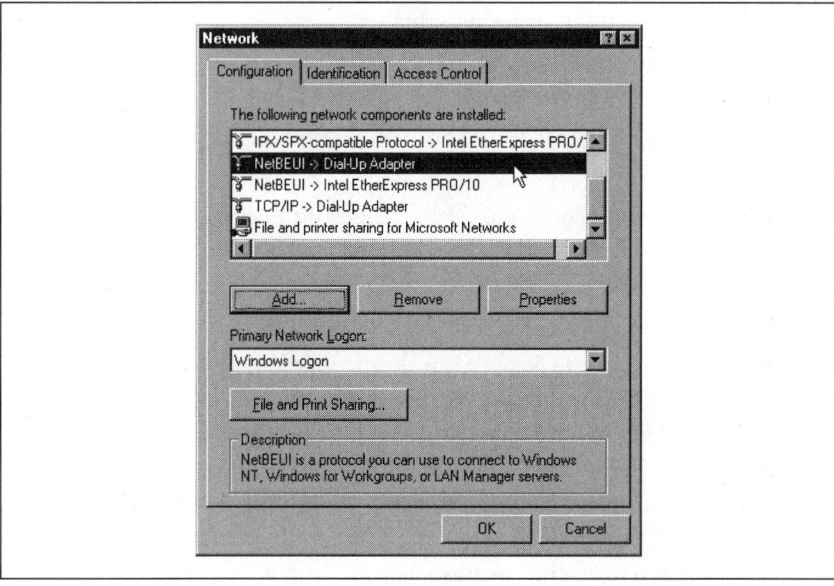

Figure 7-5: The Network properties window shows the protocols installed for each available network adapter

5. Click **OK** to close the Network Properties window when you're finished, and verify that you want to restart Windows when asked, since you're done configuring networking at this point.

Part 2: Configuring DUN connections

1. Open the Dial-Up Networking folder in Explorer or My Computer, and double-click on the **Make New Connection** icon to create a new Dial-Up Networking connection. If this is the first time you've visited this folder, the Make New Connection wizard will appear automatically.

2. Type the name of your connection in the first field. This can be anything, but it's recommended you type in the name of your ISP here to avoid confusion with other possible future connections. Select your modem from the list below (if you have more than one), and click **Configure** to make sure your modem is configured correctly. Set the maximum speed to **57,600** for 14.4 modems and **115,200** for 28.8 or faster modems. You might want to leave the speaker volume turned up until you're sure the connection works. Make sure **Only connect at this speed** is *not* checked, and click **OK** when you're done.
3. Click **Next**, and type in the area code and phone number given to you by your ISP to connect. If necessary, choose the country code from the list below the phone number.
4. Click **Next** and then **Finish**. A new icon with the name you specified should now appear in the Dial-Up Networking window. Unfortunately, this rather useless wizard only prompts you for *some* of the required information.*
5. Right-click on the new icon, and select **Properties** to complete your configuration of this connection. Figure 7-6 shows a connection properties sheet, where you'll see the information you just entered, as well as some additional settings, all of which can be changed if you wish.
6. Choose the **Server Types** tab, and turn off *all* the options here except for **Enable software compression** and **TCP/IP**. Among the options that aren't relevant to connecting to an ISP are the **Log on to network** option and the **IPX/SPX** and **NetBEUI** protocols, used only if you are dialing into an NT-based network. Your screen should look like Figure 7-7. Your modem or service provider may require that you turn off **Enable software compression** as well, but leave it enabled for now.
7. Click **TCP/IP Settings** to display a window similar to Figure 7-8. Leave all the settings as they appear, except for the name servers. Select **Specify name server addresses** and type the IP addresses of the one or two name servers given to you by your ISP in the **Primary DNS** and **Secondary DNS** fields, respectively.†

* One of the major design flaws present throughout Windows 98 is the overuse of the Wizard, often just a cop-out employed to make a dialog box seem easier to use. It's reminiscent of a quotation of Mark Twain's; after completing a 12-page letter to a friend, he is said to have written, "Sorry to have written you a 12-page letter, but I didn't have time to write a 1-page letter."

† Domain Name Server (DNS) is the service responsible for translating domain names, such as *annoyances.org*, into obscure IP addresses, such as 207.105.6.101. IP addresses are codes required for all communication across the Internet.

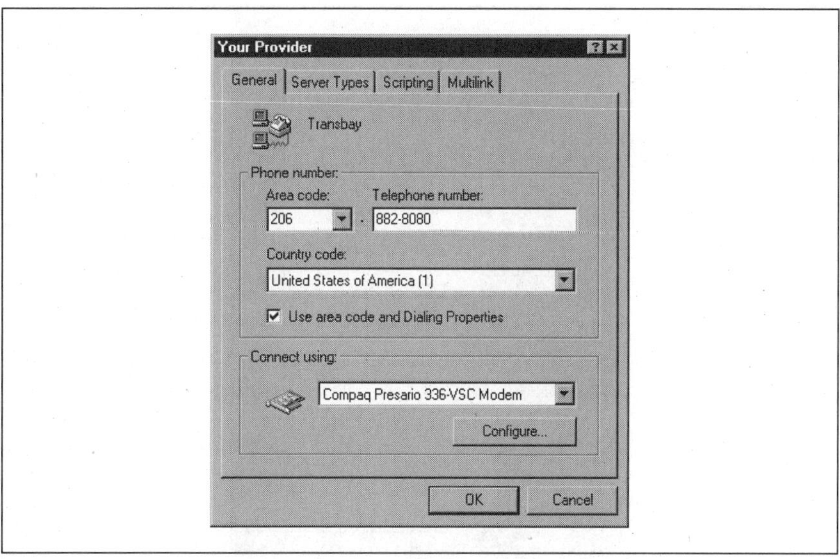

Figure 7-6: The General tab of the connection properties sheet displays the information you entered into the Make New Connection Wizard

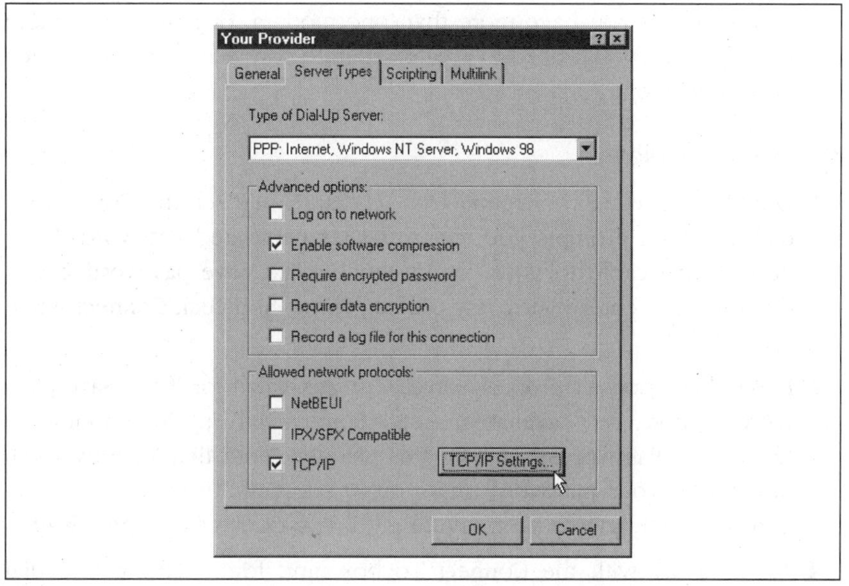

Figure 7-7: The Server Types window allows you to enter the network settings for a Dial-Up Networking connection

8. Click **OK** in each of the open dialog boxes to save your settings. If you have more than one connection, you'll need to repeat these steps for each one. If your ISP has more than one telephone number for

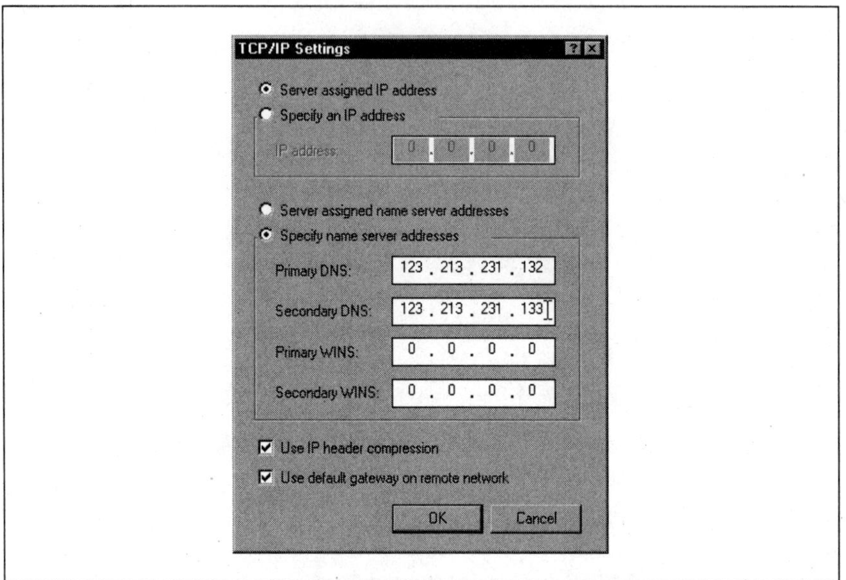

Figure 7-8: The TCP/IP Settings window allows you to input your name server addresses, required when accessing most web sites

you to use, if you have more than one modem, or if you have more than one ISP, you'll need to create separate connection icons for each implementation.

Part 3: Connecting

1. Double-click on a connection icon to dial. You'll see the Connect To dialog, which prompts you for your **User name** and **Password**. Enter both if applicable to your circumstance, click **Save password** if you don't want to enter your password each time, and click **Connect** when finished.
2. If Windows doesn't properly save your password, or if the **Save password** option isn't available, see "Force Dial-Up Networking to Remember Passwords," later in this chapter. Note that Windows will never save your password until you've successfully made a connection, so you'll have to keep entering it if you don't get in right away.

   To do away with the Connect To box, and force Windows to dial automatically whenever you double-click on a connection icon, see "Bypass the "Connect To" Dialog Box," later in this chapter.

   Depending on your modem, it may take anywhere from a few seconds to over a minute to establish a connection. Once a connection is established, a timer will start keeping track of your connect time, and you can start using your Internet software. See Appendix F, *Software to Solve Annoyances*, for more information on obtaining free software you can use on the Internet.

Troubleshooting

If your connection or any of your Internet applications don't work, or you're experiencing poor performance, the problem could be caused by any number of things. The following configuration procedures and troubleshooting tactics should help you get Dial-Up Networking up and running in most situations:

- Sometimes restarting Windows solves connection or performance problems, as it forces Dial-Up Networking to reinitialize.
- If your phone line has call waiting, you'll need to tell Windows to turn it off before dialing. Otherwise, any incoming calls can interrupt your connection. To automatically disable call waiting, double-click the **Telephony** icon in Control Panel, and turn on the **To disable call waiting, dial** option. Then, type the appropriate code to the right. The first item, *70, should work for most users, although you may need to call your phone company to get the correct code.

  If you have a laptop and dial from different locations, you'll want to configure the Telephony properties dialog for each location you use. For example, a location called "Home" may have call waiting disabled, while the location called "Bob's House" would not.

  Note that if you try to disable call waiting on a line that doesn't have call waiting, you may not be able to make a call at all (convenient, huh?). If you do configure Windows to disable call waiting, call waiting will be re-enabled the moment you hang up.
- Occasionally, conflicts with other Internet programs can cause Dial-Up Networking to fail. If you were, at one time, using another Internet dialer (such as Trumpet Winsock, a popular 16-bit dialer used on Windows 3.x), make sure you remove it completely from your system before trying to use Dial-Up Networking. See Chapter 6 for details on *Winsock.dll* and the problems caused by having multiple versions of the file on your system.
- If Windows simply won't connect, try dialing the phone number manually with your telephone and see if you hear beeps on the other end, and not an answering machine, busy signal, or massage parlor.

  Contact the phone company to see if there is a switching or routing problem (especially for ISDN customers). If you can't dial by hand, your computer can't dial either.

- Check with your Internet service provider to see if they've been having any trouble with their service, or if you need any special settings or a script (see "Dial-Up Scripting" in Chapter 9, *Scripting and Automation*) to access their service. Verify that your IP addresses and the phone number you're supposed to dial are all correct, and check your settings for typos.

  Make sure your account is actually functioning. It can take up to several days after you subscribe before you can use your account, and be prepared for the possibility of your ISP getting your password wrong.

- Don't rule out hardware problems. Make sure your modem is turned on (if it's an external model), is functioning correctly, and is configured correctly, by using HyperTerminal to dial the same number. Note: if you use another modem communications program to test the connection, it may not be Windows 95/98-compliant, meaning that you're not really testing the modem configuration! See Chapter 6 for additional modem troubleshooting techniques.

  If your modem usually works, yet has stopped functioning recently, try powering down your computer completely (not just restarting). Completely cutting power to your modem will force it to reset, which may solve the problem.

  If all else fails, you'll have to contact the manufacturer of your modem for technical support; possibly to request a driver or BIOS update, or even repairs to the unit. Newer drivers can also improve performance.

- If you're connecting, but not at a satisfactory speed, try replacing the phone cord or wall jack. A noisy phone line can cause a performance drop, although it may be beyond your power to resolve the problem. You should be able to coerce your phone company into fixing the problem if you bug them enough. See "Change the MTU and RWIN Parameters for Dial-Up Networking" later in this chapter for another solution.

Coping with Dial-Up Networking

As more of the world's populace gets hooked up to the Internet, the demand for better service and more ways to communicate drive the need for more flexible connections. Often in computing, however, more flexible means more prone to problems and confusing configuration, and networking is no exception.

Some of the following solutions mention the way it used to be in Windows 95, which was the first release of Windows to have built-in Dial-

Up Networking. Since Dial-Up Networking was one of the features beefed up for Windows 98, anyone familiar with the way things used to be may be more prone to confusion.

The following topics should be helpful in improving your experience with Dial-Up Networking.

Exporting Dial-Up Networking Connections

There's no reason why you should have to open the Dial-Up Networking (DUN) window every time you want to connect to the Internet. Windows allows you to make shortcuts to connection icons located on your desktop, in your Taskbar toolbars, or in your Start Menu, just as you can make shortcuts to any other file, folder, or Windows object (such as Control Panel applets).

The problem is that the process used to make shortcuts to DUN connections is not exactly consistent with the shortcut process in other parts of Windows 98. If you've used Windows 95,* you know that you could make a shortcut to a DUN connection just by dragging and dropping the connection icon out of the DUN window.† If you do this in Windows 98, however, you'll end up with a "Dial-Up Networking Exported File" (with the extension *.dun*) instead of a shortcut.

A Dial-Up Networking Exported File is simply an *.ini* file (see Chapter 3, *The Registry*), which, instead of just being a shortcut to the connection, contains all of the properties of the connection, allowing you to easily copy the connection to another computer by simply copying the file. Once you create an exported file, it becomes a standalone connection; you can edit it without affecting your original connection icon, and you can even dial with it.

While these files may seem more useful than traditional shortcuts, they have drawbacks. For example, if you make a change to the properties of one of your connections in the DUN window, those changes will not be reflected in exported files made from those connections. This means you'll have to re-export your exported file every time you make a change of any kind, such as to the phone number or nameserver address. If you make a

* Windows 95 OSR2 and Windows 95 with the Dial-Up Networking update 1.2 also support Dial-Up Networking Exported Files, but the default behavior of drag-and-drop is still to create shortcuts.

† By mentioning this inconsistency, I am in no way endorsing the way that shortcuts are created in Windows 95/8. The fact that shortcuts are created when you drag-drop an *.exe* file is inconvenient, confusing, and dare I say, barbaric.

shortcut to a connection, on the other hand, it will be automatically updated with any changes to its target connection.

To make a true shortcut (which should be the default, as it is more likely to be what the user wanted in the first place), you have to drag the connection out of the DUN window with the right mouse button, and select **Create Shortcut(s) Here** when asked. Figure 7-9 shows both a shortcut and an exported file made from the same dial-up connection.

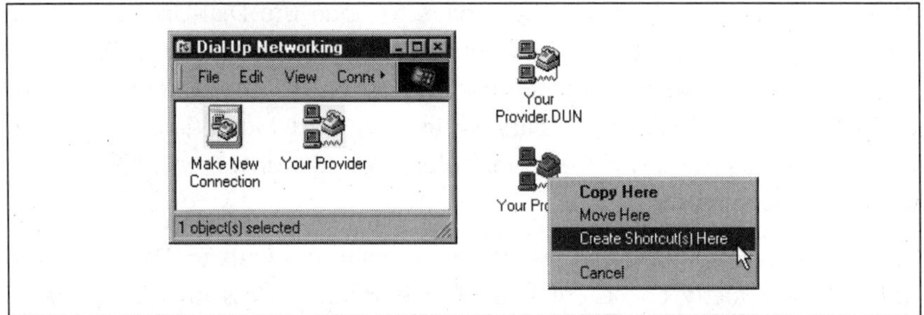

Figure 7-9: Get more control when dragging items out of and into the Dial-Up Networking folder by using the right mouse button

Shortcuts and exported files suffer the same limitation: you can't right-click on either type of file and select **Properties** to change the properties of the connection. Since shortcuts are only shortcuts, this makes sense; it's easy enough to change the properties of the target connection. However, since an exported file contains its own properties, it should stand to reason that you can change them as easily as you can change the properties of a normal connection icon. Well, you can't. Microsoft hasn't bothered to link the Dial-Up Properties sheet with the properties sheet for exported files, but this doesn't mean the files can't be edited; it just means editing them is not as easy as it should be.

Dial-Up Networking exported files use the structure of *.ini* files so that they can be edited—not only by hand with a text editor, but also from within a program. (Developers can write code to read and write *.ini* files quite easily.) You can open any exported file in a plain text editor, such as Notepad; you'll need to drag-drop it onto your text editor, or use **File → Open**, however, as its context menu has no **Edit** option.

Each section denoted by square brackets in the exported file is simply a different part of the dialog in which the parameters were originally entered. Most of the entries in this file should be self-explanatory. What doesn't quite make sense, however, is that if you try to reimport the file into the Dial-Up Networking window, the connection name it uses is *not* the name of the exported file, but rather the connection name specified inside. To change the name of the connection used in the Dial-Up Networking window, you'll need to change both the `Entry_Name` and `Import_Name` lines to reflect the new name.

A significant advantage of Dial-Up Networking exported files is that they can be imported *back* into the Dial-Up Networking window by drag-dropping. This feature, though, has its disadvantages. For example, if you drag an exported file into your DUN window, and there's another connection with the same name, Windows will overwrite the existing connection without asking—another Windows inconsistency. So before importing any exported files, you should check the `Entry_Name` and `Import_Name` lines for possible conflicts with existing connections.

There are several reasons why you might want to import an exported file. For example, you can import a *.dun* file, edit its properties visually, and then re-export it (which may be easier than editing it in Notepad). You can also export a connection, change its name in Notepad, and then reimport it; this creates a duplicate of the connection, something otherwise impossible in the Dial-Up Networking window. You might want to duplicate a connection if you have two different numbers for the same ISP, or want to access the same ISP with two different modems. If you do this, you'll have to change the exported file's connection name before reimporting; otherwise, any existing connections by the same name will be overwritten.

Naturally, the ability to import a *.dun* file also allows you to export a connection on one computer, copy the file to another, and then easily import it. ISPs have wanted this capability for years, and it should make setting up customers' systems easier for them.

Bypass the "Connect To" Dialog Box

In the original release of Windows 95, you were forced to install a third-party utility in order to skip the "Connect To" dialog box. Since this window is really only useful the first time you connect, most users want to get rid of it. Luckily, in Windows 98 (as well as in the second release of Windows 95, OSR2), this is much easier to accomplish.

The only prerequisite is that you've checked the **Save password** option in the Connect To box and already successfully connected at least once. If not, skipping the Connect To box will mean that you'll never get the chance to enter necessary information, such as your password, and your connection will never be established. For some reason, it is not possible to simply enter this information in the properties sheet of the connection.

Follow these steps to skip the Connect To box:

1. Open the Dial-Up Networking folder in Explorer or My Computer, and select **Settings** from the **Connections** menu.
2. Turn off the **Prompt for information before dialing** option
3. Next, choose the **Don't prompt to use Dial-Up Networking** option, and press **OK** when you're finished. This last option will hide the Connecting To window for Autodial, described below.

Using Autodial with Dial-Up Networking

The Autodial feature in Windows automatically connects you to the Internet with Dial-Up Networking whenever it's needed, rather than forcing you to connect manually. If you attempt any Internet communication when you're not connected, such as trying to view a web page or check your email, Windows will connect for you if Autodial is enabled.

Some users (like myself) may find the Autodial feature immensely annoying; for example, you may not want to connect to the Internet every time you open your email program or view an *.html* file on your hard disk. Likewise, some users may find it annoying when Windows *doesn't* automatically connect for them. Luckily, this is configurable; here's how to control it:

1. Double-click on the **Internet** icon in Control Panel or select **Internet Options** from Internet Explorer's **View** menu.
2. Choose the **Connection** tab, which is shown in Figure 7-10. The settings here are particularly confusing, because the phrasing of the options doesn't match what they actually do.

   If you wish to use Autodial, select the **Connect to the Internet using a modem** option. To disable Autodial, select the **Connect to the Internet using a local area network** option. The setting actually has nothing to do with the method by which you connect; by telling Windows you're using a modem, you're telling it that it needs to dial whenever you want to connect to the Internet. Likewise, the implication of connecting over a local area network is that you're always connected, and never need to dial.
3. If you're enabling Autodial, click **Settings** here; otherwise, skip to the last step. In most cases, all you'll have to do is choose the dial-up connection you wish to have Windows use when autodialing; if you have only one, it will probably already be selected. If you haven't yet successfully connected with this connection, you'll also have to enter your username and password below.

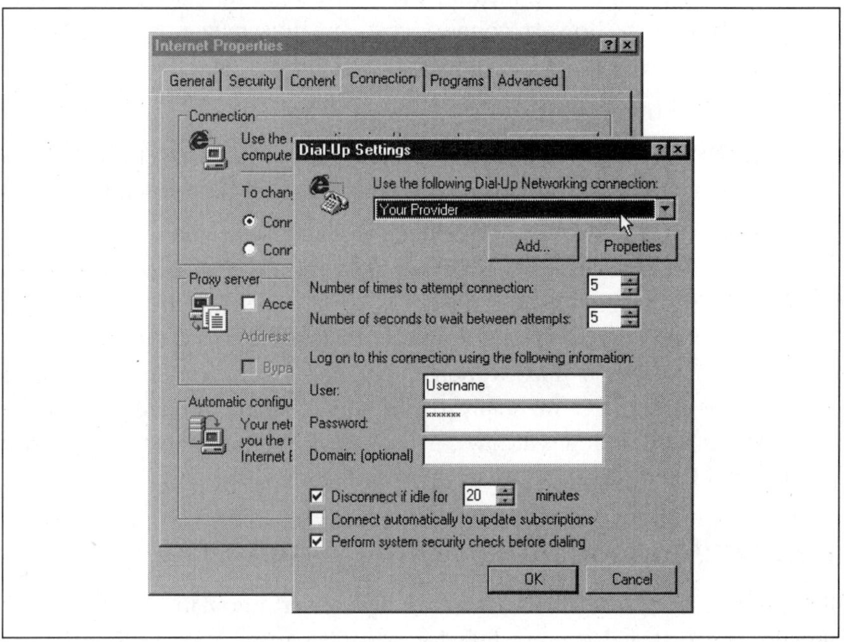

Figure 7-10: Enabling Autodial is more than just turning on an option; you must specify which connection to use

4. The only other important option here is the **Disconnect if idle** setting. If you're going to have Windows dial for you, you'll need to have it hang up for you as well. One of the problems with Autodial is that it may connect for what seems to be no reason: a program may invoke the autodialer merely by trying to initiate communication. When Windows detects that your connection is idle—that no data is being sent or received over the connection—it will disconnect for you, if enabled.

   The **Disconnect if idle** setting should conform to your needs; there's no globally optimal setting. For example, if you don't get charged for connect time and don't need the phone line for any other reason, you may want to make this value high (over 20 minutes), or even disable it. On the other hand, when many users share a phone line, they may prefer to have Windows disconnect soon after communication has ceased.

   If you are charged for connect time, you can calculate the optimal setting. For example, some users of high-speed connections are charged something like three cents for the first minute and one cent for each additional minute of connect time. Obviously, it doesn't pay to disconnect and reconnect repeatedly, since the first minute is so much more expensive. Setting the disconnect time to four minutes would yield the lowest connect cost, but this may not be the most convenient setting, so you may want to raise it a bit.

Click **OK** when you're finished with these settings.

5. Click **OK** to save your Autodial preferences. You can test the settings by first making sure you're not connected, and then opening a web browser and connecting to a web site.

   Note that some users may experience connection problems when connecting to the Internet using Autodial, such as the modem not being able to dial, and the network not working once the connection has been made. If this happens, but Dial-Up Networking still works when you connect manually (by double-clicking on an icon in the Dial-Up Networking window), try contacting the manufacturer of your modem for an updated driver or other technical support.

Enabling Auto-Redial in Dial-Up Networking

For some reason, Dial-Up Networking will never automatically attempt to redial if the first dial attempt fails for whatever reason. If the line is busy or if the computer on the other end doesn't answer the first time, you'll be forced to retry manually until a connection is made. If the line is frequently busy, you'll definitely want to turn on auto-redial. Here's how to do it:

1. Open the Dial-Up Networking folder in Explorer or My Computer, and select **Settings** from the **Connections** menu.
2. Turn on the **Redial** option, and set the **Before giving up retry** option to as high as you feel is reasonable; 100 is the maximum, but may tie up your phone line for too great a time.
3. Set the number of minutes and seconds in the **Between tries wait** setting both to zero, unless you'd rather have Windows wait before redialing. Press **OK** when finished.

   Note that this will only redial for a busy signal or failed connection. If, after a successful connection, you're disconnected for any reason (such as idle time or a noisy line), Windows will not automatically redial. Use the Dunce utility (see Appendix F) to add this functionality.

Speed Up Dial-Up Networking Initialization

Connecting with Dial-Up Networking is generally clean and straightforward, but can seem to take an eternity. If you try to use your web browser or a Telnet window, you'll notice that a connection is established long before Dial-Up Networking appears to be finished connecting. By removing unnecessary components and turning off unneeded options, you can speed up this process considerably. Try the following suggestions:

1. Right-click on an existing connection in the Dial-Up Networking folder, select **Properties**, and choose the **Server Types** tab. Figure 7-7 shows what this window should look like.
2. Turn off the options labeled **NetBEUI**, **IPX/SPX**, and **Log on to network** (make sure to leave **TCP/IP** turned on).
3. Click **OK** when you're done. You'll have to repeat this for each connection if you have more than one.
4. Next, double-click on the **Network** icon in Control Panel (see Figure 7-5). Make sure there aren't any unneeded protocols bound to the Dial-Up Networking Adapter. TCP/IP should be the only one, unless you have special requirements. Click **OK** when you're done.

Force Dial-Up Networking to Remember Passwords

One problem with Dial-Up Networking that doesn't seem to have gone away with the release of Windows 98 is Windows' inability to save passwords, although there has been some improvement. Either Windows forgets your password, or it doesn't give you the opportunity to save your password in the first place. This generally affects the Connect To dialog, which prompts for your username and password when you first try to connect to the Internet. At this point, you should be able to check the **Save password** checkbox so that you don't have to enter your password again. If you find that Windows either ignores the checkbox or grays it out, try any of the following solutions:

- Make sure you have the correct components installed for Dial-Up Networking. See "Installing Dial-Up Networking" earlier in this chapter for details.
- Double-click on the **Network** icon in Control Panel, and choose the **Identification** tab. If the **Computer Name** field doesn't match what you've typed in for your username in Dial-Up Networking, try changing it here so that they match. They don't necessarily *have* to match, but the **Computer Name** is what DUN uses for the default username; this has been known to help. Click **OK** when you're finished. You'll have to restart Windows at this point. Try connecting again when Windows starts.

- Try recreating the connection in the Dial-Up Networking window by double-clicking on the **Add New Connection** icon.
- Often, Windows can't save your password because it doesn't know that's it's supposed to. To enforce Windows' capability to save settings for each user, double-click on the **Passwords** icon in Control Panel, and choose the **User Profiles** tab. If it's not already checked, select **Users can customize their preferences**..., turn on either of the options below, if desired, and click **OK**. Restart Windows at this point; when you're asked for a username and password, enter a username, but leave the password field blank. If you're asked whether or not Windows should remember settings for this user, answer **Yes**.
- Occasionally, your Password List (a file with the *.pwl* extension) can get corrupted. Select **Find** and then **Files or Folders** from your Start Menu, look for `*.pwl`, and delete any files it finds in your *\Windows* folder. After restarting Windows, all your configured passwords should be forgotten, and Windows should allow you to start from scratch.
- Check your other connections in the Dial-Up Networking window, if any. If the **Save password** checkbox is turned off for at least one connection, it may disable all of your passwords. Make sure the checkbox is enabled for each connection.
- Open the Registry Editor (if you're not familiar with the Registry Editor, see Chapter 3). Expand the branches to `HKEY_LOCAL_MACHINE\Software\Microsoft\Windows\CurrentVersion\Network\Real Mode Net`. If you see a value named `auto-logon` in the right pane with a value of `00`, double-click on it, and replace the value with `01 00 00 00 00`. You'll have to restart Windows for this change to take effect.
- Maybe Windows isn't saving your password because your ISP uses nonstandard user authentication. In this case, you may have to configure Dial-Up Scripting to enter your password for you. See Chapter 9 for more information.

Coping with the Non-Functional Windows Update

Strangely enough, the Windows Update command accessible from your Start Menu is totally nonfunctional for many users. If you see the message "The path 'http://windowsupdate.microsoft.com' does not exist or is not a directory" whenever you try to use this feature, you've run into a problem that has existed since the feature was released.

The good news is that this problem is easy to circumvent. Just open Internet Explorer (naturally, Netscape Navigator isn't supported), and type in the following URL: *http://windowsupdate.microsoft.com/* (note the absence of the "www" prefix). The update feature technically should work as intended at this point.

Test Your Throughput

Throughput is the amount of data you can transmit over a connection in a given period of time. Now, most types of connections are classified by their throughput: a 33.6kbps modem theoretically will be able to transmit and receive 33,600 bits per second. Since there are eight bits to a byte, this should give us a throughput of 4.2KB per second. In reality, however, you're likely never to get more than about 3.6KB per second. That's a difference of about 14%; a file that you would expect to take a minute to download will actually take 70 seconds.

This discrepancy exists because the speed at which a modem is classified is the speed at which it communicates to your ISP. Since error correction, lost packets due to noise on the line, and other types of information are transferred along with your data to and from the modem on the other end of the connection, the actual throughput will always be lower. Furthermore, your PC's serial port is a bottleneck that will further throttle your connection. Unfortunately, most factors that contribute to throughput are beyond your control.

Factors within your control include the hardware and software you use and various settings and working conditions (phone line quality, distance from your ISP, etc.). It is often advantageous to test throughput under different conditions.

The simplest way to measure throughput is to transfer a binary file from your computer to another location and then back again, recording the time it takes to complete the transfer. Divide the file size by the transfer time to get the throughput, in kilobytes per second.

You shouldn't use ASCII files, such as text files and web pages, to test the throughput, since your modem's compression will yield uncharacteristic results. Note also that we test the "uplink" as well as the "downlink" speed, as many types of connections are asynchronous; 56K modems, for example, download at around 53.2kbps, but upload at only 33.6kbps.

Average throughputs for common connection speeds are shown in Table 7-2. Note that you shouldn't fret if your throughput doesn't match the values in the table. If you find that you're getting substantially slower performance, however, you should test your equipment and contact the phone company to check your line. See the next section for further information.

Table 7-2: Common Download and Upload Throughputs for Various Connection Speeds

Connection Method	Expected Throughput (kb/sec)
14.4kbps modem	1.6 down, 1.6 up
28.8kbps modem	3.2 down, 3.2 up
33.6kbps modem	3.6 down, 3.6 up
56kbps modem	5.4 down, 3.6 up
ISDN (single channel, 64kbps)	7.0 down, 7.0 up
ISDN (dual channel, 115.2kbps)[a]	11 down, 11 up
ISDN (dual channel, 128kbps)	14 down, 14 up
Cable Modem, ~800kbps synchronous	84 down, 84 up
ADSL (asynchronous 1.5Mbps/384kbps)	160 down, 42 up
T1, fast DSL (1.5Mbps)	160 down, 160 up

[a] If you have an external ISDN modem connected to a serial port, you'll be limited by the serial port's maximum speed, which is 115.2kbps.

The System Monitor utility that comes with Windows 98 now allows you to measure your Dial-Up Networking throughput, including download and upload bytes per second. Depending on your needs, this utility may be less or more accurate than a simple real-world test as described previously.

Change the MTU and RWIN Parameters for Dial-Up Networking

Part of the Winsock specification upon which Dial-Up Networking is based is the reliance on several numeric parameters, two of which are MTU and RWIN.

The maximum transmission unit (MTU) is the size of the individual packets, or blocks of information, that are sent and received by Dial-Up Networking. If this setting is too large, a router somewhere between you and the remote host that can't accept large packets may fragment the transmitted data, resulting in slower data transmission. Conversely, if the setting is too small, it won't be taking full advantage of the bandwidth available. The default is "automatic," which uses an MTU of 576 for connection speeds below 128kbps, and an MTU of 1500 otherwise.* The MTU setting can be different for each instance of TCP/IP installed.

Receive WINdow (RWIN) is the size of a buffer Windows uses to fill with packets before completing whatever communication is pending. The RWIN setting affects all network communication, and should not be changed if you're on a local area network.

Unlike in Windows 95, the default settings in Windows 98 are optimal for most situations; in most circumstances, you should have no need to change them.

If you have reason to believe that the default values are causing a problem (for example, web pages stop loading before completion), or if you find that your connection performance is sub-par (see the previous section, "Test Your Throughput"), you may want to check with your ISP to see if they recommend settings other than Windows 98's defaults.

Only change the MTU and RWIN values if your ISP recommends different settings than the defaults. Follow these directions to change these values in Windows 98.

Setting MTU: Solution 1

1. Double-click on the **Network** icon in Control Panel, and then double-click on **Dial-Up Adapter** in the list.
2. Choose the **Advanced** tab, and select **IP Packet Size** from the **Property** list. From the **Value** dropdown listbox on the right, choose the desired setting. Unfortunately, rather than typing in a value here, you must choose from **Automatic**, **Small** (576), **Medium** (1000), and **Large** (1500). If you need to specify a different value, proceed to Solution 2.
3. Click **OK** twice when you're done.

Setting MTU: Solution 2

1. Open the Registry Editor (if you're not familiar with the Registry Editor, see Chapter 3).
2. Expand the branches to `HKEY_LOCAL_MACHINE\System\CurrentControlSet\Services\Class\Net\`*`0000`*`\`, where *`0000`* is a four-digit number representing the key that we want to change. To find the right key, look in each key (there may be three or four numbered keys here); the correct key will have the `DriverDesc` string value set to

* If you're using Virtual Private Networking (discussed later in this chapter), the MTU setting will be lower to account for the extra overhead. If you're using the older SLIP technology, the MTU will be set to 58.

Networking

"Dial-Up Adapter". If there is more than one, you'll have to do this for each one.

3. The MTU parameter is specified in the `(Default)` value in the `Ndi\params\IPMTU` subkey. Double-click `(Default)` and type the desired number or `0` (zero) for automatic.
4. Close the Registry Editor when you're finished.

Setting RWIN

1. Open the Registry Editor (if you're not familiar with the Registry Editor, see Chapter 3).
2. Expand the branches to `HKEY_LOCAL_MACHINE\System\CurrentControlSet\Services\VxD\MSTCP\`.
3. If you don't see a value named `DefaultRcvWindow` in this key, select **New** and then **String Value** from the **Edit** menu, type `DefaultRcvWindow` for the name of the new value, and click **OK**.
4. Double-click on the new value and type in the desired number. If you don't know what value to use here, don't change it at all.
5. Close the Registry Editor when you're finished.

Using Multilink to Connect

The new Multilink feature in Windows 98 allows you to "bind" multiple modems or network adapters together to increase bandwidth for a single Internet connection. For example, if you have two 56K modems, Multilink will give you a theoretical connection speed of 112kbps. This idea has been around since long before Windows 98; ISDN, for example, comes with two digital 64kbps channels that can be bound together to achieve a 128kbps connection.

The downside here is that your ISP must specifically support one of the Multilink protocols, and you must have two or more compatible devices installed.

Here's how to do it:

1. First, create a Dial-Up Networking connection using a single device, as described in "Installing Dial-Up Networking," earlier in this chapter.
2. Right-click on the new connection icon, select **Properties**, and click on the **Multilink** tab. Select **Use Additional Devices**, then click **Add** to add a new entry for each additional device you wish to support. You'll be able to add any configured modem or network adapter that isn't already configured for the DUN connection.

3. If the ISP or other host to which you're connecting supports "rotary," "rollover," or "hunt group" Multilink connections, you'll be able to use the same phone number for all your devices. Otherwise, you may have to specify a different phone number for each one.

4. To use Multilink, double-click on the corresponding connection in the DUN window. After making the initial connection, Windows will attempt to connect with any configured additional devices. The **Connected** icon in the tray will keep you up to date on how many devices are actually being used.

Dial-Up Scripting

Most ISPs should support Dial-Up Networking in Windows 98 without any modifications or special settings. However, some users must endure a more complicated logon process, common with more specialized ISPs, universities, and private companies that have chosen to stick with a proprietary method. If your provider doesn't support a common authentication protocol (e.g., PAP, SPAP, CHAP), you can still fully automate your logon procedure with Dial-Up Scripting.

Dial-Up Scripting provides a way to preprogram a list of commands that you would otherwise have to type manually every time you connect. Rather than simply listing the necessary commands in a file somewhere, however, you'll need to adhere to a special scripting language. The scripting syntax is documented in the file *Script.doc*, located in your *\Windows* folder, although it is likely to be confusing for non-programmers.

The following procedure outlines the steps necessary to form a script that works with your configuration and hook it up to an existing DUN connection. For more information on DUN connections, see "Installing Dial-Up Networking" earlier in this chapter. Before you begin, you might want to contact your provider to see if they have a prewritten script you can use; due to the popularity of Windows 95/98, it's likely that someone has already come up with a solution.

Part 1: Log in manually

1. Double-click on the **Dial-Up Networking** icon in the My Computer window, right-click on the connection icon you wish to use, and select **Properties**.

2. In the **Connect using** portion, click **Configure**, and choose the **Options** tab. Turn on the **Bring up terminal window after dialing** option, click **OK** and **OK** again when you're done.

3. Start connecting to your provider by double-clicking the same connection icon.
4. *After* your modem has dialed and successfully established a call, a small window with a black background will appear, allowing you to complete the logon procedure.

   Proceed by typing in the appropriate commands, usernames, and passwords required by your provider. As you type, write down on a piece of paper each prompt you see as well as each command you type, carefully noting spelling and punctuation; capitalization doesn't count for prompts, but it may count for the text you type, such as passwords. For example, you might write the following:

   ```
   username:    billybob
   Password:    Secret5
   server781>   ppp
   LOGIN?       billybob
   passwd?      WalaWala
   ```

   This example shows five prompts with five corresponding entries; your procedure will most likely be different.
5. When you've finished typing, click **Continue** (or press **F7**) to have Windows complete the logon procedure.

Steps 4 and 5 accomplish two important tasks: testing the logon procedure to make sure you can connect, and recording the process so that you can reproduce it with a script.

Part 2: Write the script

1. Open a plain text editor, such as Notepad.
2. Start your script by typing `proc main`, which is necessary for every DUN script.
3. For each prompt displayed during the logon process, type the following command:

   ```
   waitfor "username:"
   ```

   where the text between the quotation marks matches a prompt you'd see when logging in; spelling and punctuation both count here. A good trick is to leave off the punctuation to avoid matching problems (i.e., `"username"`).
4. After each corresponding `waitfor` command, type the following for each piece of text you're supposed to enter:

   ```
   transmit "billybob^M"
   ```

where the text between the quotation marks is what is sent to the host. The `^M` (a caret, **Shift-6**, followed by a capital **M**) is interpreted as a carriage return; include it inside the quotation marks every time you'd normally press the **Enter** key. Most of the text here—especially passwords—will be case-sensitive.

5. End your script by typing `endproc`, a necessary terminator to the command typed in step 2.
6. What you should end up with is a series of pairs of `waitfor` and `transmit` commands. The following sample script is based on the example shown in Part 1:

```
proc main
  waitfor "username"
  transmit "billybob"
  waitfor "password"
  transmit "Secret5"
  waitfor ">"
  transmit "ppp"
  waitfor "login"
  transmit "billybob"
  waitfor "password"
  transmit "WalaWala"
endproc
```

   Note the sixth line, which lists the `waitfor` command, followed only by the `">"` character. This is because of the `server781>` prompt shown in the example in Part 1; the `781` implies that this prompt may be different every time you log on, due to multiple servers answering the phones. By specifying only `">"` here, we eliminate any matching errors.

7. If you want to have the script enter the username and password entered in Dial-Up Networking's "Connect To" dialog, replace the appropriate transmit command with the following:

```
transmit $USERID, raw
```

   for your username, and:

```
transmit $PASSWORD, raw
```

   for your password. The `raw` parameter accommodates any weird characters that may be in your username or password.

8. When you've finished typing your script, save it into a filename with the extension *.scp*, put it in any folder that's convenient, and close your text editor.

Part 3: Hook up the script to a connection

1. To have DUN automatically invoke the script whenever you connect, you must first turn off the **Bring up terminal window after dialing** option as described in Part 1.
2. Right-click on the DUN connection icon you wish to use, and select **Properties**.
3. Choose the **Scripting** tab, click **Browse**, and select the *.scp* file you saved in Part 2.
4. Click **OK** when you're finished. To try out the new script, double-click on the connection icon, and watch it go. If all goes well, DUN should complete its connection without any input from you.
5. However, if there's an error in the script, you'll have to go back to your text editor and try to fix the problem. You can use the **Step through script** option in the connection properties dialog to have DUN walk you through the logon procedure so you can see what went wrong.

Notes and other issues

If your provider doesn't support standard PPP authentication, don't hesitate to complain to them. If enough users are annoyed, they'll do something about it.

Once you have your script working, you'll most likely never need to do this again—unless your provider changes the logon procedure, as many ISPs do.

Note that if your logon procedure is different each time you log on, you'll have to write a more complex script than is documented here. See the *Script.doc* file that comes with Windows 98 for more information.

Dial-Up Scripting is not the type of scripting supported by the Windows Scripting Host, which is discussed in Chapter 9, but you might want to check out Chapter 9 to familiarize yourself with some basic scripting concepts such as commands and conditional statements.

The scripts used with Windows 95/98 are the same as those used in Windows NT 4 and 5. In Windows NT, the script files (*.scp*) are located in *\winnt\system32\ras*. This means that the scripts you write for Windows 98 will be usable even if you upgrade to NT. It also means that any scripts others may have written for NT will work on your system.

Special Circumstances

Since there are so many different kinds of connections, and since some ISPs and other companies don't support standard PPP, for whatever reason, it can be difficult to get Windows to work in your particular circumstances. Here are some tips for nonstandard connections:

Commercial services

If you use America Online, the Microsoft Network, Prodigy, or another proprietary commercial service, you most likely use the application that shipped with your package to dial and access the Internet. However, for the most flexibility, you may want to use standard Dial-Up Networking with your connection, which allows you to use the latest web browsers and other more specific Internet programs, such as voice and video conferencing. The problem is that most of these major players use nonstandard software. You'll have to contact the company you do business with to see if they support Dial-Up Networking in Windows 98.

ISDN

Integrated Services Digital Network (ISDN) gives Internet users a connection speed of up to 128kbps, about four times faster than common 33.6kbps modems. Each ISDN adapter requires a somewhat different installation procedure and drivers; you'll have to consult the adapter's documentation for specific setup details. See the section on troubleshooting modems in Chapter 6 for more information on the different kinds of ISDN adapters.

Mixing and Matching Networks

In this chapter, two distinctly different kinds of networks are discussed: local area networks (commonly called workgroups), and dial-up Internet connections. While the intended uses of each of these types of communication are quite different, there are several ways in which they can interact.

One useful fusion of these technologies is to connect an entire LAN to the Internet with a single connection, rather than having each computer on the LAN connect independently. The two technologies can also be used in combination to form a workgroup with two or more Internet connections, which is called Virtual Private Networking.

Share an Internet Connection on a Workgroup

A common scenario is a workgroup of two or more computers and a single phone line. Installing a modem in each machine and sharing a line is less than ideal, especially since both computers can't be connected simultaneously, and installing two phone lines is often even less desirable.

Figure 7-11 shows a diagram of two solutions for connecting a workgroup to the Internet, neither of which is supported by or documented in Windows 98 out of the box.

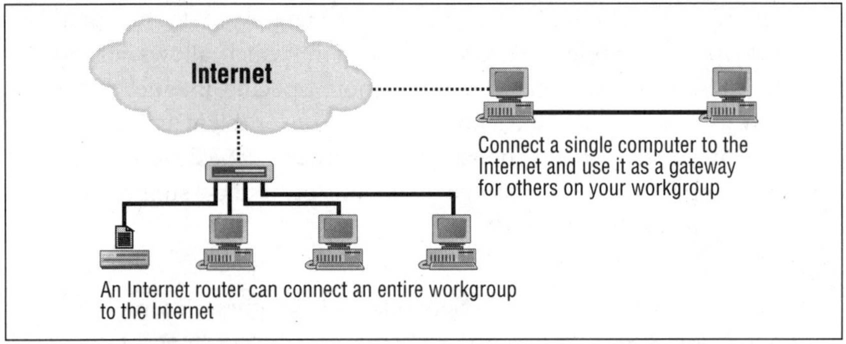

Figure 7-11: Different ways to connect a workgroup to the Internet, depending on your needs and resources

This seems more complicated than it should be because Windows is not capable of transporting one protocol (TCP/IP, in this case) over another protocol (IPX, used over the workgroup) in a way that helps us accomplish our goal. The following solutions provide the necessary pieces to complete the puzzle. Solution 1 requires special software, and Solution 2 requires special hardware.

Solution 1: Use one machine as a gateway

In order to provide Internet access to the second computer shown in the first example of Figure 7-11, the first computer must be configured to route Internet transmission to the second, while still maintaining Internet access of its own. This is accomplished by configuring the computer with Internet access as an Internet gateway, which then provides Internet access to the other computers on the workgroup. The following steps accomplish this:

1. Start by properly installing and configuring Dial-Up Networking on the computer with the modem or other type of Internet Connection. See "Installing Dial-Up Networking" earlier in this chapter for details.

2. Hook up one or more additional computers (including the one with Internet access) to form a workgroup, as described in "Setting Up a Workgroup," earlier in this chapter.

3. Obtain and install WinGate or NAT32 (see Appendix F) on the machine with Internet access, both of which will make it an Internet gateway.

4. Find the IP address of the gateway computer* by running the IP Configuration utility (*Winipcfg.exe*). Choose your network adapter (not **PPP Adapter**) from the list, and write down what it says in the **IP Address** field. Close the IP Configuration utility when you're done.

5. Configure the other computers in the workgroup so they know that they need to get TCP/IP from the gateway. Double-click on the **Network** icon in Control Panel, and choose **TCP/IP -> Dial-Up Adapter** from the list. Click **Properties**, and then choose the **Gateway** tab, as shown in Figure 7-12. Type in the IP address of the gateway you obtained in step 4, and click **Add**. Click **OK** when you're done.

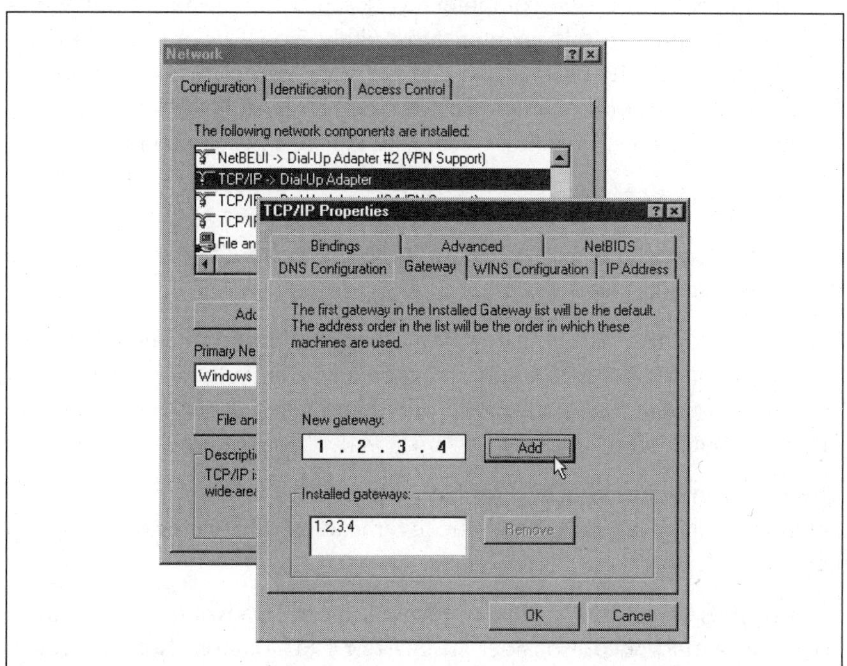

Figure 7-12: Configure each client machine to access the Internet through a gateway

* Note that the IP address of a machine on a LAN (which is what we're getting here) may not be the same as a static or dynamically assigned IP address used when connected to the Internet.

Networking

6. You may have to restart each of the computers when you're done. When you have restarted and have connected the gateway to the Internet, all computers in the workgroup should have Internet access.

Solution 2: Using an Internet router

Commonly, a router doubles as a hub, interconnecting two or more computers, as well as hooking them all up to the Internet. ISDN routers are a good choice, since they don't cost much more than single-user ISDN adapters, and are able to provide adequate bandwidth for a handful of computers. Here's how to employ an Internet router:

1. Obtain and install an Internet router, following the instructions included with the device.
2. Connect one or more computers to the router, and install any necessary client software that may be required by the router. Some routers use an HTTP interface, which means that they can be controlled with any web browser, and no special client software is needed.
3. Configure each of the computers as described in "Setting Up a Workgroup," earlier in this chapter. Most likely, you'll have to additionally bind the TCP/IP protocol to the network cards in each computer, since the network cards provide the connectivity to the Internet Router, and must be able to transport TCP/IP to each computer.

Notes and other issues

Setting one computer up as a gateway (Solution 1) will be less expensive than purchasing a router (Solution 2).

Solution 1 requires that the gateway machine be turned on and connected for the other computer(s) to have Internet access. Solution 2 gives each computer equal access; connecting one computer isn't dependent on any other computer.

The router in Solution 2 is potentially more efficient than the gateway in Solution 1, as you don't have the overhead of the gateway eating up bandwidth for the "client" computers.

Both of these solutions are likely to need more bandwidth than a single computer would need. Consider an ISDN or DSL solution. Note, however, that two or more users will rarely need full, simultaneous bandwidth.

Virtual Private Networking

Virtual Private Networking (VPN) is a system whereby you can use the Internet to connect computers as though they were attached with a cable, while theoretically maintaining all the security and privacy of a closed environment.

The technology, Point-to-Point Tunneling Protocol (PPTP), creates a private "tunnel" across the Internet connection, and allows you to accomplish tasks previously only available over a LAN, such as file and printer sharing, and even networked games. Figure 7-13 shows one scenario, with a tunnel connecting a single computer to a small workgroup.

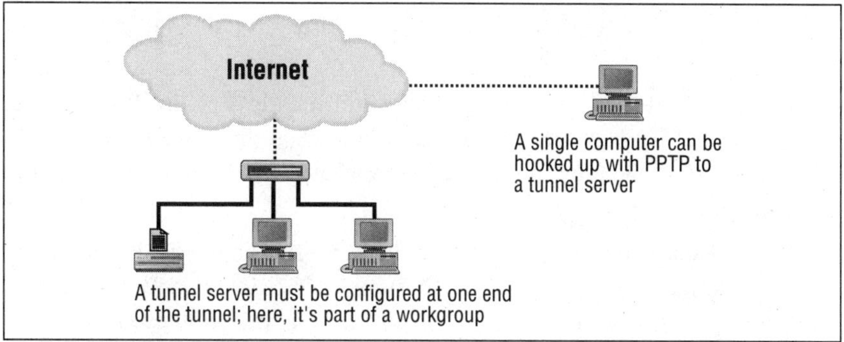

Figure 7-13: Form a virtual private workgroup through a tunnel across the Internet

The significant problem with the VPN technology included in Windows 98 is that a *tunnel server* is required to complete the virtual workgroup. Although VPN has been marketed as a feature of Windows 98, Windows 98 cannot be configured as a Tunnel Server; therefore, a VPN can not be achieved with Windows 98 alone. This means that at least one of the computers involved must be running Windows NT Server 4.0 or later.

The other significant problem with VPN is that there is virtually no documentation included with Windows 98 or Windows NT that is helpful in getting VPN to work. The following process briefly shows how to set up a simple VPN:

1. Configure Windows NT Server, running on one of the machines involved, as a tunnel server. In NT, double-click the **Network** icon in Control Panel, choose the **Protocols** tab, and then click **Add**. Select **Point To Point Tunneling Protocol** from the list and click **OK**. When asked how many simultaneous VPNs you want the server to support, choose a nice, big, healthy number, and click **OK**.

   Next, you'll need to add the VPN devices to RAS: choose the **Services** tab and select **Remote Access Service**. Click **Properties**, and then click **Add**. From the **RAS Capable Devices** list, select a VPN device and click **OK**. Once all the VPN devices have been added, select a VPN port and click **Configure**. Check the **Receive calls only** option and click

OK. Repeat for each VPN device. You'll have to restart NT at this point.

The last step with NT is to add a user for each VPN client. The username and password configured here will be entered in step 5, below.

2. Install VPN support on each Windows 98 client machine. Double-click on the **Add/Remove Programs** icon in Control Panel and choose the **Windows Setup** tab. Choose **Communications** from the list, and click **Details**. Put a checkmark next to **Virtual Private Networking**, and click **OK** twice. You may have to restart Windows for this change to take effect.

3. Create a Dial-Up Networking connection for the VPN in Windows 98. In the Dial-Up Networking folder, double-click the **Make New Connection** icon. Type any name, select **Microsoft VPN Adapter** from the **Select a device** list, and click **Next**.

   In the **Host name or IP Address** field, type the name or IP address of the Tunnel Server you set up in step 1. Click **Next** and then **Finish** when you're done. Right-click on the new connection icon and click **Properties** to change any additional settings.

4. You'll need to connect to the Internet before initiating a VPN session, if you're not already connected.

5. Once you're connected to the Internet, you can connect to the VPN server. Double-click on the new VPN connection icon and enter your username and password (as configured in NT in step 1).* Click **Connect** to initiate a connection.

   Once you connect Windows 98 to the Tunnel Server, you will be connected to that remote network as if you were physically attached to it. Therefore, you must ensure that Windows 98 has the proper protocols native to *that* network (such as IPX/SPX or NetBEUI) installed and bound to the VPN adapter in the Network Properties window.

Notes and other issues

While VPN support is included with Windows 98, Windows 95 users will need to install the Dial-Up Networking Update with PPTP, Version 1.2 or later (from Microsoft); see Appendix F.

---

* If you've used the "Bypass the 'Connect To' Dialog Box" solution earlier in this chapter, you'll need to re-enable the Connect To dialog at least temporarily before continuing. In the Dial-Up Networking folder, select **Settings** from the **Connections** menu, turn on the **Prompt for information before dialing** option, and click **OK**. Once you've successfully connected at least once, you can turn this option back off.

After installing VPN, you may see a second Dial-Up Adapter named "Dial-Up Adapter #2 (VPN Support)". Make sure not to remove this adapter, as it is required by PPTP to encapsulate its data stream.

Security and Multiple Users

The use of multiple users on a Windows platform falls into two categories:

1. One or more users are allowed to log onto a single Windows 98 system with their own settings (application toolbars, desktop wallpaper, etc.).
2. A network server running Windows NT or Unix provides mail and multiple remote user access. Since Windows 98 doesn't support multiple remote users, the following solutions apply only to the first category.

Problems arise either when you only have one user, yet run into features available for multiple users, or when you have multiple users, and encounter the limitations of this predominantly single-user environment.

Get Rid of the Logon Screen

If you've installed any networking drivers, including those for a local area network or Dial-Up Networking (both discussed earlier in this chapter), you might see a window the next time you start Windows asking for your username and password. Ideally, you should be able to type your username and leave the password field blank,* and never have to see this window again, if you so choose.

Unfortunately, this window often comes back every time you boot—even if you're the only user on the system. To remove the logon box, try any of the following solutions.

Networking

If you do not have multiple users

- Double-click on the **Network** icon in Control Panel, and from the list entitled **Primary Network Logon**, choose **Windows Logon**. Press **OK**, and confirm that you want to restart Windows when asked.
- If that doesn't work, you may have chosen a password for yourself at one point. If you did, Windows will always ask for it. To clear the

* While you can specify a password here, all it will do is prevent others from logging in with your username. Since Windows 98 has no security features to speak of, there's nothing to prevent users from entering any other username at this point. See "Prevent new users from logging in" in "How to Implement Security in Windows" later in this chapter.

password, double-click on the **Passwords** icon in Control Panel, and click **Change Windows Password**. You'll have to enter your old password, but make sure to leave the new password blank; click **OK** when you're done.

- If neither of the preceding solutions work, see "Force Dial-Up Networking to Remember Passwords" for other solutions to what could be a related problem.

If you do have multiple users

1. Open the Registry Editor. (If you're not familiar with the Registry Editor, see Chapter 3.)
2. Expand the branches to `HKEY_LOCAL_MACHINE\Network\Logon`.
3. If it's not already there, create a new value called `Process Logon Script` by selecting **New** and then **Binary Value** from the **Edit** menu.
4. Double-click on the `Process Logon Script` value and change the data from `00 00 00 00` to `01 00 00 00`. Click **OK** and close the Registry Editor when you're done; you'll have to restart Windows for this change to take effect.

   This *should* force Windows to bypass the logon screen the next time you start Windows. To change users, just select **Log Off** from the Start Menu.

Share System Folders Between Users

If you've configured multiple users in Windows 98, you'll notice that each user has his or her own *Desktop* folder, *Start Menu* folder, *Send To* folder, *Favorites* folder, as well as private copies of other system folders. Each user's personal folders are subfolders of *\Windows\Profiles\Username* (where *Username* is the name of the user).

In addition, Windows 98 also has the *All Users* folder, which contains yet other copies of the *Desktop* and *Start Menu* folders. The idea is this: any items located in the "All Users" instances of the folders will appear for each user configured on the system. And in the Start Menu, a horizontal divider separates "All Users" items from each user's personal Start Menu contents.

The problem with this system is that it causes clutter in the Start Menu, on the desktop, and in Explorer. Additionally, it can make the process of making changes to all users more difficult. To clean things up, you may want to consolidate some of the users' individual folders to create several shared folders.

This solution takes advantage of two features of Windows:

- When you rename or move a system folder with drag-drop, Windows keeps track of the change and records it.
- When you try to move a folder from one place to another in Explorer, and there is another folder in the destination with the same name, Windows combines the contents of the two folders, after asking.

Utilizing both of these features, you can, for example, drag one user's **Send To** menu onto another user's profile folder, effectively combining the contents of both folders. When you see the prompt, "This folder already contains a folder called 'Send To,'" answer **Yes** to confirm that you want to replace the existing files. When it's done, Windows will automatically update the registry settings for the currently installed user so that the new location of the *Send To* folder is used.

How to Implement Security in Windows

While Windows NT comes with more security features than the average home user requires, Windows 98 doesn't seem to come with enough. Whether you're trying to protect your computer from prying children, or trying to protect valuable data from prying coworkers, there are ways to implement various forms of security, depending on your needs and means. Although there's no way to achieve the same type of security found in Windows NT or Unix, the following are a few hints that can help add limited security to Windows 98.

Prevent new users from logging in

Anyone can simply log in to Windows 98 by choosing a new username, or even by simply clicking **Cancel** at the logon screen. Passwords in Windows 98 actually accomplish nothing besides preventing users from logging in as other existing users. The following solution prevents someone from logging in without a password for a presently configured user:

1. Double-click on the **Network** icon in Control Panel.
2. Click **Add**, choose **Client**, and click **Add**. Select **Microsoft** in the left-hand list, then **Microsoft Family Logon** in the right-hand list, and click **OK**.
3. In the main Network Properties window, select **Microsoft Family Logon** from the **Primary Network Logon** list, and click **OK** when you're finished. When Windows asks if you want to restart, answer **Yes**.

Notes and other issues

Installing the Microsoft Family Logon client causes a list of users to be displayed when Windows starts, from which you can choose one. If this is not desirable, you'll have to switch the **Primary Network Logon** option in step 3 back to the standard **Client for Microsoft Networks**.

Another way of preventing unwanted users from logging in is to obtain and install the Shutdown utility (see Appendix F).

Save settings for multiple users

1. If you've configured Windows to be used with more than one user, and want each user's desktop settings to be saved individually, double-click on the **Passwords** icon in Control Panel and choose the **User Profiles** tab.
2. Select **Users can customize their preferences**, turn on both options beneath the **Option** button, and click **OK**. You'll have to restart Windows for this change to take effect.

Limit access to unprivileged users

Windows 98 comes with several settings that remove key menu items and icons from the basic interface, making it easier to restrict access to certain users. This procedure outlines a particular scenario; your needs may differ:

1. Create two users: one called Administrator and one called Visitor, or something to that effect. Choose a password for the Administrator, but choose no password for the Visitor.
2. You'll want to restrict access to the Visitor user, yet retain all privileges for the Administrator user. Log in as the Visitor, and start the System Policy Editor (see Appendix A, *Setting Locator*).
3. Select **Open Registry** from the **File** menu, and then double-click on the **Local User** icon. Open `Local_User\Shell\Restrictions`, and go through the settings here carefully, checking the ones that interest you. Most of the settings should be fairly self-explanatory.
4. Close the Local User window, select **Save** from the **File** menu, and close the System Policy Editor when you're finished. For your reference, most of the policy changes are stored in the Registry in the key `HKEY_CURRENT_USER\Software\Microsoft\Windows\CurrentVersion\Policies\Explorer`.
5. Lastly, install the Shutdown utility (see "Prevent new users from logging in," earlier in this topic). This will prevent someone from logging in as a user other than Administrator or Visitor.

This way, you'll get full access as the administrator, and all other users will only have "Visitor" access. A word to the wise: anyone with sufficient knowledge of Windows 98 will be able to break this security; for better security, you'll either have to install a third-party add-on, or upgrade to Windows NT.

8

In this chapter:
- *A Little History and Motivation*
- *Massaging the Interface*
- *The Web View and the Active Desktop*
- *Choosing Your Defaults*

Taking Control of Web Integration

Sometime after the release of Windows 95 and before the introduction of Internet Explorer 4.0 in 1997, Microsoft decided to deliver web integration to millions of unsuspecting Windows users around the world. With the release of Windows 98 and NT 5, Microsoft stopped making it an option, and included a preinstalled copy of the integrated web browser with every copy of the operating system.

Whether you feel that Microsoft has inflicted web integration on their users, or that they've graced their users with this feature, is entirely up to you. What's for certain is that they don't give you a choice when you install Windows 98.

Of course, to say that the Internet Explorer web browser is actually *integrated* with Explorer is quite inaccurate. What Microsoft calls "integration" is a collection of otherwise unrelated features designed to make it *appear* as though the web browser is part of the operating system. What's more, most of these features don't have all that much to do with the Internet; they're in effect for everyone, whether they use the Internet or not.

The following is a list of the various components that Microsoft has put under the "integration" umbrella:

- The ability to configure icons to open with a single mouse click, rather than the traditional double-click. This makes the icons for your files and folders look and feel at least superficially like hyperlinks you might see in a web page. All your icons' captions are underlined, and even light up when you move the mouse over them—something links in web pages traditionally *don't* do.

- The *Web View* of your folders in Explorer, wherein each folder can be shown with an extra pane containing a brief description of the currently selected item. While it adds some fancy graphics, the actual information displayed is, in most cases, nothing more than you'd see by selecting **Details** from Explorer's **View** menu or **Properties** from Explorer's **File** menu—things that have been around since Windows 95. See "The Web View and the Active Desktop" later in this chapter for information on customizing the Web View.
- The *Active Desktop*, which is essentially the "Web View" of your desktop, with the following addition: the desktop can hold small, movable, resizable, window-like panes, each containing a web page. These panes aren't much different from ordinary IE windows, except they have thinner borders, appear to be "attached" to your desktop, and automatically reappear when you restart Windows.
- The *Internet Explorer* icon on the desktop. Just in case you couldn't find a web link, and didn't feel like going to the trouble of opening your Start Menu, you can open an Internet Explorer window by double-clicking on this icon.
- The *Favorites* menu on the Start Menu. This is the same as the Favorites menu in Internet Explorer, which holds all your Internet shortcuts. See "Clean Up and Customize System Folders" in Chapter 4, *Tinkering Techniques*, for information on redirecting the *Favorites* folder to another location you might find more useful, such as your desktop or *My Documents* folder.
- The *Channel Bar,* simply another place to put links to web sites. Not much more than a revenue source for Microsoft, this small box comes preconfigured with links to the web sites of companies like Disney who have purchased advertising space there.
- Web links everywhere. Links to various web sites are scattered throughout the operating system; in Help menus, the *Favorites* folder, the Channel Bar, and the "Windows Update" utility. Clicking on any of these links launches the default web browser (see "Choosing Your Defaults," later in this chapter).
- The illusion that the Windows Explorer and Internet Explorer are the same program (they do, after all, have similar names). In certain circumstances, Internet Explorer and Windows Explorer can share the same window. Assuming IE is your default browser for the HTTP protocol, when you type an Internet address in Explorer or select any links from Explorer's Favorites menu, the Explorer window appears to be transformed into an Internet Explorer window. Likewise, if you

type a folder name (e.g., *c:\program files*) in Internet Explorer, the window is transformed back into an Explorer window.

Having both programs use the same container is a good trick, but it's clear that they're two different programs; they have different menus and toolbars, and respond differently to many actions.

- The *Address Bar* on the Taskbar and in the Windows Explorer. This is, at least on the surface, a duplicate of the Address Bar found in Internet Explorer, in which you can type Internet addresses (e.g., *http://www.annoyances.org/*). While the intent is to make it appear as though all Explorer windows are Internet Explorer windows, you can easily see the difference.

  In Internet Explorer, for example, an address typed in the Address Bar will cause a web page to load in Internet Explorer. However, in the Windows Explorer and on the Taskbar, a typed address will launch the default browser. Technically, the Address Bar is identical to the **Run** command in the Start Menu; you can launch any program (e.g., Notepad) as well as any Internet address from the Address Bar. See Appendix C, *Contents of the MSDOS.SYS File*, for a way to use the Address Bar as a DOS command prompt.

- Most important of all, the fact that Internet Explorer is the *default* web browser. When you double-click on an *.html* file on your hard disk, launch a URL from Explorer or the Start Menu, or click on a link in any application, the default web browser will appear and load the link. You can very easily choose any other program to be your default web browser, replacing Internet Explorer with Netscape, for example. You can even make Solitaire your default web browser, although that obviously won't get you too far.

Now, saying that the items listed above constitute a web browser integrated with the operating system is like saying that Notepad and FreeCell are integrated because (1) they both can be launched from the Start Menu; (2) they both have rectangular windows; (3) their About boxes look the same; and (4) they both come with Windows 98. This is, of course, absurd.

A Little History and Motivation

Before Version 4.0 and its integration with Windows, Internet Explorer was marketed and distributed as a separate product, which, among other things, put it in equitable competition with its rival, Netscape. By Microsoft's own admission, the integration of the browser with Windows was a scheme engineered to gain market share in the web browser market; making the web browser seem like part of Windows, Microsoft believed, would result in fewer customers looking for a third-party browser.*

Aside from the potential ethical problems, this means that Internet integration in Windows 98 may not necessarily have been included for the user's benefit. Whether or not this is true, however, depends upon your point of view.

On one hand, the idea of an operating system coming with a free web browser and means for connecting to the Internet is, conceptually, a step in the right direction. The Internet is quickly becoming a staple of the information age, and access should be within the reach of as many people as possible, regardless of financial or intellectual limitations. If you believe that Internet integration actually makes access to the Internet easier, then Microsoft has done Windows users a service.

On the other hand, consider Microsoft's motivation in wanting to gain market share with a product they're essentially giving away for free.

The primary purpose of a web browser is to display a certain type of document: the web page. Those who design web pages make design decisions based upon the people who view them and the tools they use. Since Netscape Navigator is the most popular web browser at the time of this writing, for example, most web pages are designed to take advantage of Navigator's features as well as to accommodate its limitations.

If Microsoft succeeds in making Internet Explorer the most popular browser, more web pages will be designed to take advantage of specific IE features, like ActiveX. ActiveX, a Windows-only technology used for making building blocks that can be used in web pages, is not supported by Netscape, and therefore is not currently very popular among web page designers. As IE gains consumer acceptance, however, so will ActiveX; more web pages will be designed to utilize ActiveX, which will result in a stronger demand for IE, and therefore, for Windows. Furthermore, the products used to create ActiveX components are sold exclusively by Microsoft; proliferation of IE will mean more sales of Windows and other Microsoft products to both developers and end users.

In the end, of course, the decision is yours. While some users are required to use a particular web browser for one reason or another, due to their

* In suggesting a possible strategy to compete with Netscape, Jim Allchin, a Microsoft senior vice president, wrote to Paul Maritz, the executive in charge of Microsoft's operating system division, "We should think first about an integrated solution—that is our strength." (Source: *New York Times*, Jan. 12, 1998)

employers' standards or some other political agenda, most users have the freedom to choose their tools.

Knowledge Is Power

While writing this book, I was asked by literally hundreds of Windows 95 users if they'd still be able to use Netscape, or any other Internet programs, for that matter, in Windows 98. Even more striking was the existential angst expressed by Windows 98 users who believed they wouldn't have any choice about Internet integration—to the point that many were reluctant to upgrade for that very reason. This is precisely the intent behind Internet integration: to maintain the myth that Internet Explorer is the only choice. This chapter intends to dispel that myth.

The truth is that you *do* have a choice—not just for your default browser, but for all of the components that make up Internet integration, and indeed, all the components that make up your computer. The solutions in this chapter will enable you to disable the options you don't want, as well as customize the options you do want.

Ignorance, in this case, is not bliss. The more you understand the technology behind the tools you use, and the motivation for their design, the better you can take advantage of the entire system.

Massaging the Interface

As described in the beginning of this chapter, Internet integration is the combination of several different interface components and settings. The problem is that the configuration of these various components is scattered across about a dozen different dialog boxes. The following guidelines should help you take full control over each these features, changing or even disabling them to your liking:

Icons get single-click rather than double-click

How to change: Select **Folder Options** from Explorer's **View** menu, choose **Custom, based on settings you choose** and then click **Settings**. Choose either **Single-click to open an item** or **Double-click to open an item** and then click **OK** twice.

Notes: Selecting **Classic style** or **Web style** in the Folder Options window will override this setting.

The Web View

How to change: Select **Folder Options** from Explorer's **View** menu, choose **Custom, based on settings you choose** and then click **Settings**.

Make the desired selection in the **View Web content in folders** section and then click **OK** twice when you're done.

Notes: See "The Web View and the Active Desktop" for details on customizing the Web View.

The Active Desktop

How to change: Double-click on the **TweakUI** icon in Control Panel (see Appendix A, *Setting Locator*), and choose the **IE4** tab. You can enable or disable the Active Desktop entirely with the **Active Desktop enabled** option.

Notes: See "The Web View and the Active Desktop" for details on customizing the Active Desktop.

The Internet Explorer Icon on the Desktop

How to change: Right-click on the icon and select **Delete** to get rid of it. To get it back, open TweakUI (see Appendix A), choose the **Desktop** tab, put a checkmark next to **Internet Explorer**, and click **OK**.

Notes: If you get rid of the icon, you can still run Internet Explorer by selecting Internet Explorer using the Start Menu or by launching *Iexplore.exe*.

The Favorites Menu on the Start Menu

How to change: Double-click on the **TweakUI** icon in Control Panel (see Appendix A), and choose the **IE4** tab. You can show or hide the **Favorites** menu with the **Show Favorites on Start Menu** option.

Notes: If you remove the **Favorites** menu from the Start Menu, it will still be shown in the Windows Explorer and in Internet Explorer.

The Channel Bar

How to change: To turn it off, move the mouse over the Channel Bar until its titlebar appears, and then click the close [X] button. To get it back, double-click on the **Display** icon in Control Panel, choose the **Web** tab,* put a checkmark next to **Internet Explorer Channel Bar**, and click **OK**.

Notes: You can customize the Channel Bar, should you decide to keep it, by simply dragging items (Internet shortcuts, programs, documents, etc.) onto it. Drag items onto the Recycle Bin to remove them. Changes are recorded in the *\Windows\Favorites\Channels* folder.

Web links are everywhere

How to change: For the most part, this cannot be changed. However, since most modern Windows applications allow you to customize

* The **Web** tab will be available only if the Active Desktop is enabled.

their menus, you should be able to get rid of any unwanted web links in applications. For example, in Microsoft Word, right-click on the menu bar, select **Customize**, open the **Help** menu, and drag the **Microsoft on the Web** item off the menu to get rid of it.

Notes: To change the browser used to open these links, see "Choosing Your Defaults" later in this chapter.

The illusion that the Windows Explorer and Internet Explorer are the same program

How to change: Double-click the **internet** icon in Control Panel, choose the **Advanced** tab, turn on the **Browse in a new process** option, and click **OK**.

Notes: See "Choosing Your Defaults" later in this chapter for choosing another program to be the default browser, which is another way of disabling this behavior.

The Address Bar on the Taskbar and in the Windows Explorer

How to change: Right-click on an empty area of the Taskbar, select **Toolbars**, and then **Address** to turn on or off the Address Bar.

Notes: See Appendix E, *Interface Terminology and the Basics*, for more information on the Taskbar toolbars, and Appendix B, *DOS Lives*, for details on using the Address Bar as a DOS command prompt.

The fact that Internet Explorer is the default web browser

How to change: You can make any program your default web browser; see "Choosing Your Defaults" later in this chapter for details.

Notes: Even if you make another web browser the default, you can still use Internet Explorer by selecting **Internet Explorer** from the Start Menu.

The Web View and the Active Desktop

The Web View component in Windows 98 allows you to make any folder (including the desktop) feel like a web page, complete with hyperlinks, graphics, and even a scripting language like JavaScript. But why would someone want to do this?

Traditionally, interface designers and users alike have prized clean, unobtrusive, attractive, and simple interfaces. The Web View isn't any of these. The Web View is, on the other hand, fairly customizable; exactly *how* customizable depends on your knowledge of HTML.

Now, it's unlikely that most users will have much use for the Default Web View, which augments the fairly simple Explorer interface with a bunch of unnecessary graphics and text. Figure 8-1 shows the same folder in its classic view as well as its Web View.

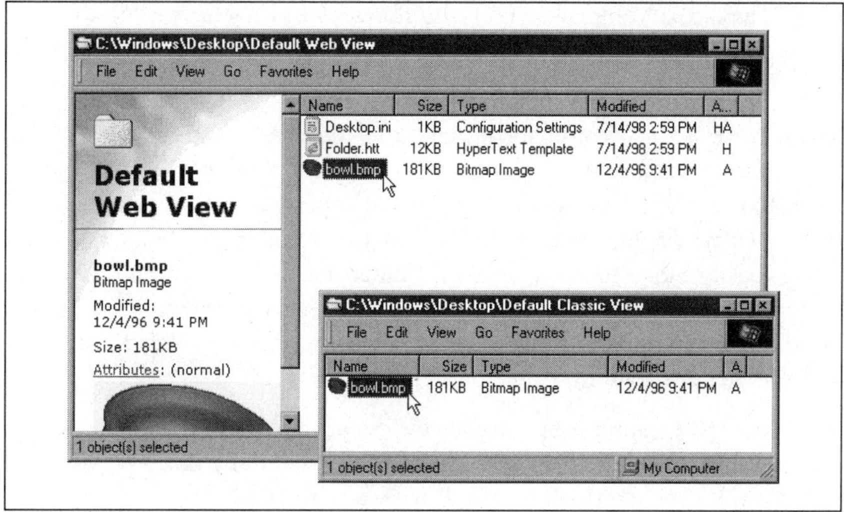

Figure 8-1: The Default Web View takes up much more space yet offers no additional information except for a full-size preview of some graphics files

When you first install Windows 98, all folders are shown in their Web View; that is, they all look similar to the larger window shown in Figure 8-1. If you turn off the Web View by unchecking **As Web Page** in Explorer's **View** menu, all folders should revert to their traditional appearance, exemplified by the smaller window in Figure 8-1.

I see a tremendous wasted opportunity here. While the Web View that Microsoft provides offers no apparent benefit to most users other than some pretty colors, the ability to customize the Web View is potentially quite useful. What's additionally confusing about the entire design is how complicated Microsoft has made the customization process.

While it's fairly easy to turn on and off the Web View for one or all of your folders, the process of customizing the Web View involves altering the template used for the Web View, which turns out to be an exercise in futility.

Using Hypertext Templates (Some Knowledge of HTML Required)

The pages that Windows uses for the Web Views of your folders and the Active Desktop are written in a somewhat bastardized version of HTML called Hypertext Templates (HTT). Windows 98 stores its *.htt* files in your *\Windows\Web* folder; for example, *Controlp.htt* is used for the Web View for Control Panel, and *Mycomp.htt* is used for My Computer.

Now, in the case of ordinary folders, the file used for the Web View is *Folder.htt* (located in the *\Windows\Web* folder). However, if you choose to customize the Web View of a particular folder, Windows places a copy of the *Folder.htt* file in that folder and creates a file called *Desktop.ini* alongside it.* Since most of us spend much more time navigating normal folder windows than the special system folders like Network Neighborhood and Printers, we'll concentrate on customizing the Web View of an average, generic folder.

I recommend creating a new folder to test out the Web View, rather than endangering the contents of an existing folder. If, at any time, you want to start over, just delete the folder and make a new one.

To set up a custom folder, first open the folder, and then select **Customize this folder** from its **View** menu. Choose **Create or edit an HTML document**, and click **Next** twice. Windows will automatically copy the necessary files, switch the folder to Web View, and open the folder's own copy of *Folder.htt* file in Notepad for editing.

Unfortunately, this is where Microsoft really screwed up. The template that's used for folders is a whopping 341 lines of nearly incomprehensible code. Although the Web View is supposedly intended to make Windows easier for less experienced users, the process involved in customizing this view is so convoluted that only the most experienced users will be able to make anything of it. And it's unlikely that experienced users are going to want to bother.

The truth is that you can cut out almost all of the code here,† and replace it with only a few lines of HTML, making it much easier—and much more desirable—to customize. The resulting Web View will not only load

* Both *Folder.htt* and *Desktop.ini* are hidden files and therefore not visible by default. To show hidden files, select **Folder Options** from Explorer's **View** menu, choose the **View** tab, and select **Show all files**.

† Most of the HTML code used to resize the folder window is JavaScript. With a little bit of thoughtful design, you can totally eliminate the need for this code. See Chapter 9, *Scripting and Automation*, for more information on JavaScript.

quicker, but the fact that's it's customized will make it instantly more useful.

There are a few things you need to know about *.htt* files used in the Web View before proceeding:

- Because of the proprietary nature of *.htt* files, it's not practical to use a WYSIWYG web page editor like FrontPage Express (the rudimentary editor that comes with Windows 98) to design your pages. You'll need to know at least some HTML and use a plain text editor like Notepad or UltraEdit-32 (see Appendix F, *Software to Solve Annoyances*) to effectively customize these files. Luckily, HTML is fairly easy and fun to learn.*
- *.htt* files are just standard HTML files, with one relevant difference: the poorly-documented FileList object. The FileList object duplicates the classic folder view, showing icons for the contents of the current folder. Since the Web View of a folder must display the contents of the current folder somewhere, the *.htt* file must include a reference to a FileList object.
- The FileList object displays the folder contents inside a rectangular box that is embedded in a web page like a picture (e.g., the <IMG> tag). The size and position of the FileList object can be specified either in pixels, which results in a fixed-size listbox, or in percentages, which allows it to resize with the window.
- The size of the FileList object *cannot* be specified with mathematical operations, such as "width of the window minus 50 pixels." This is unfortunate, as it means it's difficult to make usable space for anything else on the page. The second example (see "Making a Custom Toolbar with the Web View," later in this chapter) shows a workaround for this important limitation.
- To get the best feel for how the FileList object interacts with other objects on a web page, you'll need to build one yourself. Since the FileList object has no border, you'll want to put some files in the folder and choose **Details** from the **View** menu; that way, scrollbars will appear that will show you where the FileList object ends and the rest of the page begins.

* For more information on HTML, see *HTML: The Definitive Guide*, by Chuck Musciano and Bill Kennedy (O'Reilly & Associates).

Start by erasing all the text in the open Notepad window,* and replacing it with the code in Example 8-1. Make sure to type all lines exactly as shown.

Example 8-1: HTML Code for the Most Basic Web View

```
<html>
<body topmargin=0 leftmargin=0 rightmargin=0 bottommargin=0
      scroll=no>
<object id="FileList"
        classid="clsid:1820FED0-473E-11D0-A96C-00C04FD705A2"
        style="position: relative; width: 100%; height: 70%">
</object>
Hello World!
</body>
</html>
```

Notice the `<object></object>` structure, which shows the FileList object. You'll notice that its width is set to 100%, which makes it fill the window horizontally, but its height is only 70%, which leaves room for the text `Hello World!` at the bottom of the page. Also note the values in the `<body>` tag, which set all the margins to zero; without them, there would be an unsightly margin surrounding the entire page.

When you're done, save your changes, close Notepad, and click **Finish** in the Customize this Folder wizard. Windows will automatically update the folder, showing you the changes you've just made; it should look like Figure 8-2.

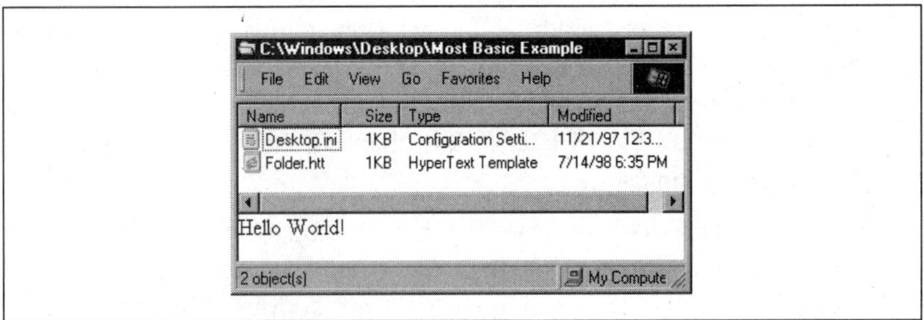

Figure 8-2: The resulting Web View using only seven lines of code (as shown in Example 8-1)

* Notepad should still be open from the beginning of this procedure. Remember, this is just a *duplicate* of the original template file located in your *\Windows\Web* folder. You can change it, delete it, or totally mess it up without affecting the original file that Windows will use for subsequent Web Views.

You can then reopen *Folder.htt* in your favorite text editor, and make any additional changes as desired. To see your changes in the folder at any time, press the **F5** key to refresh the folder window.

You'll notice when you resize the folder window (try it) that the FileList and the area containing "Hello World!" both resize proportionally. It should be apparent that this doesn't work very well; the lower area takes up too much space if the window is made larger, and is too small if the window is made smaller. For best results, we will want to engineer this so that the area outside the FileList has a constant height. The next example shows how to do this to accommodate a custom toolbar at the top of the window, for example.

Making a Custom Toolbar with the Web View

For more control over the way components in the folder window are resized, we can use frames. Frames allow us to subdivide a web page into two or more panes, each of which contains a child page. Example 8-2 shows the revised *Folder.htt* file, which specifies the necessary `frameset` structure.

Example 8-2: HTML Code for Folder.htt; the <frame> Tags Point to the Two Pages with the Actual Content

```
<html>
<frameset rows="40,*">
<frame src="c:\windows\web\toolbar\Toolbar.html"
       name="toolbar" scrolling="no" noresize>
<frame src="c:\windows\web\toolbar\Filelist.htt"
       name="filelist" scrolling="no">
</frameset>
</html>
```

This simple page has no content of its own; it simply lists the two other HTML files that are displayed in each of the two panes. The key is the `<frameset>` tag, which defines a fixed height of 40 pixels for the top pane and a variable height for the bottom pane, specified by an asterisk (*).

Note that the `src` values for both `<frame>` tags point to the *Toolbar.html* and *Filelist.htt* files, which are located in a fixed folder created for this example. This means that we can use the same custom toolbar page for all folders on the hard disk, making subsequent changes very easy. Example 8-3 contains the code for *Toolbar.html* (the upper "toolbar" pane), and Example 8-4 shows the code for *Filelist.htt* (the lower "filelist" pane). Make sure to save both of these files in the *c:\windows\web\toolbar* folder. (If you choose to save them in a different folder, make sure that change is reflected in the *Folder.htt* file as well.)

Example 8-3: HTML Code for the "toolbar" Pane to Go with Examples 8-2 and 8-4

```
<html>
<body topmargin=0 leftmargin=0 rightmargin=0 bottommargin=0
      scroll=no background="c:\windows\web\toolbar\stone.gif">
<nobr>
<a href="c:\windows\desktop" target="_top">
<img src="c:\windows\web\toolbar\desktop.gif" border=0
     hspace=3 vspace=5></a>
<a href="c:\my documents" target="_top">
<img src="c:\windows\web\toolbar\documents.gif" border=0
     hspace=3 vspace=5></a>
<a href="http://www.annoyances.org/" target="_top">
<img src="c:\windows\web\toolbar\internet.gif" border=0
     hspace=3 vspace=5></a>
</nobr>
</body>
</html>
```

The toolbar page (*Toolbar.html*) contains three graphical buttons, linked to the *Desktop* folder, the *My Documents* folder, and to a web site, respectively. A few things to note about this file:

- The `target="_top"` directive in each anchor tag forces all links to be shown in the full window; without it, followed links would only appear in the upper pane.*
- The button graphics (*Desktop.gif*, *Documents.gif*, and *Internet.gif*) are all located in the *c:\windows\web\toolbar* folder created for this example, as are *Toolbar.html* and *Filelist.htt*.
- The `<nobr></nobr>` structure disables word wrap for the buttons, and the `background` directive in the `<body>` tag gives us our nice stone background (also located in the *c:\windows\web\toolbar* folder).

Example 8-4: HTML Code for the "filelist" Pane to Go with Examples 8-2 and 8-3

```
<html>
<body topmargin=0 leftmargin=0 rightmargin=0 bottommargin=0
      scroll=no>
<object id="FileList"
        classid="clsid:1820FED0-473E-11D0-A96C-00C04FD705A2"
        style="position: relative; width: 100%; height: 100%">
```

* The web page (the **internet** button) will only be displayed within the folder window if Internet Explorer is the default browser. See "Choosing Your Defaults" later in this chapter for more information.

Example 8-4: HTML Code for the "filelist" Pane to Go with Examples 8-2 and 8-3 (continued)

```
</object>
</body>
</html>
```

Note that the *Filelist.htt* file shown in Example 8-4 is very similar to the code in Example 8-1 at the beginning of this section, except that the "Hello World!" text has been taken out, and the FileList object now has a height of `100%`. This is the beauty of the design; since the FileList object resides in its own pane (which it fills completely), we can effectively resize the folder window and keep the upper toolbar pane at a constant height.

Once you've made the changes, press the **F5** key in the open folder window to refresh. Figure 8-3 shows the finished folder window using all three files.

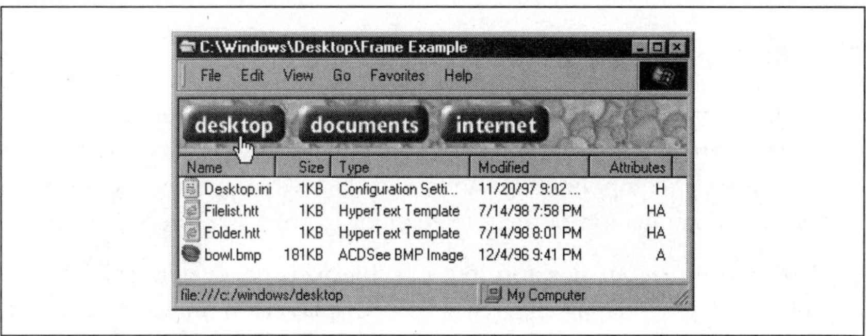

Figure 8-3: The resulting Web View, complete with functional toolbar

The other nice thing about this design is that it allows you to design a custom toolbar, something Explorer won't let you do.*

In its current implementation, the toolbar will appear only in the folder in which it was configured. However, we can easily propagate it so that it appears in every folder, with the exception of system folders such as Control Panel and My Computer. Here's how you do it:

1. Make a backup of the *original* template file, *Folder.htt*, located in your *\Windows\Web* folder (call it something like *Backup of Folder.bak*). When making the backup, create a copy of the file (see "Make a

* It's worth mentioning that while you can't customize Explorer's default toolbar, you can change the bitmap used for the toolbar background. Open the Registry Editor (see Chapter 3) to `HKEY_CURRENT_USER\Software\Microsoft\Internet Explorer\Toolbar`, and set the `BackBitmap` value to the complete filename of any bitmap on your hard disk.

Duplicate of a File or Folder" in Chapter 2, *Customizing the Interface*) instead of renaming it. If you rename it, Windows might "track" the change in the Registry.

2. Copy the customized *Folder.htt* file from your test folder into the *\Windows\Web* folder, replacing the one that's there.
3. From your custom folder's **View** menu, select **Folder Options**, and choose the **View** tab. Click **Like current folder**, and then click **OK**.

Now, the toolbar will appear at the top of every folder on your hard disk. To make a change to the toolbar, you'll only need to edit the single *Toolbar.html* file, and the change will instantly take effect in all your folders.

To remove the toolbars, first open any standard folder in which the toolbar appears. Select **Customize this Folder** from the **View** menu, choose **Remove Customization**, click **Next** twice, and then click **Finish**. Then, propagate the change across all folders by repeating step 3 above.

The Active Desktop

Although it was heralded as a breakthrough feature when it made its debut in Internet Explorer 4.0, Microsoft has somewhat downplayed the Active Desktop component in Windows 98.* What makes the desktop "active" is a combination of three features of Internet Explorer:

- You can turn your desktop into one big web page, optionally hiding all desktop icons. Double-click the **Display** icon in Control Panel, choose the **Background** tab, click **Browse**, and select any HTML or BMP file to be displayed as the backdrop.

  To hide desktop icons on the Active Desktop, select **Folder Options** from Explorer's **View** menu, choose the **View** tab, and turn on the **Hide icons when desktop is viewed as Web page** option.

- You can add "Active Desktop items" to your desktop; these are small movable and resizable boxes that contain web pages. They're very similar to ordinary IE windows, except they have thinner borders, can't float on top of normal windows, and automatically appear when you start Windows. To add a new Active Desktop item, Double-click the **Display** icon in Control Panel, choose the **Web** tab, and click **New**. Click **No** to

* Similarly, "Push" technology, once a hot topic in the industry, has all but vanished from the collective conscience of the Internet. "Push" allowed a web site to initiate communication with you, the surfer, saving you the trouble of having to click on links or type URLs to visit web sites. The idea was a passive TV-like interface, from which the Channel Bar was born. Incidentally, the Channel Bar is slated to disappear in the next release of IE.

skip Microsoft's web site, and then either type a URL of a web site, or point to an HTML file or Internet shortcut on your hard disk.

- You can subscribe to various web sites. This is essentially an extension of the Scheduled Tasks feature, whereby your computer could be configured to automatically connect to the Internet at predetermined intervals and retrieve updates to any web sites you wish.

The idea is to set up an "active" web page on your desktop that would automatically be updated at regular intervals. Common examples of this include a stock ticker that is on your screen all the time, and a weather forecast window that is always up-to-date. Suffice it to say that the potential of this system has yet to be realized.

If you have some time to kill, connect to Microsoft's web site to see the "Active Desktop Gallery," a listing of all kinds of things that you can add to your desktop, assuming you want to be connected all the time.

Choosing Your Defaults

The Internet is useless without communication tools. While Windows 98 comes with Internet Explorer, Outlook Express, Telnet, FTP, and other such programs, it's often desirable to use different programs, either from Microsoft or from a third-party manufacturer.

To take the most advantage of whatever programs you use, you'll want to make sure that each is made the *default* for the particular type of communication in which it specializes. For example, typing a URL in Explorer's Address Bar or double-clicking on an HTML file will launch the default web browser; likewise, clicking on a *mailto:* link in a web browser or using the Mail feature of your word processor will launch the default email program.

The problem is that while it may be relatively easy to change the defaults, there's virtually no way to keep other programs from making themselves the default whenever they please. The most common example, of course, is the ongoing battle between Netscape Navigator and Internet Explorer for the prestigious position of the default web browser.

The ongoing theory in the computer industry these days is that the Internet is, in simple terms, an important business opportunity. Since the web browser is the doorway to the Internet, whatever company can produce the browser used most frequently as the default—the one that pops up automatically when you want to access the Web—is the company that, theoretically, can control the Web. From the user's point of view, however, this corporate battle is nothing more than an annoyance.

There are two ways to launch Internet programs: by double-clicking on *.html* files, which are web pages on your hard disk, or by using Uniform Resource Locators (URLs), which are addresses of web pages elsewhere on the Internet. HTML file types concern only web page documents on your hard disk: the browsers are used to view them, and the editors are used to change them. URLs, on the other hand, handle all Internet protocols, including Internet Shortcuts, web links in applications, and anything entered into Windows' Address Bar.

It's important to realize that you can have different programs associated with these various URLs and file types; you don't have to hook them all up to a single browser. In fact, if you use both Netscape and Internet Explorer, it might be convenient, for example, to associate Netscape with the *.html* file type, and Internet Explorer with the *.htm* file type.

Select **Folder Options** from Explorer's **View** menu, and choose the **File Types** tab to configure all your default clients. Table 8-1 shows the common HTML file type and URL entries, and their default Windows associations. See "Customize Context Menus" in Chapter 4 for details on configuring individual applications and making them the default, and "Protect Your File Types," also in Chapter 4, for more information on keeping your preferences intact.

Table 8-1: Default URLs and HTML File Types, and Their Associated Default Internet Clients

File Type Description	Default Application
Microsoft HTML Document (**.htm, *.html, *.shtml, *.dhtml*)	Internet Explorer (*iexplore.exe*) for **Open**, Notepad for **Edit**
URL:File Protocol (*file://filename*)	Internet Explorer (*iexplore.exe*)
URL:FTP Protocol (*ftp://host*)	Internet Explorer (*iexplore.exe*)
URL:GOPHER Protocol (*gopher://host*)	Internet Explorer (*iexplore.exe*)
URL:HTTP Protocol (*http://host*)	Internet Explorer (*iexplore.exe*)
URL:HTTPS Protocol (*https://host*)	Internet Explorer (*iexplore.exe*)
URL:MAILTO Protocol (*mailto:username@host*)	Outlook Express (*msimn.exe*)
URL:NEWS Protocol (*news://host*)	Outlook Express (*msimn.exe*)
URL:RLOGIN Protocol (*rlogin://host*)	Telnet (*telnet.exe*)
URL:SNEWS Protocol (*snews://host*)	Outlook Express (*msimn.exe*)
URL:TELNET Protocol (*telnet://host*)	HyperTerminal (*hypertrm.exe*)
URL:TN3270 Protocol (*tn3270://host*)	Telnet (*telnet.exe*)

There are easier ways to make certain programs the default. The installation programs for most Internet software will either ask you if you want to make the new program the default, or do it automatically *without* asking. So, if you want to make Netscape the default web browser, for example, you may be able to do it by simply reinstalling.

On the other hand, you may wish to stop certain programs from making themselves the default even after installation, as web browsers often do. The following solutions disable the functionality in Internet Explorer and Netscape that allows these browsers to make themselves the default without asking:

- For Internet Explorer, double-click the **Internet** icon in Control Panel, choose the **Programs** tab, turn off the **Internet Explorer should check to see whether it is the default browser** option, and click **OK**. The next time you use Internet Explorer, it won't automatically grab Internet associations.
- Netscape, however, makes this process much more difficult. Make sure Netscape isn't running before proceeding. First, you'll have to open the Registry Editor (see Chapter 3) and expand the branches to `HKEY_CURRENT_USER\Software\Netscape\Netcape Navigator\Main`. Double-click the `Check_Associations` value in the right pane, and make sure it's set to `No`. Then double-click the `Ignore DefCheck` value and make sure it's set to `Yes`. If any of these values aren't there, create them by selecting **New** and then **String Value** from the Registry Editor's **Edit** menu, and then typing in the appropriate values.

  The next step is to find Netscape's *Prefs.js* file. For Netscape 3.x, it's in the main *Netscape* folder; for Netscape 4.x, it's in the current user folder (usually *c:\program files\Netscape\Navigator\Users\Default*). Open the file with a plain text editor, such as Notepad, and look for the following line:

  ```
  user_pref("browser.wfe.ignore_def_check", false);
  ```

  Change change `false` to `true` so that the line reads:

  ```
  user_pref("browser.wfe.ignore_def_check", true);
  ```

  Save the file and close your editor when you're done. The next time you start Netscape, it won't automatically make itself the default browser.

Note that the Web Browser Delegate utility, part of *O'Reilly Utilities—Quick Solutions for Windows 98 Annoyances* (see Appendix F), allows you to choose the default applications for all major file types and URL protocols. In addition, it automates all of the above settings, and allows you to create a backup registry patch to easily restore associations in the event that they are overwritten.

9

In this chapter:

- *Windows Scripting Host*
- *DOS Batch Files*
- *Scheduled Tasks*

Scripting and Automation

Programming is considered by many to be an art form; to others, it is merely a chore. Regardless, programming is sometimes the only way to solve a certain problem or complete a certain task.

To give you an example, I wanted to find a workaround for the fact that you can't rename more than one file at a time in Windows. Now, you can do this in DOS (see Appendix B, *DOS Lives*), but it involves typing, isn't as flexible as I would like, and only works with multiple files in the same directory. Since this isn't a problem that can be solved with a registry tweak or obscure setting somewhere, I decided to write the Power Rename utility (see Appendix F, *Software to Solve Annoyances*). While this took some doing, the convenience and the time I've saved in the long run have made it worthwhile.

Scripting, a simple form of programming, is well suited for quick-and-dirty tasks, such as automating repetitive procedures or simplifying file operations. Scripts are usually small plain text files that can be written and executed without using a special development environment (Notepad will suffice; see "Finding a Better Editor" later in this chapter for more information). Also, scripts don't require a compiler, which is a program that turns certain kinds of code into executables. Windows comes with two forms of scripting: DOS batch files, which have been around since the early days of DOS, and the Windows Scripting Host (WSH), which was first introduced in Windows 98.

Both technologies have their strengths and limitations. Both DOS batch files and WSH scripts can copy, move, delete, and even modify files. DOS batch files are somewhat simpler to write, but WSH scripts are more flexible and offer better user interaction. WSH scripts are Windows-based, and can even communicate with other running Windows programs; batch files are DOS-based and can run when Windows isn't running. DOS batch files run on any PC made after 1982, but WSH scripts run only on Windows 98 and Windows NT 5.0 (and on earlier versions of these two operating systems only with an add-on). Luckily, you can use both technologies in conjunction to accommodate just about any task you throw at them.

On the other end of the spectrum is the Scheduled Tasks feature, another new feature in Windows 98. It allows you to schedule the launching of a program, as well as the execution of a script or batch file. For example, you can have Scheduled Tasks run your tape backup utility at 2:00 a.m. every Wednesday, automatically run Disk Defragmenter at the end of the day, and even display an inspirational message every hour, on the hour. The ability to schedule scripts makes them even more powerful; the more you automate your work, the less time you should have to spend in front of the computer.

Microsoft's feature documentation has always left much to be desired, and scripting is not an exception. Scheduled Tasks earns only two sentences in the Windows 98 manual, and the Windows Scripting Host and DOS batch files aren't mentioned at all. Compare that to the 25 or so pages of the manual devoted to Internet Integration (discussed in Chapter 8, *Taking Control of Web Integration*). Coverage in Windows' help files isn't much different; no type of scripting is mentioned at all in any help file, although remarkably, there is a help file for Scheduled Tasks (*Mstask.chm*).

Some sample WSH scripts are included in the *C:\Windows\SAMPLES\WSH* folder of Windows 98; interestingly, they are in both the VBScript and JavaScript formats. However, they're left over from the first release of WSH (Version 3 ships with Windows 98), and don't cover most of the more useful functions mentioned later in this chapter.

Microsoft would have earned a lot of respect from me if they had done as little as include a single line somewhere in the documentation that at least acknowledged the existence of some of these features, noting simply, "For more information on the Windows Scripting Host, see *http://www.microsoft.com/you-don't-want-us-to-make-it-too-easy/do-you?.html*". Microsoft does have a great quantity of information online, but relevant information is so mind-numbingly difficult to find on Microsoft's web site* that I often just give up.

* Microsoft's web site is arranged by technology, where each product has its own branch in the hierarchy. Ideally, their web site should be *task-oriented*, where you could find information or documentation based on what you want to accomplish, rather than by the name of the product you might be using.

Suffice it to say that finding the information you need on these various technologies can be a frustrating experience. By chance, the primary goal of this chapter is to provide that documentation and show useful problem-solving applications of the different technologies. Be prepared for a pop quiz—remember, spelling counts!

Windows Scripting Host

For many people, education in computer programming ended abruptly in the seventh grade with a class in the BASIC programming language. However, if you want to take advantage of the new scripting language included in Windows 98 (and Windows NT 5.0), and you recognize code like this:

```
10 print "hello."
20 goto 10
```

your education is about to get a jump-start.

The beauty of the Windows Scripting Host (yes, I said *beauty* in regards to a Microsoft product) is that it is language-independent, meaning that it will work with any modern scripting language. It has built-in support for JavaScript and VBScript, but can be extended with third-party add-ons to use almost any other language, such as Perl and Python (see "Further Study" later in this chapter for more information). This extensibility is a welcome change from Microsoft's usual narrow support of only their own, proprietary technologies.

VBScript, based loosely on the Visual Basic language, will be used primarily in this chapter because it's easy to learn, it supports the features we need, like registry access and file operations, and its cousin, VB, is one of the most widely used programming environments in the world. The good news is that any time you spend learning VB or VBScript won't be wasted.

So where does the Windows Scripting Host end and the VBScript language begin? From the point of view of the end user, WSH starts up when you double-click on a script file, and it automatically chooses an appropriate language interpreter based upon the script filename extension. From the point of view of the developer, WSH provides special functionality to all languages through the use of objects (see "Object References" later in this chapter); that way, each WSH-supported language needn't bother including functionality for advanced functions like registry access and file system operations.

Building a Script with VBScript

The following sections offer a rapid introduction to VBScript and scripting in general. Don't let the snippets of code intimidate you. The best way to learn programming of any kind is to simply try it out. Type the code samples and then execute the scripts to see how they work. Don't be afraid to experiment. For more comprehensive documentation on scripting or any scripting language, as well as more thorough instruction, see "Further Study" later in this chapter.

Putting a script together essentially involves typing commands and then running the scripts to test them. In the next three sections, we'll cover the following background concepts necessary to complete many tasks with scripts:

- Entering code and saving scripts
- Using variables
- Asking for and displaying information with the *InputBox* and *MsgBox* commands
- Using objects (see "Object References")
- Controlling program execution using conditional statements, loops, and subroutines (see "Flow Control")

The concepts and commands presented cover only a subset of the language. Look in the examples for additional concepts and scripting techniques.

VBScript files are plain text files with the *.vbs* extension, and can be edited with any text editor, such as Notepad. To run a script, just double-click on the script file icon; you'll probably never need to run the Scripting Host program (*Wscript.exe*) directly.*

You can quickly open an existing script file for editing by right-clicking on it and selecting **Edit**. This will, by default, open Notepad, although you might want to associate the **Edit** action for *.vbs* files with a more powerful text editor (see "Finding a Better Editor" later in this chapter).

Scripts are built by typing one command on each line, and then saving the file as a *.vbs* file. When the script is run by the Scripting Host, the commands are executed in order, one by one. You can leave Notepad open to make changes and additions while you test the script.

* The WSH also comes with a DOS-based scripting host program (*Cscript.exe*), which is useful for running scripts from batch files (see "DOS Batch Files" later in this chapter). In theory, *Cscript.exe* also allows you to run scripts when Windows isn't running.

Commands are used either to carry out some action, or to set a variable or property of an object to some value. For example, the following two commands:

```
MyName = "joe user"
MyShoeSize = 12
```

sets two different variables to two different values. The first variable, *MyName*, is assigned to a text string, while the second, *MyShoeSize*, is set to a numeric value. You can also assign variables in terms of other variables:

```
MyIQ = MyShoeSize / 2
```

which, when placed after the two preceding lines, would result in the variable *MyIQ* having a value of 6. You can carry out more complex mathematical operations using various combinations of parentheses and the standard operators (+, -, *, /, and ^ for addition, subtraction, multiplication, division, and exponentiation, respectively).

Naturally, performing the same operations on static (never changing) values makes for a pretty boring script. One of the strengths of VBScript is that it allows limited user interaction. For example, the command:

```
MyName = InputBox("Please enter your name.")
```

will display a prompt on the screen when the script is run, asking for user input. When you enter some text and press **OK**, the script places the text you've typed into the variable *MyName* and continues to the next command.

Now, collecting and rearranging information does no good without the ability to spit out a result. The versatile *MsgBox* function allows you to display a message, as follows:

```
MsgBox "Hello, Hello Again."
```

Combining the principles we've covered so far, consider the following code:

```
MyAge = InputBox("Please type your age.")
NewAge = MyAge + 5
MsgBox "In 5 years, you will be " & NewAge & "."
```

The first line does two things: it first asks the user to type something, and then assigns the typed text to the variable *MyAge*. The second line creates a new variable, *NewAge*, assigns the user's input to it, and adds five. (Note the lack of any error checking: if the user enters his or her name instead of a number, this statement will cause an error.) The third line uses the & operator to concatenate (glue together) a text string to the *NewAge* variable and displays the result in a message box. Notice that plain text is always enclosed in quotation marks, but variables never are. If we were to enclose the *NewAge* variable in quotation marks, the script would simply print out the text, "NewAge" instead of the variable's value.

The *MsgBox* statement can also be used like this:

```
Response = MsgBox("Here's My Message", 17, "Message Title")
```

which allows it to be used for more than just displaying messages. The 17 is the sum of a few different values, which specify the options used when displaying the message box. Figure 9-1 shows two sample message boxes, each with different buttons and icons.

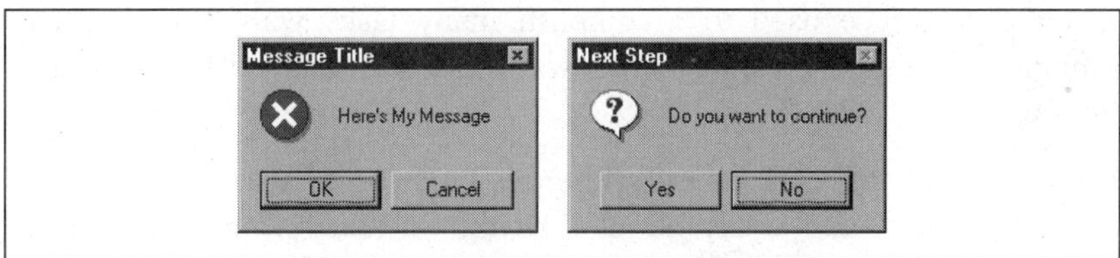

Figure 9-1: Various options can be combined to produce a variety of message boxes

To choose the buttons that are displayed by *MsgBox*, specify 0 for **OK**; 1 for **OK**, **Cancel**; 2 for **Abort**, **Retry**, **Ignore**; 3 for **Yes**, **No**, **Cancel**; 4 for **Yes**, **No**; 5 for **Retry**, **Cancel**. To choose the icon that is displayed, specify 16 for a red "X" (error); 32 for a question mark (query); 48 for an exclamation mark (warning); and 64 for a blue "I" (information). Additionally, you can add 256 to give the second button the focus, 512 to give the third button the focus, and 4096 to make the message box "system modal," meaning that all applications are suspended until the user responds to the message box.

So, to have a message box with the **Yes** and **No** buttons, the question mark icon, and to have **No** be the default, you would specify a value of 4 + 32 + 256 = 292. The two message boxes in Figure 9-1 have values of 17 (that's **OK**, **Cancel**, and "X") and 292, respectively.

When the user responds to the message box, the *Response* variable will be set to 1 if the user pressed **OK**, 2 for **Cancel**, 3 for **Abort**, 4 for **Retry**, 5 for **Ignore**, 6 for **Yes**, or 7 for **No**.

See "Conditional statements" later in this chapter for an example.

Object References

There are some operations that can be performed with the Windows Scripting Host regardless of the language being used. These operations, such as accessing the file system, are made possible by extending the language with objects. For the time being, we can consider an object to be simply a *context* that is referred to when carrying out certain commands.

Admittedly, this can make carrying out some tasks rather difficult and convoluted, but it is necessary for the modular architecture. For example, many scripts will require a line similar to the following (using VBScript syntax):

```
Set WshShell = WScript.CreateObject("WScript.Shell")
```

which creates and initializes the ***WshShell*** object. ***WshShell*** is not a visible object like a file or other component of Windows, but rather is a required reference used to accomplish many tasks with WSH, such as running programs, creating Windows shortcuts, and retrieving system information.

If you're unfamiliar with object references, your best bet is to simply type them as shown, and worry about how they actually work when you're more comfortable with the language. The "Scripting Goodies" section, later in this chapter, presents many solutions that take advantage of objects, such as ***WScript.Shell***, which has many uses, and ***Scripting.FileSystemObject***, used for accessing the file system. Since probably the greatest obstacle to using these objects is finding accurate and up-to-date documentation, you'll want to see "Finding a Better Editor" and "Further Study," both later in this chapter, for documentation resources and other information.

Flow Control

You can accomplish quite a few tasks by simply stringing together long lists of commands, but the capability of redirecting the flow of a script—making it nonlinear—adds a lot of flexibility to the language and reduces the amount of work required to accomplish many tasks.

Conditional statements

Conditional statements allow us to redirect the flow depending on a condition, such as the value of a variable. Take, for example, the following script:

```
Response = MsgBox("Do you want to continue?", 36, "Next Step")
If Response = 7 then WScript.Quit
MsgBox "Here's the next step."
```

The first statement uses the *MsgBox* function, described in "Building a Script with VBScript" earlier in this chapter, to ask a question. The value of `36` specifies **Yes** and **No** buttons, as well as the question mark icon. If the user chooses **Yes**, the value of the *Response* variable is set to 6; if **No** is chosen, *Response* is set to 7.

The next statement uses the `If` statement to test the value of the *Response* variable. If it's equal to 7 (the user clicked **No**), then the script ends (using the `WScript.Quit` statement). Otherwise, script execution continues to the next command.

Here's another example using a more complex version of the `If` statement:

```
MyShoeSize = InputBox("Please type your shoe size.")
MyIQ = InputBox("Please type your IQ.")

If MyShoeSize > MyIQ then
  MsgBox "You need to read more."
Else
  MsgBox "You need larger shoes."
End if
```

One of the nice things about VBScript is that most of the commands are in plain English; you should be able to follow the flow of the program by just reading through the commands. Before you run the script above, try to predict what will happen for different values entered at each of the *InputBox* statements.

This script uses the `If...Then` structure to redirect output depending on the two values entered at runtime, when the script is actually being executed. It should be evident that the first message is displayed if the value of *MyShoeSize* is larger than the value of *MyIQ*. In all other cases, including when both values are equal, the second message is displayed. Note also the use of `End If`, which is required if the `If...Then` structure spans more than one line.

Loops

Another useful structure is the `For...Next` loop, which allows you to repeat a series of commands a given number of times:

```
SomeNumber = InputBox("How many lumps do you want?")
TotalLumps = ""
For i = 1 To SomeNumber
  TotalLumps = TotalLumps & "lump "
Next

Rem -- The next line displays the result --
MsgBox TotalLumps
```

The `For...Next` loop repeats everything between the two statements by incrementing the value of the variable *i* until it equals the value of the variable `SomeNumber`. Each time we go through the loop, another "lump" is added to our output string variable, `TotalLumps`. When the loop is finished, the contents of the `TotalLumps` variable is displayed.

Notice the use of the concatenation operator, `&`, in the middle of the loop, which adds a new lump to the variable. Those new to programming might be put off by the fact that we have the `TotalLumps` variable on both sides of the equal sign.* This works because the scripting host *evaluates*, or adds up, everything on the right side of the equals sign, and then assigns it to the variable on the left side.

Note also the `TotalLumps=""` statement before the `For...Next` loop; this empties the variable before we start adding stuff to it. Otherwise, whatever might be assigned to that variable *before* the loop will be kept around, something we didn't expect. It's good programming practice to prepare for the unexpected.

Also good programming practice is the use of spaces and indentations, which make the code easier for you to read, though the computer won't know the difference.

Additionally, you can use the `Rem` command shown in the previous code segment to include remarks, or comments that are ignored when the script is run; this allows you to label any part of the script with pertinent information. In place of the `Rem` command, you can also use a single apostrophe (`'`), even on the same line as another command. I personally use the `Rem` command to label a section, and the apostrophe to explain smaller items, such as variables or cryptic commands.

As you write these scripts, think about formatting them as you would a word processor document; scripts that are easier to read are easier to debug and easier to come back to six months later.

Subroutines and functions

A third type of flow control, and quite a powerful one at that, is the use of subroutines and functions. A subroutine allows you to encapsulate a bit of code inside a single command, making it easy to repeat that command as many different times as you want.† Simply include the entire subroutine anywhere in a script, and then type the name of the subroutine elsewhere in the script to execute the subroutine. A function is essentially the

* In traditional algebra, we couldn't have a statement like this; it would be like saying $x=x+1$, which has no solution. However, this is not an equation; it's a *statement*.

† To those who are familiar with macros in a word processor, subroutines are similar. In fact, Microsoft Word saves its macros as VB subroutines.

same as a subroutine, except that it has a result, called a return value, that is sent back to the command that called the function.

Consider Example 9-1, which compares the contents of two text files. At the heart of this example are the two structures at the end of the script, although their position is not important. WSH separates all subroutines and functions before executing the script; they won't be executed unless they're called. Whenever it encounters the name of a subroutine or function in the script body, it executes it as though it were a separate script. Try to follow the execution of the script, command by command.

Example 9-1: Using Functions and Subroutines

```
Filename1 = InputBox("Enter the first filename")
Filename2 = InputBox("Enter the second filename")

If Not FileExists(Filename1) then
  MsgBox Filename1 & " does not exist."
ElseIf Not FileExists(Filename2) then
  MsgBox Filename2 & " does not exist."
Else
  Call RunProgram("command /c fc " & filename1 & _
                  " " & filename2 & " > c:\temp.txt")
  Call RunProgram("notepad c:\temp.txt")
End If

Function FileExists(Filename)
  Set FileObject = CreateObject("Scripting.FileSystemObject")
  FileExists = FileObject.FileExists(Filename)
End Function

Sub RunProgram(Filename)
  Set WshShell = WScript.CreateObject("WScript.Shell")
  ReturnVal = WshShell.Run(Filename, True)
End Sub
```

One of the most important aspects of both subroutines and functions is that they can accept one or more input variables, called *parameters*. The parameters a subroutine can accept are listed in parentheses after the subroutine definition, and are separated with commas, if there is more than one. Then, using the `Call` statement, the *values* you wish to pass to the subroutine, which are placed in the parameter variables when the script is run, are listed in parentheses.

In this way, the same subroutine or function can be called repeatedly, each time with one or more different variables. Functions such as *FileExists* in Example 9-1 also can *return* a single variable, which is usually dependent on the outcome of some operation.

The first structure defines the *FileExists* function, which is passed a filename and returns a value of `True` (–1) if the file exists and `False` (0) if it does not. The *FileExists* function is called twice, once for each filename entered when the script is run (***`Filename1`*** and ***`Filename2`***). The `If` commands (see "Conditional statements" earlier in this chapter) first call the function, then redirect the flow based on the result of the function.

The second structure defines the *RunProgram* subroutine, also called twice from the script. *RunProgram* runs the program filename passed to it, but returns no data.

In *FileExists* and *RunProgram*, **`Filename`** is a variable (shown in parentheses) in which passed data is placed so that it can be used inside the subroutine or function. It's considered a *local* variable; that is, it has no value outside of the subroutine or function.

The most important consequence of this design—the separation of the code into subroutines and functions—is that it makes it easy to reuse portions of code. Experienced programmers will intentionally separate code into useful subroutines that can be copied and pasted to other scripts. The following section, "Scripting Goodies," presents solutions as subroutines and functions, allowing you to easily integrate the code into your projects.

Scripting Goodies

Now, I've only covered a few basics with the past few examples. You should be able to use these simple building blocks to create more useful or complex scripts. However, some of the more juicy stuff is yet to come, such as accessing the Registry, launching programs, and writing and reading files.

The following solutions are presented as either subroutines or functions (see "Subroutines and functions" earlier in this chapter for an explanation of the structures). Subroutines are used for code that performs an action, such as copying a file or writing information to the Registry. When a result is expected, such as reading information from the Registry or finding the date of a file, a function is used instead.

You should be able to place the subroutines and functions directly into your scripts and call them with a single command. It's up to you to put the pieces together to accomplish whatever tasks you have in mind. Feel free, also, to alter these routines to suit your needs.

Running programs

This code is used to run a program, which can be a DOS program, a Windows application, an Internet URL, or anything else you could normally type in the Start Menu's **Run** command. Place this subroutine in your scripts:

```
Sub RunProgram(Filename, Wait)
  Set WshShell = WScript.CreateObject("WScript.Shell")
  RetVal = WshShell.Run(Filename, Wait)
End Sub
```

and call the routine like this:

```
Call RunProgram("c:\windows\notepad.exe", True)
```

You can replace `True` with `False` if you don't want to wait for the program to finish before the next script command is executed.

Registry access

The following code is used to write, read, and delete information in the Registry. Include the following three routines in your script:

```
Sub RegistryWrite(KeyName, ValueName, ValueData, ValueType)
  ValueType = UCase(ValueType)
  If ValueType <> "REG_DWORD" and ValueType <> "REG_BINARY" _
    then ValueType = "REG_SZ"
  Set WshShell = WScript.CreateObject("WScript.Shell")
  WshShell.RegWrite KeyName & "\" & ValueName, ValueData, _
    ValueType
End Sub

Function RegistryRead(KeyName, ValueName)
  Set WshShell = WScript.CreateObject("WScript.Shell")
  RegistryRead = WSHShell.RegRead(KeyName & "\" & ValueName)
End Function

Sub RegistryDelete(KeyName, ValueName)
  Set WshShell = WScript.CreateObject("WScript.Shell")
  WshShell.RegWrite KeyName & "\" & ValueName, ""
  WshShell.RegDelete KeyName & "\" & ValueName
End Sub
```

Using these three routines, you can accomplish most registry tasks. To create a registry key, type this (note that all `HKEY...` roots must appear in uppercase):

```
Call RegistryWrite("HKEY_LOCAL_MACHINE\New Key", "", "", "")
```

To set the `(Default)` value in a key:

```
Call RegistryWrite("HKEY_LOCAL_MACHINE\My Key", "", _
                   "Some Data", "")
```

To set any value in a key:

```
Call RegistryWrite("HKEY_LOCAL_MACHINE\My Key", "Some Value", _
                   "Some Data", "")
```

To read the (`Default`) value in a key:

```
Variable = RegistryRead("HKEY_LOCAL_MACHINE\My Key", "")
```

To read any value in a key:

```
Variable = RegistryRead("HKEY_LOCAL_MACHINE\My Key", _
                   "Some Value")
```

To delete a key:

```
Call RegistryDelete("HKEY_LOCAL_MACHINE\My Key", "")
```

To delete a value:

```
Call RegistryDelete("HKEY_LOCAL_MACHINE\My Key", "Some Value")
```

To delete the `(Default)` value in a key, we set the value to nothing:

```
Call RegistryWrite("HKEY_LOCAL_MACHINE\My Key", "", "", "")
```

You'll notice in the *RegistryDelete* subroutine above, there's a *RegWrite* statement. This is necessary to ensure that the key or value that you're trying to delete actually exists. If you don't include this statement and try to delete a nonexistent key or value from the Registry, the Windows Scripting Host will give an error to the effect that "The system cannot find the file specified." Helpful, huh? Instead, with *RegWrite*, the subroutine will create the key or value entry to be deleted if it doesn't already exist.

See Chapter 3, *The Registry*, for more information on the Registry, and in particular, "Automate the Deletion of Registry Items," which explains the need to use scripting to remove a registry key, a task otherwise impossible with registry patches.

File operations

One of the myths surrounding the Windows Scripting Host, and VBScript in particular, is that there's no provision for accessing the file system to copy, delete, and write to files. This assumption is based on the fact that VBScript, when used in web pages, is not permitted to access the file system for security reasons.

The following routines rely on the `FileSystemObject` object, and provide most necessary file operations. The names I've chosen for these functions and subroutines are based on what they act upon and what they're used for; for example, the *FolderCopy* subroutine is used to copy a folder, while the *FileCopy* subroutine is used to copy a file:

```
Function DriveExists(DriveLetter)
  Set FileObject = CreateObject("Scripting.FileSystemObject")
  DriveExists = FileObject.DriveExists(DriveLetter)
End Function

Function DriveFreeSpace(DriveLetter)
  If Left(DriveLetter,1) <> ":" then _
      DriveLetter = DriveLetter & ":"
  Set FileObject = CreateObject("Scripting.FileSystemObject")
  Set DriveHandle = _
      FileObject.GetDrive(FileObject.GetDriveName(DriveLetter))
  DriveFreeSpace = DriveHandle.FreeSpace
End Function

Sub FileCopy(Source, Destination)
  Set FileObject = CreateObject("Scripting.FileSystemObject")
  FileObject.CopyFile Source, Destination
End Sub

Function FileDate(Filename)
  Set FileObject = CreateObject("Scripting.FileSystemObject")
  Set FileHandle = FileObject.GetFile(Filename)
  GetFileDate = FileHandle.DateCreated
End Function

Sub FileDelete(Filename)
  Set FileObject = CreateObject("Scripting.FileSystemObject")
  FileObject.DeleteFile(Filename)
End Sub

Function FileExists(Filename)
  Set FileObject = CreateObject("Scripting.FileSystemObject")
  FileExists = FileObject.FileExists(Filename)
End Function

Function FileExtension(Filename)
  Set FileObject = CreateObject("Scripting.FileSystemObject")
  GetFileExtension = FileObject.GetExtensionName(Filename)
End Function

Sub FileMove(Source, Destination)
  Set FileObject = CreateObject("Scripting.FileSystemObject")
  FileObject.MoveFile Source, Destination
End Sub

Function FileSize(Filename)
  Set FileObject = CreateObject("Scripting.FileSystemObject")
  Set FileHandle = FileObject.GetFile(Filename)
  FileSize = FileHandle.Size
End Function
```

```
Sub FolderCopy(Source, Destination)
  Set FileObject = CreateObject("Scripting.FileSystemObject")
  FileObject.CopyFolder Source, Destination
End Sub

Function FolderCreate(Foldername)
  Set FileObject = CreateObject("Scripting.FileSystemObject")
  Set Result = FileObject.CreateFolder(FolderName)
  If Result.Path = "" then
    FolderCreate = False   'failure
  Else
    FolderCreate = True    'success
  End If
End Function

Sub FolderDelete(Foldername)
  Set FileObject = CreateObject("Scripting.FileSystemObject")
  FileObject.DeleteFolder(Foldername)
End Sub

Function FolderExists(Foldername)
  Set FileObject = CreateObject("Scripting.FileSystemObject")
  FolderExists = FileObject.FolderExists(Foldername)
End Function

Sub FolderMove(Source, Destination)
  Set FileObject = CreateObject("Scripting.FileSystemObject")
  FileObject.MoveFolder Source, Destination
End Sub

Function FolderSize(Foldername)
  Set FileObject = CreateObject("Scripting.FileSystemObject")
  Set FolderHandle = FileObject.GetFolder(Foldername)
  FolderSize = FolderHandle.Size
End Function

Function FolderParent(Foldername)
  Set FileObject = CreateObject("Scripting.FileSystemObject")
  FolderParent = FileObject.GetParentFolderName(Foldername)
End Function

Function GetSystemFolder()
  Set FileObject = CreateObject("Scripting.FileSystemObject")
  GetSystemFolder = FileObject.GetSpecialFolder(1) & "\"
End Function

Function GetTempFilename()
  Set FileObject = CreateObject("Scripting.FileSystemObject")
  GetTempFile = FileObject.GetSpecialFolder(2) & "\" _
              & FileObject.GetTempName
End Function

Function GetWindowsFolder()
  Set FileObject = CreateObject("Scripting.FileSystemObject")
  GetWindowsFolder = FileObject.GetSpecialFolder(0) & "\"
End Function
```

```
Function ReadFromFile(Filename)
  Const ForReading = 1, ForWriting = 2, ForAppending = 8
  Set FileObject = CreateObject("Scripting.FileSystemObject")
  Set FileHandle = FileObject.OpenTextFile(Filename, _
                   ForReading)
  Buffer=""
  Do Until FileHandle.AtEndOfStream
    Buffer = Buffer & FileHandle.ReadLine & vbCrLf
  Loop
  FileHandle.Close
  ReadFromFile = Buffer
End Function

Sub WriteToFile(Filename, Text)
  Const ForReading = 1, ForWriting = 2, ForAppending = 8
  Set FileObject = CreateObject("Scripting.FileSystemObject")
  If FileObject.FileExists(Filename) Then
    Set FileHandle = FileObject.OpenTextFile(Filename, _
                                             ForAppending)
    FileHandle.Write vbCrLf
  Else
    Set FileHandle = FileObject.CreateTextFile(Filename)
  End If
  FileHandle.Write Text
  FileHandle.Close
End Sub
```

The following script illustrates the use of several of these routines; you'll need to include the above subroutines and functions in the script file for it to work. The script first prompts for a folder name and checks to see if it exists. If not, it gives you the opportunity to enter another folder name. Then, it creates a backup of the entire folder on your floppy drive:

```
On Error Resume Next
Accepted = False
Do Until Accepted
  MyFolder = InputBox("Please enter the name of the folder "& _
                      "you want to backup.")
  If Not FolderExists(MyFolder) Then
    Answer = MsgBox("The folder you typed doesn't exist. "& _
                    "Try again?", 36, "")
    If Answer = 7 then WScript.Quit
  Else
    Accepted = True
  End If
Loop

Answer = MsgBox("Please put a diskette in your floppy "& _
                "drive.", 33, "")
If FolderSize(MyFolder) > DriveFreeSpace("a") Then
  MsgBox "The folder you specified won't fit on the floppy.",_
                16
  WScript.Quit
End If
```

```
If FolderCreate("a:\Backup\") = False Then
  MsgBox "There was a problem writing to the diskette.", 16
  WScript.Quit
End If

Call FolderCopy(MyFolder, "a:\Backup\")

If Right(MyFolder, 1) <> "\" then MyFolder = MyFolder & "\"
Call WriteToFile(MyFolder & "backuplog.txt", _
                 "Last backed up: " & Now)
```

This script uses several *MsgBox* prompts, which will probably irritate most users. However, it also shows part of the power of interactive scripting. A little intelligent planning and error trapping can keep your scripts running smoothly, interrupting you only when necessary. Note the use of the *FolderExists* function at the beginning of the script; rather than risk encountering an error, the script checks for a potential missing file problem and takes the necessary steps to resolve it. Note also that if the file doesn't exist, the user is given the option of entering it again or quitting; always give your users a choice to get out if they want.

Since we have implemented some degree of error checking in this script, we include the line `On Error Resume Next`. This statement instructs WSH to simply ignore any errors it finds. This doesn't automatically resolve any errors; it just eliminates the error message that would otherwise appear in the event of an error. This way, we're only bothered with the errors that concern us.

This example also uses the `Do...Loop` loop, which is similar to the `For...Next` loop. The code inside such a loop is repeated until a specific condition is met; in this case, the loop will repeat until the *`Accepted`* variable has a value of `True` (notice that it's set to `False` at the beginning of the script). The `If` statements insure that the `Accepted` variable is set to `True` only if the folder actually exists.

The second part of the script compares the total size of the folder and all its contents with the amount of free space on the diskette currently inserted in the floppy drive. You could expand the script, so that if the diskette is not sufficient to store the folder, the user is given the opportunity to insert another diskette and try again. You'd need to use a `Do...Loop` similar to the one described above.

Once the script has gone through all of the tests, eliminating the possibility of many errors, the *FolderCopy* subroutine is used to copy the folder to the floppy. Finally, the *WriteToFile* subroutine is used to record in a log file that the folder was backed up. Note also the proceeding line that adds a backslash to the end of the *`MyFolder`* variable; this way, we can pass a valid filename (the folder name followed by a backslash and then the filename) to the *WriteToFile* subroutine.

The use of all file operations subroutines and functions listed in this section should be fairly self-explanatory. While only a few of the routines documented above are used in the example script, all of the routines documented in this section work similarly. For example, the *FolderExists* function and the *FileExists* function are nearly identical, except that *FolderExists* checks for the existence of a folder, while *FileExists* checks for the existence of a single file.

Windows and Internet shortcuts

Include the following subroutine in your script to allow easy creation of Internet shortcuts (**.url*) and Windows shortcuts (**.lnk*):

```
Sub Shortcut(LinkFile, CommandLine)
  Set WshShell = WScript.CreateObjesct("WScript.Shell")
  If LCase(Right(LinkFile, 4)) <> ".lnk" and _
     LCase(Right(LinkFile, 4)) <>".url" then _
     LinkFile = LinkFile & ".LNK"
  Set ShortcutHandle = WshShell.CreateShortcut(LinkFile)
  ShortcutHandle.TargetPath = CommandLine
  ShortcutHandle.Save
End Sub
```

To create a shortcut to a program or file, use the following statement:

```
Call Shortcut("c:\Windows\sendto\Notepad.lnk", "Notepad.exe")
```

To create a shortcut to an Internet address:

```
Call Shortcut("c:\Windows\desktop\Annoyances.url", _
              "http://www.annoyances.org/")
```

If the first parameter (***LinkFile***) ends in `.LNK` (case doesn't matter), the `Shortcut` subroutine will automatically create a standard Windows shortcut; if ***LinkFile*** ends in `.URL`, however, an Internet shortcut will be created. Note the `If` statement in the routine, which automatically adds `.LNK` to any shortcut filenames that aren't properly named.

If you specify a nonexistent folder in the path for the new shortcut file, an "Unspecified Error" will occur. You may want to use the *FolderExists* function detailed in the "File operations" section earlier in this chapter to eliminate the possibility of this error.

Networking

VBScript has a few limited networking functions built in, which can be used for mapping network drives and connecting to network printers. For advanced network functionality, you'll have to look into a different scripting language (see "Further Study" later in this chapter). For more information on networking, see Chapter 7, *Networking*.

The following routines provide access to some of the more useful network-related functions in VBScript:

```
Function AlreadyMapped(DriveLetter)
  Set WshShell = WScript.CreateObject("WScript.Shell")
  Set WshNetwork = WScript.CreateObject("WScript.Network")
  Set AllDrives = WshNetwork.EnumNetworkDrives()

  If Left(DriveLetter,1) <> ":" then DriveLetter = _
    DriveLetter & ":"
  ConnectedFlag = False
  For i = 0 To AllDrives.Count - 1 Step 2
    If AllDrives.Item(i) = UCase(DriveLetter) Then _
      ConnectedFlag = True
  Next

  AlreadyMapped = ConnectedFlag
End Function

Sub MapNetDrive(DriveLetter, RemotePath)
  Set WshShell = WScript.CreateObject("WScript.Shell")
  Set WshNetwork = WScript.CreateObject("WScript.Network")
  WShNetwork.MapNetworkDrive DriveLetter, RemotePath
End Sub

Sub MapNetPrinter(Port, RemotePath)
  Set WshShell = WScript.CreateObject("WScript.Shell")
  Set WshNetwork = WScript.CreateObject("WScript.Network")
  WshNetwork.AddPrinterConnection Port, RemotePath
End Sub

Sub UnMapNetDrive(DriveLetter)
  Set WshShell = WScript.CreateObject("WScript.Shell")
  Set WshNetwork = WScript.CreateObject("WScript.Network")
  WShNetwork.RemoveNetworkDrive DriveLetter
End Sub

Sub UnMapNetPrinter(Port)
  Set WshShell = WScript.CreateObject("WScript.Shell")
  Set WshNetwork = WScript.CreateObject("WScript.Network")
  WshNetwork.RemovePrinterConnection Port
End Sub
```

The following script serves as an example for these subroutines. It's used to map a network drive if it's not already mapped, or disconnect a currently mapped drive. The above routines are required:

```
DriveLetter = "N:"
RemotePath = "\\server\c"

If AlreadyMapped(DriveLetter) then
  Call UnMapNetDrive(DriveLetter)
```

```
    Msgbox "Drive " & DriveLetter & " disconnected."
  Else
    Call MapNetDrive(DriveLetter, RemotePath)
    Msgbox "Drive " & DriveLetter & " connected."
  End if
```

This script requires no user interaction once it has been executed, and displays only a single confirmation message when it's done. The first two lines contain the drive letter and network path to be mapped together. The *AlreadyMapped* function is used to determine if the drive mapping already exists. The script then maps or disconnects the drive, depending on what's needed.

Command-line parameters

A command-line parameter is a bit of text specified after the filename of a script when it is executed from a command prompt. Although the command line may seem to be an antiquated concept, it's still very much a part of Windows. When you double-click on a *.vbs* file, for example, Windows executes the following:

```
wscript.exe filename.vbs
```

where ***`filename.vbs`*** (the file that was double-clicked) is the command-line parameter for *WScript.exe*, telling it which script to run. Scripts also accept command-line parameters, which is accomplished like this:

```
wscript.exe filename.vbs param1 param2
```

The two additional parameters, ***`param1`*** and ***`param2`***, are both passed to the script as command-line parameters when it is run.

The function to convert a single command-line parameter into a variable is the following:

```
Function CommandLine(Number)
  Set Arguments = WScript.Arguments
  If Number <= Arguments.Count Then
    CommandLine = Arguments(Number - 1)
  Else
    CommandLine = ""
  End If
End Function
```

For example, to display the second command-line parameter passed to a script, issue the following statement:

```
MsgBox CommandLine(2)
```

The problem with providing command-line arguments to your script is that Windows considers scripts to be documents instead of executables. This means that you can't run a script with a command-line parameter without typing; you can't drag a file onto a script icon, or put a script directly into your **Send To** menu.

Luckily, there's a slightly convoluted workaround. Since the syntax required to launch a script with command-line parameters must be typed, it can be put into a DOS batch file.* The batch file simply passes on the command-line parameters to the script (see "Command-line parameters" in the "DOS Batch Files" section, later in this chapter).

Consider the following example, which uses a single-line batch file and a Windows shortcut, in conjunction with a script, to make any filename lowercase. It is assumed that all files are saved in a folder called *c:\scripts*):

1. Type the following into a text editor and save it as *rename.bat*:

   ```
   @echo off
   del c:\temp.txt
   dir /b %1 > c:\temp.txt
   wscript c:\scripts\rename.vbs %1
   ```

2. Close the text editor, then right-click on *rename.bat* and select **Properties**. From the **Run** dropdown list, choose **Minimized**. Lastly, turn on the **Close on exit** option, and click **OK**.

3. A file called *rename.pif* will then appear in the same folder; this contains the batch file properties. Move this file into your *\Windows\SendTo* folder, and rename it to *Make lower case.pif.*

4. Then, in a plain text editor, type the following:

   ```
   LongFileName = ReadFromFile("c:\temp.txt")
   Call FileDelete("c:\temp.txt")
   Call FileMove(CommandLine(1), LCase(LongFileName))
   ```

   You'll also include the following functions and subroutines, listed earlier in this chapter: *ReadFromFile*, *FileMove*, *FileDelete*, and *CommandLine.* Save the completed script as *rename.vbs.*

   The first two lines of this script read and then delete a temporary text file created by the batch file. The purpose of this temporary file is to preserve any long filenames that are passed to the batch file. Without it, if you try to rename a file with a long filename, it will be renamed to its short filename!

   This script uses the *CommandLine* function described at the beginning of this topic, which turns command lines into variables, as well

* While one would expect that a Windows shortcut could be used to launch the script as well, this unfortunately doesn't work; Windows shortcuts don't handle command-line parameters properly.

as the *FileMove* subroutine described in "File operations" earlier in this chapter, which performs the actual file renaming. This script also uses the *LCase* function built into VBScript, which makes any variable lowercase.

5. Once the three files (*rename.bat*, *rename.vbs*, and *Make lower case.pif*) are all in place, you can test the script out. Right-click on any file in Explorer and select **Make lower case** from the **Send To** menu.

One caveat to this script is that if you select multiple files in Explorer, only one of them will be renamed. While this problem can be fixed with additional code, this is as far as it will be taken here.

Make a startup script

The process of making a startup script that is executed automatically when Windows starts is quite simple. There are two ways to do it:

Use the StartUp folder

Put a shortcut to the script in your *StartUp* folder, which is usually *\Windows\Start Menu\Programs\StartUp*. This method is by far the easiest to implement, but also the most fragile, as it's equally as easy to disable. Additionally, if you have multiple users configured, this will only work for the current user.

Use the Registry

Open the Registry Editor (if you're not familiar with the Registry Editor, see Chapter 3), and expand the branches to `HKEY_LOCAL_MACHINE\Software\Microsoft\Windows\CurrentVersion\Run`.

Select **New** and then **String Value** from the **Edit** menu, and type `Startup Script`. Double-click on the new `Startup Script` value, type the name of your script (e.g., `c:\scripts\myscript.vbs`), and click **OK**.

This has a similar effect to using the *StartUp* folder, except that it's harder to disable, and it works for every user configured on the system.

Regardless of how you do it, there's an additional use of startup scripts that may not be immediately apparent. If you have several computers interconnected through a network, the problem of remote administration often comes up. Assuming that one of the computers on the network is taking on the role of server, and therefore is always on, you can place a script on the server that is automatically run by each client machine whenever they boot.

For example, if you place the script *Startup.vbs* on a machine called Server in a folder called *c:\scripts*, then each client machine should be configured to execute `\\server\c\scripts\startup.vbs`.

The beauty of this is that when you don't want the script to do anything, you can simply leave it intact and empty. If you find that you need to, say, make a registry change to each computer, just type the appropriate commands into the script, and turn on all the client computers. This can turn some administration tasks into very short work.

Deciphering Errors

One of the general disadvantages of scripts is that you don't use a rich debugging environment to edit them (see "Finding a Better Editor" later in this chapter). Since Notepad doesn't understand VBScript, it can't offer any assistance with syntax or errors while you're editing. Therefore, you must wait until you run the script to see if there are any problems. If WSH encounters an error, it will display a message similar to that shown in Figure 9-2.

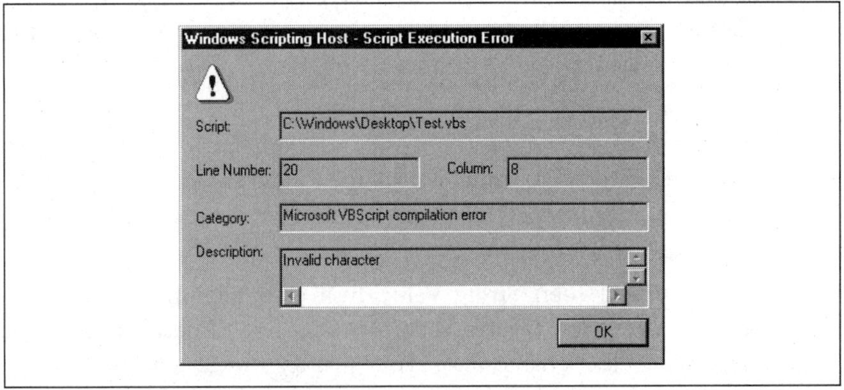

Figure 9-2: The Windows Scripting Host will display a message like this whenever it encounters an error

This sparse message box actually provides enough information to resolve most problems. Naturally, the first field, Script, shows the script filename in which the error occurred; this is especially useful if the script was run from a scheduled task or from your StartUp group, and you might otherwise not know which script caused the error.

The Line Number and Column fields show exactly where in the script the error occurred. Unfortunately, Notepad doesn't tell you what line the cursor is on, so you'll either have to count down from the top and then count columns, or use a better text editor.

The Category field describes more than anything else what WSH was doing when it encountered the error. A *compilation error* occurs when WSH is first reading the file and making sure all of the commands are correctly entered; you'll see this if you forgot a parenthesis or quotation mark, or left out some other important command. A *runtime error*, on the other hand, is an error encountered while the script is being executed. This is caused by commands that WSH doesn't know are errors until it actually tries to execute them; for example, if your script tries to read from a file that doesn't exist or calculate the square root of a negative number, it will cause a runtime error.

Lastly, the Description field has a brief explanation of the error encountered. Sometimes it's helpful, but most of the time it's either too general or too cryptic to be of much help. Programming experience comes in handy for interpreting these messages and figuring out what caused them. The following are a few of the more common error descriptions, and what they mean:

Expected ')'.
: *Compilation error*: You left out a closing parenthesis, such as at the end of an *InputBox* statement. Note that sometimes you can have nested parentheses: `x=1+(6+7*(3-4))`. You need to make sure that you have an equal number of open and close parentheses, and that they're all placed correctly.

Expected 'End'.
: *Compilation error*: You left out a closing statement for a structure, such as `If`, `Sub`, or `For`. Make sure you include `End If`, `End Sub`, and `Next`, respectively. Note that WSH might report that the error occurred on line 37 of a 35-line file; when it's looking for a closing statement, it searches all the way to the end, and only then will it report the error. You'll have to look through the entire script for the *unpaired* beginning statement. See "Flow Control" earlier in this chapter for more information on these commands.

Unterminated string constant.
: *Compilation error*: You left out a closing quotation mark, usually required at the end of a string of text.

Invalid procedure call or argument.
: *Runtime error*: This usually means that a subroutine or function has been called with one or more improper parameters. This can occur, for example, if you try to do something WSH isn't capable of, such as calculating the square root of a negative number.

Type mismatch: '[undefined]'.

Runtime error: This means you've tried to use a command or function that VBScript doesn't recognize. I get this error whenever I try to use a VB command that doesn't exist in VBScript.

Object doesn't support this property or method.

Runtime error: Since it can be difficult to find documentation on the various objects used in VBScript, you're likely to encounter this error frequently. It means that you've tried to refer to a property or method that isn't supported by a particular object.

The system cannot find the file specified.

Runtime error: This error, obviously reporting that you've tried to access a file on your hard disk that doesn't exist, also appears when you try to delete a registry key that doesn't exist. See "Scripting Goodies" earlier in this chapter for a registry function that solves this problem.

If you plan on distributing your scripts, you'll want to eliminate any errors that may pop up. See the "File operations" example script in "Scripting Goodies" earlier in this chapter for more information on error trapping and the `On Error Resume Next` statement.

Finding a Better Editor

Notepad is a very rudimentary text editor. While it serves our purpose, allowing us to write and save VBScript files, it doesn't go any further than it absolutely needs to. If you find yourself writing VBScript files often, you'll want to use a better editor. Now, Windows 98 also comes with WordPad, although it doesn't do much more than Notepad in helping to write scripts, and it has that creepy Microsoft Word-like interface.

One direction to go is simply to use a better plain text editor, such as UltraEdit-32 (see Appendix F). It has many features prized by programmers, such as column selections, line numbering, good search-and-replace, and other goodies. However, it's still just a text editor, and therefore doesn't provide any VBScript-specific assistance.

Most full-featured programming languages come with a rich programming environment that provides real-time syntax checking (it tells you right away if you missed a parenthesis) as well as context-sensitive help (you can get technical assistance as you're typing code). The problem is that Windows doesn't come with such an editor, nor am I aware of any decent VBScript editor at the time of this writing.

Some may suggest that you can use either the Visual Basic editor or the VBA editor that comes with Microsoft Office 97 to write your scripts, but this should be taken with a grain of salt. While VB and VBA do have a similar syntax to VBScript, and even share many commands, the environments are different enough that it's more trouble than it's worth.

Further Study

Since programming for the Windows Scripting Host is a language-dependent endeavor, the most helpful reference material will be about the particular language you're using. For starters, take a look at Microsoft's Windows Scripting Host page* at:

> *http://www.microsoft.com/scripting/windowshost/default.htm*

And for more information on some of the WSH object references, including the `WshShell` object, see:

> *http://www.microsoft.com/msdn/sdk/inetsdk/help/wsh/wobj.htm*

Before committing to VBScript for a project, you may want to do some research on other supported languages listed here. Due to VBScript's heritage in web pages, security concerns have resulted in some limitations in the VBScript language, such as its inability to access the clipboard or link to external *.dll* files. Perl, for example, is much more powerful and efficient than VBScript, although it requires a third-party add-on module.

The following is a list of resources and research tips for each of the more common scripting languages used with WSH. Check the *Windows 98 Annoyances* web site (see Appendix F) for additional links.

VBScript

The preceding section covers some of the elementary concepts of scripting with VBScript, as well as some otherwise hard to find solutions. One problem you'll encounter when trying to find more information on VBScript is that most print and online resources devoted to VBScript describe how it is used in web pages rather than in the Windows Scripting Host.

As WSH gains popularity, however, that will change. The first place to look for VBScript information pertaining both to VBScript and WSH in

* If you want to run your scripts on a Win95 or NT 4 machine, you'll want to download the Windows Scripting Host engine from this site as well. Note that it may not support all of the additional features found in WSH 3.0, the version included in Windows 98. This is yet another reason to test your scripts on each platform before giving them to others.

general is Microsoft's web site. In particular, you can download a nearly complete VBScript language reference at:

http://www.microsoft.com/scripting/vbscript/default.htm

For a more comprehensive study of programming in VBScript, check out *Learning VBScript*, by Paul Lomax (O'Reilly & Associates).

JavaScript

Support for JavaScript is also built into the Windows Scripting Host. Due to JavaScript's popularity on the Web, you'll find far more documentation and examples of JavaScript than of VBScript on the Web and in books. Note that JavaScript is supported by both Netscape and Internet Explorer, while VBScript is only supported by IE.

Microsoft calls their version of JavaScript "JScript." More information on JScript is available at:

http://www.microsoft.com/scripting/jscript/default.htm

Also take a look at Netscape's web site for additional, more general JavaScript information:

http://developer.netscape.com/tech/javascript/

For a more comprehensive JavaScript reference and tutorial, read *JavaScript: The Definitive Guide*, by David Flanagan (O'Reilly & Associates).

Perl

Perl (Practical Extract and Report Language) is probably the most powerful and flexible scripting language available for the Windows Scripting Host at the time of this writing. It's traditionally very popular among the Unix crowd, and has gained tremendous popularity for its use in writing Common Gateway Interface (CGI) programs for web servers.

Unfortunately, Windows 98 doesn't come with the Perl engine; you'll have to obtain and install it separately. It's available from:

http://www.activestate.com/

As "PerlScript," it's also available as part of the *Perl Resource Kit, Win32 Edition* (O'Reilly & Associates).

You can also find just about any information, sample scripts, and add-ons for Perl from:

http://www.perl.com/

If you want to learn more about Perl, you definitely should not be without *Programming Perl* (affectionately known as the Camel book), by Larry Wall, Tom Christiansen, and Randal L. Schwartz (O'Reilly & Associates). Newcomers to Perl will probably prefer *Learning Perl on Win32 Systems*, by Schwartz, Erik Olson, and Christiansen (O'Reilly & Associates).

Python

More information on the Python language is available at *http://www.python.org/*, as well as in the book *Programming Python*, by Mark Lutz (O'Reilly & Associates).

DOS Batch Files

When it comes to quick and dirty scripting, it's hard to beat DOS batch files. Batch files, like WSH scripts (discussed earlier in this chapter), are plain text files, but have the extension *.bat*. However, rather than relying on a complex, unfamiliar scripting language, batch files are comprised simply of one or more DOS commands.

One of the problems with Windows-based scripting (see "Windows Scripting Host" earlier in this chapter) is that it tries to control a graphical environment with a command-based language. Since DOS has a command-based interface, DOS-based batch files are a natural extension of the environment.

Consider the following DOS commands:

```
c:
CD \windows\temp
ATTRIB -r *.tmp
DEL *.tmp
```

If you type these commands into a plain text editor, such as Notepad, and save it all into a *.bat* file, executing the batch file will have the same effect as if the commands were manually typed consecutively at the DOS prompt. Obviously, this can be a tremendous time-saver if you find yourself entering the same DOS commands repeatedly.

Batch files can be executed by double-clicking them in Explorer, or by typing their names in DOS. You'll want to put more frequently used, general-purpose batch files in a folder specified in the system path (see "The path less traveled" in Chapter 6, *Troubleshooting*), so that they can be executed from DOS regardless of the current working directory.

When you run a batch file, each command in the file will be printed (or *echoed*) to the screen before it's executed, which can be unsightly. To turn off the echoing of any given command, precede it with the `@` character. To turn off the printing of *all* commands in a batch file, include the command `@ECHO OFF` at the beginning.

Although batch files can run Windows programs (just type **`NOTEPAD`** to launch Notepad), it's preferable to run Windows programs with Windows Scripting Host scripts, as they'll be able to run without having to first load a DOS window.

To change the way a batch file runs in Windows, right-click on it and select **Properties**. This will allow you to set various options, such as if Windows should shut down before running the batch file, if programs run from the batch file can detect that Windows is running, and if the command prompt window is automatically closed when the batch file completes. For the most part, you won't have to bother with these options, although the **Close on exit** option can come in handy.

In addition to the standard DOS commands, most of which are documented in Appendix C, *Contents of the MSDOS.SYS File*, batch files use a couple of extra statements to fill the holes. Variables, conditional statements, and `For...Next` loops are all implemented with statements that are ordinarily not of much use at the DOS prompt.

The following topics cover the concepts used to turn a task or a string of DOS commands into a capable batch file.

Variables and the environment

The use of variables in batch files can be somewhat confusing. All variables used in a batch file, with the exception of command-line parameters, are stored in the DOS *environment*, an area of memory that is created when you first boot, and kept around until the computer is turned off.

Note that if you start the command prompt from within Windows, the environment is imported from the DOS session initiated at system startup. However, any changes to this "temporary" version of the environment are lost when the command prompt is closed. To add data to the environment that won't be lost, it must be done before Windows is started.

To view the contents of the environment, type **`SET`** at the command prompt. To set a variable to a particular value, type this command:

```
SET VariableName=Some Data
```

Note that, unlike VBScript, the **`SET`** command *is* required and no quotation marks are used when setting the value of a variable. To remove the variable from memory, you set its value to nothing, like this:

```
SET VariableName=
```

To display the contents of the variable, use the `ECHO` command, as follows:

```
ECHO %VariableName%
```

Here, the percent signs (`%`) on both ends of the variable name are necessary; otherwise, the `ECHO` command would take its arguments literally, and display the name of the variable rather than the data it contains.

What's confusing is that sometimes variables need no percent signs, sometimes they need one, two at the beginning, or one on each end. See the following topics for details.

Flow control

Batch files have a very rudimentary flow control structure. The following example exhibits the use of the `GOTO` command:

```
@ECHO OFF
ECHO Rock
GOTO LaterOn
ECHO Scissors
:LaterOn
ECHO Paper
```

The `:LaterOn` line (note the mandatory colon prefix) is called a label, which is used as a target for the `GOTO` command. If you follow the flow of the script, you should expect the following output:

```
Rock
Paper
```

as the `GOTO` command has caused the `Scissors` line to be skipped.

Command-line parameters

Suppose you executed a batch file called *Demo.bat* by typing the following at the DOS prompt:

```
Demo file1.txt file2.txt
```

Both `file1.txt` and `file2.txt` are command-line parameters, and are automatically stored in two variables, *%1* and *%2*, respectively, when the batch file is run.

The implication is that you could run a batch file which would then act with the parameters that have been passed to it. A common use of this feature, shown in the above example, is to specify one or more filenames that are then manipulated or used in some way by the batch file.

The following two-line example uses command-line parameters and the `FC` utility to compare two text files. A similar example using the Window

Scripting Host, shown in "Subroutines and functions" earlier in this chapter, takes 18 lines to accomplish approximately the same task:

```
fc %1 %2 >c:\windows\temp\output.txt
notepad c:\windows\temp\output.txt
```

Save this batch file as *compare.bat*, and execute it like this:

```
compare c:\autoexec.bat c:\config.sys
```

which will compare the two files, *autoexec.bat* and *config.sys*, and then open the output in Notepad. Note that the > character on the first line redirects the output of the `FC` program, which would otherwise be displayed on the screen, and instead saves it in the *output.txt* file. The second line opens the *output.txt* file in Notepad for easy viewing.

There are ways, other than typing, to take advantage of command-line parameters. If you place a shortcut to a batch file (say, *Demo.bat*) in your *\Windows\SendTo* folder, then right-click on a file in Explorer, select **Send To** and then **Demo**, the *Demo.bat* batch file will be executed with the file you've selected as the first command-line parameter. Likewise, if you drag-drop any file onto the batch file icon in Explorer, the dropped file will be used as the command-line parameter.*

Batch files have a limit of nine command-line parameters (`%1` through `%9`), although there's a way to have more if you need them. Say you need to accept 12 parameters at the command line. Your batch file should start by acting on the first parameter. Then, you would issue the `SHIFT` command, which eliminates the first parameter, putting the second in its place. `%2` becomes `%1`, `%3` becomes `%2`, and so on. Just repeat the process until there are no parameters left. Here's an example of this process:

```
:StartOfLoop
IF "%1"=="" EXIT
DEL %1
SHIFT
GOTO StartOfLoop
```

Save these commands into *MultiDel.bat*. This simple batch file deletes one or more filenames with a single command; it's used like this:

```
MultiDel file1.txt another.doc third.log
```

The program works by cycling through the command-line parameters one by one using `SHIFT`. It repeats the same two lines (`DEL %1` and `SHIFT`) until the `%1` variable is empty (see the next section, "Conditional state-

* If you drop more than one file on a batch file icon, their order as arguments will be seemingly random, theoretically mirroring their ordering in your hard disk's file table.

ments," for the use of the IF statement), at which point the batch file ends (using the EXIT command).

Conditional statements

There are three versions of the IF statement, each of which allows you to test a condition and redirect the flow of the batch file. The first version is usually used to test the value of a variable, as follows:

```
IF "%1"=="help" GOTO SkipIt
```

Note the use of quotation marks around the variable name and the help text, as well as the double equals signs, all of which are necessary. Notice also there's no THEN keyword, which those familiar with Visual Basic might expect. If the batch file finds that the two sides are equal, it executes everything on the right side of the statement; in this case, it issues the GOTO command.

The second use of the IF command is to test the existence of a file:

```
IF EXIST c:\autoexec.bat GOTO SkipIt
```

If the file *c:\autoexec.bat* exists, the GOTO command will be executed. Similarly, you can you can test for the *absence* of a file, as follows:

```
IF NOT EXIST c:\autoexec.bat GOTO SkipIt
```

The third use of the IF command is to test the outcome of the previous command, as follows:

```
IF ERRORLEVEL 0 GOTO SkipIt
```

If there was any problem with the statement immediately *before* this line, the ERRORLEVEL (which is similar to a system-defined variable) will be set to some nonzero number. The IF statement shown here tests for any ERRORLEVEL that is greater than zero; if there was no error, execution will simply continue to the next command.

Here's a revised version of the file compare example first shown in the "Command-line parameters" section earlier in this chapter:

```
IF "%1"=="" GOTO Problem
IF "%2"=="" GOTO Problem
IF NOT EXIST %1 GOTO Problem
IF NOT EXIST %2 GOTO Problem
fc %1 %2 >c:\windows\temp\output.txt
IF ERRORLEVEL 0 GOTO Problem
IF NOT EXIST c:\windows\temp\output.txt GOTO Problem
notepad c:\windows\temp\output.txt
EXIT
:Problem
ECHO "A problem has been encountered."
```

This batch file is essentially the same as the original two-line example shown earlier, except that it adds some error-checking statements that utilize the `IF` statement. If you neglect to enter one or both command-line parameters, or if the files you specify as command-line parameters don't exist, the batch file will display the error message. An even more useful version might have multiple error messages that accurately describe the specific problem that was encountered.

Loops

Batch files have a very simple looping mechanism, based loosely on the `For...Next` loop used in other programming languages. The main difference is that the batch file `FOR` loop doesn't increment a variable regularly, but rather cycles it through a list of values. Its syntax is as follows:

```
FOR %%i IN ("Rock","Scissors","Paper") DO ECHO %%i
```

Here, the variable syntax gets even more confusing; the reference to the *`i`* variable when used in conjunction with the `FOR...IN...DO` statement gets two percent signs *before* the variable name, and none after. Note also that only single-letter variables can be used here.

If you execute this batch file, you'll get the following output:

```
Rock
Scissors
Paper
```

Note also the use of the quotation marks; although they aren't strictly necessary, they're helpful if one or more of the values in the list has a comma in it.

To simulate a more traditional `For...Next` statement in a batch file, type the following:

```
FOR %%i IN (1,2,3,4,5) DO ECHO %%i
```

Simulating subroutines

Batch files have no support for named subroutines (as described in "Subroutines and functions" in the "Windows Scripting Host" section earlier in this chapter). However, you can *simulate* subroutines by creating several batch files: one main file, and one or more subfiles, each of which can accept command line parameters. Don't try this if performance is an issue, however.

This is useful in cases like the `FOR...IN...DO` statement (described in the preceding section), which can only loop a single command. Consider the following example.

In one batch file, called *WriteIt.bat*, type:

```
IF "%1"=="" EXIT
IF EXIST %1.txt DEL %1.txt
ECHO This is a text > %1.txt
```

Then, in another batch file, called *Main.bat*, type the following:

```
FOR %%i IN ("Rock","Scissors","Paper") DO CALL WriteIt.bat %%i
```

The single-line *Main.bat* batch file uses the `CALL` command to run the other batch file, *WriteIt.bat*, three times. The `CALL` command allows one batch file to run another batch file; if it's omitted, one batch file can still run another, but the first batch file will abruptly end as it runs the second batch file.

When this pair of batch files is run, you should end up with three files, *Rock.txt*, *Scissors.txt*, and *Paper.txt*, all containing the text, "This is a text." The `IF` statement as well as the `For...In...Do` loop are explained in preceding sections.

Startup batch file: Autoexec.bat

The *Autoexec.bat* file, a feature as old as batch files themselves, is nothing more than a standard batch file that has been placed in the root directory of the boot drive (usually *c:*). This batch file is run automatically when you start your computer, and before Windows is loaded.

See "Do I Still Need Config.sys and Autoexec.bat?" and "The path less traveled," both in Chapter 6, for more information.

Scheduled Tasks

The Scheduled Tasks feature introduced in Windows 98 is fairly simple, allowing you to schedule any program or, more importantly, any script.

What's nice about the Scheduled Tasks feature is that it's actually a technology that is somewhat well-integrated into the operating system. For example, there are a few tools (the Maintenance Wizard, for one) that automate the creation of scheduled tasks to complete various automated functions, such as running Scandisk once a day.

The Scheduled Tasks feature also has its pitfalls. The logging option is limited, and only tells you if the task has been performed. It can be hard to tell whether a scheduled task has actually been performed successfully or not, unless you specifically implement logging in a script. Also, any scheduled tasks will not be performed if you've selected the **Stop Using Task Scheduler** option, if your computer is turned off, or if Windows isn't running. These may be obvious points, but they can be easy to forget. Lastly, you must disable the Task Scheduler to get rid of its tray icon (see Appendix A, *Setting Locator*).

To create a new scheduled task, open the Scheduled Tasks folder in Explorer or from My Computer, and double-click **Add Scheduled Task**. The overly verbose wizard should then walk you through the process of creating a new task. When the wizard prompts you to select a program (it just displays a list of all the applications listed in your Start Menu), click **Browse**, select an existing script or batch file on your hard disk, and click **OK** when you're done.

I recommend just clicking **Next** repeatedly here until the wizard is finished; then right-click on the new task and select **Properties** to configure the task with the more suitable tabbed interface. One thing to note is the two **Power Management** settings in the **Settings** tab of the task's properties dialog. By default, tasks won't be run if your computer is running on batteries, a setting you may want to change if you need the task performed regardless of your computer's power source.

This opens up some interesting possibilities. One of the most powerful uses of scripting is to automate repetitive tasks, and probably the most important task to automate is that of backing up your system, something that most people don't bother to do at all. Now, most backup programs come with rudimentary schedulers, but they can't do the things the following example can do:

1. Run Scandisk to check the disk for errors and repair any errors found.
2. Delete all the files left over in your temporary directory.
3. Connect to a network drive, so you can include your coworker's documents in your backup
4. Launch your backup software and back up your entire system.
5. Disconnect from your coworker's networked drive when finished.
6. Write a log file to verify that the backup was completed successfully.
7. Repeat this process automatically every Thursday at 3:00 a.m. while you are peacefully passed out on your couch.

And here's the script that accomplishes steps 1 through 6 (step 7 is done with Scheduled Tasks, as described above):

```
On Error Resume Next
```

```
Call RunProgram("Scandisk.exe", True)
Call FileDelete("C:\Windows\Temp\*.tmp")
If Not AlreadyMapped("N:") then Call MapNetDrive("N:", _
      "\\torey\\c\)
Call RunProgram("C:\Program
Files\Accessories\BACKUP\MSBACKUP.EXE", True)
Call UnMapNetDrive("N:")
Call WriteToFile("C:\MyBackup.log", "Successful Backup on " _
     & Now())
```

This script also requires that you include the following subroutines and functions, listed earlier in this chapter: *RunProgram* in "Running programs," *FileDelete* in "File operations," *AlreadyMapped* in "Networking," *MapNetDrive* in "Networking," *UnMapNetDrive* in "Networking," and *WriteToFile* in "File operations."

One of the things I like about this example is that it puts a lot of pieces discussed elsewhere in this book together in a way that can save your data. See Chapter 6 for more information on backing up, and what it can do for you.

Note that you'll need to consult the documentation of your backup software to make it automatically perform the backup when it's launched. For example, many backup programs allow you to save a backup job into a file that contains your preferences and selected files to back up. Instead of launching the *.exe* file from the script, you would launch the job file (often with the extension *.set*) from the script, which would automatically perform the backup rather than just sitting there.

Setting Locator

It shouldn't take you too long to find that the various options, switches, and adjustments that allow you to customize Windows are scattered throughout dozens of dialog boxes, property sheets, and add-on utilities. Understandably, this can turn a simple task into a monumental wild goose chase. This appendix lists over 200 Windows settings and where to find them.

The settings are arranged in several categories, listed alphabetically, and named in such a way that they should be easy to locate by context. For example, to find out how to turn off the power management icon in the tray, look for the **Power Management Icon** entry in the **Tray** section. Note that a few settings have been duplicated with different labels to make them easier to find.

Registry entries are not included here due to the complexity associated with their use, and because most of the more basic settings can be changed without editing the Registry. Settings associated with the Registry are described elsewhere in the book; see Chapter 3 for more information.

Some of the solutions below require one of the following programs, which all come with Windows, but for one reason or another, aren't immediately accessible in the Start Menu:

TweakUI

One of Microsoft's Power Toys, which provides some advanced settings otherwise not available in Windows. It's located in the *\tools\reskit\powertoy* folder of the Windows 98 CD. To install it, right-click on the *tweakui.inf* file, and select **Install**. Once TweakUI is installed, you can access it through the Control Panel.

System Policy Editor

A utility providing access to settings that relate to security and multiple users. To install, double-click on the **Add/Remove Programs** icon in Control Panel, select the **Windows Setup** tab, and click **Have Disk**. Click **Browse**, point to the *\tools\reskit\netadmin\poledit* folder on the Windows CD, and click **OK**. Check both options that appear, and click **OK** again. Once the System Policy Editor is installed, you can access it by selecting **Run** from the Start Menu, typing `poledit`, and clicking **OK**.

To get more categories and settings in the System Policy Editor, select **Policy Template** from PolEdit's **Options** menu. Click **Add**, and select any *.adm* file that doesn't already appear in the **Current Templates** list—you'll have to do it for each *.adm* file until you've got them all. All the *.adm* files that come with PolEdit are located in your *\Windows\INF* folder.

System Configuration Utility

A new component in Windows 98, and yet another collection of obscure Windows settings, mostly intended for advanced troubleshooting. The program is installed by default, and located in your *\Windows\System* folder. Select **Run** from the Start Menu, type `msconfig` and click **OK** to run this program.

To conserve space, the setting locations below are described in a form of computerese: Consecutive actions are separated by an arrow (→). For example, **Control Panel → TweakUI → Desktop tab** means you should first double-click on the **Control Panel** icon, then double-click on the **TweakUI** icon, then choose the **Desktop** tab. The setting you're seeking will then be in plain sight. All directions assume the My Computer window as a starting point, unless otherwise stated.

Explorer and the Start Menu

Active Desktop—allow changes

Control Panel → TweakUI → IE4 tab

Active Desktop—customize

Start Menu → Settings → Active Desktop

Active Desktop—show channel bar at startup if Active Desktop is off

Control Panel → Internet → Advanced tab

Active Desktop—view as web page
Control Panel → Display → Web tab

Active Desktop—view as web page
Start Menu → Settings → Active Desktop

Active Desktop enabled
Control Panel → TweakUI → IE4 tab

Control Panel—show/hide icons
Control Panel → TweakUI → Control Panel tab

Desktop—folder location
Control Panel → TweakUI → General tab

Display settings in Control Panel—restrict
System Policy Editor → File → Open Registry → Local User\Control Panel\Display

Display the full path in title bar
View menu → Folder Options → View tab

Documents menu—add new documents
Control Panel → TweakUI → IE4 tab

Documents menu—clear at logon
Control Panel → TweakUI → Paranoia tab

Documents menu—clear on exit
Control Panel → TweakUI → IE4 tab

Documents Menu—folder location
Control Panel → TweakUI → General tab

Documents menu—show on Start Menu
Control Panel → TweakUI → IE4 tab

Enable all web-related content on desktop
View menu → Folder Options → choose Custom option → Settings

Favorites menu—show on Start Menu
Control Panel → TweakUI → IE4 tab

Find command—show/hide
System Policy Editor → File → Open Registry → Local User\Windows 98 System\Shell\ Restrictions\Remove 'Find' command

Find Computer history—clear at logon
Control Panel → TweakUI → Paranoia tab

Find Files history—clear at logon
Control Panel → TweakUI → Paranoia tab

Folders settings—show/hide
System Policy Editor → File → Open Registry → Local User\Windows 98 System\Shell\Restrictions\Remove folders from 'Settings' on Start Menu

Hide all icons on desktop
System Policy Editor → File → Open Registry → Local User\Windows 98 System\Shell\Restrictions\Hide all items on desktop

Hide all icons when desktop is viewed as web page
Control Panel → Display → Effects tab

Hide all icons when desktop is viewed as web page
View menu → Folder Options → View tab

Internet Explorer—show on desktop
Control Panel → Internet → Advanced tab

Internet icon—show on Desktop
Control Panel → TweakUI → IE4 tab → Show Internet icon on desktop

My Computer—change icon
Control Panel → Display → Effects tab → Desktop icons

My Computer—show/hide all drives
System Policy Editor → File → Open Registry → Local User\Windows 98 System\Shell\Restrictions\Hide Drives in 'My Computer'

My Computer—show/hide individual drives
Control Panel → TweakUI → My Computer tab

My Documents folder—change icon
Control Panel → Display → Effects tab → Desktop icons

Network Neighborhood—change icon
Control Panel → Display → Effects tab → Desktop icons

Network Neighborhood—Entire Network icon—show/hide
System Policy Editor → File → Open Registry → Local User\Windows 98 System\Shell\Restrictions\No 'Entire Network' in Network Neighborhood

Network Neighborhood icon—show/hide
Control Panel → TweakUI → Desktop tab

Network Neighborhood icon—show/hide
System Policy Editor → File → Open Registry → Local User\Windows 98 System\Shell\Restrictions\Hide Network Neighborhood

Network settings in Control Panel—restrict
System Policy Editor → File → Open Registry → Local User\Control Panel\Network

Open each folder in its own window
View menu → Folder Options → choose Custom, click Settings

Open each folder in the same window
View menu → Folder Options → choose Custom, click Settings

Passwords settings in Control Panel—restrict
System Policy Editor → File → Open Registry → Local User\Control Panel\Passwords

Printers settings in Control Panel—restrict
System Policy Editor → File → Open Registry → Local User\Control Panel\Printers

Recycle Bin—change icon
Control Panel → Display → Effects tab → Desktop icons

Recycle Bin—show/hide
Control Panel → TweakUI → Desktop tab

Remember each folder's view settings
View menu → Folder Options → View tab

Reset defaults for all folders
View menu → Folder Options → View tab → Reset All Folders

Reset defaults for view settings
View menu → Folder Options → View tab → Restore Defaults

Run command—show/hide
System Policy Editor → File → Open Registry → Local User\Windows 98 System\Shell\Restrictions\Remove 'Run' command

Run history—clear at logon
Control Panel → Display → Settings tab → Advanced → Adapter Tab

Run history—clear on exit
Control Panel → TweakUI → Paranoia tab

Save Explorer windows (for next bootup)
Control Panel → TweakUI → Explorer tab

Save Explorer windows (for next bootup)
System Policy Editor → File → Open Registry → Local User\Windows 98 System\Shell\Restrictions\Don't save settings at exit

Set new defaults for all folders
View menu → Folder Options → View tab → Like Current Folder

Show file attributes in Detail View
View menu → Folder Options → View tab

Show Map Network Drive button in toolbar
View menu → Folder Options → View tab

Show pop-up description (tooltip) for folder and desktop items
View menu → Folder Options → View tab

Show pop-up description (tooltip) for folder and desktop items
View menu → Folder Options → View tab

Show Windows version on desktop
Control Panel → TweakUI → General tab

Shut Down command—enable/disable
System Policy Editor → File → Open Registry → Local User\Windows 98 System\Shell\Restrictions\Disable Shut Down command

Start Menu—folder location
Control Panel → TweakUI → General tab

Start Menu—folder location
System Policy Editor → File → Open Registry → Local User\Windows 98 System\Shell\Custom Folders\Custom Start Menu

Startup—folder location
Control Panel → TweakUI → General tab

Startup—folder location
System Policy Editor → File → Open Registry → Local User\Windows 98 System\Shell\Custom Folders\Custom Startup Folder

System settings in Control Panel—restrict
System Policy Editor → File → Open Registry → Local User\Control Panel\System

Taskbar—always on top
Control Panel → TweakUI → General tab

Taskbar—auto-hide
Start Menu → Settings → Taskbar

Taskbar—show clock
Start Menu → Settings → Taskbar

Taskbar—show small icons
Start Menu → Settings → Taskbar

Taskbar settings—show/hide
System Policy Editor → File → Open Registry → Local User\Windows 98 System\Shell\Restrictions\Remove Taskbar from 'Settings' on Start Menu

Tip of the day
Control Panel → TweakUI → IE4 tab

Toolbar(s)
Start Menu → Settings → Taskbar

Toolbar(s)
View menu → Toolbars

Tooltip font / color
Control Panel → Display → Appearance tab → choose Tooltip from Item list

Use large icons
Control Panel → Display → Effects tab → Desktop icons

Use windows classic interface
View menu → Folder Options → choose Custom, click Settings

View web content in all folders
View menu → Folder Options → choose Custom, click Settings

View web content only where I select "as Web Page"
View menu → Folder Options → choose Custom, click Settings

Files and Icons

Allow all uppercase 8.3 filenames
Control Panel → TweakUI → Explorer tab

Allow all uppercase 8.3 filenames
View menu → Folder Options → View tab

Compressed files color
Control Panel → TweakUI → Explorer tab

Double-click sensitivity
Control Panel → TweakUI → Mouse tab

Double-click speed
Control Panel → Mouse → Buttons tab

Double-click to open icons, single-click to select
View menu → Folder Options → choose Custom option → Settings

Drag sensitivity
Control Panel → TweakUI → Mouse tab

Hidden files—show/hide
View menu → Folder Options → View tab

Hide file extensions for known file types
View menu → Folder Options → View tab

Hide icons when desktop is viewed as web page
View menu → Folder Options → View tab

Icon size
View menu → Large Icons or View menu → Small Icons

Icon spacing
Control Panel → Display → Appearance tab → choose Icon Spacing from Item list

Icon text font
Control Panel → Display → Appearance tab → choose Icon from Item list

Menu font
Control Panel → Display → Appearance tab → choose Menu from Item list

Message Box font
Control Panel → Display → Appearance tab → choose Message Box from Item list

New menu—add/remove items
Control Panel → TweakUI → New tab

Reset default file associations
Control Panel → TweakUI → Repair tab

Reset defaults for view settings
View menu → Folder Options → View tab → Restore Defaults

Shortcut overlay—change icon
Control Panel → TweakUI → Explorer tab

Shortcut to... prefix on new shortcuts
Control Panel → TweakUI → Explorer tab

Show all files (including hidden and system)
View menu → Folder Options → View tab

Show icons using all possible colors (256 colors)
Control Panel → Display → Effects tab → Desktop icons

Single-click to open, point to select
View menu → Folder Options → choose Custom, click Settings

Sort (name, extension, date, type)
View menu → Arrange Icons

System files—show/hide
View menu → Folder Options → View tab

Interface

Click here to begin... animation
Control Panel → TweakUI → Explorer tab

Combo box (drop-down list) animation
Control Panel → TweakUI → General tab

Font scaling
Control Panel → Display → Settings tab → Advanced → General Tab

List box animation
Control Panel → TweakUI → General tab

Menu animation
Control Panel → TweakUI → General tab

Menu speed
Control Panel → TweakUI → Mouse tab

Menu underlines (for accelerator keys)
Control Panel → TweakUI → General tab

Mouse AutoRaise (x-mouse window activation)
Control Panel → TweakUI → General Tab

Mouse pointer speed
Control Panel → Mouse → Motion tab

Mouse trails—enable/disable
Control Panel → Mouse → Motion tab

Refresh rate
Control Panel → TweakUI → Paranoia tab

Show window contents while dragging
Control Panel → Display → Effects tab → Desktop icons

Show window contents while dragging
Control Panel → TweakUI → My Computer tab

Smooth edges of screen fonts
Control Panel → Display → Effects tab → Desktop icons

Smooth edges of screen fonts
View menu → Folder Options → View tab

Smooth scrolling
View menu → Folder Options → View tab

Tooltips—enable/disable
Control Panel → TweakUI → General tab → Mouse hot tracking effects

Use mouse wheel for scrolling
View menu → Toolbars

Window Animation (minimizing, restoring, maximizing)
Control Panel → TweakUI → Mouse tab

Internet and Network

Default Search Engine
Control Panel → TweakUI → Mouse tab

Detect accidental double-clicks
Control Panel → TweakUI → General tab

IE4 enabled
Control Panel → TweakUI → IE4 tab

Internet Explorer—open browser in full-screen view
Control Panel → Internet → Advanced tab

Internet Explorer—open channels in full-screen view
Control Panel → Internet → Advanced tab

Internet Explorer—show font button
Control Panel → Internet → Advanced tab

Internet Explorer—show on desktop
Control Panel → Internet → Advanced tab

Internet Explorer—use small icons on toolbar
Control Panel → Internet → Advanced tab

Internet Explorer history—clear at logon
Control Panel → TweakUI → IE4 tab

Internet Explorer should check to see if it is the default browser
Control Panel → Internet → Programs tab

Last user list—clear at logon
Control Panel → TweakUI → Paranoia tab

Network Connection history—clear at logon
Control Panel → TweakUI → Paranoia tab

Telnet history menu—clear at logon
Control Panel → TweakUI → Paranoia tab

Temporary Internet Files—folder location
Control Panel → Internet → General tab → Settings (Temporary Internet Files section) → Move Folder

System

Add/Remove Programs—add/remove items
Control Panel → TweakUI → Explorer tab

Allow F4 to boot to previous operating system
Control Panel → TweakUI → Add/Remove tab

Allow logoff
Control Panel → TweakUI → Boot tab

Apply display settings without restarting
Control Panel → TweakUI → IE4 tab

Autorun CDs
Control Panel → Display → Settings tab → Advanced → General Tab

Beep on errors
Control Panel → TweakUI → Paranoia tab

Boot function keys available
Control Panel → TweakUI → General tab

Boot menu—show always
Control Panel → TweakUI → Boot tab

Cache—CD-ROM cache settings
Control Panel → System → Performance tab → File System → CD-ROM tab

Cache—disable write-behind caching for all drives (for troubleshooting only)
Control Panel → System → Performance tab → File System → Troubleshooting tab

Cache—hard disk cache settings
Control Panel → System → Performance tab → File System → Hard Disk tab

Cache—removable drive cache settings (Syquest, Zip, Jaz, MO drives)
Control Panel → System → Performance tab → File System → Removable Disk tab

CD-ROM autorun
Control Panel → TweakUI → Boot tab

Common Files (in Program Files)—folder location
Control Panel → TweakUI → General tab

Desktop—folder location
Control Panel → TweakUI → General tab

Document Templates—folder location
Control Panel → TweakUI → General tab

Documents Menu—folder location
Control Panel → TweakUI → General tab

Don't show last user at logon
System Policy Editor → File → Open Registry → Local Computer\Windows 98 System\Windows Update

DOS startup menu—enable/disable
System Configuration Utility → General → Advanced

Fast shutdown—enable/disable
System Configuration Utility → General → Advanced

Favorites—folder location
Control Panel → TweakUI → General tab

File sharing—disable file sharing and locking (for troubleshooting only)
Control Panel → System → Performance tab → File System → Troubleshooting tab

Floppy disk—search for new drives at startup
Control Panel → System → Performance tab → File System → Floppy Disk tab

Installation Path (where Setup looks for Windows)—folder location
Control Panel → TweakUI → General tab

Installation Path (where Setup looks for Windows)—network folder location
System Policy Editor → File → Open Registry → Local Computer\Windows 98 System\Network Paths

Load Windows at system startup
Control Panel → TweakUI → Paranoia tab

Minimum Windows password length
System Policy Editor → File → Open Registry → Local Computer\Windows 98 Network\Logon

MS-DOS Prompt—enable/disable
System Policy Editor → File → Open Registry → Local User\Restrictions\Disable MS-DOS prompt

MS-DOS single mode applications—enable/disable
System Policy Editor → File → Open Registry → Local User\Restrictions\Disable single-mode MS-DOS applications

My Documents—folder location
Control Panel → TweakUI → General tab

Network Neighborhood—folder location
System Policy Editor → File → Open Registry → Local User\Windows 98 System\Shell\Custom Folders\Custom Network Neighborhood

Program Files—folder location
Control Panel → TweakUI → General tab

Programs (in Start Menu)—folder location
Control Panel → TweakUI → General tab

Programs (in Start Menu)—folder location
System Policy Editor → File → Open Registry → Local User\Windows 98 System\Shell\Custom Folders\Custom Programs Folder

Registry Editor—enable/disable
System Policy Editor → File → Open Registry → Local User\Restrictions\Disable Registry editing tools

Restart Windows after changing display settings
Control Panel → TweakUI → Boot tab

Scandisk—autorun after crash
Control Panel → Display → Settings tab → Advanced → General Tab

Scandisk—autorun after crash
System Configuration Utility → General → Advanced

Send To—folder location
Control Panel → TweakUI → General tab

Start Menu—folder location
Control Panel → TweakUI → General tab

Start Menu—folder location
System Policy Editor → File → Open Registry → Local User\Windows 98 System\Shell\Custom Folders\Custom Start Menu

Startup—folder location
Control Panel → TweakUI → General tab

Startup—folder location
System Policy Editor → File → Open Registry → Local User\Windows 98 System\Shell\Custom Folders\Custom Startup Folder

Startup logo—show while booting
Control Panel → TweakUI → Boot tab

Swap file (virtual memory) settings
Control Panel → System → Performance tab → Virtual Memory

System startup configuration files—selective enable/disable
System Configuration Utility → Any of the six top-level tabs

User Profiles—enable/disable
Control Panel → Multimedia → Show volume control on the Taskbar

Users—all users share same preferences
Control Panel → Passwords → User Profiles tab

Users—each user can customize their preferences
Control Panel → Passwords → User Profiles tab

Video hardware acceleration setting
Control Panel → System → Performance tab → Graphics

Virtual memory (swap file) settings
Control Panel → System → Performance tab → Virtual Memory

Welcome message—show at every logon
Control Panel → Internet → Advanced tab

Windows Update—enable/disable
System Policy Editor → File → Open Registry → Local Computer\Windows 98 System\User Profiles

Tray

Dial-Up Networking—modem status icon
Control Panel → TweakUI → Boot tab

Dial-Up Networking icon
Dial-Up Networking → Properties sheet of a connection → Configure → Options tab → Display modem status

Display settings icon
Dial-Up Networking → Connections → Settings → Show an icon on Taskbar after connected

FilterKeys icon
Control Panel → Display → Settings tab → Advanced → General Tab → Show settings icon on Taskbar

HyperTerminal—modem status icon
Control Panel → Accessibility Options → Keyboard tab → Settings (FilterKeys) → Show FilterKey status on screen

Keyboard Language
HyperTerminal → Properties sheet of a connection → Connect To tab → Configure → Options tab → Display modem status

MouseKeys icon
Control Panel → Keyboard → Language tab → Enable indicator on Taskbar

PC Card (PCMCIA) icon

Control Panel → Accessibility Options → Mouse tab → Settings → Show MouseKey status on screen

Power management icon

Control Panel → PC Card (PCMCIA) → Show control on Taskbar

Scheduled tasks icon

Control Panel → Power Management → Advanced tab → Show power meter on Taskbar

Show/hide printer icon

Scheduled Tasks → Advanced → Stop using Task Scheduler

StickeyKeys icon

Not possible; icons are shown when printing, disappear when printing is finished

Taskbar—show clock

Control Panel → Accessibility Options → Keyboard tab → Settings (StickeyKeys) → Show StickeyKeys status on screen

Volume control icon

Start Menu → Settings → Taskbar

Yellow speaker volume control icon

Control Panel → Multimedia → Show volume control on the Taskbar

B

DOS Lives

Many solutions in this book require that you type commands into a DOS Window. If you don't quite have a grasp on this concept, here's a crash course on MS-DOS (short for Microsoft Disk Operating System). DOS is the operating system that has been included with PCs since the very first IBM PCs appeared in the early 1980s, before Microsoft Windows became the standard; even the newest PCs still use it to some extent. All versions of Windows from 1.0 to 3.11 relied on DOS; Windows was thought of only as an extension, as one needed to load DOS before starting Windows. Windows 98 is still based somewhat on MS-DOS for compatibility with the vast majority of available software and hardware products, but it does a good job of hiding this dependence. Microsoft has made Windows NT completely independent of MS-DOS, but still makes the command prompt available from within Windows for those who need the functionality.

Rather than unloading Windows to access the command prompt, you can simply load another command prompt while remaining in Windows; this is often referred to as a *DOS Box* or *DOS Window*. If you don't have a **Command Prompt** item in your Start Menu, you can use the Start Menu's **Run** command to execute `command.com`. You can also get to the command prompt by selecting **Shut Down** from the Start Menu, and choosing **Restart the computer in MS-DOS mode**. See "Boot directly into DOS" in Chapter 5 for more information. For more information on using the command prompt, see *Windows 95 in a Nutshell*, by Tim O'Reilly and Troy Mott (O'Reilly & Associates).

When you open a command prompt window, you'll see a window that looks like the one shown in Figure B-1. The cursor indicates the command line (where commands are typed), and the prompt usually shows the current working directory (here, *C:\Windows*).

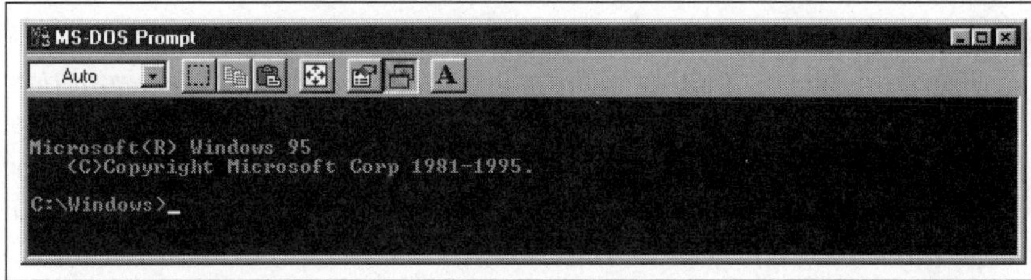

Figure B-1: The Command Prompt is used to complete some of the solutions in this book

To run programs in a DOS box, type the name of the program or command at the command line (also called the "C prompt" because it usually appears as **C:\>**) and press **Enter**.

MS-DOS Crash Course

You should know the following basic DOS commands to be able to complete the solutions in this book and get by in the world of Windows. The commands shown here are in uppercase, and any parameters (the information you supply to the command) are in lowercase, although it doesn't matter which case you use when you type them in DOS (DOS, like Windows, is not case-sensitive). If there is more than one parameter, each is separated by a space.

ATTRIB filename

Changes the attributes (also called properties) of a file. In Explorer, you can right-click on a file or group of files to change the attributes (R for *read only*, S for *system*, A for *archive*, and H for *hidden*); `ATTRIB` is the DOS counterpart to this functionality. In addition, `ATTRIB` lets you change the 'S' (system) attribute, something Explorer doesn't let you do. Here are some examples:

— `ATTRIB +H MYFILE.TXT` turns on the `H` parameter for the file *myfile.txt*, making the file hidden.

— `ATTRIB -R "ANOTHER FILE.DOC"` turns *off* the `R` (read-only) parameter for the file *another file.doc* (note that quotation marks are used because of the space in the filename).

— Type `ATTRIB /?` for additional options.

CD foldername

Changes the working directory to *foldername*. If the prompt indicates you are in *C:\Windows*, and you want to run a DOS program located in *C:\Files*, type `CD C:\FILES`. Type `CD` by itself to display the current directory.

COPY filename destination

Copies a file to another directory or drive, specified as *destination*. This is the same as dragging and dropping files in Explorer, except that the keyboard is used instead of the mouse. For example, to copy the file *myfile.txt* (located in the current working directory) to your floppy drive, type `COPY MYFILE.TXT A:\`. Type `COPY /?` for additional options.

DEL filename

Deletes a file. For example, to delete the file *myfile.txt*, type `DEL MYFILE.TXT`. This is not the same as deleting a file in Windows, as the file will *not* be stored in the Recycle Bin. The advantage of the DOS variant is that you can easily and quickly delete a group of files, such as all the files with the *.tmp* extension: `DEL *.TMP`. Type `DEL /?` for additional options.

DELTREE foldername

Deletes a directory and all of its contents, including all subdirectories. This, obviously, can be a dangerous command, so use it with caution. However, deleting a large number of files can often be done much faster with `DELTREE` than using Windows. Type `DELTREE /?` for additional options.

DIR name

Displays a listing of all the files and directories in the current working directory. Use `CD` to change to a different directory. Type `DIR C:\FILES` to display the contents of *C:\Files* without having to first use the CD command. Type `DIR /?` for additional options.

EDIT filename

Opens the DOS counterpart of Notepad, allowing you to edit a text file. It's especially useful if Windows isn't running. You may have to use `ATTRIB` first if the file is a hidden or system file.

EXIT

Closes the command prompt window. In most situations, you can just click the close button [X] at the upper-right corner of the Window, but the `EXIT` command is safer. If you've gotten to the command prompt by selecting **Restart the computer in MS-DOS mode**, typing `EXIT` will get you back into Windows. If Windows isn't running, the `EXIT` command will have no effect.

MD foldername

Make directory. This command creates a new directory with the name *foldername*. The command won't work if there's already a directory or file with the same name.

MOVE filename destination

The same as `COPY`, except that the file is moved instead of copied. Type `MOVE /?` for additional options.

RD foldername

Remove directory. This command removes an existing directory with the name *foldername*. The command won't work if the directory is not empty. To remove a directory and all of its contents, use `DELTREE`.

REN oldfilename newfilename

Renames a file to *newfilename*. This is especially useful since you can use the `REN` command to rename more than one file at once—something Explorer doesn't let you do. For example, to rename *myfile.txt* to *herfile.txt*, type `REN MYFILE.TXT HERFILE.TXT`. To change the extensions of all the files in the current working directory from *.TXT* to *.DOC*, type `REN *.TXT *.DOC`. Type `REN /?` for additional options.

For a more powerful Windows-based file renaming utility, get Power Rename, part of the *O'Reilly Utilities—Quick Solutions for Windows 98 Annoyances* (see Appendix F).

START name

Allows you to open a folder window and execute a Windows shortcut from the command prompt or from a DOS batch file. For example, `START C:\WINDOWS` opens the *c:\Windows* folder. `START` only works if Windows is running.

TYPE filename

Displays the contents of a text file. Type `TYPE filename | MORE` to display the file and pause between each page of information rather than displaying the whole file at once.

Using the Command Prompt in Windows

The following are a few tidbits that should help you accomplish nearly all command prompt tasks. Some familiarity with DOS is assumed, but not required. See Chapter 9 for information on writing DOS batch files, which allow you to automate DOS commands.

Using long filenames

- When using the `DIR` command in DOS, the names of files or folders in the current directory with long filenames will appear truncated. That is, a file with the name *My List of Things.TXT* will be appear as *MYLIST~1.TXT* in the left column. Look to the right to see the long filenames, or type `DIR /b` to view only the long filenames.
- If the name of a file or folder with a long filename does not contain a space, you should be able to type it normally. That is, you can type the name of an *.exe* file to run the program, and include the name of a document file after a command (such as `DEL`).
- Say, for example, you want to use the `CD` command to change the current working directory to *c:\Program Files*. If you type `CD Program Files`, it obviously won't work, since DOS will only look for a folder named *Program* (actually, CD will complain that you passed too many parameters). To get around this, you can either use the short version:

  ```
  CD PROGRA~1
  ```

  or enclose the folder name in quotation marks:

  ```
  CD "Program Files"
  ```

Run a shortcut from the command prompt

- While shortcuts linked to files, folders, applications, and other system objects can be opened from Windows, they aren't recognized by DOS. However, by using the `START` command-prompt utility, either from the DOS prompt or from a batch file, you can run any Windows shortcut. Note the use of quotation marks from the previous topic.

  Type the following:

  ```
  start "c:\directory\Shortcut to Some Program.lnk"
  ```

  where *c:\directory* is the full path containing the shortcut, and *Shortcut to Someprog.exe.lnk* is the filename of the shortcut. You can also open a folder window with the following:

  ```
  start "c:\Program Files\"
  ```

Notes and other issues

When using long filenames, if you're especially lazy, you can drop the closing quotation mark in most situations.

Using quotation marks to accommodate long filenames should work in most circumstances. If not, you can use the short version (with the ~1).

Turn the Address Bar into a Command Prompt

If you select **Run** from the Start Menu, you are given a limited command prompt; you can execute any program, open any folder, or launch any Internet URL simply by typing it here. Windows 98 also comes with the Address Bar, which was originally intended to extend Web Integration (see Chapter 8) to the desktop, but actually accomplishes the same thing as the **Run** command. The problem with both the **Run** command and the Address Bar is that they can only be used to launch programs; they don't understand intrinsic DOS commands, like `DIR` and `COPY`. However, there is a way to have the Address Bar mimic all the functions of the command prompt, and therefore have a true command prompt always within reach:

1. Start by making the Address Bar visible, if it's not already. Right-click on an empty area of your Taskbar, select **Toolbars** and then **Address Bar**. Your Taskbar will then contain the Address Bar, which is dockable, resizable, and removable: you can move it around the Taskbar, or even tear it off by dragging it. Your Taskbar will look something like Figure B-2.

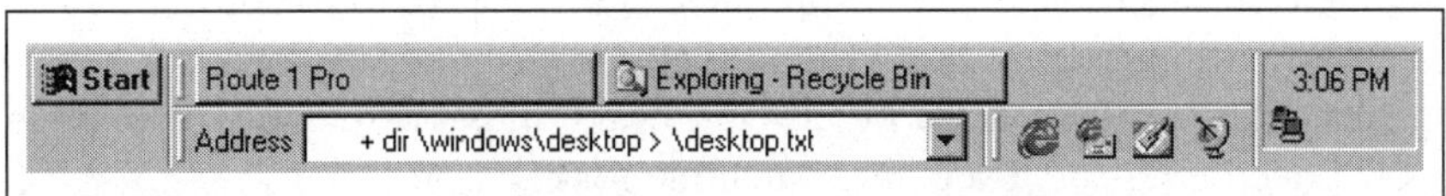

Figure B-2: The Address Bar can be put to good use as a handy Command Prompt. Also shown is the standard Quick Launch toolbar

   You'll immediately be able to run programs, open folders, and launch URLs simply by typing them and pressing **Enter**.

2. To add DOS command functionality, you'll need the assistance of a DOS batch file (see Chapter 9 for more information on batch files). Open a text editor, such as Notepad, and type the following:

```
@echo off
if "%1"=="" exit
if exist c:\windows\temp\temp.bat del c:\windows\temp\temp.bat
echo %1 %2 %3 %4 %5 %6 %7 %8 %9 > c:\windows\temp\temp.bat
call c:\windows\temp\temp.bat
if exist c:\windows\temp\temp.bat del c:\windows\temp\temp.bat
```

   (You may have to change the *c:\Windows\Temp* references according to the location of these folders on your computer.)

3. Save this file as *+.bat* (the plus sign, followed by *.bat*) in your *\Windows\Command* folder. See Chapter 9 for more information on DOS batch files.

4. Now, to run a DOS command from the Address Bar, simply precede it with a plus sign (+) and a single space, like this:

```
+ copy c:\bootlog.txt a:\
```

5. You can even have the output of a DOS command redirected to a file, as follows:

```
+ dir c:\windows > c:\windows\desktop
```

Notes and other issues

Here's how it works: the batch file reads what you've typed after the + and writes it to a new but temporary batch file. The new batch file is then executed, and the command you've typed is carried out. When it's finished, the temporary batch file is deleted (the file is also deleted at the beginning of *+.bat* if it exists).

The plus key on your keyboard's numeric keypad is usually more convenient than the one near your backspace key (Shift-=). However, you can certainly replace + with any other character, such as ` or -, as long as you rename the batch file accordingly.

To configure the default directory for all commands issued through *+.bat*, right-click on the file, select **Properties**, and select the **Program** tab. Enter the desired directory in the **Working** field—*\Windows\Desktop* is a convenient folder for this purpose. If you want multiple default directories, you'll need to create a separate batch file for each one.

To configure the window to close automatically when it's finished with the command, right-click on the *+.bat* file, select **Properties**, select the **Program** tab, and turn on the **Close on exit** option. If it closes automatically, you won't be able to see the output from commands like `DIR`—you might want to create two batch files, one that closes, and one that doesn't, depending on the command you issue.

There are some limitations to this design. While it does mimic the command prompt, it only allows a single command at a time, after which the context is forgotten. This means that commands like `CD` won't have much meaning—you can certainly type `+ cd directoryname`, but the "current directory" will be forgotten once the command has been executed. To get around this, include the full path with your commands—instead of the following series of statements:

```
d:
cd \myfolder
del *.tmp
```

just type this:

```
+ del d:\myfolder\*.tmp
```

Of course, if you find that you need to type several consecutive commands, you can always just type `command.com` in the Address Bar to launch a full-fledged command prompt window.

C

Contents of the MSDOS.SYS File

When you install Windows 98, a file called *MSDOS.SYS* is created in the root directory of your boot drive (usually *C:*). While this file was a system file in previous versions of MS-DOS (one of the binary files that composed the operating system), it's now a text file used to store various settings for Windows 98 initialization.

To edit this file, you need to first unhide it by typing the following command from the command prompt:

```
attrib -r -s -h c:\msdos.sys
```

You can then edit the file with a plain text editor, such as **Notepad**. The file layout is the same as for standard Windows initialization (**.ini*) files; see Chapter 4 for details.

The file consists of settings divided into two sections: **[Paths]**, which lists the locations for certain Windows files, and **[Options]**, which allows you to customize the boot process. Any settings not already found in your *MSDOS.SYS* file can be manually inserted.

The **[Paths]** section can contain the following settings:

HostWinBootDrv={Root of Boot Drive}

Default: C

Purpose: Specifies the drive letter of the boot drive. Usually "C," unless you have DriveSpace loaded.

WinBootDir={Windows Directory}

Default: Windows directory specified during Setup (usually *C:\Windows*)

Purpose: Specifies the location of the required startup files, usually located in the Windows directory.

WinDir={Windows Directory}

Default: Windows directory specified during Setup (should be the same as **WinBootDir**)

Purpose: Specifies the location of Windows.

The **[Options]** section can contain the following settings:

AutoScan={Number}

Default: 1

Purpose: Specifies whether Scandisk should be run automatically, after prompting, or not at all after improper shutdown (usually a crash). A setting of 0 means no scanning. A setting of 1 (the default) means prompt the user, but scan automatically if there is no response within 60 seconds. A setting of 2 means scan automatically without prompting.

BootDelay={Seconds}

Default: 2

Purpose: Specifies the amount of time to display the "Starting Windows" message before continuing to boot Windows.

BootFailSafe={Boolean}

Default: 0

Purpose: A setting of 1 forces your computer to boot in safe mode.

BootGUI={Boolean}

Default: 1

Purpose: A setting of 1 forces the loading of the graphical user interface (GUI), more commonly known as Windows. A setting of 0 (zero) will allow you to boot directly into MS-DOS (see Chapter 3 for more information).

BootKeys={Boolean}

Default: 1

Purpose: A setting of 1 allows you to use the function key to choose from the various boot options (see "Create a Startup Menu" in Chapter 6). A setting of 0 disables these function keys.

Note: A setting of BootKeys=0 overrides the BootDelay setting.

BootMenu={Boolean}

Default: 0

Purpose: A setting of 1 enables the startup menu (see "Create a Startup Menu" in Chapter 6). A setting of 0 means that you must press the **F8** key when "Starting Windows" appears to display the startup menu.

BootMenuDefault={Number}

Default: 1

Purpose: This setting is automatically set to 4 (safe mode) if your system hangs when trying to load Windows. Use this setting to set the default menu item—see "Create a Startup Menu" in Chapter 6 for all possible menu choices.

BootMenuDelay={Number}

Default: 30

Purpose: This setting is used to set the number of seconds your system will pause on the startup menu (see "Create a Startup Menu" in Chapter 6). If the number of seconds counts down to 0 without user intervention, the option specified in **BootMenuDefault** is activated.

BootMulti={Boolean}

Default: 0

Purpose: A setting of 0 disables the multi-boot option, meaning that you will not be allowed to boot your previous operating system even if your system is set up to do so. A setting of 1 allows you to boot your previous operating system with the **F4** and **F8** keys.

Note: This setting is set to 0 by default to avoid problems encountered by loading certain programs intended for earlier versions of MS-DOS.

BootWarn={Boolean}

Default: 1

Purpose: A setting of 0 disables the safe mode warning message at boot time as well as the startup menu (see "Create a Startup Menu" in Chapter 6).

BootWin={Boolean}

Default: 1

Purpose: A setting of 1 forces Windows to load at startup. A setting of 0 (zero) disables Windows as your default operating system, allowing you to load MS-DOS version 5.x or 6.

Note: Pressing **F4** during startup changes this setting temporarily only if **BootMulti**=1. (For example, pressing the **F4** key with a setting of 0 forces Windows to load.)

DisableLog={Boolean}

Default: 0

Purpose: A setting of 0 disables creation of the *bootlog.txt* file during startup.

DoubleBuffer={Boolean}

Default: 0

Purpose: A setting of 1 enables double-buffering for disk controllers that need it (for example, some older SCSI controllers). A setting of 2 forces double-buffering regardless of whether the controller needs it or not. A setting of 0 disables double-buffering. Don't change this setting unless your controller specifically requires it.

DBLSpace={Boolean}

Default: 1

Purpose: A setting of 1 allows the automatic loading of the *DBLSPACE.BIN* file if the DoubleSpace disk compression utility is in use. A setting of 0 prevents this program from loading, and may make any DoubleSpace drives inaccessible.

DRVSpace={Boolean}

Default: 1

Purpose: A setting of 1 allows the automatic loading of the *DRV-SPACE.BIN* file if the DriveSpace disk compression utility is in use. A setting of 0 prevents this program from loading, and may make any DriveSpace drives inaccessible.

LoadTop={Boolean}

Default: 1

Purpose: A setting of 0 (zero) prevents Windows from loading *COMMAND.COM* or *DRVSPACE.BIN/DBLSPACE.BIN* at the top of conventional memory (the first 640K). If you are having problems with software that may be making assumptions about the available memory, try setting this to 0; otherwise leave it alone.

Logo={Boolean}

Default: 1

Purpose: A setting of 1 forces the ugly Windows logo to appear while Windows is loading. A setting of 0 (zero) prevents the animated logo from being displayed, which can have the added benefit of avoiding incompatibilities with certain third-party memory managers. See Chapter 2 for information on customizing the Startup logo.

Network={Boolean}

Default: 0

Purpose: A setting of 1 means that network drivers have been installed, and that the "Start Windows, bypassing startup files, with network support" option should appear in the Windows startup menu (see "Create a Startup Menu" in Chapter 6).

WinVer={Number}

Default: 4.10.xxxx (This depends on your version of Windows.)

Purpose: This should automatically reflect the currently installed version of Windows.

The *Msdos.sys* file also contains a section that contains seemingly useless information. This information is necessary to support older programs that expect the *Msdos.sys* file to be at least 1024 bytes in length. For example, if an antivirus program detects that the *Msdos.sys* file is less than 1024 bytes, it may assume that the *Msdos.sys* file is infected with a virus. If you delete the *Msdos.sys* file, your computer will not start. The following statement, followed by a series of Xs, appears in the *Msdos.sys* file:

```
;The following lines are required for compatibility
;with other programs.
;Do not remove them (MSDOS.SYS needs to be >1024 bytes).
```

Since each line begins with a semicolon (;), the standard initialization file comment character, the lines are not read by the system.

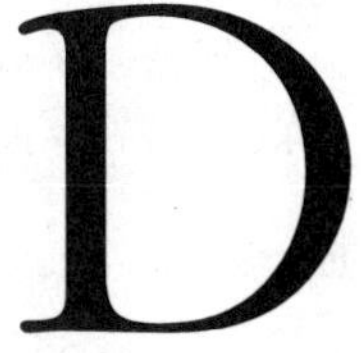

Class IDs of System Objects

Windows keeps track of its various components with Class IDs, 33-digit codes consisting of both letters and numbers, enclosed in curly braces {}. What follows is a list of the commonly used system objects and their corresponding Class IDs (sometimes called namespace IDs).

System Object	Class ID
ActiveX Cache Folder	{88C6C381-2E85-11d0-94DE-444553540000}
Briefcase	{85BBD920-42A0-1069-A2E4-08002B30309D}
Compressed Folder	{E88DCCE0-B7B3-11d1-A9F0-00AA0060FA31}
Control Panel	{21EC2020-3AEA-1069-A2DD-08002B30309D}
Desktop	{00021400-0000-0000-C000-000000000046}
Dial-Up Networking	{992CFFA0-F557-101A-88EC-00DD010CCC48}
Favorites	{1A9BA3A0-143A-11CF-8350-444553540000}
Fonts	{BD84B380-8CA2-1069-AB1D-08000948F534}
Internet Cache	{7BD29E00-76C1-11CF-9DD0-00A0C9034933}
Internet Explorer	{FBF23B42-E3F0-101B-8488-00AA003E56F8}
My Computer	{20D04FE0-3AEA-1069-A2D8-08002B30309D}
My Documents	{450D8FBA-AD25-11D0-98A8-0800361B1103}
Network Neighborhood	{208D2C60-3AEA-1069-A2D7-08002B30309D}
Printers	{2227A280-3AEA-1069-A2DE-08002B30309D}
Recycle Bin	{645FF040-5081-101B-9F08-00AA002F954E}
Scheduled Tasks	{D6277990-4C6A-11CF-8D87-00AA0060F5BF}
Subscriptions	{F5175861-2688-11d0-9C5E-00AA00A45957}
The Internet	{3DC7A020-0ACD-11CF-A9BB-00AA004AE837}

System Object	Class ID
The Microsoft Network	{00028B00-0000-0000-C000-000000000046}
URL History Folder	{FF393560-C2A7-11CF-BFF4-444553540000}

There are several ways to use Class IDs in Windows. They are as follows:

- Class IDs are stored in the Registry under `HKEY_CLASSES_ROOT\CLSID`. Locate the key named for a Class ID under this branch to change any settings or behavior of the corresponding object. Use the Registry Editor's search feature to find the Class ID for an object not listed here by searching for the name of the object.
- A good way to avoid having to type these codes is to do a search in the Registry. For example, if you're looking for the Recycle Bin Class ID, do a search in the Registry Editor for `Recycle Bin`. When it's found, make sure the code matches the one listed above (as there may be more than one). Right-click on the key named for the code, and select **Rename**. Then, right-click on the highlighted text in the rename field, and select **Copy**. The Class ID will then be placed on the clipboard, waiting to be copied anywhere you please.
- To create a copy of a virtual folder system object, such as **Dial-Up Networking**, create a new folder anywhere (on your Desktop, or somewhere in the file system), and call it *Dial-Up Networking.{992CFFA0-F557-101A-88EC-00DD010CCC48}*. Make sure to include the dot between the name and the Class ID. Replace the name and ID with any others from the table. Note that *all* objects listed above except for **Network Neighborhood** should be able to exist as movable folders. See "Make Control Panel Applets More Accessible" in Chapter 2 for more information.
- By placing references to Class IDs in other parts of the Registry, you can make Windows do cool tricks—see "Customize My Computer" in Chapter 4 for more information.

E

Interface Terminology and the Basics

In order to set a context for the solutions in this book, as well as provide a visual "glossary" of the basic building blocks of Windows, what follows is an examination of the Windows 98 interface, as well as some coverage of some basic concepts, such as *.zip* files, shortcuts, and mouse feedback. Many of the Windows 98 user interface elements are shown in Figure E-1.

Some of the most rudimentary interface components (also known as widgets or controls) can be the source of the most irritating aspects of Windows 98. Since nearly all applications, dialog boxes, and Windows components are made up of these components, a good understanding of their use and intended purpose is very helpful in diagnosing many problems.

The colors, fonts, and sizes of most of these interface elements can be changed to your liking by double-clicking on the **Display** icon in Control Panel and choosing the **Appearance** tab.

The Interface Experience

Title bar

The title bar is more than just window dressing. At any given time, only one window can be the active window, and the title bar is its most obvious visual indicator. That is, it's easy to tell where keyboard input will be directed, since, by default, the title bar of the "active" window is dark blue, while all others are gray. A notable exception is

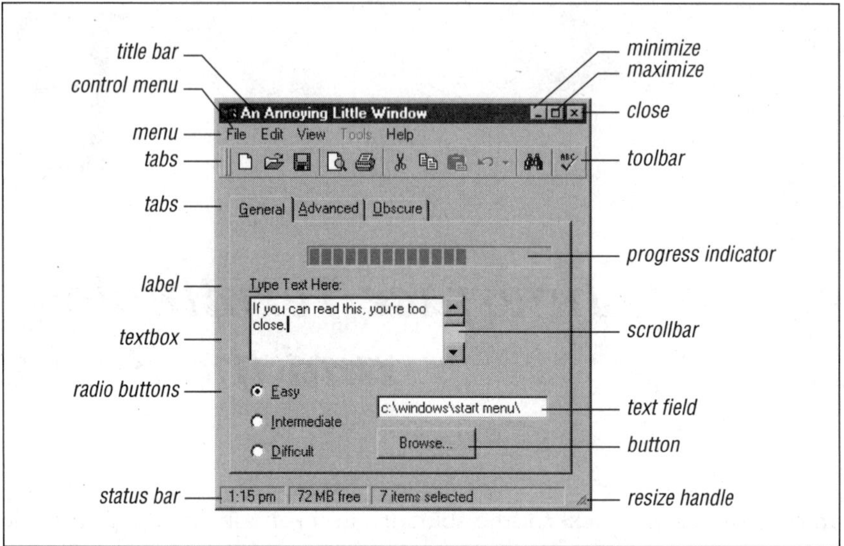

Figure E-1: This example dialog box doesn't actually exist in real life, but it contains nearly all of the building blocks of the Windows 98 interface

the little floating toolbars (discussed later in this list) that clutter most larger applications, but we'll just ignore those for the time being. One problem that many users encounter is that at some time the colors might have been changed inadvertently to make inactive and active title bars indistinguishable. If this is the case in your system, fix it by opening the display properties in Control Panel, and clicking the **Appearance** tab.

You can reposition any moveable window by dragging the title bar.

Shortcut: Double-click on the title bar of a resizable window to maximize it (see "Minimize, Maximize, and Close" later in this list).

Control menu

This is left over from the old days of Windows, before pointing devices like our beloved mice became ubiquitous. The control menu is simply a list of the basic window functions (Minimize, Maximize, Resize, Move, and Close) that is hidden behind a small icon in the upper-left corner of a window and is accessible with the keyboard. Occasionally, you can find other items in the control menu, such as extra settings or "about" screens. Of course, the designers think they are being clever by hiding things in there, but we know better.

If you see two control menus, one on top of the other, you're using an application such as a word processor that can have one or more document windows open inside of it. See the next item, "Minimize, Maximize, and Close," for more information.

Shortcuts: Press **Alt-Space** to display the control menu for the active window, and then press the key of any underlined letter to carry out that action (i.e., **C** for Close). If you choose **Move** or **Size**, you can then use the cursor keys to adjust the window position or size. You can also double-click on the icon to close a window.

Minimize, Maximize, and Close

These three tiny buttons are conveniently placed extremely close together in the top-right corner. The **Minimize** button hides a window without stopping the program; just click the corresponding button on the Taskbar to make it visible again. The **Maximize** button makes a window fill the entire screen, which is nice for word processors, but not so good for folder windows. Finally, the **Close** button—big surprise here—closes the window.

If you see two rows of these buttons, you're using an application such as a word processor that can have one or more document windows open inside of it. The top row of buttons applies to the application itself, while the lower row applies to the active document window. For example, press the lower **[X]** to close the document without exiting the program.

Shortcuts: Rather than risk hitting **Close** when you're trying to maximize, you can double-click on the title bar. A window can be closed by pressing **Alt-F4** as well. All three are also available in the control menu.

Resize handle

The resize handle is nothing special; it's just an easy place to grab the lower-right corner of a window with your mouse. You usually won't see it unless there's a status bar. Regardless of this little grip, you can resize a window by grabbing any side or corner of a resizable window (not all windows can be resized) and dragging.

Shortcut: Press **Alt-Space** and then **S** to resize a window with the cursor keys.

Menu

The menu is a nice, neat place to cram all the functionality of a program. Rather than littering your screen, all available commands are categorically arranged into cascading lists. Modern applications have become so elaborate, however, that menus are often very complex, which makes it a pain to sift through them all to find the command you want. So designers invented toolbars as shortcuts for the items we actually use. It makes you wonder why we need menus in the first place.

Anyway, if you ever get lost, menus tend to be pretty consistent across applications. For example, you can almost always find **Open**, **Save**, **Print**, and **Exit** in the **File** menu, just as **Cut**, **Copy**, **Paste**, and **Undo** are always in the **Edit** menu.

Figure E-1 shows a Tools menu that has been grayed out, meaning that it cannot be used until some other criteria are met. Gray menu items don't respond at all when clicked, and it is often not obvious what action must be taken in order to "un-gray" a menu item. If you're stuck, try to imagine in what context the menu item is used, and then try to put the application in the correct state for that menu item to be appropriate. For example, some menu items in your word processor will be grayed out when graphics are selected, or the spelling checker is open.

Shortcuts: Press **F10** or **Alt** (by itself) to enter the menu, then use the cursor keys to navigate, and press **Enter** to select an item. Once you're in the menus, press the underlined letter of a menu item to quickly jump to that item, or if no letter is underlined, press the first letter of the item's caption. You can also jump right to a specific menu from anywhere else in the application by pressing the key of the underlined letter while pressing **Alt**.

Toolbar

Toolbars vary from application to application, mostly because Microsoft has changed the standard look and feel of the toolbar four times since the release of Windows 95. However, they're not especially difficult to use, regardless of the style—just click a button to carry out the corresponding action. Some buttons are simply switches, such as **Bold** in a word processor; click it to turn it on, and click again to turn it off. There is no visual distinction between action buttons, switch buttons, and buttons that display more buttons, except that switch buttons usually look pushed in when they're turned on.

The toolbars in most modern applications are configurable; that is, you can rearrange the tools to your liking, add new items, and remove the ones you don't use. It's definitely worth it to take a few minutes with the applications you use and configure the toolbar with the features that you use most. You can usually right-click on a toolbar to display its configuration options, although every application does this a bit differently. Also, most toolbars are "dockable," meaning that they can be moved to a different location by dragging an empty portion of the toolbar. If they are dragged near a window edge, they're automatically docked and become part of the window at that location rather than floating above it. At one time or another, you've probably been annoyed by a toolbar that was moved accidentally when you tried to simply press a button; at present, there's no way of disabling a toolbar's mobility or dockability.

Shortcuts: Toolbars are almost never usable with the keyboard, although the individual tools may have keyboard shortcuts; for example, **Ctrl-S** is oven used for Save, and **Ctrl-B** is often used to turn Bold on or off.

Status bar

The status bar is an often overlooked display of pertinent information. The standard status bar shown has several sections, each of which shows a relevant statistic or setting. Some elements of the status bar respond to clicks and double-clicks, although there's no standard for any user interaction. If an application has a status bar, it can usually be hidden or made visible by an entry in the **View** menu. Some programs even let you configure the status bar with the information that is important to you; try right-clicking on the status bar for configuration options.

Shortcut: None.

Tabs

Tabbed dialog boxes like the ones in Figure E-1 are a commonly used cop-out, implemented to subdivide the available options in a program when there are too many to fit in a single window. By far the worst implementation of tabbed dialogs is found in the Microsoft Office suite of applications, which use multiple rows of tabs. You can activate a tab by clicking on it; the active tab (or page) is visibly more prominent than the rest. Usually, all settings in the various tabbed pages apply to the same thing, and moving from one tab to another doesn't discard any settings.

Shortcuts: Press **Ctrl-Tab** to move to the next tabbed page, or **Shift-Ctrl-Tab** to move in reverse.

Label

This is a piece of text used to describe a control (in the case of Figure E-1, the text box) that doesn't have a place for a description. Clicking labels usually has no effect.

Shortcut: The important thing to note about labels is that they often contain a single underlined letter; holding **Alt** and pressing the key for that letter will send the focus to the next control. This is useful, since the textbox in Figure E-1, for example, doesn't have a shortcut key of its own.

Textbox

Essentially a mini word processor, the textbox is used for—surprise!—entering text. It's functionally the same as the text field, except that it allows multiple lines of text, and usually wraps text that flows past the width of the control. You can usually right-click in a textbox to display a quick menu for **Cut**, **Copy**, **Paste**, and **Undo**.

Shortcuts: Press the **Tab** key to move to the next control, or **Shift-Tab** to go in reverse. If you actually want to type a tab at this point, try pressing **Ctrl-Tab** or just insert five spaces. If pressing the **Enter** key moves to the next control, try pressing **Ctrl-Enter** to insert a new line in the textbox. Press **Ctrl-X** for Cut, **Ctrl-C** for Copy, **Ctrl-V** for Paste, and **Ctrl-Z** for Undo.

Radio buttons

They're called radio buttons because 25 years ago, most automobile radios used large buttons to jump to different radio stations, and these controls work in kind of the same way. In a single group of radio buttons, only one can be "lit"—click one, and the others go off.

Shortcuts: The radio button with the focus, indicated by a thin, dotted rectangle around the text, will always be the one that is selected. To choose a different radio button, use the cursor keys, as pressing Tab will move to the next group of radio buttons or the next control.

Progress indicator

The progress indicator is a gauge that graphically shows the completion of a particular task. The annoying part is that programmers are often not diligent enough to ensure that the progress indicator is accurate. For example, the Add New Hardware dialog in Control Panel shows a completion of about 95% in the first 20 to 30 seconds. The remaining 5% might take another two minutes, meaning that the indicator is not at all useful in helping you determine how long you have to wait before it's done. My advice: go outside and take a walk, and it should be finished when you get back.

Shortcut: None.

Scroll bar

Before computers, "scroll" was not a verb. We use the scroll bar not only to set the position of something (in this case, the text cursor in this textbox), but to give us visual feedback of where we are, and how much stuff there is that we can't see. The little box called the *thumb* shows us where we are in the entire piece of text, and the size of the thumb shows us what percentage we're viewing: a large thumb means that most of what's there is visible, and a small thumb means that there's a lot we can't see. The scroll bar usually becomes disabled (grayed out) if there's no scrolling to be done.

Click the up or down arrows to move the scroll bar incrementally, or drag the thumb with the mouse to move to the desired position. You can also click in the gray areas between the arrows and the thumb to move up or down a page at a time.

Shortcut: If the scroll bar is part of another control, such as the textbox shown in Figure E-1, then it cannot receive keyboard input. However, if the scroll bar stands alone, you can use the cursor keys and **PgUp**/**PgDn** keys to adjust it. The thumb blinks if it has the focus.

Text field

This is the same as the textbox, but accepts only a single line of text. In this context, it is used in conjunction with the **Browse** button.

Shortcut: See "Textbox," earlier in this list.

Button

Just click a button to make it do what it's supposed to. In Figure E-1, the **Browse** button is used to display a file dialog box. When you choose a file and click **OK**, the name and location (path) of the file are automatically entered into the text field. This synergy of controls is common, and saves typing, which prevents typos. Some applications place a small folder icon next to a text field rather than the full-sized text field, but the usage is the same.

Shortcut: If the button has the focus, indicated by a thin, dotted line surrounding the caption of the button, press the space bar to activate it. In dialogs with more than one button, one button (usually the **OK** button) often has a thicker border than the rest—this is the default button, and can be activated by pressing **Enter**, regardless of which control has the focus. Similarly, there is usually a **Cancel** button that responds to the **ESC** key, but has no visual distinction. If in doubt, use **Tab** to cycle through the buttons, and then press the space bar.

The Shell: Basics of Explorer

Desktop

The desktop is the basis for the modern graphical user interface (GUI) paradigm. Figure E-2 shows a portion of the Windows 98 desktop. The desktop is considered a container for all other resources on your computer, as well as a backdrop for your Windows workspace. The

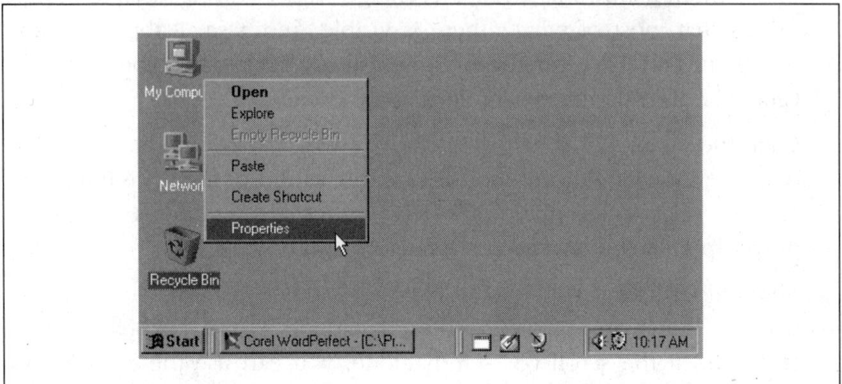

Figure E-2: A Windows context menu in its natural habitat; available by right-clicking on an icon on the desktop

desktop is always underneath any open windows—to access the desktop if it's covered, you need to minimize or close any open windows (right-click on the Taskbar and select **Minimize All Windows** to accomplish this quickly).

The desktop contains two types of icons; namespace icons and file icons. File icons can be files or folders that are actually located in the *\Windows\Desktop* directory on your hard disk. You can drag-drop them to and from the desktop as though they were ordinary folders. The desktop is a good place to store newly downloaded files from the Internet, email attachments, stuff from floppies, and other files you're currently working on.

Namespace icons, on the other hand, such as My Computer, Network Neighborhood, and the Recycle Bin, aren't files, but rather specific resources built into Windows. All of these icons can be renamed or even hidden, although the process isn't always obvious; see Chapters 2 and 4 and Appendix D for more information.

As with most other components of the Windows interface, the desktop has properties that you can customize. Right-click on an empty portion of the desktop and click **Properties** to change the wallpaper, color, screen saver, and settings for the display (this is also accessible by double-clicking on the **Display** icon in Control Panel).

Shortcut: Press **Ctrl-ESC** to show the Start Menu, then press **ESC**, **Tab**, and **Tab** again. Once the desktop has the focus, you can use the cursor keys to navigate. See the discussion of Explorer windows for keystrokes used with icons. Note that if you want to access the desktop with the keyboard—or even with the mouse—it's usually easier to open an Explorer window, and move to the top of the tree by pressing the **Home** key.

My Computer

Double-clicking the **My Computer** desktop icon opens a folder with icons for all of the drives on your computer, including all floppies, hard disks, CD-ROM drives, and removables, as well as the Control Panel folder, Dial-Up Networking, Printers, and Scheduled Tasks. While you can't drag anything into the My Computer window, you can drag items from My Computer to other locations to make shortcuts to those items. See Chapter 4 for methods for adding items to My Computer, as well as removing and customizing the desktop icon.

Right-click on the **My Computer** icon and select **Properties** for quick access to the System Properties dialog (also accessible through Control Panel), which contains, among other things, Device Manager.

Shortcut: None, directly. However, you can follow the shortcut for the desktop, move the focus to the **My Computer** icon, and press **Enter**. Or, press **Alt-Enter** to access its properties. It's usually easier just to open Explorer, and locate **My Computer** on the tree.

Network Neighborhood

The Network Neighborhood icon is displayed on your desktop if you have any network drivers loaded, including those for Dial-Up Networking and the Direct Cable Connection. The Network Neighborhood contains all of the shared resources for any other computers to which you're connected over a network. For example, if another computer on your network is configured to share its hard drive and printer, you'll have access to that hard drive through the Network Neighborhood icon, accessible as though it were another hard disk on your computer. As long as the icon is visible on the desktop, the Network Neighborhood is also accessible through the Explorer window. If the only networking you do is using Dial-Up Networking to connect to the Internet, the Network Neighborhood icon is of no use to you. See Chapter 4 for details on removing this icon, and Chapter 7 for more information on networking.

Right-click on the **Network Neighborhood** icon and select **Properties** for quick access to the Network Properties window (also accessible through Control Panel), which allows you to add, remove, and configure the various network drivers and protocols that are installed.

Shortcut: None, directly. However, you can follow the shortcut for the desktop, move the focus to the **Network Neighborhood** icon, and press **Enter**. Or, press **Alt-Enter** to access its properties. It's usually easier just to open Explorer, and locate Network Neighborhood on the tree.

Recycle Bin

The Recycle Bin is a trashcan for your data, which can be configured to either delete files and folders immediately, or can serve as a temporary holding place for files and folders until you finalize your decision to throw them out. Double-click on the **Recycle Bin** icon to view a list of recently deleted files—any files shown here haven't actually been erased yet, and are still taking up disk space. Right-click on the **Recycle Bin** icon and select **Empty Recycle Bin** to permanently erase all files in the Recycle Bin. If you open it up, you'll be able to selectively erase files by right-clicking on them and selecting **Delete**, or restore files to their original locations by selecting **Restore**.

While you can send a file or folder to the Recycle Bin by drag-drop, you can also right-click on an item and select **Delete**, or highlight a file and hit the **Del** key. Right-click on the **Recycle Bin** and select **Properties** to choose whether deleted files are actually deleted on the spot, or stored in the Recycle Bin. Regardless of whether you delete a file in Explorer with the keyboard, by using menus, or with drag-drop, the file obeys the Recycle Bin setting. That is, items are either *always* deleted right away, or *always* stored in the bin, regardless of the method.

Shortcut: None, directly. However, you can follow the shortcut for the desktop, move the focus to the **Recycle Bin** icon, and press **Enter**. Or, press **Alt-Enter** to access its properties. It's usually easier just to open Explorer, and locate Recycle Bin on the tree.

Context Menu

In Figure E-2, I've right-clicked on the Recycle Bin icon to display its context menu, which is simply a list of all the things I can do at that point with that item. The idea is that the options available for any given object in Windows depend upon the *context*, or the set of circumstances under which you're operating. The **Empty Recycle Bin** option is shown here, since it is relevant to the context of the Recycle Bin; since the Recycle Bin is currently empty here, the option is grayed out (disabled). Nearly all objects in Windows have their own context menus, almost always accessible with the right mouse button. See Chapter 4 for details on customizing the context menus for your files, folders, and certain desktop items.

Shortcut: When a file or other object is selected, press **Shift-F10** to display the context menu. If you have a special Windows keyboard, there is a special key for this purpose, usually located to the right of the space bar. The most frequently used item in most context menus is **Properties**, which can be accessed more quickly by pressing **Alt-Enter**. Other shortcuts for context menu items include **Del**, **F2**, **Ctrl-X**, **Ctrl-C**, and **Ctrl-V** for Delete, Rename, Cut, Copy, and Paste, respectively.

Taskbar

The Taskbar contains the **Start Menu** button, all minimized applications, the quick launch toolbar, and the tray (all described later in this list). You can make the Taskbar larger or smaller by grabbing the edge closest to the center of the screen with the mouse and dragging. The Taskbar can be moved to any of the four sides of your screen by clicking down on an empty portion of the Taskbar and dragging. Right-click on an empty area of the Taskbar and click **Properties** to configure certain aspects, such as the **Auto-hide** feature (where the Taskbar moves off-screen when it's not being used) and whether or not other windows can be displayed on top of the Taskbar. See Chapter 4 for details on getting rid of the obnoxious "Click here to begin" animation displayed on the Taskbar every time you start Windows.

Shortcut: None, since the Taskbar can't have the focus directly. See "Start Menu" and "Minimized application (running task)," later in this list, for specific shortcuts for those items.

Start Menu

The Start Menu is a user interface design disaster. All of the most frequently used features in Windows are hidden under this tiny, unsuspecting button on the Taskbar, including **Shut Down**, **Help**, **Find**, **Settings**, and icons for most of your installed programs. Just click the **Start** button to access the Start Menu, and then carefully move the mouse to choose the item you want, being careful not to let your hand stray more than a tenth of an inch, or else the menu you want might disappear from sight. See "What to Do if You Hate the Start Menu" in Chapter 2 for alternatives.

While you aren't allowed to configure most of the intrinsic items in the Start Menu (see Chapter 4 for exceptions and devious workarounds), you can configure items in the upper region of the Start Menu (above **Programs**), as well as items inside the **Programs** submenu. Just like the desktop, the Start Menu is actually a folder on your hard disk, located in *\Windows\Start Menu*. Any items added, removed, or changed in the *Start Menu* folder will show up in the actual Start Menu. To quickly access the *Start Menu* folder, right-click on the **Start** button, and select **Open** or **Explore** to see the folder or tree view, respectively. The easiest way to add an item to the Start Menu is to drag an *.exe* file (usually the main executable from an application) directly into the *\Windows\Start Menu\Programs* folder, or a subfolder thereof, which will create a shortcut to the program.

New in Windows 98 is the capability of adding, removing, or rearranging Start Menu items by simply dragging them right into and out of the menu itself. This may not be immediately evident, as it requires that you hold the mouse button down for a few seconds from time to time. Here's an example: Start by dragging an item from Explorer or the desktop onto the **Start Menu** button, and hold it there for about two seconds. The Start Menu will open automatically, at which time you must continue to hold the item being dragged until you find a place to put it. Move the cursor to the top of the Start Menu or into the **Programs** submenu, continuing to hold the mouse button down. A black dividing line will appear where the new item will be inserted; when you're ready, let go, and it will be inserted accordingly. You can similarly rearrange existing Start Menu items, and even drag them directly into the **Recycle Bin** icon (if it's not covered). Figure E-3 shows an item being added to the **Programs** submenu.

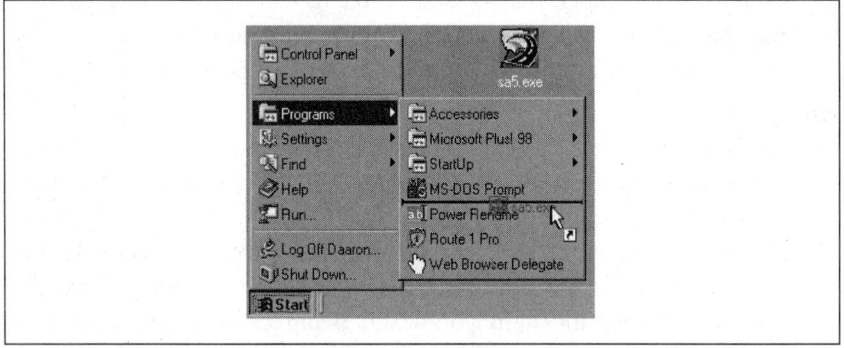

Figure E-3: Windows 98 allows you to add, remove, and rearrange items in the Start Menu without having to use a wizard or open Explorer

By default, dragging any files or other objects directly into the Start Menu as shown in Figure E-3 will create shortcuts to those items, which is inconsistent with the way that Windows handles drag-drop elsewhere (outside of the Start Menu, only dragging *.exe* files and system objects creates shortcuts). If you're dragging an existing shortcut or a folder full of shortcuts into the Start Menu, hold the **Shift** key to force Windows to move (or the **Ctrl** key to copy) the items, rather than create shortcuts to them.

One of the annoyances regarding the drag-drop of Start Menu items is that their ordering is stored in the Registry (see Chapter 3). If you rename a Start Menu item, it will be moved to the end of the list; you'll have to manually drag it to alphabetize the menu. To reset the ordering of any Start Menu folder, move all of its contents to another folder temporarily; then, move them all back. They'll be alphabetized, at least until you add something new.

Something else which can be very frustrating about this feature is that there's no way to turn it off; it's easy to unintentionally rearrange items in the Start Menu. Furthermore, the **ESC** key doesn't cancel a drag in progress here like it does everywhere else in Explorer. The only way to cancel a drag operation like this once it has begun is to drop the item onto one of the "intrinsic" Start Menu items, such as **Run** or **Shut Down**. When your cursor changes to a circle with a line through it, release the mouse button.

See Chapter 2 for more information on dragging and dropping files, and to learn why dragging *.exe* files to create shortcuts is such an awful design, even though it happens to be convenient here. Also in Chapter 2 is a way of making items in Control Panel more accessible through the Start Menu.

The other common annoyance with the Start Menu in Windows 98 is what happens when a particular menu gets too big for the screen. In Windows 95, the menu simply expanded to multiple columns, which was confusing and awkward to use. This has been changed in Windows 98, although not improved. Now, if a menu is too big for the screen, tiny arrows appear at the bottom and top of the menu, allowing you to scroll up or down. There's no scrollbar in sight, so this won't be immediately evident; additionally, the lack of a scrollbar forces you to hold down the mouse button to wait for the menu items to slowly scroll and become visible. Unfortunately, there's no way to prevent this from happening, short of rearranging your Start Menu items so that no menu is too large for the screen.

Shortcut: Press **Ctrl-ESC** to show the Start Menu, regardless of what program you're in. Once you're in the Start Menu, you can navigate with the cursor keys, and select an item by pressing **Enter**. Press the underlined letter of a menu item to quickly jump to that item, or if no letter is underlined, press the first letter of the item's caption.

Minimized application (running task)

You can keep tabs on all running applications by looking in this portion of the Taskbar. Nearly every currently open window is represented by a button on your Taskbar. Click the button of a corresponding window to bring that window to the top (if it happens to be obscured) and shift focus to that window. The currently active window appears pushed in, while any others appear as normal buttons. If a window has been minimized, it will also appear as a normal button, indistinguishable from those for visible windows. Press the button of a minimized window to restore it to its visible state.

You can right-click on a Taskbar button to access the window's control menu, allowing you, among other things, to close a window without restoring it.

Shortcut: Press **Ctrl-ESC** to show the Start Menu, then **ESC**, and then **Tab** to send focus to the application buttons. Use the cursor keys to navigate, and press the space bar to activate a window or **Shift-F10** to display its control menu. It's usually preferable to simply use **Alt-Tab** (or **Shift-Alt-Tab** to go in reverse) to cycle through the open windows rather than dealing with the Taskbar. While we're at it, press **Alt-ESC** to send a window to the bottom of the pile.

Quick Launch Toolbar

As a result of many users' dissatisfaction with the Start Menu, Windows 98 now comes with configurable, "dockable" toolbars. They're configurable, in that you can drag-drop program icons and other shortcuts directly onto or off these toolbars. By placing icons for your most frequently used applications, folders, and documents directly on the Taskbar, you can make it easier and quicker to open the tasks you need.

To display one of the preconfigured toolbars, right-click on an empty area of the Taskbar, select **Toolbar**, and choose the one you want. In addition to the **Address** and **Links** toolbars from Internet Explorer, there's a **Desktop** toolbar that mirrors the contents of your desktop, and the customizable **Quick Launch** bar—or you can select **New Toolbar** to make a new one.

While the Address Bar is intended for launching Internet URLs, it's really just a simpler version of the **Run** command in the Start Menu; for quick launches, type program filenames, such as *telnet*, *command.com* (for the DOS prompt), and *notepad*. See Appendix C for another use of the Address Bar.

Icons on the customizable toolbars, as on the Start Menu, are shortcuts on your hard disk located in subfolders of the *\Windows\Application Data\Microsoft\Internet Explorer* folder. You can drag items into these folders as well as directly onto the toolbars to add them. Note that right-clicking on toolbar icons allows you to open them, change their properties, and even delete them, as though you were right-clicking on the actual shortcuts in Explorer.

Take a look at the discussion of toolbars earlier in this list, as well as "What to Do if You Hate the Start Menu" in Chapter 2 for more information.

Shortcut: None.

Tray

The tray is the small area at the far-right or bottom of the Taskbar that by default holds the clock and the tiny, yellow speaker icon. With the exception of the clock, the tray holds icons placed there by Windows and other running applications. Hold the mouse cursor over the clock to see the date temporarily (sorry, you can't get a permanent date without a third-party utility—see Appendix F), or right-click on an empty area of the Taskbar and click **Properties** to turn the clock on or off. There's no way to turn the tray off entirely, but most icons can be removed individually.

Shortcut: None

Tray Icon

The tray can be a convenient place for applications to display information and for quick access to certain features, but the problem is that Microsoft never bothered to create a standard for tray icons. Some icons are clicked, others double-clicked, while others require a right-click, and some don't get clicked at all. Some flash, some don't, Most icons can be disabled, but some just won't go away. See Chapter 2 and Appendix A for more information on clearing the clutter in the tray.

Shortcut: None

Getting up to Speed

To ensure that you can follow most of the material in this book, there are some additional basic concepts you'll need to know. At the very least, keep this section in mind if you encounter a concept that doesn't quite make sense.

First-time users

If you've never used a Windows PC before, probably the first thing you should do is start Solitaire—yes, the card game. It's fun, easy, and perfect for training you on the basic mouse functions, including clicking, dragging and dropping, and double-clicking. Besides, it's a good way to kill time while you're on the phone with Microsoft technical support.

Files and folders

Your hard drive contains hundreds, perhaps thousands, of files. Your files make up your programs and hold your documents, letters, and spreadsheets. Files are organized into folders, sometimes called directories, and these files and folders live together in peace on your hard drive. Folders can contain files as well other folders. In Windows 98, you can give your files long filenames. This probably means nothing to you, unless you're used to DOS or Windows 3.x, and were forced to name your letter to your mom something like *LTR2MOM.DOC*. Get used to giving files names like *A letter to my mom where I finally gain my independence.doc* from now on. See "Transition to Windows 98" in Chapter 1 for more information.

Objects

The word *object* by itself is essentially meaningless, but in the context of an operating system interface, an object is something that you can expect to behave in predictable ways. In Windows 98, for example, the icons on your screen are objects, whether they represent files, folders, drives, printers, or network connections. You can double-click on any of them to open them, or right-click on them to see what else they'll do. All objects behave similarly in response to your actions, and share many of the same properties. Most of them have a **Properties** entry in the context menu; learn to use this menu, because most of the good stuff is in there. See "Customize Context Menus" in Chapter 4 for more information.

Mouse cursors

Your mouse cursor tells you what's happening. Look closely at your mouse cursor while you're moving it around; it's not always a plain, white arrow. For example, when you're dragging a file, Windows gives you a clue as to what's going to happen when you drop it depending on where you're dragging it and what's currently underneath the cursor.

Help is near

Pressing the **F1** key in most situations will either display detailed instructions of an application or a brief description of the currently selected control, depending on how well the application's help system has been designed. If you open help with a menu item or a button labeled **Help**, you'll have access to the search feature, too, allowing you to find desired information by typing in a keyword.

Shortcuts

A shortcut is a little file that lets you open a program without having to find the actual program on your hard disk. You can make a shortcut for any program, document, drive, or folder by dragging and dropping the icon onto the desktop or onto any folder with the right mouse button. See the discussion of the Start Menu in the previous section for a common use for shortcuts, or see "Move or Copy Files at Will" in Chapter 2 for more details on controlling drag-drop.

Drivers

A driver is a software program that's used to help your computer work with a particular piece of hardware, such as a sound card or scanner. Many problems and errors in Windows are caused by buggy or outdated drivers. If you're having trouble, make sure you contact the manufacturer to see if they have any newer drivers for your hardware. See Chapter 6 for more information.

.zip files

Occasionally, one of the solutions in this book requires you to obtain and install software from the Internet. More often than not, this software is squeezed into a *.zip* file. A single *.zip* file can contain an entire directory of files, while only occupying a fraction of the disk space. This definitely helps to reduce download time, but you'll need to obtain the program used to deal with such files. You'll need a program like WinZip (32-bit) for Windows or PKZIP for DOS (Version 2.04g or later) to create *.zip* files as well as to extract the files stored as *.zip* files. See Appendix F for more information on downloading files from the Internet, as well as obtaining Zip utilities.

Regular maintenance

Windows 98 comes with several maintenance utilities, the two most useful of which are Scandisk and Disk Defragmenter. Scandisk is used to find and correct many types of errors on your hard disk, and Disk Defragmenter is used to optimize your files (rearrange them so they aren't scattered in pieces). Using each of these on a regular basis (such as once a week) will not only improve performance, but will reduce the likelihood of a disk crash or other loss of important stuff. See Chapter 6 for more information.

The Registry

The Registry is a central database containing all of the settings for Windows and most of the applications you run. Many of the solutions in this book require a basic working knowledge of the Registry and the Registry Editor. Chapter 3 covers the Registry in detail, and includes several solutions and examples to get you up to speed.

Plug-and-Play

Plug-and-Play is a catch phrase describing a particular design that allows Windows to automatically detect and configure the hardware installed inside and attached outside your computer. For example, if you plug a CD-ROM drive into a system with Windows 98 installed, the drive will automatically show up in *My Computer* (the folder providing access to all your drives) when the machine is powered up. If you've ever tried to install a CD-ROM drive onto a system running DOS and Windows 3.x, you understand what how helpful this is. However, Plug-and-Play isn't all peaches and cream. See Chapter 6 for troubleshooting information relating to the advantages and pitfalls of Plug-and-Play.

Keyboard Shortcuts

Keyboard shortcuts can enable you to complete many simple tasks far more quickly and comfortably than if you switch repeatedly between the keyboard and mouse. The following keyboard shortcuts work in nearly all circumstances in Windows 98.

General keystrokes

- Press **F1** at almost any time to get help. If you're lucky, and not using a Microsoft application, you may actually get a useful help screen at this point, rather than a little yellow post-it.
- It's usually much faster to use the keyboard equivalents of **Undo**, **Cut**, **Copy**, and **Paste** than to use menus or toolbars. Hold **Ctrl** while pressing **Z**, **X**, **C**, and **V**, respectively. In most circumstances, the following older keystrokes will also work: **Alt-Backspace**, **Shift-Del**, **Ctrl-Ins**, and **Shift-Ins**, respectively.

Files and folders

- In Explorer, use the **Tab** key to go back and forth between the tree pane and the file pane.
- In Explorer (as well as the Registry Editor) use the left and right arrow keys while the tree has the focus to expand or contract any branches you wish. Press * (the asterisk key) to expand all of the branches (you won't want to do this in the Registry Editor, though) under the currently highlighted folder. If you press * while viewing the desktop in Explorer, all directories in all drives will be expanded.
- In Explorer, use the **Backspace** key to go to the parent folder (go up one level). This works in file dialog boxes, folder windows, and the

Registry Editor, as well as in most other Windows hierarchical structures.

- To display an object's context (right-click) menu with the keyboard, highlight the file, folder, or other item, and press **Shift-F10**.
- When you're in a file dialog (for example, when opening or saving a file), press **F4** to shift the focus to and open the drive and directory drop-down listbox at the top of the window.

Managing windows and applications

- Switch between running applications without minimizing applications and bothering with the Taskbar. Press **Tab** repeatedly while holding the **Alt** key. Hold the **Shift** key along with **Alt** to go in reverse.
- Send the active window to the bottom of the pile by pressing **Alt-Esc**. This is similar to **Alt-Tab**, above, except that pressing **Alt-Tab**, letting go, and pressing **Alt-Tab** again, will cycle between the two most recently used windows. Pressing **Alt-ESC** repeatedly will cycle through the entire pile of Windows.
- To switch between open documents within a single application (such as in Excel), press **Ctrl-Tab**. If an application such as Word or most other word processors decides to interpret this keystroke differently, you can use **Ctrl-F6** to accomplish the same thing. Hold the **Shift** key along with **Ctrl** to go in reverse.
- Press **Alt-F4** to close the current application window, or **Ctrl-F4** to close the active document window without closing the entire application.
- In a tabbed dialog (such as Display Properties in Control Panel), move to the next tab by pressing **Ctrl-Tab**. Hold the **Shift** key to go in reverse.
- When entering data in a window with multiple fields (small textboxes), you can move quickly from field to field by pressing **Tab**. Hold the **Shift** key to go in reverse. This also moves between other controls, such as buttons (not toolbars, though), checkboxes, and listboxes.
- Go to an application's menu without opening any specific menu by pressing **F10** or the **Alt** key by itself. Use the cursor keys to navigate, and press **Enter** to make a selection.
- Open the Start Menu from any application by pressing **Ctrl-ESC**, or by using the Windows logo key (near the space bar) on some newer keyboards.

- If you're used to switching to the Taskbar or desktop with keystrokes in Windows 95, you'll be disappointed to find that Microsoft has prevented this action in Windows 98. However, there's another way to get to the desktop: press the **D** key while holding the Windows logo key to immediately minimize all open windows, which in turn, sends the focus to the desktop. There's no longer a way to get to the Taskbar buttons with the keyboard, although with **Alt-Tab** and **Ctrl-ESC**, this isn't really necessary.
- To display the control menu (the little box in the upper-left of most windows) for the active window, press **Alt-Space**. You can then use the cursor keys to move, resize, minimize, maximize, or close the window.
- Switch easily between a full-screen and windowed DOS prompt by pressing **Alt-Enter** at any time. This only works if Windows is running.
- Lastly, press **Ctrl-Alt-Del** at any time to display the **Close Program** box, which allows you to end a program that has stopped responding. If the whole system appears to be crashing, press **Ctrl-Alt-Del** to restart Windows.

F

Software to Solve Annoyances

Wherever possible throughout *Windows 98 Annoyances*, solutions to problems are offered that can be implemented without obtaining a third-party program or purchasing any other products. However, in some cases, a third-party software solution is either preferable or the only recourse. Consequently, various software utilities, patches, and add-ons are mentioned throughout the book as offering solutions to various problems.

All of the software utilities, patches, and add-ons mentioned in *Windows 98 Annoyances* are available on the Internet, but including a separate address for each piece of software would be silly. Instead, point your web browser to this address:

http://www.annoyances.org/

In addition to links for the downloadable software, you'll find updates and additional information for this book, related web sites and articles, and recent news.

So, What's on the CD?

We decided to put something useful on the CD that comes with this book instead of including a bunch of *shovelware*.* First, you'll find copies of all the code examples from the book, such as the registry patches in Chapter

* It's common practice these days to sell CDs with hundreds of megabytes of unsorted, untested freeware and shareware "shoveled" onto it. Since all this stuff is available for free on the Internet, where it is constantly updated and improved, we figured the best solution was to simply provide links on the *Windows 98 Annoyances* web site.

3 and the various VBScript functions in Chapter 9, in the *\Book Examples* folder.

Also, you'll find an evaluation copy of *O'Reilly Utilities—Quick Solutions for Windows 98 Annoyances*, a software product developed to complement this book. The software provides an automated way of implementing many of the fixes mentioned in this book, and goes beyond that to give you many useful add-ons to customize Windows 98. The software includes point-and-click features that perform many functions, including the following:

- Ensure the fastest possible switching between applications by optimizing the Windows virtual memory settings.
- Improve your productivity with dozens of Windows extensions that make common tasks easier, such as group file renaming, file copying, and customizing the desktop.
- Easily turn off features in the product if you decide not to keep changes you've made to your Windows configuration.

The enclosed evaluation software is a trial version of the software. When you install the trial software, it will record and save your current Windows registry settings. During the 30-day evaluation period, any changes you make to Windows 98 using this software will be implemented and your new settings will be saved. At the end of the evaluation period, your original Windows 98 settings will be restored.

If you decide to purchase the software during or after the trial period, simply install the licensed version of the software you receive over the trial version and it will restore the customized settings you created with the trial version.

Instructions for purchasing the software can be found in the back of this book. As an owner of *Windows 98 Annoyances*, you get a $10.00 discount on *O'Reilly Utilities—Quick Solutions for Windows 98 Annoyances*.

Index

Symbols, Numbers

A

B

D

E

F

G

H

I

J

K

L

Q

R

S

T

X

Y

Z

About the Author

David A. Karp, a graduate from the University of California at Berkeley in mechanical engineering, is a specialist in user-interface design and software engineering. He currently consults on Internet technology and web site production, and has written for a number of magazines, most recently *Windows Sources*, *Windows Pro Magazine*, and *New Media*.

Author of the bestselling book *Windows Annoyances*, he created the Windows 95 Annoyances web site, as well as the Windows 98 Annoyances web site, upon which this book is based. Both Annoyances web sites have been cited repeatedly as among the best technical resources on the Web. Noted recognition includes *PC Computing* magazine, *Windows Magazine*, the *San Francisco Examiner*, and the *New York Times*.

When David's not writing, you can usually find him outdoors or getting his hands dirty with yet another project.

Colophon

The animal featured on the cover of *Windows 98 Annoyances* is a European common toad (*Bufo Bufo*). There are more than 200 species of toads found in all continents except Australia and Antarctica. Toads are closely related to frogs, but they generally have shorter, squatter bodies and wartier skin than frogs.

The European common toad is greenish-brown in color, with a dusty white belly. Its thick skin is covered in warts both big and small. It grows to approximately 8 to 12 centimeters long. The toad's preferred habitats are large ponds or lakes. As tadpoles, European common toads eat plankton and single-celled animals. Their adult diet expands to includes insects, especially ants, and invertebrates, and they occasionally eat small lizards and frogs. A less savory ingredient of their diet is their own skin, which these toads sometimes eat after shedding.

Like many toads, the European common toad secretes a foul-tasting substance from its skin, making it less appetizing to potential predators. They are occasionally eaten by snakes, hedgehogs, and birds.

Madeleine Newell was the production editor and copyeditor for *Windows 98 Annoyances*; Sheryl Avruch was the production manager. Jane Ellin, Ellie Fountain Maden, and Nancy Kotary provided quality control; Sebastian Banker and Kimo Carter provided production assistance, and Mike Sierra provided FrameMaker technical support. Seth Maislin created the index.

Edie Freedman designed the cover of this book, as well as the CD label. The cover layout was produced by Kathleen Wilson with QuarkXPress 3.32 using the ITC Garamond font. Whenever possible, our books use RepKover™, a durable and flexible lay-flat binding. If the page count exceeds RepKover's limit, perfect binding is used.

The inside layout was designed by Nancy Priest and implemented in FrameMaker 5.5 by Mike Sierra. The text and heading fonts are ITC Garamond Light and Garamond Book. The screen shots that appear in the book were provided by David Karp and prepared for print by Robert Romano using Adobe Photoshop 5.0. The figures were created by Robert Romano using Macromedia FreeHand 7.0. This colophon was written by Clairemarie Fisher O'Leary.

More Titles from O'Reilly

Eliminating Annoyances

Windows Annoyances

By David A. Karp
1st Edition June 1997
300 pages, ISBN 1-56592-266-2

Windows Annoyances is a comprehensive, detailed resource for all intermediate to advanced users of Windows 95 and NT version 4.0. This book shows step-by-step how to customize the Win95/NT operating systems through an extensive collection of tips, tricks, and workarounds. Covers **Registry**, **Plug and Play**, networking, security, multiple-user settings, and third-party software.

Office 97 Annoyances

By Woody Leonhard, Lee Hudspeth & T.J. Lee
1st Edition October 1997
396 pages, ISBN 1-56592-310-3

Office 97 Annoyances illustrates step-by-step how to get control over the chaotic settings of Office 97 and shows how to turn the vast array of applications into a simplified list of customized tools. It focuses on the major components of Office 97, examines their integration or lack of it, and shows how to use this new Office suite in the most efficient way.

Outlook Annoyances

By Woody Leonhard,
Lee Hudspeth & T. J. Lee
1st Edition June 1998
400 pages, ISBN 1-56592-384-7

Like the other Microsoft Office-related titles in the Annoyances series, this book points out and conquers the annoying features of Microsoft Outlook, the personal information management software included with Office. It is the definitive guide for those who want to take full advantage of Outlook and transform it into the useful tool that it was intended to be.

Excel 97 Annoyances

By Woody Leonhard, Lee Hudspeth & T.J. Lee
1st Edition September 1997
336 pages, ISBN 1-56592-309-X

Excel 97 Annoyances uncovers Excel 97's hard-to-find features and tells how to eliminate the annoyances of data analysis. It shows how to easily retrieve data from the Web, details step-by-step construction of a perfect toolbar, includes tips for working around the most annoying gotchas of auditing, and shows how to use VBA to control Excel in powerful ways.

Word 97 Annoyances

By Woody Leonhard, Lee Hudspeth & T.J. Lee
1st Edition August 1997
356 pages, ISBN 1-56592-308-1

Word 97 contains hundreds of annoying idiosyncrasies that can be either eliminated or worked around. *Word 97 Annoyances* takes an in-depth look at what makes Word 97 tick and shows you how to transform this software into a powerful, customized tool.

O'Reilly Utilities: Quick Solutions for Windows 98 Annoyances

Software developed by
Mark Bracewell & David A. Karp
1st Edition October 1998 (est.)
CD-ROM with full online Help
ISBN 1-56592-549-1

O'Reilly Utilities: Quick Solutions for Windows 98 Annoyances is the stand-alone software companion to David Karp's *Windows 98 Annoyances* book. This software provides immediate, automated solutions for many of the key annoyances described in the book, as well as other important new enhancements to Windows 98.

Developed in cooperation with *Windows Annoyances* author David Karp, *O'Reilly Utilities* allows you to immediately improve your productivity with dozens of Windows extensions that go beyond Tweak UI and make common tasks easier, such as group file renaming, file copying, and customizing the desktop. Even better, we've built programs into this package that solve some of the most aggravating behaviors of Windows and other applications.

Internet for Everyone

The Whole Internet for Windows 95

By Ed Krol & Paula Ferguson
1st Edition October 1995
650 pages, ISBN 1-56592-155-0

The Whole Internet for Windows 95, the most comprehensive introduction to the Internet available today, shows you how to take advantage of the vast resources of the Internet with Microsoft Internet Explorer, Netscape Navigator, Microsoft Exchange, and many of the best free software programs available from the Net. Also includes an introduction to multimedia for PCs and a catalog of interesting sites to explore.

Bandits on the Information Superhighway

By Daniel J. Barrett
1st Edition February 1996
246 pages, ISBN 1-56592-156-9

Most people on the Internet behave honestly, but there are always some troublemakers. *Bandits* provides a crash course in Internet "street smarts," describing practical risks that every user should know about. Filled with anecdotes, technical tips, and the advice of experts from diverse fields, *Bandits* helps you identify and avoid risks online, so you can have a more productive and enjoyable time on the Internet.

AOL in a Nutshell

By Curt Degenhart & Jen Muehlbauer
1st Edition June 1998
536 pages, ISBN 1-56592-424-X

This definitive reference breaks through the hype and shows advanced AOL users and sophisticated beginners how to get the most out of AOL's tools and features. You'll learn how to customize AOL to meet your needs, work around annoying idiosyncrasies, avoid unwanted email and Instant Messages, understand Parental Controls, and turn off intrusive advertisements. It's an indispensable guide for users who aren't dummies.

Internet in a Nutshell

By Valerie Quercia
1st Edition October 1997
450 pages, ISBN 1-56592-323-5

Internet in a Nutshell is a quick-moving guide that goes beyond the "hype" and right to the heart of the matter: how to get the Internet to work for you. This is a second-generation Internet book for readers who have already taken a spin around the Net and now want to learn the shortcuts.

How to stay in touch with O'Reilly

1. Visit Our Award-Winning Site

http://www.oreilly.com/

★ "Top 100 Sites on the Web" —*PC Magazine*
★ "Top 5% Web sites" —*Point Communications*
★ "3-Star site" —*The McKinley Group*

Our web site contains a library of comprehensive product information (including book excerpts and tables of contents), downloadable software, background articles, interviews with technology leaders, links to relevant sites, book cover art, and more. File us in your Bookmarks or Hotlist!

2. Join Our Email Mailing Lists

New Product Releases

To receive automatic email with brief descriptions of all new O'Reilly products as they are released, send email to:
listproc@online.oreilly.com
Put the following information in the first line of your message (*not* in the Subject field):
subscribe oreilly-news

O'Reilly Events

If you'd also like us to send information about trade show events, special promotions, and other O'Reilly events, send email to:
listproc@online.oreilly.com
Put the following information in the first line of your message (*not* in the Subject field):
subscribe oreilly-events

3. Get Examples from Our Books via FTP

There are two ways to access an archive of example files from our books:

Regular FTP

- ftp to:
  ftp.oreilly.com
  (login: anonymous
  password: your email address)
- Point your web browser to:
  ftp://ftp.oreilly.com/

FTPMAIL

- Send an email message to:
  ftpmail@online.oreilly.com
  (Write "help" in the message body)

4. Contact Us via Email

order@oreilly.com
To place a book or software order online. Good for North American and international customers.

subscriptions@oreilly.com
To place an order for any of our newsletters or periodicals.

books@oreilly.com
General questions about any of our books.

software@oreilly.com
For general questions and product information about our software. Check out O'Reilly Software Online at **http://software.oreilly.com/** for software and technical support information. Registered O'Reilly software users send your questions to:
website-support@oreilly.com

cs@oreilly.com
For answers to problems regarding your order or our products.

booktech@oreilly.com
For book content technical questions or corrections.

proposals@oreilly.com
To submit new book or software proposals to our editors and product managers.

international@oreilly.com
For information about our international distributors or translation queries. For a list of our distributors outside of North America check out:
http://www.oreilly.com/www/order/country.html

O'Reilly & Associates, Inc.
101 Morris Street, Sebastopol, CA 95472 USA
TEL 707-829-0515 or 800-998-9938
(6am to 5pm PST)
FAX 707-829-0104

Titles from O'Reilly

WEB

Advanced Perl Programming
Apache: The Definitive Guide
Building Your Own Web Conferences
Building Your Own Website™
CGI Programming for the World Wide Web
Designing for the Web
Designing Sound for the Web
Designing with Animation
Designing with JavaScript
Dynamic HTML: The Definitive Reference
Frontier: The Definitive Guide
Gif Animation Studio
HTML: The Definitive Guide, 2nd Edition
Information Architecture for the World Wide Web
JavaScript: The Definitive Guide, 3nd Edition
Mastering Regular Expressions
Netscape IFC in a Nutshell
Photoshop for the Web
Shockwave Studio
WebMaster in a Nutshell
WebMaster in a Nutshell, Deluxe Edition
Web Navigation: Designing the User Experience
Web Security & Commerce

PERL

Learning Perl, 2nd Edition
Learning Perl for Win32 Systems
Perl5 Desktop Reference
Perl Cookbook
Perl in a Nutshell
Perl Resource Kit—UNIX Edition
Perl Resource Kit—Win32 Edition
Programming Perl, 2nd Edition
Web Client Programming with Perl

JAVA SERIES

Database Programming with JDBC and Java
Developing Java Beans
Exploring Java, 2nd Edition
Java AWT Reference
Java Cryptography
Java Distributed Computing
Java Examples in a Nutshell
Java Fundamental Classes Reference
Java in a Nutshell, 2nd Edition
Java in a Nutshell, Deluxe Edition
Java Language Reference, 2nd Edition
Java Native Methods
Java Network Programming
Java Security
Java Threads
Java Virtual Machine

SYSTEM ADMINISTRATION

Building Internet Firewalls
Computer Crime: A Crimefighter's Handbook
Computer Security Basics
DNS and BIND, 2nd Edition
Essential System Administration, 2nd Edition
Essential WindowsNT System Administration
Getting Connected: The Internet at 56K and Up
High Performance Computing, 2nd Edition
Linux Network Administrator's Guide
Managing Internet Information Services, 2nd Edition
Managing IP Networks with Cisco Routers
Managing Mailing Lists
Managing NFS and NIS
Managing the WinNT Registry
Managing Usenet
MCSE: The Core Exams in a Nutshell
MCSE: The Electives in a Nutshell
Networking Personal Computers with TCP/IP
PalmPilot: The Ultimate Guide
Practical UNIX & Internet Security, 2nd Edition
PGP: Pretty Good Privacy
Protecting Networks with SATAN
sendmail, 2nd Edition
sendmail Desktop Reference
System Performance Tuning
TCP/IP Network Administration, 2nd Edition
termcap & terminfo
Using & Managing PPP
Using & Managing UUCP
Virtual Private Networks
Volume 8: X Window System Administrator's Guide
Web Security & Commerce
WindowsNT Backup & Restore
WindowsNT Desktop Reference
WindowsNT in a Nutshell
WindowsNT Server 4.0 for Netware Administrators
WindowsNT SNMP
WindowsNT User Administration

GRAPHICS & MULTIMEDIA

Director in a Nutshell
Photoshop in a Nutshell
QuarkXPress in a Nutshell

UNIX

Exploring Expect
Learning VBScript
Learning GNU Emacs, 2nd Edition
Learning the bash Shell, 2nd Edition
Learning the Korn Shell
Learning the UNIX Operating System, 4th Edition
Learning the vi Editor, 5th Edition
Linux Device Drivers
Linux in a Nutshell
Linux Multimedia Guide
Running Linux, 2nd Edition
SCO UNIX in a Nutshell
sed & awk, 2nd Edition
Tcl/Tk Tools
UNIX in a Nutshell, Deluxe Edition
UNIX in a Nutshell, System V Edition
UNIX Power Tools, 2nd Edition
Using csh & tsch
What You Need To Know: When You Can't Find Your UNIX System Administrator
Writing GNU Emacs Extensions

WINDOWS

Access Database Design and Programming
Developing Windows Error Messages
Inside the Windows 95 File System
Inside the Windows 95 Registry
VB/VBA in a Nutshell: The Languages
Win32 Multithreaded Programming
Windows95 in a Nutshell
Windows NT File System Internals
Windows NT in a Nutshell

USING THE INTERNET

AOL in a Nutshell
Bandits on the Information Superhighway
Internet in a Nutshell
Smileys
The Whole Internet for Windows95
The Whole Internet: The Next Generation
The Whole Internet User's Guide & Catalog

ANNOYANCES

Excel97 Annoyances
Office97 Annoyances
Outlook Annoyances
Windows97 Annoyances
Word97 Annoyances

SONGLINE GUIDES

NetLaw
NetLearning
NetLessons
NetResearch
NetSuccess
NetTravel

PROGRAMMING

Advanced Oracle PL/SQL Programming with Packages
Applying RCS and SCCS
BE Developer's Guide
BE Advanced Topics
C++: The Core Language
Checking C Programs with lint
Encyclopedia of Graphics File Formats, 2nd Edition
Guide to Writing DCE Applications
lex & yacc, 2nd Edition
Managing Projects with make
Mastering Oracle Power Objects
Oracle8 Design Tips
Oracle Built-in Packages
Oracle Design
Oracle Performance Tuning, 2nd Edition
Oracle PL/SQL Programming, 2nd Edition
Oracle Scripts
Porting UNIX Software
POSIX Programmer's Guide
POSIX.4: Programming for the Real World
Power Programming with RPC
Practical C Programming, 3rd Edition
Practical C++ Programming
Programming Python
Programming with curses
Programming with GNU Software
Pthreads Programming
Software Portability with imake, 2nd Edition
Understanding DCE
UNIX Systems Programming for SVR4

X PROGRAMMING

Vol. 0: X Protocol Reference Manual
Vol. 1: Xlib Programming Manual
Vol. 2: Xlib Reference Manual
Vol. 3M: X Window System User's Guide, Motif Edition
Vol. 4M: X Toolkit Intrinsics Programming Manual, Motif Edition
Vol. 5: X Toolkit Intrinsics Reference Manual
Vol. 6A: Motif Programming Manual
Vol. 6B: Motif Reference Manual
Vol. 8 : X Window System Administrator's Guide

SOFTWARE

Building Your Own WebSite™
Building Your Own Web Conference
WebBoard™ 3.0
WebSite Professional™ 2.0
PolyForm™

International Distributors

UK, Europe, Middle East and Northern Africa *(except France, Germany, Switzerland, & Austria)*

INQUIRIES
International Thomson Publishing Europe
Berkshire House
168-173 High Holborn
London WC1V 7AA, UK
Telephone: 44-171-497-1422
Fax: 44-171-497-1426
Email: itpint@itps.co.uk

ORDERS
International Thomson Publishing Services, Ltd.
Cheriton House, North Way
Andover, Hampshire SP10 5BE,
United Kingdom
Telephone: 44-264-342-832 (UK)
Telephone: 44-264-342-806 (outside UK)
Fax: 44-264-364418 (UK)
Fax: 44-264-342761 (outside UK)
UK & Eire orders: itpuk@itps.co.uk
International orders: itpint@itps.co.uk

France

Editions Eyrolles
61 bd Saint-Germain
75240 Paris Cedex 05
France
Fax: 33-01-44-41-11-44

FRENCH LANGUAGE BOOKS
All countries except Canada
Telephone: 33-01-44-41-46-16
Email: geodif@eyrolles.com

ENGLISH LANGUAGE BOOKS
Telephone: 33-01-44-41-11-87
Email: distribution@eyrolles.com

Germany, Switzerland, and Austria

INQUIRIES
O'Reilly Verlag
Balthasarstr. 81
D-50670 Köln
Germany
Telephone: 49-221-97-31-60-0
Fax: 49-221-97-31-60-8
Email: anfragen@oreilly.de

ORDERS
International Thomson Publishing
Königswinterer Straße 418
53227 Bonn, Germany
Telephone: 49-228-97024 0
Fax: 49-228-441342
Email: order@oreilly.de

Japan

O'Reilly Japan, Inc.
Kiyoshige Building 2F
12-Banchi, Sanei-cho
Shinjuku-ku
Tokyo 160 Japan
Tel: 81-3-3356-5227
Fax: 81-3-3356-5261
Email: kenji@oreilly.com

India

Computer Bookshop (India) PVT. Ltd.
190 Dr. D.N. Road, Fort
Bombay 400 001 India
Tel: 91-22-207-0989
Fax: 91-22-262-3551
Email: cbsbom@giasbm01.vsnl.net.in

Hong Kong

City Discount Subscription Service Ltd.
Unit D, 3rd Floor, Yan's Tower
27 Wong Chuk Hang Road
Aberdeen, Hong Kong
Telephone: 852-2580-3539
Fax: 852-2580-6463
Email: citydis@ppn.com.hk

Korea

Hanbit Publishing, Inc.
Sonyoung Bldg. 202
Yeksam-dong 736-36
Kangnam-ku
Seoul, Korea
Telephone: 822-554-9610
Fax: 822-556-0363
Email: hant93@chollian.dacom.co.kr

Taiwan

ImageArt Publishing, Inc.
4/fl. No. 65 Shinyi Road Sec. 4
Taipei, Taiwan, R.O.C.
Telephone: 886-2708-5770
Fax: 886-2705-6690
Email: marie@ms1.hinet.net

Singapore, Malaysia, and Thailand

Longman Singapore
25 First Lok Yan Road
Singapore 2262
Telephone: 65-268-2666
Fax: 65-268-7023
Email: daniel@longman.com.sg

Philippines

Mutual Books, Inc.
429-D Shaw Boulevard
Mandaluyong City, Metro
Manila, Philippines
Telephone: 632-725-7538
Fax: 632-721-3056
Email: mbikikog@mnl.sequel.net

China

Ron's DataCom Co., Ltd.
79 Dongwu Avenue
Dongxihu District
Wuhan 430040
China
Telephone: 86-27-83892568
Fax: 86-27-83222108
Email: hongfeng@public.wh.hb.cn

Australia

WoodsLane Pty. Ltd.
7/5 Vuko Place, Warriewood NSW 2102
P.O. Box 935,
Mona Vale NSW 2103
Australia
Telephone: 61-2-9970-5111
Fax: 61-2-9970-5002
Email: info@woodslane.com.au

All Other Asia Countries

O'Reilly & Associates, Inc.
101 Morris Street
Sebastopol, CA 95472 USA
Telephone: 707-829-0515
Fax: 707-829-0104
Email: order@oreilly.com

The Americas

McGraw-Hill Interamericana Editores, S.A. de C.V.
Cedro No. 512
Col. Atlampa 06450
Mexico, D.F.
Telephone: 52-5-541-3155
Fax: 52-5-541-4913
Email: mcgraw-hill@infosel.net.mx

Southern Africa

International Thomson Publishing Southern Africa
Building 18, Constantia Park
138 Sixteenth Road
P.O. Box 2459
Halfway House, 1685 South Africa
Tel: 27-11-805-4819
Fax: 27-11-805-3648

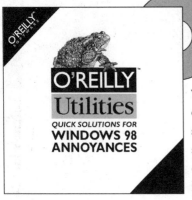